CRICKET

Cricket

C.L.R. JAMES
Edited by Anna Grimshaw

Allison & Busby
Published by W.H. Allen & Co. Plc

An Allison & Busby book
Published in 1989 by
W.H. Allen & Co Plc
Sekforde House
175/9 St John Street
London EC1V 4LL

Printed in Great Britain by
Anchor Press Ltd, Tiptree, Essex.

ISBN 0 85031 786 X

Contents

Preface and Acknowledgements   ix
Introduction by C.L.R. James (1985)   xi

Notes: 1901-32   1
Notes: 1930s   4

1. The Greatest of All Bowlers: An   7
   Impressionist Sketch of S.F. Barnes (1932)
2. A Great West Indian Batsman: Headley's   10
   Remarkable Rise to Fame (1933)
3. West Indies Cricket (1933)   12
4. Chances of West Indies in First Test (1933)   34
5. Lancashire's Bleak Cricket (1934)   39
6. Spirited Batting by Kent (1934)   41
7. Lancashire Draw with Kent (1934)   43
8. Bradman's Remarkable Century at   45
   Scarborough (1934)
9. Australian Bowling Can be Hit (1934)   47
10. Australians' Easy Victory (1934)   49
11. Lancashire Collapses at Aigburth (1935)   51
12. Exciting Cricket Depends upon Exciting   53
    Personalities (1937)
13. Freer Style of Cricket Promised (1937)   56
14. E.A. McDonald's Example of Perfection   58
    of Style (1937)
15. Bradman's One Palpable Weakness; Hassett   62
    Sets a Problem (1938)
16. Cricket is Losing a Supreme Artist — Frank   64
    Woolley (1938)

Notes: 1950s   69

17. Return of a Wanderer: Comparisons   71
    between 1938 and 1953 (1953)
18. Letter to George Headley (1954)   74
19. Letter from George Headley (1954)   74
20. Pakistanis in Good Form (1954)   75
21. Pakistanis Far Ahead; Khalid's Leg-Breaks   77
    (1954)

22. Fazal's Fine Bowling at Worcester (1954)   79
23. "Neither Toss, Weather nor Wicket were   81
     Decisive Elements in the Defeat of
     Australia Last Season" (1957)
24. Letter to Facing Reality Group (1957)   87
25. That Worrell Tour (1959)   88
26. Without Malice (1959)   90
27. Gilchrist Before and Gilchrist After (1959)   92
28. The MCC Players as I Knew Them (1959)   94

Notes: 1960s   99

29. The Captain for Australia (1960)   101
30. Letter to J.H. Fingleton (1960)   103
31. Letter to J.H. Fingleton (1960)   104
32. Letter from John Arlott (1960)   106
33. Letter to John Arlott (1960)   106
34. Letter from J.H. Fingleton (1961)   107
35. Letter to Robert Lusty (1961)   108
36. Letter to John Arlott (1962)   109
37. Body-line (1963)   111
38. Letter to Berkeley Gaskin (1963)   115
39. Letter to V.S. Naipaul (1963)   116
40. Letter to V.S. Naipaul (1963)   118
41. Cricket in West Indian Culture (1963)   118
42. Letter to Frank Worrell (1963)   124
43. Letter to Garfield Sobers (1963)   125
44. The Departure of the West Indians (1963)   125
45. Dexter and Sobers (1963)   127
46. Letter to V.S. Naipaul (1963)   130
47. The 1963 West Indians (1964)   134
48. Reflections on the Late Series (1964)   147
49. Sir J.B. Hobbs (1964)   154
50. Sobers' Greatest Days are Ahead (1964)   156
51. West Indies (1966)   158
52. Kanhai: A Study in Confidence (1966)   165
53. Long may Windies Flourish (1966)   171
54. After that Nottingham Defeat (1966)   174
55. A Question of Cricket Approach . . . (1966)   178
56. Why Windies Fade in the End (1966)   182
57. Two Cricketing Societies (1966)   186

58. George Headley (1967) 190
59. Sir Frank Worrell: The Man Whose 202
  Leadership Made History (1967)
60. Letter to Colin Cowdrey (1968) 205
61. Letter to E.W. Swanton (1968) 206
62. Letter to Colin Cowdrey (1968) 207
63. Letter to John Arlott (1968) 208
64. Not Cricket (1968) 209
65. Letter to John Arlott (1968) 213
66. Driving the Ball is a Tradition in the West 215
  Indies (1968)
67. Letter to Learie Constantine 217
68. Garfield Sobers (1969) 218
69. Learie Constantine (1969) 232
70. Letter to Rowland Bowen (1969) 245
71. Letter to Rowland Bowen (1969) 246
72. West Indian Cricketers in County Cricket 247
  (1960s)

Notes: 1970s 252

73. Walter Hammond — An Anniversary 253
  Tribute (1970)
74. Sir Frank Worrell (1970) 255
75. The History of Cricket (1970) 270
76. Not Just Cricket (1975) 277
77. Cricket and Race (1975) 278

Notes: 1980s 280

78. A Majestic Innings with Few Peers (1982) 281
79. Gower to Lead England (1983) 284
80. The Captain and his Team: An Injustice to 287
  Gower (1983)
81. George Headley, 1909-83 (1984) 291
82. MacGregor (1984) 295
83. West Indies *vs* England (1984) 298
84. The Decline of English Cricket (1985) 301
85. Botham Hitting Sixes (1985) 303

Bibliography 305
Index 313

Preface and Acknowledgements

For over half a century C.L.R. James has distinguished himself
as a writer on cricket. This volume offers, for the first time, a
comprehensive selection of this aspect of his work: portraits of
cricketers, reports on Test and county matches, reflections on
the history and development of the game internationally,
correspondence with other experts and enthusiasts and unpublished articles from his personal archives.

C.L.R. James has always approached cricket in the same
rigorous manner as he has dealt with questions of history,
politics and aesthetics. The game is a critical component in his
total conception of the world, and therefore this collection has
a significant place alongside those of his publications already
available.

The chronological arrangement of the articles, grouped in
decades, indicates the development in range and scope of
James's thinking about cricket (although unfortunately, it has
not been possible to include material from his early years in the
Caribbean, the period before he left for England in 1932). The
bibliography is a provisional listing of his cricket writings, and
additions or corrections would be welcome. The notes preceding different sections aim to place the articles in the context of
James's other work: concerns in cricket are frequently part of
his more general preoccupations. As James himself observed in
his classic *Beyond a Boundary*: "What do they know of cricket
who only cricket know?"

I would like to thank the following for their assistance: Stephen
Green, curator of MCC; Clive Porter, editor of *The Journal of the
Cricket Society*; the staff of the British Newspaper Library,
Colindale; and the many other individuals who responded to
my enquiries.

ANNA GRIMSHAW
January 1986

Introduction

An artistic, a social event does not reflect the age. It is the age. Cricket, I want to say most clearly, is not an addition or a decoration or some specific unit that one adds to what really constitutes the history of a period. Cricket is as much part of the history as books written are part of the history. And that raises questions which I will pose, but not attempt to solve here.

Far more people play cricket, look at cricket and scan the cricket news in the morning paper, far more take part in these activities than those who read books.

The real problem is that we maintain that ancient distinction between social life and games. Today, and for some years, that distinction has been false. Workers carrying out negotiations with employers calculate so many hours of the day for work in the plant and so many hours of the day for recreation, including chiefly periods when the sun is shining.

I have been driven to make these observations because I have been thinking, and believe it would help if I could indicate a historical development in the business of batting. The dangers of this kind of thinking I shall leave for later.

Meanwhile, in the second half of the nineteenth century W.G. Grace followed by Arthur Shrewsbury, William Gunn and that generation laid the foundations of batting. That is to say playing cricket day after day and scoring runs at a regular rate. At its best it was, let us say, between 1885 and 1895. But in 1895 a change took place, symbolized by Ranjitsinhji.

Now people like to read about the oriental suppleness of his play, his eagle eyesight and such-like fiction. Ranjitsinhji may or may not have had such qualities. What he was doing was altering a style of batting of which people were tired. And the proof of this was that in Australia at the same time Victor Trumper and others of that generation were changing the batting style. The emphasis was on scoring off the back foot, which Ranjitsinhji had introduced. This brilliant play was at its best betwen 1900 and 1914. Grace knew it only a few years before he died.

The war put an end to this blaze, and the batsmen after the war had to fight to restore what had been lost. This struggle took place during the 1930s, but by 1929 the Australians had reorganized batting, strengthened it and at the same time made it more aggressive. The British followed them and during the 1930s players in England developed batting to a high standard.

After World War Two cricket became less standardized. For one thing, whereas from number eight down in the old days consisted chiefly of men who had made runs by hitting out, in the last years that has not remained. Batsmen from number eight to eleven nowadays can bat and make steady runs. On the whole the batting is not as brilliant as in the old days, but by and large the general standard is higher.

If I can sum up: for brilliance there has been substituted competence.

One last word about approaching cricket in this way. What I have set down are not laws. They are not a logical construction. They are guidelines and from using them the careful historian can work historically at individual batsmen and emerge with certain hard facts in their hard places. These usurp the name of History. There is another history — the unrecorded hundreds and hundreds of games and thousands of players, boys, men and even some old men.

This from the heart of English literature has not an obtrusive place here:

Let not Ambition mock their useful toil,
Their homely joys, and destiny obscure;
Nor Grandeur hear with a disdainful smile,
The short and simple annals of the poor. . . .

Perhaps in this neglected spot is laid
Some heart once pregnant with celestial fire;
Hands, that the rod of empire might have sway'd,
Or wak'd to extasy the living lyre. . . .

Some village-Hampden, that with dauntless breast
The little Tyrant of his fields withstood;
Some mute inglorious Milton here may rest,
Some Cromwell guiltless of his country's blood.*

But 1985 is not 1885. Our rurals are not mute, they are not inglorious and they are not in any way guiltless of their country's blood and other precious substances.

C.L.R. JAMES
London, 1985

---

*"Elegy written in a Country Church-yard", Thomas Gray (1716-71).

"Our house was superbly situated, exactly behind the wicket. A huge tree on one side and another house on the other limited the view of the ground, but an umpire could have stood at the bedroom window. By standing on a chair a small boy of six could watch practice every afternoon and matches on Saturdays. . . ."

C.L.R. James opened his classic book *Beyond a Boundary* with a description of the circumstances of his childhood. He was born in 1901 to black middle-class parents and he grew up in Tunapuna, a small town outside Port of Spain, Trinidad. His father was a schoolteacher, his mother a voracious reader who introduced James early to literature, and in particular to Thackeray. On both sides of the family, including James's aunts, cricket was an integral part of their heritage in a West Indian island where the game dominated all aspects of social and cultural life. Closely tied to the game and its code was a Puritan mentality and outlook with which James's family was deeply imbued.

In this context, then, cricket could hardly have failed to be a major force in the development of James's life and thought. He himself was an unusual boy: precociously bright, he was from a young age drawn to the intellectual aspects of cricket as much as to a physical participation in it. As a boy he had stored in his mind's eye clear images of local cricket personalities. Over many years he built up a whole collection of newspaper clippings which he studied in order to increase his understanding of the intricacies of the game. However, James also played cricket. He was a right-arm fast-medium bowler and a good defensive right-hand batsman. In his youth he was viewed as a cricketer with potential.

In 1910, under the tutorship of his father, James won one of the island exhibitions to Queen's Royal College. Here he was schooled by Oxford and Cambridge masters in the classics: Greek, Latin, English and European history and literature. It was this kind of education, with its public-school ethic, which gave James his early affinity with ancient Greek civilization. This later influenced much of his writing, particularly its social and aesthetic dimensions, on sport in general and on cricket in particular.

But once at Queen's Royal College, James very quickly succumbed to the temptations of cricket. His academic career

C.L.R. James

proved to be a great disappointment to his family, who had
hoped that it would lead him into the professions expected of
scholarship boys.

When he left school in 1918 James was already playing
cricket to a good standard, first of all for the Old Collegians and
later for Maple Club. He was also well known among the
island's prominent players — Constantine, Senior and Junior,
Wilton St Hill and Clifford Roach — for his intellectual grasp of
the game and his strong historical sense of its development.

Cricket clubs at this time in Trinidad expressed the wider
social stratification based upon wealth, but more importantly
upon colour. James, a member of the black middle class, was
faced with a choice between the Maple and Shannon Clubs. He
chose Maple, the club of the brown-skinned. This was an early
political decision which distanced him from what he later
recognized as the creative forces in the West Indies. Players
from the black lower-middle classes, like Constantine and W.
St Hill, played for Shannon. They were laying important
foundations for the subsequent development of cricket as a
political and social expression of the West Indian personality.

During the 1920s James earned his living as a schoolmaster.
He returned to Queen's Royal College for a short time to teach
English and History. Notable among his pupils was Eric Williams, later to lead Trinidad to independence; Victor Stollmeyer, brother of Jeffrey and a talented cricketer in his own
right; and MacGregor, an unusual cricketer of potential whom
James spotted early.*

James was beginning to develop into a serious writer. He
continued his interest in cricket and reported matches for local
newspapers. He also began to write fiction. He became part of a
literary circle in Trinidad which included such writers as
Alfred Mendes, Albert Gomes and Ralph de Boissière. They
founded two important, if shortlived, journals: Trinidad (1929–
30) and The Beacon (1931–3). These provided a forum for an
emerging, indigenous West Indian literature. James published
here both general articles on literature and philosophy as well
as a number of short stories.

The 1920s were particularly significant years in the history of
Trinidad. The First World War had a profound effect upon the
thinking and expectations of the people in Britain's Caribbean
colonies. There was a growth and development in workers'
organizations (specifically related to the oil industry) and

*below pp 295-8.

2

agitation intensified against colonial government. The literary movement with which James was identified was very much part of the gathering political momentum. In this climate his attention was caught by the personality of Captain André Cipriani, a French Creole who was building a powerful labour movement that posed a serious challenge to colonial authority, and James began work on a biography of him.

Although James had made the decision in 1918 to play cricket for the Maple Club and not Shannon, the club for which Learie Constantine played, they remained close cricketing companions. Both generations of Constantine's family had been well known to James's family, and Learie had been a pupil of James's father.

Constantine had left Trinidad to play as a Lancashire League cricket professional in 1929. He had been signed up while touring England with the West Indies team in 1928. He returned to the West Indies during the winter months, resuming his lengthy conversations on cricket with James which had been developing over many years. Constantine was preparing to write his autobiography and he proposed that James join him in Nelson to assist in the research and writing of the book.

For a black man of his talents, emigration was the only road open to James if he wished to fulfil his considerable potential. In fact he stayed in the West Indies much longer than many of his contemporaries (Constantine had first left in 1923, George Padmore, one of the founders of Pan-Africanism, had left for the United States in 1924). At the time James accepted Constantine's invitation, 1932, he could not be described as an impressionable youth, rather he was a mature and developed man of thirty-one years of age. He had, however, still a great deal to learn. Constantine's experience abroad had expanded his horizons and had given him a political awareness beyond the intellectual conceptions of James.

In 1932 James left Trinidad and sailed to England. It was the beginning of a journey which was to take him, intellectually and politically, to the heart of many of the major historical movements of the twentieth century.

1930s

C.L.R. James arrived in Britain in March 1932 with two manuscripts in his baggage. These were the draft of Constantine's autobiography, much of it based upon conversations between James and Constantine, and a biography of the West Indian political activist, Captain Cipriani. The two manuscripts were very closely linked and James completed them during his stay in Nelson, Lancashire.

The first weeks in London formed the basis for a series of articles which James published in the *Port of Spain Gazette*, Trinidad, during 1932. These pieces dealt with different aspects of English life and culture as they appeared to a British-educated colonial subject just arrived in the metropolis.

In May 1932 James moved to Nelson, the town where Learie Constantine was playing cricket as a Lancashire League professional. He shared Constantine's house in Meredith Street for the next eleven months.

James himself was granted permission to play with Nelson at cricket, but the only record of his doing so appeared in the local newspaper, *The Leader* of 17 June 1932. He had played in a friendly match against Radcliffe, another Lancashire town, had taken one wicket for 35 runs and had scored six runs.

These months in Nelson, however, were devoted primarily to writing. James completed *The Life of Captain Cipriani*; Constantine put up the money for its publication and its appearance in September 1932 caused a considerable stir in the Caribbean.

James also continued to send articles to different West Indian newspapers. An early article in the *Sporting Chronicle*, dated 8 July 1932, set the scene of Lancashire League cricket for his readers:

I am at present staying with Learie Constantine, and on Saturday I saw one of the big matches in the Lancashire League versus Burnley. Nelson is a town of about 40 thousand inhabitants; Burnley has about 103 thousand and is about 20 minutes' run from Nelson. Burnley had not lost a match in the league up to Saturday, and they and Nelson were as keen rivals as only near neighbours can be. The question was one of rain. If the rain held off there might be a gate of over £200; it did not they might do no more than £20. Fortunately the rain held off, but the weather was rather bleak and the gate was only somewhere between £100 and £200, I cannot remember exactly, and it does not matter. The Nelson ground is, I expect, as pretty a cricket ground as you could see anywhere. I had imagined a small piece of grass, fighting for its life against the gradual encroaching of cotton factories, menacing with black smoke, machine shops and tenement houses. The ground is nothing of the kind. It is full-size, level and when you sit in the pavilion, you see on three sides a hill rising gradually covered with green grass, clumps of trees, houses here and there, beautiful as it seems only the English countryside can be beautiful.*

It was at this time that a piece James wrote on Sydney Barnes, the Lancashire bowler, came to the notice of Neville Cardus at the *Manchester Guardian*. It so impressed Cardus that he took James on as his assistant for the cricket season of 1933. This continued for the following two seasons, 1934 and 1935.

In 1933 Constantine's book *Cricket and I* appeared, the fruit of his close collaboration with James in Nelson. It was reviewed as one of the first serious cricket autobiographies. Importantly, too, it was an autobiography of a West Indian. At around the same time, Virginia and Leonard Woolf reissued in a shortened version James's biography of Cipriani under the title *A Case for West Indian Self-Government*. Both publications were significant statements and contributions to the political growth of the West Indies.

1933 was the year in which a West Indies cricket team arrived in Britain for a series of Test matches. James had moved to London in the April of that year and watched them carefully as they practised in the nets. His first articles for the *Manchester Guardian* assessed the strengths and weaknesses of this West Indies team, and included a notable essay on George Headley.

Employing a method that was to become characteristic, James placed the 1933 West Indies cricket team firmly within a historical tradition which he explored in a series of articles published in *The Cricketer*.

The majority of James's reporting for the *Manchester Guardian* in the seasons of 1933, 1934 and 1935, however, was of county cricket matches. He travelled extensively between the different grounds, thereby greatly broadening his knowledge of English life. His sense of occasion, his understanding of both the styles and idiosyncracies of particular players and their interaction with the crowd, have given his match reports a vividness undimmed after fifty years.

Sporting Chronicle, Trinidad, reprinted in *The Leader*, Nelson, 8 July 1932.

Life as a cricket reporter suited James well, since it left the winter months free for him to pursue his researches, often in Paris, on the San Domingo revolution of 1791. He was also reading seriously the Marxist classics and becoming involved in the struggles of various left-wing groups associated with the Independent Labour Party.

He left the *Manchester Guardian* after the season of 1935, and in 1937 he resumed employment as a cricket reporter, with the *Glasgow Herald*. The year in which James was not employed by a national newspaper, 1936, was in many ways the climax of his career in radical British politics. His break from cricket reporting at this time meant he could concentrate solely upon the issues which had been thrown up by the Italian invasion of Abyssinia in 1935.

Following the split and upheaval in the Independent Labour Party in 1936 over the Abyssinian crisis, James's political career took a new direction. It became focused in a small group, the Revolutionary Socialist League, which agitated from without rather than from within the mainstream labour movement. James also began to publish the results of his years of research and writing: *Minty Alley* (1936), *World Revolution* (1937), *The Black Jacobins* (1938) and *A History of Negro Revolt* (1938).

As the political momentum of 1935 and 1936 declined James returned to full-time cricket writing in the season of 1937. In contrast to his earlier submissions to the *Manchester Guardian*, his articles in the *Glasgow Herald* were not reports of county cricket matches, but essays on the nature of the game itself.

In 1938 he covered the Australian tour for the *Glasgow Herald*, but it was to be his last season of cricket reporting. James left Britain for the United States of America in November 1938 and he was not to see a cricket match for the next fifteen years.

The Greatest of All Bowlers:
An Impressionist Sketch of S.F. Barnes

(*Manchester Guardian*, 1 September 1932)

Sydney Barnes is generally admitted to be the greatest bowler cricket has yet seen. I had a glimpse of him the other day in action. He is fifty-nine years of age (the date of his birth given in *Wisden's Almanack* is incorrect). Yet the man is still a fine bowler. It was an experience to watch him.

To begin with, Barnes not only is fifty-nine, but looks it. Some cricketers at fifty-nine look and move like men in their thirties. Not so Barnes. You can almost hear the old bones creaking. He is tall and thin, well over six feet, with strong features. It is rather a remarkable face in its way, and could belong to a great lawyer or a statesman without incongruity. He holds his head well back, with the rather long chin lifted. He looks like a man who has seen as much of the world as he wants to see.

I saw him first before the match began, bowling to one of his own side without wickets. He carried his arm over as straight as a post, spinning a leg-break in the orthodox way. Then he had a knock himself. But although the distance was only a dozen yards and the ball was being bowled at a very slow pace, Barnes put a glove on. He was not going to run the risk of those precious fingers being struck by the ball. When the preliminary practice stopped he walked in, by himself, with his head in the air, a man intent on his own affairs.

His own side, Rawtenstall, took the field to get Nelson out. League sides will sometimes treat the new ball with Saturday-afternoon carelessness; not so Rawtenstall. Ten of them played about with an old ball: Barnes held the new. He fixed his field, two slips close in and the old-fashioned point, close in. Mid-off was rather wide. When every man was placed to the nearest centimetre Barnes walked back and set the old machinery in motion. As he forced himself to the crease you could see every year of the fifty-nine; but the arm swung over gallantly, high and straight. The wicket was slow, but a ball whipped hot from the pitch in the first over, and second slip took a neat catch. When the over was finished he walked a certain number of steps and took up his position in the slips. He stood as straight as his right arm, with his hands behind his back. The bowler began his run — a long run — Barnes still immovable. Just as

the ball was about to be delivered Barnes bent forward slightly
with his hands ready in front of him. To go right down as a
normal slip fieldsman goes was for him, obviously, a physical
impossibility. But he looked alert, and I got the impression that
whatever went into his hands would stay there. As the ball
reached the wicket-keeper's hands or was played by the batsman, Barnes straightened himself and again put his hands
behind his back. That was his procedure in the field right
through the afternoon. Now and then by way of variety he
would move a leg an inch or two and point it on the toe for a
second or two. Apart from that, he husbanded his strength.

He took 7 wickets for about 30 runs, and it is impossible to
imagine better bowling of its kind. The batsmen opposed to
him were not of high rank, most of them, but good bowling is
good bowling, whoever plays it. Armistead, a sound batsman,
was obviously on his mettle. Barnes kept him playing; then he
bowled one of his most dangerous balls — a flighted one,
dropping feet shorter without any change of action and, what is
so much more dangerous, pitching on the middle wicket and
missing the off. Armistead, magnetized into playing forward,
had the good sense to keep his right toe firm. The wicket-keeper
observed Armistead's toe regretfully, and threw the ball back to
Barnes. Up to this time Armistead had relied almost entirely on
the back stroke. It had carried him to where he was without
mishap. A forward stroke had imperilled his innings. Behold
there the elements of a tragedy, obvious, no doubt, but as Mr
Desmond MacCarthy says, the obvious is the crowning glory of
art. Armistead played back to the next ball. But he couldn't get
his bat to it in time. Barnes hit him hard on the pads with a
straight ball, and the pads were in front of the wicket.

He went from triumph to triumph, aided, no doubt, by the
terror of his name. When Constantine came in I looked for a
duel. Constantine was not going to be drawn into playing
forward. Barnes was not going to bowl short to be hooked over
the pavilion, or over-pitch to be hit into the football field.
Constantine also was not going to chance it. For on that turning
wicket, to such accurate bowling, who chanced it was lost.

Constantine jumped to him once, and a long field picked the
ball up from the ground, where it had been from the time it left
the bat. Barnes bowled a slow one, that might almost be called
short. It pitched on the leg stump. Constantine shaped for the
forcing back-stroke. The field was open. But even as he raised
himself for the stroke he held his hand, and wisely. The ball
popped up and turned many inches. Another ball or two, and

again Barnes dropped another on the same spot. It was a sore temptation. Constantine shaped again for his stroke, his own stroke, and again he held his hand; wisely, for the ball broke and popped up again. So the pair watched one another, like two fencers sparring for an opening. The crowd sat tense. Was this recitative suddenly to burst into the melody of fours and sixes to all parts of the field? The Nelson crowd at least hoped so. But it was not to be. Some insignificant trundler at the other end who bowled mediocre balls bowled Constantine with one of them.

After that it was a case of the boa constrictor and the rabbits, the only matter of interest being how long he would take to dispose of them. But, nevertheless, old campaigner as he is, Barnes took no chances. Slip would stand on the exact spot where the bowler wanted him, there and nowhere else. When a batsman who had once hit him for two or three fours came in, Barnes put two men out immediately. As soon as a single was made, the out-fieldsmen were drawn in again and carefully fixed in their original positions, although the score might be about 50 for 8 or something of the kind. Barnes had lived long enough in the world of cricket to know that there at any rate it does not pay to give anything away. Nelson failed to reach 70. As the Rawtenstall team came in, the crowd applauded his fine bowling mightily. Barnes walked through it intent on his own affairs. He had had much of that all his life.

Constantine, running seventeen yards and hurling the ball violently through the air, began sending back the Rawtenstall batsmen. One, two, three, wickets and bails flying every time. Forth from the pavilion came Barnes. He faced the West Indian fast bowler. He was older than Constantine's father and the wicket was faster now. Barnes got behind the ball, the pitched-up ball, and played it back along the pitch to the bowler. He judged the ball quickly and so got there in time. He kept his left shoulder forward and that kept the bat straight. He played the slower bowlers with equal skill, and whenever there was a single to be taken he took it. He never lost one, and he was in difficulties to get into his crease once only. "Yes" and "No" he said decisively in a deep voice which could be heard all over the ground. His bones were too stiff to force the ball away. But his bat swung true to the drive and he got over the short ball to cut. He stayed there some forty minutes for 10, and as long as he was there his side was winning. But Constantine bowled him behind his back. Barnes satisfied himself that he was out, and then he left the crease. He came in slowly amidst the plaudits of the Nelson crowd, applauding his innings and their satisfaction at his having been dismissed. Courtesy acknowledged the applause. For the rest he continued as he had begun, a man unconsciously scornful of his milieu. After he left, Rawtenstall collapsed.

Since then, Barnes has taken 5 for a few and startled Lancashire a few days ago by taking 9 for 20. In the years to come, it will be something to say that we have seen him.

A Great West Indian Batsman: Headley's Remarkable Rise to Fame

(*Manchester Guardian*, 18 April 1933)

"Statistics prove — " began a speaker on the wireless the other night, and I turned him off at once. Yet in George Headley's case the bare statistics are the best introduction to his cricket. He was born in Jamaica in 1909, and in 1926 emerged from the village green into good club cricket. Tradition has it that he still wore short trousers. The youthful Bradman, it is related, astonished a big club in Australia both by his batting and by his black trousers. Victor Trumper also banged a Test-match bowler about when clad in other than the regulation white flannel. Some forty years ago Ephraim Lockwood, hastily summoned to fill a breach, went in to bat at the Oval in a check shirt and short pants. The Ovalites were convulsed with laughter. They had a lot of time in which to laugh, for Ephraim made over eighty. Constantine relates that his father objected to his coming too early into first-class cricket and would not help him to buy flannels, wherefore he had to save the money sixpence by sixpence. So the material gathers for an essay on "The nether garments of budding Test cricketers". Remains only he who, wearing none at all, makes his mark in a match: the prospect is not so remote in these nudist days.

The next year, 1927, Headley attracted the notice of the local authorities and earned a place in the Jamaica side against the Hon. L.H. Tennyson's Eleven. Against Clark, M.J.C. Allom, Lee (G.M.), A.L. Hilder and T. Arnott, Headley made 16 and 71, 211 40 and 71. In the long innings he gave one chance, a hard one, early in the innings, and scored the 211 out of 348.

As is the sad lot of the West Indian batsman, he got no more first-class cricket until the next year, 1929, when Sir Julian Cahn took a team including Astill, Mercer, Durston and Nichols. Headley made 57 and 22, 17 and 43, 41 and 143. He had therefore played in six first-class matches and was not yet twenty-one years old when the MCC team under Calthorpe went to the West Indies in 1930. The bowlers on this team were Calthorpe himself, Voce, Astill, Wilfred Rhodes, Nigel Haig, G.T.S. Stevens. Limited as was his experience, they could do nothing at all with Headley. It was his first trip away to play, and he travelled from island to island for the Tests. In Barbados in the first Test he made 21 and 176; in Trinidad, 8 and 36; and in the British Guiana Test, 114 and 112. Going back home to meet them in Jamaica, he made 64 and 72 and 52; and in the fourth Test, 10 and 223.

In the autumn of that year he went to Australia. He began with 25 and 82 against New South Wales and followed them up with 131 against Victoria on the Melbourne wicket on the first day, batting before lunch. He made 1,000 runs in the season, scored a century in the third Test, and one in the fifth. Last year Lord Tennyson again took a team to Jamaica. Headley made 344 not out, 84 and 155 not out, and 140. His figures to date are 30 matches, 54 innings, 3,507 runs, highest score 344 not out, average 70.14. He has made in all thirteen centuries, including two double and one treble century, and a century in each innings of a Test match.

Whatever statistics may or may not prove, such scoring has only itself to blame if it arouses abnormal expectations. Moreover, he is as great a master of style as he is of runs.

He is a Negro, finely built but short and small, and only a careful judge of physique would notice him in a crowd. But at the wicket no one can miss his mastery. He is of that type which uses a bat as if it is an extension of the arm. Ease, poise and balance, he has them all. Good as his footwork is for defensive play, it is even better in the way he makes ground to the ball. He and Edwin St Hill, the Lowerhouse professional, are great friends, a friendship which began at the nets before the first Test at Barbados in 1930. Edwin St Hill, bowling strong fast-medium, was amazed to see the little Jamaican wristing the good-length ball away between mid-on and short leg or jumping in to drive it. Though he makes all the strokes, these are the two in which he specializes — forcing the ball away on the on side with a back stroke and getting to the pitch to drive. In a bright summer the slow bowlers will be glad to see him go.

As will be noticed from the scores enumerated, he is always

in form, and it was noted that he never batted better during the whole of the Australian trip than in the first innings of all — against New South Wales. Hugh Trumble said that the Melbourne innings was one of the best that he had ever seen, and many habitués of the Melbourne ground thought that no finer innings had ever been played there. Headley is a good field. Formerly, he was brilliant, but in Australia, for some reason, the edge of his keenness left him. I have seen him bowl Hendren, well set, three off-breaks and then send one away from the edge of Hendren's bat into the slips, where it was dropped. After that, however, he had shot his bolt.

Headley is a commercial clerk in ordinary life, but is devoted to cricket and is "a good lad". If he has to bat tomorrow, he goes to bed tonight. In Australia he failed to get runs against Grimmett. "I have to make a century against Grimmett," he told his friend St Hill. Batting very carefully, he made it in the third Test. "Satisfied?" asked St Hill. "Not yet; I have to master him now." In the fifth Test Headley made another century in a little over two hours, playing so brilliantly that even Bradman, Kippax and the rest joined in the applause. "Satisfied?" asked St Hill. "Ye-es," said Headley, hesitatingly. He had been brilliant, but it galled him that he had had to treat Grimmett with some respect. It is the genuine artistic instinct faithful to an inner ideal.

West Indies Cricket

(*The Cricketer*, 6 May–24 June 1933)

In the old, old days the men from the wild North came down to London to play a cricket match and found themselves one man short. They sent a hasty telegram for Ephraim Lockwood, who came, still in his teens, in a check shirt and a weird pair of trousers. The West Indies in England have always worn immaculate flannels, but in their early visits to England there was a touch of the rustic coming up to town. Lockwood made 91 runs, and, though the West Indies have not done as well as that, they have, all things considered, fared extraordinarily well.

The islands are a scattered chain in the Gulf of Mexico, stretching from Jamaica in the north, a few hours from Miami, Florida, to Trinidad in the south, a few hours from Venezuela.

British Guiana, on the mainland, is West Indian in everything except geography. The islands differ widely from one another. Thus Jamaica is over 4,000 square miles in area with nearly a million people; Barbados is 166 square miles in area, and at one time had nearly 200,000 people, though the population is less today. Trinidad, nearly eighteen hundred square miles, about the size of Lancashire, has over 400,000 people. Despite many other points of difference, however, in certain essentials they are all similar. Their population is mainly Negro or Negroid, with a small number of Europeans; sugar and other tropical products form the staple industries; in other words, the islands for many years have not been rich. They export most of their produce to Europe and America, and import their manufactured goods from the same sources; which means that there is no compelling demand towards inter-island communication.

Apart from Port of Spain in Trinidad (70,000), Kingston in Jamaica (35,000), Georgetown in British Guiana (55,000), most of the two million population live in small towns and villages. Even Bridgetown, the capital of Barbados, has only 13,000 people. Until the buses came transport was difficult. The organization of cricket on any extensive scale is therefore impracticable. Cricket is a profession only for those who prepare pitches, clean pads and boots and bowl at the nets. England having lost the wealthy amateur leans more and more heavily on the professional. The West Indies have never had and are not likely to have any of these.

Australia and South Africa through the size of their big towns can organize leagues able to reach and maintain a high standard. What sort of high grade league can be expected from a town of 13,000 inhabitants? Whereas in Australia, Queensland can arrive in Sydney the day before a match and leave the day after, in the West Indies Barbados has to wait for a Canadian or British or French liner whose programme is arranged for other purposes than the needs of enthusiastic cricketers. The league cricketer in the North of England today with his good ground, his highly organized system of matches, his experienced professional and his enthusiastic (and generous crowds) enjoys advantages which not one in twenty of international West Indian cricketers enjoy. Yet if West Indians lack artificial aids Nature is on their side.

We can play and often do play right through the year. In Barbados one gets the fastest wickets in the world; in British Guiana and in Jamaica there are good tropical turf wickets. Trinidad and some of the smaller islands use matting stretched

13

on hard clay, which at least possesses the virtue of being ready for ordinary use with less than a quarter of an hour's preparation. The people are not keen to watch, but they play. Trinidad, for instance, has had a curious history, and English, French, Spaniards, Chinese, Portuguese, Negroes and East Indians are represented there. All except the Portuguese play. There was a Chinese team fifty years ago. There is one today. The East Indians have many teams. Besides which various nationalities play together in the same teams. The little village of fifty houses may not have a church. It may lack a schoolhouse, but the cricket pitch is there.

It is possible that Mr Alfred Jingle had never played cricket in his life nor ever visited Jamaica, but at least he must have heard that people played cricket there before he chose that island as the scene of his great exploit against Sir Thomas Blazo.

During the long peace which followed Waterloo, the British officers in the West Indies relieved the tedium of those remote spots by playing cricket, and it is certain that in that hot climate the "natives", that is to say, the Negroes, did most of the practice-bowling and fielding. Fifty years ago in Trinidad a relation of mine, a blacksmith, a tremendous hitter and wicket-keeper, played with a team composed of the doctor, the warden, the magistrate and the other white notabilities of the district, ten white men and a Negro. His mother had been a slave on an estate still owned by some of the brothers who played in the team. He had also played as a child. It is very likely that for many years the white Creoles and Englishmen played together, the free Mulattos by themselves, and the swarming Negroes at first looked on, and in time developed their little village clubs. Then in 1863 the Kingston Club of Jamaica was formed, as far as we know at present the oldest club in the West Indies today. (The old Trinidad CC, however, already had a history behind it as early as 1844.) Two years after, a team from British Guiana visited Barbados to play the first inter-colonial match. British Guiana lost, but a few months later when Barbados paid them a return visit they won. After eight years they played again, Barbados winning. Scoring was low in these games, but one batsman scored 50 and another 51. A dozen years passed. Then in 1882 a Trinidad team went to British Guiana to play and the first great name in West Indian cricket emerges.

He was an Englishman, E.F. Wright, and had played for Gloucestershire, at that time with the Graces the most romantic cricketing centre in England. In this tournament he scored the first century in big cricket in the West Indies, 123 out of 168. The next highest score was 14. Highest of Trinidad's small scorers was Thornton Warner with 31, who thus brought into cricket prominence a name that has remained there since that time. A year or two after, British Guiana went to Barbados and lost again. Regular intercolonial matches were not far off. But first Barbados and British Guiana joined with Jamaica, and sent a West Indies team to Canada.

Since the formation of the Kingston Club, Jamaica had been playing steadily, and in 1880 Sabina Park, the present chief ground in Jamaica, was rented. But Jamaica, being a thousand miles away, could not send teams to play in the southern colonies. The presence of Jamaican players in this team was, therefore, a welcome step in the right direction. Trinidad, strangely, was not represented! Wright did not go, neither did P.J.T. Henry (Cambridge and Middlesex), but the team was strong enough to win five matches out of the six played in Canada. Going to Philadelphia they won only one, a minor fixture, lost three and drew one, Morley, the Notts bowler, taking 10 for 32 in one match. Few took any interest in them, for the total gate receipts of the tour were short of £50. Four years later an American team, including a few who had toured England with previous Philadelphia teams, visited the West Indies. In five busy weeks they played eleven matches, won five, drew four, and lost two. Cricket was greatly stimulated, and in 1891 in Barbados the three colonies played the first triangular tournament. The regular series began in 1893–4, at first biennial, but afterwards annual.

In the 1880s there was some suggestion of sending a team to England, but the idea dropped through. Later, however, it was suggested that an English team should go out instead, and in Jamaica in 1895 the first English team under R. Slade Lucas landed in Barbados. This team played in Barbados, Trinidad, British Guiana and Jamaica. Jamaica, Barbados, Trinidad, each won a match, and the English team, though it only contained three cricketers of county rank — Slade-Lucas, Bush, who had played for Surrey, and Bromley-Davenport, a Cambridge Blue — was by no means a weak team. Cricket leapt forward. In 1895–6 there was the yearly tournament in British Guiana. Jamaica sent a team to British Guiana early in 1896–7 to play two games, and then played Barbados on the way home. Late in 1896–7, owing to a misunderstanding, not one but two English teams toured the West Indies, one under Lord Hawke, and the

15

other under the late Sir Arthur Priestley. Lord Hawke's team had P.F. Warner (born in the West Indies), H.D.G. Leveson-Gower, G.R. Bardswell, C. Heseltine and H.R. Bromley-Davenport. Priestley had A.E. Stoddart, S.M.J. Woods, R.C.N. Palairet and C.A. Beldam.

Priestley's team won ten and lost five. Lord Hawke's won nine and lost two, Trinidad beating each team twice. For Priestley's team Stoddart was the outstanding batsman, making over a thousand runs. For Lord Hawke's P.F. Warner fell short of that number only by 16. But a scrutiny of the scores made by these batsmen is revealing. In Barbados in his first innings Stoddart made 42, and then was out to Clifford Goodman. In the second innings Goodman bowled him for 16. He fell for 16 to Somers-Cocks in his next innings; then Goodman got him out for 6, 18 and 5, bowling him out for both the smaller scores. The team went next to Trinidad. In those days English teams in Trinidad usually began with a match against the Queen's Park Club which manages all big cricket in Trinidad. Stoddart got 108 not out, but against a combined West Indies team, after making 38 in the first innings he fell to Goodman again for 6. Nor was he more successful against the Trinidad XI. Woods had him out for 4 and 3, and Cumberbatch for 5. These failures were no accident. In Clifford Goodman, Woods and Cumberbatch, the West Indies possessed three bowlers of outstanding ability. Clifford Goodman was a white man, member of a cricketing family which has done an immense amount for Barbados cricket, his brother being Percy Goodman, one of the finest of Barbados batsmen and a first-class slip. Goodman, tall and heavily built, bowled fast-medium pace with a quick off-break. P.F. Warner thought he bowled a little too much at the leg-stump and rather short. But he was a master of all the arts of the medium-pace bowler, and against these English teams he had (vs Slade-Lucas) 6 for 14, 8 for 71, 6 for 104, and 1 for 121 (62 overs); (vs Priestley's) 5 for 45, and 7 for 59; 5 for 69 and 5 for 37; 8 for 40, and 6 for 50; and for all the West Indies in Trinidad 5 for 72, and 4 for 53; against Lord Hawke's team he did not do so well, and, though a young man, dropped out of cricket soon after. In the All-West Indies match in Trinidad Stoddart seemed to have mastered him at last, and made 38 before he was dismissed by another bowler. But Stoddart, as Englishmen of the last generation will remember, made the old-fashioned hit to square-leg with tremendous power, and early in his second innings Goodman motioned d'Ade the Trinidadian out to the leg-boundary and sent up the required ball. Straight and true, hard and low. Stoddart hit to the fieldsman, who, with up-raised right arm, brought off a spectacular catch which is remembered in Trinidad to this day, though nearly forty years have past.

Woods, of Trinidad, was another type of bowler altogether. He was a Negro, who, taking two or three steps to the wicket, swung them in round arm as fast as Mold. Subtlety he despised, but at times he bowled very fast, and on any wicket which gave him help he was a dangerous bowler. Cumberbatch of Trinidad was another Negro, who, with great command of length, bowled medium-pace, turning a little either way. When Lord Hawke was going into bat Mr Vincent-Brown, the Attorney-General, said to Cumberbatch, "If you give him a duck I'll give you five dollars." "Very well, sir," replied Cumberbatch, and bowled Lord Hawke out first ball. In these matches Woods had 3 for 14, 3 for 56, 6 for 64, 5 for 51, 4 for 74, 5 for 25, 7 for 46, and 3 for 21; and Cumberbatch 4 for 66, 5 for 67, 6 for 11, 5 for 48, 4 for 82, and 3 for 70. It is difficult to see how any bowlers in the circumstances could have done better, and Woods and Cumberbatch with no opportunities had made themselves bowlers whom most English counties would have been glad to have. P.F. Warner did not fare very well against them. He got 74 before falling to Cumberbatch in his first innings against the pair, and in his next three innings Cumberbatch had him twice for small scores. The pity was that only Woods came to England, for Cumberbatch would surely have succeeded. During his tour Lord Hawke had said that a team of West Indian cricketers was good enough to go to England, and play against the counties, and on this hint a tour was arranged. The team would get half the gate receipts in all matches except those against Lancashire, Surrey, York, MCC and London County, each of these guaranteeing £100. The trip was not hopefully looked upon, and the MCC decided that the matches should not rank as first-class. H.B.G. Austin, one of the finest of Barbados batsmen and captain-designate of the team, had gone to South Africa to fight. But Percy Goodman and P.J. Cox, of Barbados, and L.S. Constantine, of Trinidad, G.W. Sproston, of British Guiana, had all batted very well against the English teams and in the inter-colonial tournaments. C.A. Ollivierre came from the small island of St Vincent, while there were two representatives from Jamaica. Burton, a medium-paced bowler, was another British Guiana representative. Constantine, Ollivierre, Woods and Burton were coloured men.

Though the batsmen in the team did not come up to expectations, though H.B.G. Austin as captain and player was a great loss, yet where the team suffered most was in the absence of Clifford Goodman and Cumberbatch. Those two bowlers and Woods had laid the foundation of the successes against the English teams and of the three, Woods, though he did very well, was the least likely to repeat those successes against a line of first-class batsmen. Summarized tours are at best poor stuff to read. The West Indies played seventeen games, lost eight and drew four. The team was not taken too seriously, and the *Star* published a cartoon showing Dr Grace, huge, towering, bat in hand, while around him crouched six black men all shedding tears, and saying to the doctor: "We have come to learn, sah!" The biggest event of the tour was the defeat by an innings of the Surrey team, weakened, but still containing many first-class men. Ollivierre and Cox made 218 to start off with, Ollivierre leaving first for 94. Cox got 142, and then the team collapsed for 328. But Woods took his first five wickets for 8 runs, finished up with 7 for 48, and Surrey could only get 117. Surrey followed on, but again Woods, helped this time by Burton, bowled them down, and they reached 177, losing by an innings and 34 runs. Woods had 5 for 68, making him 12 for 116 in the match.

On the whole tour Woods took 72 wickets at a cost of 21.54 each, and Burton 78 at a cost of 21.55, this in a season of very heavy scoring. The bowling of the others was feeble. The batting, too, was moderate. Ollivierre, Constantine and P.I. Cox averaged over 30 and Goodman 28. Goodman, an excellent bat, should have done better, but Constantine and Ollivierre both played good cricket. Constantine, a batsman of great resolution, combined dogged defence with considerable punishing power. He made a great century *vs* MCC at Lord's, 113 in ninety minutes with a five and seventeen fours. Up to a few years ago there were experienced West Indian cricketers who believed that Ollivierre was the best batsman the West Indies had ever produced. He was a big powerful man who at school threw 126 yards and cut one-handed for 6. He made most of the strokes with a few of his own, chiefly a glorious lofting drive over extra-cover's head. After this season he stayed in England to qualify for Derbyshire, thus beginning that undermining of West Indies cricket by English money which has continued into our own day and done so much to prevent us developing to our fullest extent. In 1900 English cricket took Ollivierre; in 1906 it took S.G. Smith; in 1923 it nearly took Francis and John; in 1928 it took Francis and Constantine; and now in 1933 when an English tour may mark the complete emergence of one of the greatest bastmen of the post-War period all good West Indians tremble to think that George Headley may use his great powers in spheres far removed from West Indian Test cricket. Charity begins at home, and on the whole we may say that the team had not done too badly. Said the *Sun*: "They field fairly well, but their bowling is weak and their batting crude and possessing little style. None of them seem to have any idea of forward play, and there is little variety in their strokes. Few of them score freely on the off-side, but one and all are good at the old-fashioned leg stroke and time the ball admirably." It is a curious commentary on the cricket ideals of those days. One might say the same of some of the most successful batsmen of the present day. The team suffered one terrible experience which should not be omitted. Against Gloucestershire they met Jessop. He made 50 in twenty-three minutes, 100 runs in forty-three, and 157 in an hour. Unfortunately for Jessop the match was not counted as first-class. With the possible exception of Alletson's innings against Sussex in 1911, this is perhaps the greatest piece of hitting in the recognized history of the game, and thus early the West Indies had earned a place among the records.

With the men back home, the tournaments continued. In 1901 R.A. Bennett took out a team of university players, including eight blues, among them B.J.T. Bosanquet, F.L. Fane, E.W. Dillon, E.M. Dowson and E.R. Wilson. They did fairly well, but were not taken as sternly as the previous teams. Tournaments again and 1904–5 saw Lord Brackley taking out a team. Hayes, of Surrey, and Thompson, of Northants, Captain E.G. Wynyard, G.H. Simpson-Hayward, A. Hesketh-Pritchard (who had played that year for the Gentlemen) and C.P. Foley formed the nucleus of a really first-class side. This team, unlike the others, went to Jamaica first. Barbados won once, and Trinidad beat them twice, but the English team won both the matches against the West Indies XI, though then (as to this day) the All-West Indies sides in the West Indies were far from being representative. For Lord Brackley's team both Hayes and Wynyard scored over 900 runs, and Thompson took over 100 wickets. Simpson-Hayward's underhands took 50, and three other bowlers had over 30 wickets each.

For the West Indies, H.B.G. Austin, Percy Goodman and Constantine advanced their previous reputations, and Burton and Woods continued to bowl effectively; but new names appeared: S.G. Smith, a white Trinidadian, who became so familiar a figure for Northamptonshire; C.P. Cumberbatch, a Negro, who bowled well for Trinidad, A.E. Harragin, a white man, hard hitter, and one of the greatest all-round athletes. Layne, a Negro fast bowler, and Richard Ollivierre. Cumberbatch, medium-pace right-hand, had among his analyses 8 for 27 and 5 for 30; and 6 for 70; but he was not to be classed with the earlier Cumberbatch. In one respect Richard Ollivierre, though he failed in the representative games, rather stood out among the newcomers. He played for St Vincent, and perhaps a glimpse at St Vincent's history in these matches will be both entertaining and instructive.

St Vincent is a little island of 50,000 scattered agriculturalists, the chief town possessing perhaps three or four thousand people. Forty years ago the population was less, and even more scattered than it is today. Still, like all British West Indians, the St Vincentians play cricket. Slade-Lucas visited them in 1896. Slade-Lucas's team made 63. St Vincent, led by J. Vanloo, a Negro, made 139 for 8, five men making double figures, and both the not-outs being over 20. Lord Hawke's team went there, and scored 138 in the first innings. St Vincent replied with 154. Lord Hawke's team made 287 in the second innings, and, though St Vincent lost, they made a highly creditable fourth innings score of 136. In 1901 Bennett's team played a combined team from St Vincent and Grenada, another small island. In the first, Bennett's team won by an innings and 19 runs. In the second Bennett's team made 140 and 120 to win by a bare 65 runs, and Richard Ollivierre, a brother of Charlie, took in the first innings 9 wickets for 79 runs. In 1905 Lord Brackley went to St Vincent to play two matches. Lord Brackley's team had 72 for 3 at lunch, but all fell for 147, Richard Ollivierre taking 7 for 38. St Vincent before close of play had 61 for 3. Next day the score was 150 before the third wicket fell, and St Vincent reached 250 for 9, Ollivierre getting 99 and Helon Ollivierre, another brother, 45. The Englishmen had lost 4 for 77, when the two-day match came to a close. In the return match St Vincent batted first, and scored 230, Helon Ollivierre 47; and Osment 83 in thirty minutes. He hit five sixes and eight fours; the last wicket putting on 60. The Englishmen lost 4 for 70, and were all out for 210, Richard Ollivierre taking 5 for 93.

In 1906 another West Indies team came to England, including all the stars mentioned above and Layne, who bowled for Barbados, but was a native of St Vincent, and had taken his part in the fine showing against Brackley's team. Jamaica, whose cricket against these touring teams was of a rather low standard, sent C.S. Morrison and Dr Cameron. The team, supposed to be so much stronger than the last, began depressingly, losing match after match, and gaining one or two meagre victories. E.H.D. Sewell under the heading, "What is the matter with the West Indies team?" wrote: "Once again the West Indies team have failed to do themselves justice as a side. . . . It is a most extraordinary thing that the side as a side cannot 'get going', in cricketer's phraseology. Is it just all the difference between first- and second-class, I wonder? I was chatting with one of the Kent XI, and he wondered why they did not get more runs. He said their field was badly placed, and only the coloured men are good catchers. They are certainly a mysterious side — and I cannot help thinking they may one day do something surprising." They did. Twice in quick succession they showed first-class form.

The first time was against an English XI with A.P. Day, A.E. Lawton, E.H.D. Sewell, Kinneir, Quaife, Lilley, Warren, the England fast bowler, and Hargreaves, the left-hand bowler, whose misfortune it was to be at his best when Rhodes was in his prime. The West Indies made 201, Constantine hitting 54 in seventy minutes. The Englishmen made only 138, Ollivierre bowling unchanged, and getting 4 for 71. West Indies made 158, Constantine 51. With England 4 for 82 on a wicket that had gone, rain put a stop to play. That was on July 26, 27 and 28, and after taking Northumberland and Durham in their stride the West Indies gave Yorkshire a smashing defeat. The match is worth recalling in some detail.

Yorkshire, though not at full strength, had Rhodes, Denton, Tunnicliffe, T.L. Taylor, E. Smith, Sedgwick, Myers and Dolphin. The West Indies lost one for 32, and then Constantine and Layne hit 139 in sixty-five minutes when Constantine left for 79. He made some dashing hook strokes and hit twelve fours, punishing Sedgwick for twenty in one over. Layne made 63, Sydney Smith 31, and the innings closed for 270. Then on a perfect wicket Ollivierre and Sydney Smith bowled down Yorkshire for 50. In 12.5 overs Ollivierre had 7 wickets for 23 runs. Yorkshire did not follow on. George Challenor, nineteen years old, opened again with Constantine and sent up 50 in twenty-five minutes. Then came Percy Goodman to score 102 in ninety minutes with sixteen fours and the innings was declared closed at 306 for 6. Yorkshire, in the hour and a half left for play, lost 4 for 119, and were all out the next day for 263, of which three men made 227. A team that could do that was not second-rate. Yet in first-class matches Goodman averaged

21

only 31 with a total of 607. That he had it in him to do better is the opinion of all good judges, for with all his brilliancy he was sound. Constantine made 776 with an average of 29, and, fine as were the innings he played, yet he had more cricket in him than that. Harragin showed himself one of the hardest hitters playing, but he suffered from ill-health. H.B.G. Austin did not reproduce his home form, and even Ollivierre, who in first-class matches took 51 wickets at a cost of 21 each and scored nearly 500 runs with an average of 20, could hardly be said to have done his absolute best. In his case, however, as always with the West Indian fast bowling, the fielding in the slips often let him down badly. Good slips would have given him quite a few more analyses like his 7 for 23.

There on the whole we have certain characteristics of West Indies cricket which have remained to the present day. Bats-men obviously of high class even if they do moderately well fail to reproduce their form consistently; fast bowlers who are let down by bad slip-fielding; and a side which somehow rarely finds itself. It has been hinted that the temperament of the coloured men is against them, but Goodman, Austin and Harragin in 1906, Ince and Tarilton in 1923, the Wrights and de Caires in later years were white men. The reason may be found, it seems to me, in the cricket that our cricketers regularly play at home.

The general standard is too low. That unremitting concentra-tion which becomes second nature to the county cricket bats-men or the players in high-grade club cricket in Australia is very hard for the West Indian batsman to develop. Even in inter-colonial cricket after he has managed the opening bowlers and the first change, he can afford to take things easily, especially as professionals are not permitted to take part in inter-colonial games. The best bowlers in the islands are snapped up by the wealthy clubs to bowl at practice, and local players are thus deprived of playing against these in the inter-colonial games. Furthermore, inter-colonial games are rare; many a batsman gets one first-class match a year; even when English teams come they play only two matches against island teams, and a so-called Test match. A batsman is keyed up for those brief occasions, but soon slips back if not into slack at least into easygoing habits. It is therefore a strain for him to score consistently against the unremitting deadliness (compa-ratively speaking) of good first-class cricket. L.S. Constantine is a case in point. He had a remarkably sound defence, great command of a fine array of strokes, and was never intimidated by any occasion. In 1906 he started off with 89, and then in 19 innings he passed 50 only once, 40 three times, and failed over and over again. Late in the season he found himself and made 68, 13, 54, 51, 1, 27, 79, 31, 92, 50, 41. Note that, though he was so often over 50, yet on such a beginning he never went on to make the 120 or 160 which the English or Australian batsmen who had reached thus far would probably have gone on to make on at least two or three occasions.

It seems that the habit of making long scores against first-class bowling like most other useful habits owes much to environment. Constantine I choose in particular, because I have heard him say of his playing in England against a certain bowler — Thompson, I think, it was — that he bowled you a good-length, an off-break, a good yorker, one that left the pitch with a little pace, etc., and then when you thought you were well settled came an extra special that bit the pitch and took a lot of playing. You had to watch all the time. He agreed that you got into it after a time, but complained that after the tour he dropped back into second-rate club cricket and the habitual concentration soon vanished. This explanation does not attempt to explain completely all failures of all batsmen who play below their home form, but it is probably the major cause of it. Should the West Indies team of 1906 have played in England in 1907, it would conceivably have startled many more counties besides Yorkshire.

Why the slip-fielding in England is bad is hard to tell. In the West Indies one sees any number of potentially fine slip-fieldsmen. The Negro's eye is quick, his body lissom, his anticipation keen. But on cold mornings in the early summer a few balls flying through the slips and smacking the tropical hands are enough to destroy confidence, without which no catching can ever be reliable.

Of the failure of West Indies sides to do themselves justice as a whole notice will be taken later. Their 1906 side lost and lost and lost, winning only a minor match here and there until the game against an England XI at the very end of July. After the great victory against Yorkshire, they made 326 of the 351 required to win against Lancashire, 292 for 7 out of 328 required to win when stumps were drawn against Notts, and then in a small scoring match beat Northamptonshire by 153 runs. The team had found itself, but too late.

Two men deserve special mention, Sydney Smith and George Challenor. Sydney Smith in all matches made a thousand runs and took a hundred wickets, showing first-class form in both departments. He qualified later for Northamptonshire. A year or so before the War he played successfully for the Gentlemen, and would have stood a very good chance of playing on any England side. George Challenor made a thousand runs in all matches, and in first-class matches 684 with an average of 28 and a century against Notts. W.G. Grace, watching him at the nets, asked who he was, and said that an eye should be kept on him.

In the West Indies between 1907 and 1911 the tournaments continued. Percy Goodman in 1909 made two centuries in each match. Tarilton, a white Barbadian, and George Challenor began to make their innumerable runs for Barbados. André Cipriani, a Trinidadian coloured man, who had learnt a lot of cricket in Essex while studying law in England, brought home his fine back play and glorious strokes, and there emerged a new race of coloured bowlers like George John and Small, fast bowlers, and Rogers, a clever slow bowler, good batsman and magnificent cover-point. Constantine was now at his very best. H.B.G. Austin was both stylish and reliable, especially at a crisis, and the brothers Browne from Barbados, young men, both established themselves, C.A. as one of the most glorious off-side hitters the West Indies has known and C.R. as a googly bowler. In his first inter-colonial match, while still a boy at Harrison College, he bowled 74 overs for 192 runs and 7 wickets.

In February 1911, the MCC for the first time sent a team to the West Indies. Sydney Smith came with it, and the professionals were George Brown, H. Young and J.W. Hearne. Hearne had not yet made his subsequent reputation, but it must be remembered that in the autumn of that very year he was playing Test cricket for P.F. Warner's team in Australia.

This English side was weak. Twice Barbados and Trinidad beat it badly, and, although it won matches against the West Indies eleven, these sides were far from being representative. Two games against Jamaica were drawn. Austin, Challenor, Constantine, Layne, of the old brigade, did well. André Cipriani, Tarilton, C.A. Browne showed splendid form, George John and C.R. Browne shone as bowlers, and Rogers had striking all-round success. Whittington and Holloway as batsmen, Hearne and Young as bowlers, and S.G. Smith in both departments, did best for the Englishmen, but the team as a side of cricketers was a failure.

So much was that so that in 1913 the MCC sent another team — the most powerful that had hitherto visited the West Indies

— T.A.L. Whittington and S.G. Smith, who had done so well
with the 1911 team, came again; also W.C. (Razor) Smith, A.E.
Relf, whose career coincided so unfortunately for himself with
that of S.F. Barnes, E. Humphreys, of Kent, and D.C.F. Burton. It
was a very good team, but West Indies cricket was now of a
high standard. Barbados, by itself as powerful in batting as most
English counties, made scores of 520 for 6 and 447, winning by
an innings each time. Tarilton and Gibbs each scored a century,
and George Challenor two. Challenor's 109 was a grand innings, the first half played on a tricky wicket, the batsman
opening out as the wicket improved. But R. Challenor, C.A.
Browne and H.W. Ince (like the Austins, the Challenors were
all fine cricketers) all scored heavily, and the English bowling
could do little with them. As usual, a ragged West Indies team
lost the representative game. Humphreys had analyses of 6 for
92, 7 for 75, and 6 for 70, and Razor Smith and A.F. Somerset
put on 167 for the last wicket in one match, Smith scoring his
only century in first-class cricket.

In Trinidad MCC won the first game by 8 wickets, Relf and
S.G. Smith batting finely for 91 and 95, and the same pair
bowling well. But in the next game Trinidad made 334,
Constantine and André Cipriani retrieving failures in the first
game. Then John and Rogers bowled the MCC down for 87, and,
though Burton, S.G. Smith and Dobson helped their side to
score 315 for 8, only time saved MCC. In the All-West Indies
match another unrepresentative team beat MCC by an innings.
C.P. Cumberbatch, the 1906 bowler, had learnt to bat, and made
63. Ince from Barbados, made 167, and four batsmen made over
30. A welcome visitor from St Vincent was R. Ollivierre of the
1906 team, who scored 34, and in the first innings took 5
wickets for 68 runs. British Guiana, under a cloud for many
years, could not do much against MCC, who not only scored
heavily against the British Guiana team, but made 441 against a
West Indies team that had such good bowlers as Ollivierre,
John and Rogers. For MCC Relf bowled very effectively in
British Guiana. An instructive anecdote deals with Rogers, the
Trinidad slow bowler. On the matting wicket in Trinidad he got
a lot of spin on both ways, and tied up the MCC batsmen. Relf
told him that they would meet again on the turf in British
Guiana. There Rogers could not get this spin, and his 12 overs
cost 61 runs. E.R.D. Moulder carried his bat through the West
Indies first innings for 104 out of 264. Moulder had had an
unfortunate career. A successful batsman in inter-colonial
cricket in 1901, against Bennett's team, he had 64, 64 and 94

not out. He failed completely against Brackley's team, averaging less than three in four innings. But now he came again and scored well against MCC with the fine innings mentioned above as his best. Of the English team, Humphreys, Smith and Relf did best in bowling, and Smith, Relf, Whittington and Burton in batting. But there is no doubt that West Indies cricket with the uninterrupted sequence of inter-colonial and international matches from 1897 to 1913 was now very strong, how strong may be seen from the fact that Richard Ollivierre, who bowled so finely in Trinidad, scored 45 and 56 for all West Indies in the game at Bourda, British Guiana. John, who had 6 for 93 in the British Guiana representative game, was a superb fast bowler. There were many good medium-paced bowlers, and in Barbados and elsewhere any number of good batsmen. Still it must be said that Relf, after the fine showing of MCC in British Guiana, expressed the wish that he could take this team back to Barbados then.

Cricket began again in 1920 with an informal tournament between Trinidad and Barbados. Barbados won both games handsomely — Challenor, Tarilton, Ince, H.B.G. Austin, all doing well, and some of them very well. Barbados in one game scored no less than 623 for 5, Tarilton 304 not out. On the perfect wicket and against the great array of Barbados batsmen John bowled magnificently. On the Trinidad side W. St Hill, who had been coming into prominence before the War, batted finely; but the chief success of the Trinidad side was that of Small. Small before the War had been a round-arm fast bowler and had had one astonishing success against the 1913 MCC side, 7 for 49, but he had gone to Egypt with the B.W.I., had played a lot of cricket there, and improved out of all knowledge as a batsman with the strokes on the off-side off the left foot made with amazing freedom and power.

Two tournaments followed in which Pascall, Wiles and St Hill were among the new stars, but, in as much as Wiles and St Hill failed in the tournament immediately preceding the selection of the 1923 team for England, they were dropped, thus emphasizing another of the difficulties of the West Indies snap selection.

The team that finally came is worthy of being set down in detail. H.B.G. Austin, now well over forty but still a fine batsman, was the captain; G. Challenor, H.W. Ince, P.H. Tarilton and G. Francis (Barbados), C.V. Hunter, M.P. Fernandes, C.R. Browne (British Guiana), G. John, V. Pascall, G.A. Dewhurst, L.N. Constantine, and J.A. Small (Trinidad), J.K. Holt, R.K. Nunes, and R.L. Phillips (Jamaica). C.R. Browne while studying law in England had played a lot of cricket for Surrey Club and Ground, but on coming back to the West Indies had elected to practise in British Guiana instead of in Barbados. L.N. Constantine, a son of the 1900 and 1906 stalwart, was picked to play on the score of some splendid fielding at cover in the 1922 tournament, coupled with useful fast bowling. Fernandes, very young, and having played in but one first-class match, came in, it was thought, chiefly to give British Guiana a third player. The real surprise was G.N. Francis of the ground staff at the Kensington Oval in Barbados. Griffith, of Barbados, had been bowling fast and well in inter-colonial cricket, and it was thought that he should have been chosen instead. H.B.G. Austin, however, took Francis.

The team had a terribly wet summer to contend with, and was severely handicapped by it. It lost many of the earlier games, and it seemed at first as if there would be a repetition of the earlier tours — good cricketers failing to reproduce their form. But a magnificent innings of 94 by Small against Lancashire seemed to give the team good luck, and from that time, though a match here and there was lost, it had an almost triumphant progress, the culminating point of which was a ten-wicket victory over Surrey. Challenor with 1,556 runs and an average of 51 took undisputed rank as one of the finest batsmen playing that season, and his off-side hitting was as beautiful as his defence was sound. None of the others reached that standard, but Small had a great run of success, and M.P. Fernandes and H.B.G. Austin made many good scores. Small had the highest total which was only 776, but he averaged 31, Fernandes 34, and Austin 25. The failures were Tarilton and Ince, Tarilton, a master of defensive play, who left the West Indies as the best batsman on the side, being unable to reproduce anything like his home form.

If the batting, except for George Challenor, was not of the highest county standard, the bowling was fully up to it. Francis and John each took a hundred wickets, and in first-class matches Francis had 87 for 15 runs apiece. Both he and Challenor were very high in the English averages. P.F. Warner and a few others said quite openly that an England side of that year would have been glad to have Francis and John. Francis was the deadlier, and from his first match had a series of astonishing analyses, clean bowling an unusual number of batsmen for under double figures. John at the start was not so

27

deadly, but John was approaching forty and past his best. In 1917, 1918, 1919, there could have been few finer fast bowlers. C.R. Browne, medium right hand, took 75 wickets in first-class matches and maintained a high level of excellence all through, while Pascall the left-hander, if not always deadly, took 51, and bowled very well. Dewhurst behind the wicket earned general admiration and L.N. Constantine, besides being a useful change bowler, was considered by many sound judges to be the finest cover-point the game had yet seen. Others might have exceeded him in finesse, but in pace to the ball, fierce energy and the deadliness of his return he had no equal.

The finest performance was in the last match at Scarborough against an England XI which included Hobbs, Rhodes, G.T.S. Stevens, Ernest Tyldesley, J.W.H.T. Douglas, P.G.H. Fender, in fact a team not far removed from an English Test side. Having 31 to win, Francis and John bowled against the English XI in so determined a fashion that six wickets were lost before the runs were made, and that only with the help of all the luck that was going.

In 1926 the MCC sent a team to the West Indies, and its strength reflected the impression the West Indies had made in England. There were Hammond, Holmes, Roy Kilner, Root, Astill, Collins, Watson, E.J. Smith, Hon. F.S.G. Calthorpe (captain), L.G. Crawley, H.L. Dales, Hon. L.H. Tennyson, and Captain T.O. Jameson. Yet the tourists could do little with individual colonies. The weather was against them in Barbados, and they not only lost the first match by an innings, but narrowly escaped a similar fate in the second game. Trinidad drew both games with nothing in it each time. Against British Guiana, formerly a rather weak side, MCC got 350 and 46 for 0 wickets; British Guiana, 373; MCC, 385 and 124 for 2; British Guiana, 348. Yet in the Tests the West Indies, though they got together more representative sides than formerly, failed to maintain this standard. In Barbados the Englishmen made 597 for 8 declared, Hammond playing a great innings of 238. Challenor and Tarilton replied gallantly with 76 for 0 wickets at the drawing of stumps; then rain spoilt the wicket, and further rain alone saved the West Indies from a crushing defeat by an innings. In Trinidad MCC won by 5 wickets, H.B.G. Austin, who had played against English teams thirty years before, scoring 69 and 45. Wiles made 75 for West Indies, and C.R. Browne, now batsman as well as bowler, played a superb forcing innings of 74, hit in an hour. In British Guiana the West Indies made 462, C.R. Browne scoring a century again at the rate of a run per minute. The English side fell for 264 and 243 for 8, Constantine getting 5 for 52.

In this series, Tarilton, Challenor, St Hill, Fernandes, all scored well, Challenor batting superbly, but no bowler stood out, John, Pascall and Browne rather failing to maintain their 1923 form, though Browne's dashing and consistent batting and the fact that all three were near forty probably accounted for this.

The MCC team then played three matches in Jamaica. Jamaica has not figured largely in this sketch. A Trinidad team had played there in 1906, and a team from Philadelphia (including H.V. Hordern) in 1909. Also some of the English teams had included Jamaica in their itinerary. But Jamaican cricket, particularly the batting, had not been of as high a standard as that of the other cricketing centres. Of Jamaica cricketers the best was Holt, a coloured man, a fine natural batsman who had been a member of the 1923 team to England, and had rather failed to show his skill. In 1911 O.C. Scott, a slow right-hand spin bowler, had bowled with deadly effect against Somerset's first team. The vice-captain of the 1923 team had been R.K. Nunes, an old Dulwich boy. C.S. Morrison had also bowled well on many occasions.

In 1924, however, a Jamaican team visited Barbados. Challenor and Tarilton helped to add another to the long list of Barbados batting triumphs, and they were ably supported by Hoad and Bartlett, two new men. Jamaica, however, showed vastly improved form. Nunes, Holt, Scott batted very well; Scott bowled successfully; but the find of the tour was Martin, who in his first first-class match made 195 run out. A left-hander, impregnable in defence, imperturbable in temperament, Martin has ever since that good beginning been one of the first of West Indies batsmen.

Against this 1926 English team, Jamaica showed that she had come to stay. MCC won the first game by 5 wickets. In the second, Jamaica made only 253 in the first innings, but faced in the second with a large deficit reached 277 for 5, and drew creditably. In the last game 15 wickets gave nearly a thousand runs, Jamaica 445 for 9, MCC 510 for 6. Nunes had scores of 140 and 83; Martin 66, 44, and 80; and Scott, the bowler, not only scored 54, 58, 72, 62, but played fine free cricket for his runs. Martin, who bowls slow left-hand, had 6 for 104 in the first game.

Hammond and Holmes with between seven and eight hundred runs each did best for the MCC, Hammond averaging 48 and Holmes 46. Jameson and Watson batted well, and Astill was the best all-rounder. The MCC bowlers failed against the fine batting. Root, for instance, though he could swing the ball appreciably, was severely punished, while the 34 wickets of Roy Kilner cost him nearly 30 runs each. Yet both Root and Kilner were first choices for England on their return home, and Kilner played in four Test matches against Collins's teams.

We have not given much attention to tournaments. On the whole Barbados had produced the best sides, with British Guiana a pretty bad third. The 1927 tournament in Barbados, the eighteenth of the series, provided some extraordinary cricket, which deserves notice here. Barbados touched the peak of that colossal scoring which had so distinguished her cricket during the preceding years. Trinidad having won the cup in 1925, British Guiana met Barbados in the first game. British Guiana made 265. Barbados replied with 715 for 8; Tarilton, 120; Challenor, 104; C.A. Browne, 131 not out, and Hoad 115, the first four men on the batting list. Young Bartlett got 88. British Guiana made 336 and lost by an innings and 114 runs. The final for the cup was a splendid cricket match of the Marathon variety. Barbados, sent in on a bad wicket, got only 175, C.A. Browne 49. Trinidad made 559, Small 100, Ben Sealey, 98 not out, and Wiles 192, Wiles thus passing Percy Goodman's record inter-colonial score of 180. Then Barbados showed perhaps the finest batting ever seen in the West Indies. Against the powerful and varied Trinidad attack consisting of Constantine, Edwin St Hill, Pascall, Small and Ben Sealey, Challenor and Tarilton made 292 for the first wicket, when Tarilton left for 123 run out. Challenor cut short Wiles's triumph by scoring 220. Bartlett made 74, Hoad 174, not out, and Barbados declared the innings closed at 726 for 7. Trinidad on a wearing, rain-affected wicket did well to make 217.

Early in 1928 the Hon. L.H. Tennyson took a team to Jamaica with players such as the Rev. Gillingham, P.G.H. Fender, Ernest Tyldesley and many good first-class cricketers. Jamaica did well. Nunes scored 200 not out and 108, Martin 204 not out, Ray 98 and 84, and was not out in two other innings of over 20 each. Trial matches in Barbados in the spring of 1928 showed much fine cricket, and everything seemed well set for the 1928 tour in England when the West Indies were for the first time to play three Tests against the full strength of England.

The tour is probably fresh in the minds of all readers of this article. In varying degrees Challenor, Browne and Small fell short of their form of 1923; Bartlett just to show what he could do made a great century in two hours against Larwood and the full strength of the Notts bowling, but he did little else to justify the high opinion deservedly held of his cricket; and Francis, though he bowled well, was not the destructive bowler of 1923. On the other hand, Roach, a young player, got going from the start, and improved steadily. He made over a thousand runs and played many innings of sterling value. Hoad started very badly, but in the latter part of the tour was making runs against any bowling. Griffith took over a hundred wickets for the season and 6 in the one innings in the Test at the Oval. But the outstanding successes of the tour were Constantine and, in a lesser degree, Martin. But for Constantine, indeed, the tour would have been a sorry affair, and he created quite a sensation. He beat Middlesex almost single-handed in a schoolboy-fiction match. With only one interval of failure he hit with great power and certainty, bowled at an intimidating pace, and, while retaining all his brilliance at cover-point, was now dazzling in the slips, or for that matter wherever he was placed. In first-class matches he did the double of a thousand runs and a hundred wickets which, added to his untiring fielding, would have given his work a fair claim to being one of the most brilliant all-round displays of any cricketer visiting England. Unfortunately, he did not come up to expectations in the Test matches. Martin, on the other hand, was not a great player in any sense of the term. He had few strokes, and his method was pedestrian, but on a side which failed so grievously in the big games he could generally be depended upon for runs, and in one respect he was invaluable. His six innings in the Tests were 44, 12, 21, 32, 25, and 41. Nothing startling in themselves, but the West Indies without them would have cut a pitiable figure.

Two more series of matches remain. The first was the MCC tour in 1929–30. Calthorpe led another powerful team, Hendren, Sandham, George Gunn, Ames, O'Connor, Townsend, Wilfred Rhodes, Astill and Voce; R.E.S. Wyatt, G.T.S. Stevens and Major Stanyforth. For once Barbados got the worst of the opening exchanges, both matches being drawn in favour of MCC. The first Test was also drawn, West Indies 369 and 384; MCC 467, and 167 for 3. Trinidad beat MCC by 102 runs and a weakened Trinidad side lost the second game by only 23 runs. This tempted the Selection Committee to indulge in fantastic experiments for the Test, and the West Indies side was deservedly beaten. British Guiana could do nothing against the MCC, but the West Indies won the Test there by nearly three hundred runs. Roach, who had made a century in the Barbados

C.L.R. James

Test, made 209, Headley 114 and 112, and Constantine and Francis bowled down MCC for 145 on a perfect wicket, this ranking with Voce's bowling in the Trinidad Test as the finest bowling feat of the tour. Jamaica drew two matches creditably, and then came another extraordinary match. MCC made 849, Sandham 325, and West Indies replied with 286. Calthorpe, though nearly 500 runs ahead, was afraid to declare. He batted again and declared at 272 for 9. West Indies had scored 408 for 5 when rain caused the match to be abandoned. Never did a West Indies side meet the visitors. The four Test teams were selected by four different committees and led by four different players, and in various matches Hoad, Francis, Constantine, C.R. Browne, Martin and O.C. Scott, indispensable members of any West Indian side, were not available.

Hendren on the MCC side averaged over 100 per innings, and scored four double centuries, being not out each time. Ames also batted very finely, and Voce at times had great success. On the West Indies side Derek Sealy, a Barbados schoolboy, made 100, 77, 75, 58 and 15, but the most interesting cricketer of these Tests was George Headley, a young Jamaican coloured man.

When still only eighteen Headley had walked almost unannounced into big cricket in 1929, and scored 211 against one of the English teams which Jamaica has invited so frequently of recent years with such profitable results to her cricket. Later he made a magnificent century against another visiting team. Now, still short of his majority, he came south to play for All-West Indies against MCC, his first trip abroad. In Barbados he made 21 and 176; in Trinidad 8 and 39; in British Guiana 114 and 112; in the MCC vs Jamaica matches 64 and 72 and 52; in the last Test 10 and 223, the 223 being more than half the 408 for 5 made when the West Indies was over 500 runs behind. For freedom and the style which is no style and yet all style his method was fully equal to his colossal scoring.

In the autumn of 1930 a West Indies team went to Australia. It consisted of G.C. Grant (captain), L.S. Birkett, L.N. Constantine, E.A. Hunte, C.A. Roach, E. St Hill (Trinidad), F.I. de Caires, O.S. Wight (British Guiana), H.C. Griffith, E.L. Bartlett, G. Francis, J.E.D. Sealy (Barbados), O.C. Scott, F.R. Martin, G. Headley, I. Barrow (Jamaica). The team started well by chasing New South Wales to within 4 wickets. Then, save for a barren victory against Queensland, it failed against every State, and in every Test until it met New South Wales just before the final Test. New South Wales were beaten in a heavy scoring game.

And in the last Test the West Indies declared in both innings and won a well-deserved victory by 30 runs, so that the last appearance of the West Indies on the cricket stage showed the team at its best in big cricket.

Few players on the side added materially to their reputations. Constantine fielded with his usual amazing brilliance, scored 748 runs, and headed the bowling averages with 47 wickets at 20 runs each. This was an extremely good double, besides which he delighted the crowd, and was a great drawing card. In the Tests, however, he did little. Griffith, Francis and Scott had some good analyses in these games, but Griffith, who did best both in aggregate and average, had only 14 wickets which cost nearly 30 runs each. Grant, a Cambridge Blue, had a difficult task as captain, most of the men being quite unknown to him as cricketers. But both as captain and batsman he made great progress during the tour. His average of 42.5 in the Tests, though flattering, nevertheless represented value, and in the opinion of the best Australian critics near the end of the tour he was playing like a fully-fledged Test player. Headley, however, in the very first match against New South Wales scored 25 and 82, and made a thousand runs in the Australian first-class season, a feat that has been accomplished by very few cricketers either native Australian, or touring. Against Victoria, he played an innings of 131 out of 212, scoring at the rate of a run a minute. His variety of strokes and mastery of the bowling astonished the spectators. Hugh Trumble described the innings as one of the finest he had ever seen, and by common consent no finer innings has ever been played on the Melbourne ground. Then he had a bad patch, but ran into form with a century in the third Test, after which his first-class scores were 77, 113, 75, 39, 33, 11, 70, 2, 105, 30, the 105 being a Test innings made in 146 minutes in such brilliant style as to draw applause from even the players on the field.

An English team visited Jamaica early in 1932. Headley made a century in each of the three matches, and at lunch on the second day of the first game had scored 346 and was still not out. For all who know him and are interested in West Indies cricket the present season is one of absorbing interest. Jamaica cricket, West Indies Test cricket, the stern Test of an Australian season all have seen runs flowing from his bat in a limpid, never-ending stream. Whatever secret doubts may have been felt as to his real quality were set aside by his play in Australia and the unfettered praise of the Australian critics.

Chances of West Indies in First Test

(*Port of Spain Gazette*, 15 June 1933)

I could not go to the Oval on either Saturday or on Monday. On Monday night I was talking to the best cricket correspondent in England. We discussed the chances of the West Indies pretty thoroughly. Air mail is expensive and I cannot go into too much detail but he said that A.C. MacLaren, who saw the West Indies at Lord's, thinks that given a fast wicket and Constantine to help, anything may happen in the first Test. That also was his own opinion. The English batsmen were childishly helpless against the fast bowling. And it was not body-line because there was only one man forward short leg on the on side. The change bowling, however, was weak. Whether Grant will allow himself to be frightened by these English critics is an important question. If he breaks the morale of his fast bowlers by expressing doubts as to whether the tactics of Constantine and Martindale are fair, the West Indies should flay him alive. The English had no mercy on the Australians. Now that the tour is over and the Ashes won, nearly every English writer and cricketer with the most bare-faced effrontery condemns body-line bowling, but when the Australians protested they shrieked to high heaven that there was nothing in it and the Australians were merely squealing. This is our chance and if weakness and lack of a sense of realism in the high command makes us lose it, then our blood be upon our own head.

The spirit of the team is pretty good. Jack Grant is doing very well. If there is any trouble it is likely to come over the question of the vice-captaincy. The Board knew, I suppose, why it did not appoint one. If anything happens to Grant and there is any monkeying about, there are the prospects of a fine row. It would be a pity, because the correspondent whom I spoke to told me that on the last day at Lord's vs MCC when the West Indies realized that they had a chance to force a victory, it was splendid to see how they went at it. He had never noticed that in the 1928 team. Why the Board did not officially appoint the only choice of vice-captain I do not know. At any rate that and a lot of other things will come some day and quicker than they think. Then and only then will the West Indies take its rightful place in the scheme of things. For let every good West Indian know that, after watching cricket here and carefully weighing my words, I have no hesitation in saying that in cricket, as in many other things, West Indians are among the most highly gifted people one can find anywhere. The English have money, thirty times our population, vast organization, every conceivable advantage. Yet with all that, we could hold our own. Our trouble is that we have not yet learned to subordinate everything to winning. Under modern conditions to win you have got to make up your mind to win. The day West Indians White, Brown and Black learn to be West Indians, to see nothing in front to right or left but West Indian success and the means to it, that day they begin to be grown up. Along with that it will be necessary to cultivate any number of fine speeches, noble sentiments and unimpeachable principles. But these you must indulge in before the struggle, cricket or whatever it may be, and also after the struggle is over. Anyway, more of this later. Let me describe as accurately as I can the day's cricket, and the boys as I saw them.

Hobbs, not out 167, and Brown were batting to Griffith and Valentine. The wicket was perfect and somewhat slow. Martindale had pulled a muscle and could not bowl. Hobbs is the coolest thing alive. He is always in front of the wicket even before the ball is delivered and from there will play forward. Valentine and Griffith had not the faintest shadow of a ghost of a chance of getting him out. He simply played all the good balls, and as soon as he got anything loose he hit for four directly between two fieldsmen. I watched him for about an hour and a half and these are three things that struck me. 1: He never flurried but went in front of the wicket and pushed forward from there. 2: When he did raise his bat it was a four all the way. 3: You felt, as I found out afterwards, the bowlers felt also, that it was no use. Let me go into some detail over these fours. In the first over he cut Valentine for four past third man. But he was there for some half an hour afterwards for eight. He could not take the slightest chance. Then Da Costa bowled him a full pitch. Da Costa had mid-on and long field, square leg and a very wide long-on. Hobbs shoved the ball between mid-on and the man at square leg. Neither moved. The two long fields watched it. It was no use, not that it was hit so hard but it was just the correct distance away from each of them. That, of course, quite a number of batsmen can do. It is only when you watch him closely over a period that you can see how regularly he does it. It was when Achong bowled that I could see it clearly. Long-off, long-on and extra cover were on the boundary. And mid-on not too wide. Achong bowled one or two full pitches. Hobbs hit him just past his right hand in between himself and mid-on. He had to shape to hit the ball there. But the result was that both long-off and long-on went running after the ball and both reached too late. That went on until he had 200, then he hit everybody about for an over or two, jumping out to Achong, and jumping to Valentine and murdering him past mid-off. Finally Valentine bowled him, but with all due respects, it is my opinion that although he may not actually have given the wicket away, yet if he had wanted to remain in, nothing like Valentine or anybody else of the West Indies had could have got him out. The same cricket correspondent mentioned above tells me that Hobbs broke the West Indies team in 1928. If he had not been there the West Indian fast bowling was so good that, even with the bad slips in one or two innings of the Tests, they would have carried all before them. And all the time he is as peaceable as if he is playing with his little son on the lawn.

Fender made some good strokes. The rest of the Surrey batting was pretty bad and the West Indies nearly led on the first innings. As it was, Surrey headed them by ten. I do not think Grant made the best use of his fast bowlers. In fact I am sure he did not. At a quarter past eleven when the game began the score was 336; he bowled Griffith and Valentine till 12 o'clock. Naturally, when he took them off they were tired. But it would not have been so bad if the score had not been inevitably only thirty or forty short of 400. Achong, Da Costa and Merry bowled only for half an hour, by which time 400 came on, out came the new ball and Griffith and Valentine, after forty-five minutes' bowling with only half an hour's rest, had to come on again. Their first spell in view of the fact that the 400 was so near should have been no more than half an hour or even less. As it was, Griffith, trying to get some pace, bowled no-balls and a wide and was obviously unable to use the ball properly. Achong seemed to me very easy to play and, despite the success at Lord's, critics don't think that he will be much of a danger on hard wickets in the Tests. Da Costa was fair and so was Merry. Martin got some wickets at the end, but none of them were anything like Test-class Martindale and Constantine and no quarter. Barrow behind was wonderfully safe and sound. The fielding was brilliant and Grant at cover is as good as Roach and Valentine were elsewhere. He picked up and threw a batsman out in a most brilliant way and then grinned and was very happy about it in a most likeable manner. He is rather nervous and runs after balls which he should not. But he is very, very keen and, though excitable, when the situation is serious, pulls himself together and bats like a hero. Wiles was very heavy in the field but Martin in the long field ran after the ball and threw it in all things considered most satisfactorily.

Roach and Barrow came out and Barrow soon went. Roach was quiet for an over or so. Then he got going and though he only made 29, I realize what it was that made my critic friend tell me that Roach is one of the finest players of the day, not unworthy to be mentioned in the same rank with MacCartney. Certainly no Trinidadian has ever seen Roach bat. Glover, the fast bowler, sent down a short ball outside the off stump. Let any cricketer who wishes to understand what happened take a bat or a walking-stick and assume position. Then let him move his right foot back and across as far as it can go to reach a rather wide ball, then let him lift his bat or stick as high as he possibly can, and from that position let it go like a piston at the unfortunate ball. Third man on the boundary might as well have been in the slips for all the use he was. It was a tremendous stroke at the opposite pole to Jack Hobbs's careful middle-aged sedate cut. I know Roach's batting as well as anybody else and I was amazed. The next thing was a defensive stroke. At least he shaped for one but was there so long before the ball reached that it was the easiest thing in the world to push it behind short leg for a very comfortable four. Then he made another outrageous cut to the left of third man, and when that clever fellow edged in that direction Roach, lifting up the bat as in the first stroke, banged the ball past point as if to say to the man on the boundary: "What have you to say to this now?" Then he went to the other end and made one magnificent stroke which deserved ten runs. Glover the fast bowler was swinging in from leg rather late. To one fairly well pitched up, Roach shuffled the right foot in front of the wicket without extending it down the wicket at all. Then from there, putting his weight into it he played a short sharp wristy jerk and the ball flew to the boundary between short leg and mid-on. Glover bowled him after, but all he wants is luck. And he will make hundreds and hundreds of runs. When I saw him at Northampton he was bending his knees in the defensive strokes. A sure sign that concentration was a bit of an effort. At the Oval he was as straight as a wicket, right on the top of the ball and playing back in the way that we West Indians call rocking.

Wiles batted badly. He played forward and missed, and cut and missed, though when he got out it was to a fairly good stroke close in on the leg side and rather hard. But Wiles on the Saturday when he made fifty was no more run out than I was.

However, he and Roach had reached a stage where Surrey were going absolutely to pieces and it was lucky for them that the umpire made such a fortunate mistake.

To return to the match. The West Indians now seemed to be on the verge of one of their usual collapses, all out for 95 or something like that. But this team has something more than that in it. From the time that Grant came in it was clear that he meant business, though I don't think he is in his best form as yet. Martin, who came in to join him, shaped in really beautiful style. For the tummy that he has, he is very quick on his feet and he handles his bat like a swordsman. He was at home from the start and it looked as if those two would save the match.

I was, however, nervous. I hoped that both of them would keep the ball from off their feet. Martin was foolish enough not to play at one ball which hit him and flew off towards the leg. He picked it up and threw it to the bowler and then saw that the umpire was giving him out. He had to go and Surrey had victory within their grasp. But Merry pointed Grant and showed admirable defence. He was beaten once or twice but he played back and back and back and would not be tempted. Grant at the other end showed him the way and when Merry was very properly given out to one from Fender the game was saved.

But it was not finished. In came Da Costa and he nearly manslaughtered a short leg with a ferocious square-leg hit off his first ball. Grant had about 20. Da Costa soon had 20, the cleanest strokes you ever saw, and the ball humming to the boundary. When the last over began he had 42 and J. Grant 34, for Grant had been making quite a few strokes now that the game was saved. Grant had the over, and off the first ball he got a single. Everyone wished that Da Costa would get his 50. Da Costa wished it too, it seemed. He on-drove for 4, 46. Then he off-drove for 4, 50, then he straight-drove for 4, 54, then he cut through the slips for 4, 58, he played the last ball quietly. The crowd lined up to cheer them in, Grant was happy as a baby, and smiling all over at the way his side had proved itself and, I suppose, as is human, at the part he had taken in it.

Lancashire's Bleak Cricket

(*Manchester Guardian*, 20 August 1934)

Today has been a sorry day for Lancashire cricket. Into the sun and gaiety, the tents, summer dresses and music of the Dover festival, the Lancashire team brought a bleak Northern blast which made one long to hide his head and disavow the connection. Lancashire won the toss, and Watson and Hopwood began on a beautiful wicket. Watt and Valentine bowled for 22 in twenty minutes, then came Freeman and Marriott, and cricket went to sleep for the day; Freeman in this spell bowled fourteen overs, seven maidens, for 12 runs and no wicket, Marriott bowled ten maiden overs in succession. Freeman spun the ball both ways in his usual busy style, Marriott kept a fine length and dropped the ball on the leg stump to hit the off. Neither bowled short; it was extremely good bowling. No doubt it is fit that we should praise famous men, but the wicket was an admirable wicket. Neither bowler had any man out nor ever needed one. Chapman, at silly mid-off, amused the crowd for a while; he picked up everything within yards and rolled the ball off his foot to one hand, into Freeman's hand, straight from the foot into Marriott's hand, and similar refinements, all with a disarming casualness which almost hid the consummate skill of hand and eye.

But even that crowd could not hold interest for ever; the crowd grew restive, then barracked. Off two bad balls from Davies, Hopwood cut two fours. And yet all this restraint and stoicism came to nothing: just before luncheon, after nearly two hours, Hopwood was clean-bowled by Watt. He had scored but 30, Watson 34, the score was 66. After luncheon Iddon joined Watson, actually and spiritually. Marriott bowled his wonderful length and his fine leg-break and Lancashire were helpless. As soon as the band began to play, Watson cut for three — the first real stroke of his innings.

> Since nought so stockish, hard, and full of rage,
> But music for the time doth change his nature.

But the game grew limpid again, and what a wonderful day and setting for cricket it was! The Dover ground is one of the most beautiful in England and was at its best: flag-topped tents to either side of the sleek, green turf, a belt of trees and rows of houses shading into the rolling downs and surrounding the

C.L.R. James

pavilion, high-rising terrace after terrace dotted with people looking lazily on and talking of Woolley. The ancient Athenians had terraced seats in the open air, and if they looked on at Aeschylus and Sophocles, they had their Olympic Games too. What would an Athenian have thought of the day's play? Probably that the white-flannelled actors moving so sedately from place to place were performing the funeral rites over the corpse of a hero buried between the wickets. Watson and Iddon, from their garb and movements, he would have supposed to be the priests waving the sacrificial wands with solemn dignity.

Suddenly, as a sorely tried man raps out an oath, Iddon jumped at Freeman and drove him to the screen for four, but he went back playing forward at Marriott, who hit him on the pad and dismissed him lbw, amid the relief and delight of the crowd. True, Woolley had made a hundred before lunch and had made another hundred in sixty-three minutes, but there are other fish in the sea besides Woolley, and perhaps Ernest would show them. Marriott made him look unhappy and then hit him on the pad — lbw. Tyldesley had not even scored a single; as he walked out, the band played a slow tango full of drums, trombones and Spanish melancholy. Paynter, the left-hander, would deal with Marriott's leg-break. For nearly two overs he nibbled at it and then was caught behind the wicket, beaten all over. He also had made no runs.

Lister was nearly caught at slip, first off Marriott and then off Freeman. He made a good hook, then a good drive, but it was pretty certain that he would ultimately go the way of the rest — lbw to Marriott. Marriott kept the ball up, spinning it away, the batsmen played carefully; then would come one which went through a little faster with less break, and Marriott would ask how it was. At tea the score was 148 for five and Watson 73. If Watson had stayed in the better part of four hours, at least he had stayed in, and perhaps later he would hit a century in sixty-three minutes like Woolley; there were still Parkinson and Duckworth behind.

First ball after tea Parkinson cut Marriott quickly to the boundary; the ball went for four through the crowd which had not yet had time to go off the field. Parkinson, one felt, could do it. Marriott was bowling magnificently, but it would be good to see how he would react to being driven hard to the boundary and having to put a man out. Vain hope! Parkinson made no more strokes, but for the weakness of Kent in the slips he would have failed as ignominiously as the others. Knott came

40

on to bowl — high easy ones — and as the batsmen looked suspiciously even at these the crowd leaned back and laughed heartily. Between half-past four and half-past five Watson took his score from 73 to 89.

There was an interval for refreshment, and now surely Parkinson would do something. Beginning with the donkey-drops which Knott continued to send down, he hit a full pitch past cover and hit the next, another full pitch, to Chapman at square-leg by the umpire. The result of hitting? Nothing of the sort. The Parkinson who won the match against Derbyshire at Blackpool would have hit that ball into the Band of Brothers' tent. Watson went to his hundred at six o'clock; the crowd applauded him generously, as indeed they had applauded his fifty. Eckersley, all things considered, played admirably; he got his eye in and, though taking care, was not afraid to hit. Marriott and the Kent ground fielding have provided most of the fun, but Duckworth is still to come. Watson has shown what Lancashire can do in the minor key; surely Duckworth will do something in the major!

Spirited Batting by Kent

(*Manchester Guardian*, 21 August 1934)

Eckersley played such dashing cricket against Kent here this morning that there could barely have been a soul on the ground who was not sorry that he missed his century by only nine. The morning was cloudy, and after forty minutes' play down came the rain. In that forty minutes Watson made only 17, but Eckersley made 30. He jumped to Freeman and drove him straight for four, a sight to make the heart glad, and when Freeman dropped the next ball short he was ready to hook him round; only the brilliant fielding of Davies on the boundary robbed him of another four. Kent continued to field in the rain until it would have been absurd to go on, wherein they are a model to many county sides who only need to see a cloud five miles away before they begin to consider the possibilities of running to the pavilion.

Soon after the game began again, Watt bowled Watson. Bookmakers giving odds on the possibility of this would have been completely ruined; Watson had seemed invulnerable.

Probably it was the little extra pace given by the wind which caught him unawares. He had been batting seven hours for his 145 and seemed sorry to go. Duckworth failed, but Eckersley made some more brilliant strokes. He drove Watt on to the boundary; the next ball he stepped forward and slashed him on the rise past cover for another four; he played the next ball, and then drove Watt twice in succession to the on boundary, swinging strokes so directed that not a fieldsman moved. At 68 he gave a sharp chance to Marriott at square-leg by the umpire — a fair chance, but off a good stroke. He hit his way to 91, then ran out to Davies almost before he bowled, tried to get back, and failed. His 91 took thirteen fours and showed once more how important in batting is the right attitude to bowlers. Marriott bowled 68 overs, 31 maidens, for 83 runs and five wickets, and his bowling was as fine as his average.

Eckersley gave the new ball to Phillipson, who bowled with the wind. Levett and Fagg played quietly for 16, and then lunch was taken. After lunch Phillipson routed the early Kent batsmen. When the score was four for 54 he had four wickets for 24 runs in nine overs. Kent were five for 66 when Chalk and Davies made a fine stand. Chalk hit Watson to leg for four. Davies cut Pollard magnificently for four and drove him straight for another four. These two played delightfully; their side was in trouble, and they were on their mettle, but when they saw the loose ball they hit it hard and did not wait for it to be too loose. They were still together at tea and had brought the score from 66 for five to 128.

In the first over after tea, Chalk was caught off Phillipson, and the spectre of the follow-on assumed substantiability. Chapman began unconvincingly; to a fast ball he retired a pace. But he played himself in while Davies, batting better and better, went to a beautiful 50 with a grand straight drive off Phillipson. As soon as Chapman got going he settled the question of the follow-on; he hit Watson for 14 in an over, including one big straight drive for six. A few minutes later came another big on-drive for four. Soon he hit Watson for 17 in an over, including yet another six. He was 50 in an hour, with five fours and three sixes. He hit the boundaries with as much ease as other batsmen hit twos, but it is to be doubted whether he would have got them so easily off either Pollard or Phillipson.

Meanwhile Davies had settled down to confident defence, varied with a brilliant cut or equally brilliant off-drive; he was batting now with the aplomb and finish of a great batsman, and it was an exceedingly good ball from Phillipson which hastened from the pitch past his obstructing pads and bowled him. His 66 was an admirable innings.

Watt broke his duck by hitting Phillipson for six on the leg side. He then drove him happily over mid-off's head for four, and, having scored 17 in less than ten minutes, was bowled hitting out as if he was the last man in a Saturday-afternoon club match. Freeman drove Phillipson past extra cover for four as if he were Bradman himself, but his bails were soon flying. Marriott got a single, and from the applause which followed it seems that grave doubts had been entertained as to his ability to get that far; then he drove for three, giving Chapman the over. Chapman had one wholehearted stroke and got two, and another wholehearted swipe, in the course of which his bails were scattered.

Almost one forgot to ask what the score from the Oval was, so cheerful was everything; Kent were a hundred behind, nobody minded. These later Kent batsmen knew what was expected of them. Perhaps Watt could have gripped his bat handle tight and batted one hour for ten instead of eight minutes for 17. The game of cricket flourishes in Kent. Here again, as in Southend, the little boys were playing all over the field during the interval, and the Kent team were in their places and Hopwood was taking guard while the field was still dotted with people going back to their places. Does this lighthearted attitude make for a lower standard of cricket? Kent can point to Woolley, Freeman, Ames, Chapman, Valentine, Levett, Marriott. How many counties today can show such a list?

Phillipson had eight for 100, a spirited piece of fast bowling; he attacked the batsmen's wickets with the disciplined intemperance of a genuine fast bowler. Watson and Hopwood put on 27 before the close. To win the match, Lancashire will have to score fast tomorrow, so that for once duty and pleasure are both pointing in the same direction.

Lancashire Draw with Kent

(*Manchester Guardian*, 22 August 1934)

The case, it would seem, was a simple one. Lancashire were 100 ahead; the day's play began at eleven, it would end at 4.15, if necessary at 4.45; Lancashire would score as many as possible between eleven o'clock and 12.45, say 150 in the 105 minutes, then give Kent 250 to make in 180 minutes; they would get two wickets in the half-hour before lunch and frighten Kent out of their lives. This from the Lancashire point of view. Kent, on the other hand, are known to be always spoiling for a fight and would make a serious attempt to do anything that could be fairly considered reasonable.

Alas! the match did not go at all like that. Watson and Hopwood went stolidly along; they put on 19 with here and there a stroke, but what the spectators had envisaged was obviously entirely different from their plans, and, of course, one has to trust the men on the spot. Watson got out when still short of his fifty.

Iddon tried hard to score fast and made a particularly good pull, getting down on one knee and sweeping to the pitch of the ball, but he was stumped before he was properly in command of the bowling.

It was left to Paynter to show what might have been done. Paynter abandoned defence; he came in to hit, and 66 grand runs came from his bat. Fifty-one came in forty minutes, two high pulls to long-on, off-drives flying along through extra cover, a mighty straight drive over the screen. Hopwood, after being steadiness itself, was stumped when he had scored 82. Lister hit hard for 13 not out, and Lancashire at lunch were 231 for four. The 231 had taken 150 minutes, but too many of them had come in the last hour. With the wicket good and only two and a half hours left for play at the most, the match was as nearly as possible dead, strangled.

Phillipson bowled well; again he pitched the ball on or near the off stump and swung it away so quickly that two or three fours went off the edge through the slips. At intervals a wicket fell; at a quarter to four Kent were 75 for three.

A sparkling sun shone down on the beautiful ground as the match trailed its predestined way into futility through a deepening atmosphere of frustration and waste. Lister and Ernest Tyldesley must have been the only persons sorry when the drawing of stumps at four o'clock cut short their bowling.

Bradman's Remarkable Century at Scarborough

(*Manchester Guardian*, 10 September 1934)

In good cricket weather and before an immense crowd the Australians made a huge score here today. The wicket was admirable, the arrangements perfect, and the Australians could wish no better farewell match than this game of cricket which Mr H.D.G. Leveson-Gower arranges tour after tour with such unwavering success.

Wyatt could have had the new ball before luncheon today if he had wanted it; a captain usually has tentative plans laid for all emergencies, but it was unlikely that Wyatt was prepared for this one. The chief cause of the abnormality, in fact the only cause, was Bradman. Farnes, bowling at a good pace, seemed to be in-swinging the new ball. Brown edged a short one past his leg stump and soon after played on; Bradman tried to drive a half-volley wide outside the off-stump with a horizontal bat and barely dug it out of the wicket with the inside edge. He stood away to hit another splendid ball from Farnes and just snicked it off his leg stump. At the other end Bowes swung a ball away from his drive and Sutcliffe either just got to it or just failed, the ball going extremely low and wide to his left. With his score still under twenty, Bradman gave a chance that Wyatt dropped, off Farnes. Wyatt and Bradman are the only persons who can give any opinion about the merits of this chance: it was straight to Wyatt in the gully, between his legs a foot from the ground, but it was no mis-hit; it was a cut from the centre of the bat, and there ends the list of Bradman's delinquencies.

His excellences were multifarious and unique. He drove Farnes's fastest half-volleys past mid-off for four; he would stand back to Nichols and if Nichols turned from the off put him to the on boundary, and if from the leg through the covers. Verity he stretched down to and pulled to the on boundary twice in an over, with an extra-cover boundary thrown in. Nichols, changing ends, left the slips open. Bradman tapped him through them; it was much easier than hitting, and the ball went down to the boundary just the same. Furthermore, Bradman was nursing a sore right hand, which gave him a lot of trouble.

After the first excitement, this sort of thing becomes slightly monotonous. A bowler bowls, Bradman makes a stroke, not a single fieldsman moves, and the ball is returned from the boundary. The essence of any game is conflict, and there was no conflict here; the superiority on one side was too over-whelming. Bradman was 50 in thirty-eight minutes and 100 in eighty; then he started running out to Verity, and either drove him high to the on-boundary or along the ground past cover. He hit him for 19 runs in an over, and scored 32 in ten minutes before he was stumped. Just as he begins his innings Bradman will occasionally show uncertainty for ten minutes, sometimes for only two or three balls. Bowlers must get him out then, otherwise he will bat until he feels inclined to go. There is not the slightest doubt that, had he wished, he could have continued to play quietly — that is to say, at a mere 80 per hour — and made 200 before tea.

Ponsford batted till luncheon for 63, canny, solid, lifting his bat only to cut; for the rest, he watched the ball on to the bat and then, using weight and forearm, pushed it past mid-on or square-leg. At luncheon the bowling of Leveson-Gower's eleven became splendid, the fielding — or, rather, the catching — abominable. Nichols, using the new ball, attacked Ponsford in gallant style. Ponsford cut him finely, but some of the strokes past square-leg must have given heart to Nichols, who persisted and finally got an easy return when Ponsford needed only ten for the century. Ponsford made a halfhearted drive, and the catch was the culmination of a sustained piece of fine bowling.

Farnes, at the other end, pitched up to McCabe and made him put the ball to Verity at short-leg. An over or two later, McCabe again gave Verity an easy catch in the same spot; a remarkably fine ball this, pitching a good length and rising so that McCabe had to play. Farnes did not lose courage and made McCabe edge more than once through the slips when playing strictly defensive strokes, but though the balls flew high enough none came to hand. McCabe also edged Nichols badly through the slips, and altogether seemed extremely lucky to get even the 46 he required for his 2,000, but he was always making fine cuts and jumping to Verity to drive. Late in the innings he made a series of magnificent hooks off bumping balls from the fast bowlers. After he had made his hundred Leyland, placed at long-leg specially to catch him off a hook, threw quite a few in from the boundary, and when the catch did come dropped it. This was doubly unfortunate, for Leyland had fielded with brilliance and sureness all through the day. Bowes continued to bowl short balls, with most of his men on the off side, and McCabe and Chipperfield also made brilliant strokes on the off side from the tired bowling, and both men are still not out.

There were two significant points about the Australians' batting. The first was the way all of them played the fast bowlers past cover point or straight past the bowler. Farnes and Bowes sometimes used three slips, a gully and only one other man in front of the wicket on the off side. At cover J.H. Human worked fast and tirelessly all the day, but batsman after batsman could frequently get the ball past him for twos. The second point was the freedom and strength with which the Australians cut just behind point, with third man in the usual place. They got many fours here and gave no chances. The ball got through the slips sometimes, but off defensive strokes, never from a cut that was botched. These things should be remembered, representing as they do a fundamental difference between English and Australian batsmen not in the ability of individual players but in the whole method of approach.

Australian Bowling Can Be Hit

(*Manchester Guardian*, 11 September 1934)

The game between the Australians and H.D.G. Leveson-Gower's eleven, which threatened to degenerate into boredom, if not misery, was made memorable by a superb innings by Nichols and Bradman's fielding.

Farnes routed the remaining Australians in the morning. On Saturday he had bowled finely with no luck; today he had a little — not much — and in eight overs and three balls took four wickets for 19 runs. He had a new ball, and in the first over McCabe tried to hook and spooned. Chipperfield was rattled by a good-length rising ball and played on. Ebeling, who is an admirable batsman, had his bails shaved once and was caught in the slips. O'Reilly, after being morally out at least six times in twelve balls, was caught by Duckworth. Except for two humorous balls in his first over on Saturday, Farnes's bowling was unimpeachable; he used only a mid-on and a short-leg. Here, if England wants one, is an England fast bowler. It was not only his four for 19 today; he bowled equally well on Saturday. Despite all theories of wicket and modern batting, good length and really fast bowling to slips who can catch will deal satisfactorily with most bastmen and, more than anything else, are likely to dismiss Bradman in the vulnerable first five minutes. Duckworth kept wicket splendidly; in the long score he allowed only two byes, frequently earned applause by the way he got to wide balls on the leg side and caught and stumped like the great player he is.

Mr Leveson-Gower's eleven cracked badly. It is difficult to reconcile oneself to McCabe as an opening bowler for an Australian team, but Ebeling, after a poor beginning, knocked Wyatt's leg stump out of the ground with a fine off-break, and just on luncheon came tragedy. Fleetwood-Smith was bowling over the wicket, and his left-handed off-breaks, varied with one that went through, were a source of bother to both Sutcliffe and Leyland. After a trying period Sutcliffe drove Fleetwood-Smith almost straight and followed up his stroke. Fleetwood-Smith looked as if he might stop the ball, and Leyland stood and watched him miss it; as soon as it got through, Sutcliffe called and ran, Leyland moved not an inch, and Bradman, having come across from mid-off, gave Oldfield the perfect return. So far was Sutcliffe out that Oldfield, a very human cricketer, could hardly bring himself to knock a bail off. It was Sutcliffe's call true enough, but even if Bradman had been utterly unknown what he had been doing on the boundary should have been warning enough that no tricks were to be tried in that direction. One could not help thinking that Fleetwood-Smith's off-breaks over the wicket had caused the whole business.

After luncheon Human played charming cricket for 31. The off-break on the off-stump had bowled Hendren for nothing; Human did not quite know what to do with it at first, but he ended by driving it, and then hit boundaries wherever he chose. He made a particularly fine late cut off Fleetwood-Smith, and the crowd cheered his courageous innings enthusiastically. He was the first batsman to show any challenge to the Australian bowling. Leyland was curiously subdued, gave a chance, and then was out playing the ball easily back to Ebeling off the edge.

Nichols came in and started so badly that not a soul on the ground except, perhaps, himself, and even this is not certain, would have insured his life against death from Fleetwood-Smith for three overs. He pottered about and seemed unable either to judge the flight or see the ball off the pitch. This must be stated clearly and thoroughly understood in view of what happened afterwards. Nichols made the left-hander's drive between point and cover for four off his enemy; he swept him round to long-leg, but then these seemed to be no more than incidental delays before the inevitable execution. They were nothing of the kind. Nichols started to put an extremely solid forward stroke to Fleetwood-Smith and soon began to play one of the great innings of the 1934 season. He made every stroke except the hook — late cuts, off-drives, leg-glances, pulls, ball after ball racing to the boundary unchallenged by any fieldsman. Every bowler was severely punished, Fleetwood-Smith taking his full share with the rest. The quality of Nichols's stroke-play may be judged from the fact that against the speedy Australian fielding 58 of his 75 came from boundaries — thirteen fours and a six. He was helped nobly by Townsend, who himself began shakily but hit freely for 37, including one six.

The partnership between Nichols and Townsend was beautiful, and they were not parted for long: O'Reilly quickly got them both leg-before-wicket in a later spell of bowling. Nichols 75, Townsend 37, Human 31; they saved their side from ignominy and delighted the great crowd by attacking the Australian bowling and hitting it to the boundary. But for this Fleetwood-Smith would have made them look small, as he did all who stood trembling and poked at him.

Australians' Easy Victory

(*Manchester Guardian*, 12 September 1934)

The Australians beat H.D.G. Leveson-Gower's eleven by an innings today a few minutes before the tea interval. Sutcliffe began brightly, driving Ebeling through extra cover for four in the first over and playing the ball strongly from the bat even in defensive strokes. Then Sutcliffe played a ball towards Ebeling at square-leg in front of the umpire; Ebeling failed to stop it and Sutcliffe started, the ball perversely hit Dolphin, the umpire, and bounced back to Ebeling. Sutcliffe turned and ran back, but Wyatt had come straight through, and he and Sutcliffe found themselves on the same crease; Ebeling threw the ball to McCabe, and, after a word with Sutcliffe, Wyatt started cheerfully on his way to the pavilion, but McCabe stood with the ball in his hand and declined to break the wicket. So Wyatt changed direction and walked back into his crease amidst round after round of applause. Wyatt should now have made fifty at least.

Alas! McCabe soon clean-bowled him a well-pitched-up ball going away, which seemed to be delivered with the arm lower. Wyatt played forward both inside and over it and had his off stump knocked back.

Sutcliffe played cheerfully. He drove Ebeling; he played Fleetwood-Smith as if he had known all about that kind of bowling before Fleetwood-Smith was born; he forced him through the covers and swung him to leg. Leyland drove Ebeling for two boundaries on the off in his Test-match vein, and 69 came in the hour, of which Sutcliffe scored 36. Then Fleetwood-Smith dropped a slightly flighted ball on the off stump, Sutcliffe played quickly forward, and the ball turned in and bowled him. Hendren played himself in carefully. His method in defence is very good to watch; his bat is as broad and confident as his person. He did not force the game, but picked his ball and lifted O'Reilly into the unguarded long-field for four, did the same to Fleetwood-Smith and drove him through the covers for another boundary.

Leyland had quietened down, but was obviously in for a long innings when there was another piece of confusion which ended in his dismissal. Hendren cut powerfully, and Woodfull, at backward point, covering a lot of ground, picked up magnificently. He was not in a position to throw at once, but the shot had travelled extremely fast; Hendren turned and saw Leyland halfway up the pitch insisting on a run, he refused to move, Leyland could not get back in time and had to go. It was a grave loss to the English eleven, but Hendren remained in his crease all through, justly unrepentant. At lunch the score was 116 for three, Hendren 27.

After lunch, Hendren continued to play fine cricket, taking his time but hitting his boundaries with ripe discernment. He made a great squre cut off Fleetwood-Smith, who bowled interminably, and two hits to the square-leg boundary off O'Reilly, which made Woodfull put a man out. Ball after ball in the afternoon had turned from leg, and Hendren, playing forward and back, was judging the leg-break when O'Reilly bowled a slower one on the off stump, rather over-pitched. Hendren played confidently forward as usual, the ball turned in from the off, Hendren's bails flew off, and Oldfield explained to all around how the ball had come the opposite way.

Human, who stayed a long time for a few runs, was caught at deep mid-on off a full-pitch. Nichols was again in much trouble with Fleetwood-Smith and, before he could find himself, was finely caught one-handed by Ebeling at square-leg. Townsend was left with Bowes at the fall of the ninth wicket and only 175 on the board. Bowes is prime favourite with the Scarborough crowd and they like to see him make at least one, but today he soared above the most enthusiastic expectations. Batting quite well, he hit both Fleetwood-Smith and O'Reilly, lifting O'Reilly out into the country for four and then driving him straight for a towering six. Townsend played his own strong game but treated Bowes with the respect of not trying to force the pace unduly. He made some splendid strokes, and the pair scored 43 before Bowes was bowled for a sound and vigorous 20. Townsend was 39 not out.

Woodfull, as in recent matches, made excessive use of Fleetwood-Smith, who stood up to it well. There can be little doubt that the Australians are hoping for a lot from him in a future tour, and they are not likely to be disappointed.

Lancashire Collapse at Aigburth

(*Manchester Guardian*, 20 June 1935)

Rain fell here before half-past eleven, not too much to prevent hopes that Lancashire and the South Africans would start at 12.30. Before 12.30 a drizzle caused the covering to be put on, and play could not begin until after lunch. The wicket took spin and was on the slow side, but the ball played few tricks. Duckworth and Iddon came in for Booth and Hawkwood, and Bell and Balaskas for Tomlinson and Crisp, who is damaged.

Bell, from the pavilion end, and Langton began the bowling. Bell bowled fairly fast and short, outside the off-stump, with an off-break even with the new ball. His dangerous ball was overpitched and swung in almost off the pitch. Hopwood quickly drove this ball for what would have been a four on an outfield less dead. Another of them went quickly off Watson's bat almost straight to Nourse, short-leg, who dropped it.

Langton, with an action as beautiful and easy as anything on view in England today, swung the ball in and varied this with another which straightened itself from the off-stump. He had seven fieldsmen packed close to the wicket on both sides, and Hopwood, thank heaven, lifted him twice into the long-field.

Hopwood was aggressive. He failed to get Bell's short off-ball through the covers two or three times, but caught well hold of a rising ball and cut it to the third-man boundary. He had done most of the scoring when Watson tried to hook Langton, mistimed, and gave short mid-on an easy catch. The ball rose and was probably faster. With a delivery and oiled arm-swing like Langton's the change of pace is most difficult to detect even from the ring.

The first wicket had gone at 49 and the second nearly fell at the same total. Iddon played forward to his second ball, and Nourse, so brilliant in the country, dropped a still easier catch at second slip. Hopwood continued to attack. He cut Vincent square, hitting freely across the ball, and also tapping him late between the slips. He hit Langton three times over the heads of the short-legs. Perhaps he did not catch hold of them fairly, but at any rate they gave runs and were well out of harm's way.

Bell relieved Langton, and Iddon drove him straight to Wade, standing back and rather straight at mid-off. Paynter for his first ball played forward to Bell, and Wade at once put a silly mid-off to join silly mid-on. Paynter defended calmly until he got what he wanted and drove Bell straight back to the screen. One characteristic of the great Paynter frequently shows — holding his bat until the ball is almost on him and then loosing it into a powerful stroke. He was soon out to a great catch. Bell continued to bowl rather short. Paynter swung to long leg at one of these, pitched outside his legs, and missed. To the same loose-looking ball he tried the same stroke again, and hit the ball fairly. It travelled fast and waist high to the right of Langton, who was fielding at that most awkward position second slip on the leg-side. Langton took it one-handed and in a way which promised that he would do it six times out of six.

Vincent, bowling faster than usual, was now keeping Hopwood quiet. But except for a little uncertainty at the very start, Hopwood played all the South African bowlers confidently and well, especially in defence. Vincent's length wore him down, however, and after being a long time in the forties he tried a drive and lifted the ball to mid-off. Vincent next made Washbrook reach forward as far as he possibly could, which was yet not far enough. He edged the ball into Cameron's hands.

Langton, on again in place of Bell, bowled his in-swinger to Lister, and then held the ball for the one on the off-stump which does not come in; true to plan Lister played inside, and was caught at the wicket for nothing.

Farrimond, quite untroubled by these disasters and playing well, was joined by Eckersley, but at 3.55 bad light stopped play.

By the time the players reached the pavilion the rain was coming down in a drizzle. A cornet-player who must have been waiting his chance began to play "If I had a million dollars", beguiling meditation for the few hundred spectators who were being so scurvily rewarded for their enthusiasm. But though a million dollars could have done many things, there was one thing it could not possibly do, and that was stop the rain. By five minutes past four it was raining a million gallons. Even the cornet-player's game was interrupted. He began to play "God save the King". A gloomy day for everybody. At five o'clock came the now familiar announcement: "Abandoned for the day."

Exciting Cricket Depends upon Exciting Personalities

(*Glasgow Herald*, 28 April 1937)

Allen's men in Australia have done one thing for English cricket. They have restored its morale. There is no longer the mournful chorus of "What is wrong with our cricket?" — meaning: "Why do we make such a poor showing against other sides?" Everyone feels that English cricketers are as good as Australian, except for Bradman. And Bradman has to be accepted as we accept the Atlantic Ocean or the five-shilling income tax. It cannot be helped.

This is going to have a fine tonic effect on the 1937 season. One can only imagine what this season would have been like if, as many in their hearts feared, Australia had won all five Tests. Then rejoicing at a century by Hammond or a fine performance by Verity would have been embittered by the secret fear that all this fine play was perhaps not so fine after all, but only the mediocre standing out above the still more mediocre. That feeling, however, is gone.

And yet something is wrong; county cricket has been losing appeal, and a commission has been appointed (one had almost written a Royal Commission). The personnel of this commission is "emeritus, sagacious, learned, venerable". Yet the sphere in which they can usefully function is, in my opinion, strictly defined and limited, and it would be a mistake to expect too much from this or any other commission.

Cricket today is the result of a slow evolution which has made it the wonderfully complex game that it is. Any legislation which will radically alter the appeal it makes to the public must be radical in that it will have to strike at the roots of the game as we know it. And then, whatever that will be, it will not be the game that Grace, Ranjitsinhji, Hobbs and Trumper played.

In recent years we have had the wicket enlarged, the lbw rule changed; in Australia the eight-ball over. None has brought the millennium, and the simple reason is that all such changes are bound to be minor adjustments only. To make the wicket twice as large as it is at present would, without doubt, change the game radically and finish off all county matches in a day. But who wants to do that?

No. Where the commission can, and undoubtedly will, make change is in the regulations which govern county cricket. And here most people are hoping for a drastic cut in first-class county games.

In the last analysis it is the players who will make or unmake county cricket, and the changes should aim at giving the players the best chance. I believe if during every fortnight a team had three days off there would be a wonderful change in the spirit with which the players would approach their matches. The enthusiasm which the crowds lack today must come from the players, and the players must step on to the field as anxious to bowl and bat and field as is the club cricketer on his one half-day a week.

The average county cricketer cannot do this in the weary grind of match after match without intervals of rest. Of necessity, and in spite of himself, he settles down to a technique which is essentially defensive and stereotyped. Who can expect a man to be adventurous without respite day after day?

So far we can reasonably hope for some striking recommendations from the commission and some good to follow. Meanwhile, and especially for 1937, we must recognize that exciting cricket depends upon exciting personalities and exciting teams. And exciting personalities are, I think, accidents. Not altogether, perhaps. We live in a standardized age, means of communication multiply, we hear and see the same things, and therefore think and act far more alike than our parents did. The result is a mastery of elementary technique by an increasingly greater number, a general raising of the standard. But the striking personality is perhaps more rare as a result. How many competent novelists are there today! But Dickenses do not abound. There are many more good cricketers than there were, all-rounders in particular. But the men whose names fill the ground are fewer. The novel-reading public is quite prepared to put up with the second-rate. The cricket-going public, alas, is not.

Yet, on the whole, the great personality remains an accident. What law ordained Maurice Tate? How did a Hammond suddenly blossom forth some eight or ten years ago? What immortal hand or eye shaped the fearful symmetry of Bradman exactly in 1929? We do not and cannot know. But the law of averages indicates that it is about time two or three of these appeared in England.

Perhaps 1937 will see a flowering. There is Gimblett, of Somerset, young Compton, of Middlesex. We shall watch them and their like closely.

And yet in regard to what I call the exciting personality — and two or three of them can make a season — there is one point which should be clarified. Do all of us mean the same thing with the same word? I doubt it. And here comes the case of Philip Mead to prove it. Mead is to go this year. It is complained that he is too slow. Mead in 1936 made 1,000 runs with an average of 30 and two centuries. He is still, as figures go, one of the best batsmen of the side. But, they say, he was not exciting enough. Well, I part company from all critics of Mead, even long past his prime. How I loved to see the man: his stance, his pulling at his cap, his sound foundation, his pawkiness, his deep enjoyment of every minute. In the field he rolled from short-slip like a sailor on deck. Of course he was slow. But for me it didn't matter. And I wonder for how many more.

I devoutly hope the last word has not been said on Mead's retirement. As a run-getter he is still worth his place, and I am thinking that perhaps Hampshire may find it necessary to call on him again. May I be there to see; or, if not, the Post Office receipts for 1937 will be increased by the cost of one congratulatory telegram.

The legislators have their work cut out, for how is one to legislate for people who find so grand and weather-beaten an old character as Mead dull and unexciting?

Freer Style of Cricket Promised

(*Glasgow Herald*, 12 May 1937)

Times change. But the man who says that is usually referring to past times. The implication, even though unexpressed, is that these wretched times we are in will never change. And yet I believe that there is going to be now and in the coming years a gradual return to an older and freer style of cricket.

One can feel it in the air. It is not only the serious financial question. It is in the very names which are before the public eye: Allen, the England captain, fast bowler and hard-hitting batsman; Robins, all-rounder and hard-hitting batsman; Mitchell-Innes, a university player of the old school, who will drive straight or over extra cover's head for 6 without any fuss.

E.R.T. Holmes, of Surrey, is certain to play a big part in cricket during the coming years, both on and off the field, and he is of the Allen/Robins type.

Better still, the young professionals are increasingly men of enterprise and stroke play. Edrich and Compton, of Middlesex, have been batting for the MCC and making runs as if they were playing club games. Cooper, the Worcestershire find, is a player of strokes.

Faster cricket is in the air. I believe that the England players can and probably will concretize this tendency, make it "the thing", even in a Test match. Barnett's form this season may do a great deal towards this.

For years Barnett has been a thoroughly good cricketer and a Gloucestershire pillar. He played for England against the West Indies in 1933 at the Oval, and he went to India that winter. But somehow, though always on the fringe, he could not get himself definitely recognized as one of the elect. I think that against him was the fact that he always hit the ball, and too often got out driving past cover instead of pushing the ball into short-leg's hands. The result of each is that you are inside the pavilion. But whereas the one is interpreted as recklessness, the other can be attributed to good bowling. "He's keeping such a length that you simply can't get the ball away."

Well, last year Barnett made thousands of runs and went to Australia. He made in Tests 69 and 26, 57, 11 and 23, 129 and 21, 18 and 41 — 395 runs with an average of 43.88 without a not-out innings to help him. He made 259 against Queensland. He was the outstanding success of the newcomers. It was true he did not hit as brilliantly as he usually does in county cricket. It would have been a wonder if he had.

A heavy handicap was the fact that no one could ever stay with him in opening stands. The English batting was not such as to give confidence to a young player opening the innings. But Barnett has his strokes. He hasn't got to learn them. And we ought to have henceforth and for years to come a No.1 of the old-fashioned type. He hit Hampshire for a terrific century last week. It is good to see an England opening batsman scoring a century in an hour.

Curiously enough, apart from Sutcliffe, the two men in running to partner Barnett are both pronounced hitters of the ball — Gimblett, of Somerset, and Paynter, of Lancashire. Paynter went to Australia with the team previous to the last, and rose from a sick bed to score a gallant 83 in the decisive Test. No one has ever queried his courage.

But he made his reputation as a hard-hitting left-hander. He is a little man with all the little man's agility in pulling and playing on the leg-side. But he is a colossal driver, and he leaps at a loose ball like a proverbial tiger. You can almost see him spit on his hands as a full pitch looms in the air.

When he came back from Australia, however, a change came over his batting. It may have been the result of his illness in Australia, but Paynter became a careful player. He used to go feeling out for the ball with a long forward stroke. He became a good average county player, and no more.

Then last year Watson, Lancashire's No.1, could not find his form, and Paynter was promoted to No.1. In August he made 964 runs, scoring three centuries in succession. He was closely considered for the Australian tour, and (with that wisdom which we all have after the event) it is a pity that he didn't go.

Now, this season, still at No.1, Paynter is off again. With the Lancashire batting falling around him. Paynter is the old Paynter, going out of his crease to drive the faster bowlers and scoring 40, 150, 62, and 66. It is not only the runs he makes, but how he makes them, and where. Doing this sort of thing at No.1 or No.2 had almost dropped out of fashion.

That opening batsmen must be "steady" is a modern retrogression. England puts Hammond in at No.3, Australia does the same to Bradman, the West Indies the same with George Headley. Before the war one of the opening pairs was always a forcing batsman, sometimes both. Trumper and Duff were always out for runs from the first ball. And when Hobbs and Hayward or Hobbs and Rhodes broke the hearts of opposing bowlers, Hobbs was always on the look-out to punish bowlers. But the post-war Hobbs and Sutcliffe for England and Woodfull and Ponsford for Australia set a new fashion.

Down the pavilion steps they came to open the innings, the fieldsmen clustered round at silly slip, silly point, silly mid-on, and the game of patience began. I think it is going. C.F.Walters was breaking it up during the last series of Tests against Australia in England, and I am convinced that Barnett and Paynter or Gimblett will finish with it for years to come.

Test matches and Test match players set the tone today. That England lost her chances in Australia by playing too slowly when she was on top is pretty generally recognized.

And if Test players or potential Test players, by natural gifts and in response to an atmosphere, play a faster game, then the young will follow.

On Saturday Gover came out to bowl against New Zealand, put three men in the slips and a man in the gully, deep third man and fine leg, two men at short leg, and a short cover. There was not a man behind the bowler himself, and Gover pitched up and pitched back with impunity.

Time was when such an arrangement of the field would have been heresy. Nineteen hundred and thirty-seven may mark the beginning of a period when such an arrangement will again be looked upon as a relic of a bygone age.

E.A. McDonald's Example of Perfection of Style

(*Glasgow Herald*, 28 July 1937)

With E.A. McDonald passes the greatest of modern fast bowlers. It is hard to believe that there were ever fast bowlers near whom this Australian would not have been what we knew him to be — a great master of his craft.

Allen Hill and Freeman are legendary figures of two generations ago. Dr W.G. Grace, who played many of the moderns, gave them the palm. A generation ago Tom Richardson and Lockwood (both on one county side — how incredible it sounds!) were unchallenged. Both were masters of the off-break, Lockwood on the most perfect wicket. Lockwood had more devil; Richardson had a physique of iron, an unconquerable spirit, which bowled itself to a standstill by 6.30 and came back next morning ready to try again. They had the essential in a fast bowler, pace, and the essential in all bowlers, length.

But McDonald, it seems to me, could have bowled for England or Australia at any time these sixty years.

He had the physique — and it was not mere size. I played in a friendly match with him about three years ago, when he was long past his best. Standing at mid-on, I watched him closely, as well I might. Mere scribes do not often get the chance to watch such men in action at close quarters. He was no ascetic, and yet there was not an inch of superfluous flesh on him. His 6ft and tremendous breadth seemed all bone and muscle. There was no hint of rotundity at his waist and, despite his size, he had the lank, loose movements of limbs which one associates with long, lean men. He was taking things easily that day, and his action had already dropped a little, but it was still the most perfect thing on the cricket field, and half his success was due to it.

Anything more unlike Gover, for instance, could hardly be imagined. He took a long run, easy and controlled, his arm swung over as if on an oiled spring, describing the complete circle, and he finished without the slightest strain.

The best hurdlers, I am told, know to within a few inches every step that they will take in a short hurdle race, where they will jump, the number of steps between each hurdle, and in the final burst McDonald gave me that impression when bowling. The result was that he had perfect command of length and direction, he got full advantage from every ounce of weight and inch of height, he was always bowling well within himself, and the ferocious pace of the extra-fast ball came from a mere inward impulse which merely set the whole machine moving more powerfully but did not disrupt its smoothness and precision.

The afternoon I watched him he was merely bowling medium pace, but a local boy made some 50 runs and was giving trouble. "Mac" seemed to be still as careless as ever, he picked up the ball and walked his deliberate walk back to his starting point. He delivered as usual, but two balls pitched on the off-stump and flew over them at a startling pace. It was as if a bit of Test cricket had suddenly intruded itself into this pleasant village game. But nobody knew that he intended it, nobody had an inkling until the first ball had left the pitch, and his manner and action were so calm that it was only after the second ball that we realized he was on the warpath. Slips dropped back, the keeper crouched low and the batsman clenched his bat tighter.

He could hardly be called one of the ferocious fast bowlers. His action was too easy to be terrifying. He could let the ball fly, but he was by instinct and preference a length bowler. Yet he had the hostility without which a fast bowler is not a fast bowler.

After our game the boy who had made 50 was being praised, someone even suggesting that he might be tried for the county (Lancashire, it was). Mac showed an apparently unreasonable hostility. "You play as well as you are allowed to play," he growled between the intervals of his eternal cigarette-smoking. Easygoing as he was, his standards were high.

I never quite appreciated the remark until, some years after, I heard something similar from a famous international cricketer, a great batsman noted for his modesty. Some of his fellows were discussing ways and means of dealing with a certain slow bowler on a nasty wicket.

"The trouble," said one, "is that man he puts just in front of you, almost under the bat. He keeps him there all the time."

X, who is a silent man, had taken no part in the conversation, but at the "keeps him there all the time" he turned round in sudden wrath — "Keeps him there for who will let him stay there; he wouldn't keep him there for me!" — and relapsed into silence.

To both there was the same intolerance of low standards, the hallmark of high performance.

Yet McDonald was not a personality in the true sense of that word. His smooth elegance and equable temperament did not allow for that excess which distinguishes. One can see that by comparing him with the men who shared his fame — Gregory first, and Parkin and Dick Tyldesley after.

What a cargo of vitality was Gregory! You had to take notice of him. And yet he was never the bowler McDonald was. Gregory frightened them and, while they were watching Gregory, McDonald bowled them out.

But if Mac enjoyed his days with Gregory in 1921, surely the happiest times of his life (and for spectators) were his years with Cecil Parkin and Dick Tyldesley in the great post-war years of Lancashire. On the field they devastated opposing sides — Parkin with his fast ball (nearly as fast as Mac's), the slow ball (much slower than Dick Tyldesley's), his own enormous off-break, and the quips and cranks and wreathed smiles of his fantastic bowling.

A batsman had to bat against those three when they were determined to get him out. But Mac was the spearhead and the backbone.

He had, as every good man must have, an "enemy", no less a person than Walter Hammond.

One grand and glamorous day Hammond, who used to set about Mac as if his life depended on banging him about, at once, hit him for over 250 in four hours, with five fours in one over! Woolley was another who hit Mac all over Old Trafford. Hobbs, at the Oval, used to have great duels with him.

But Mac was always game. He might get these well-equipped foes out early, or they might get set and pound him. He fought them always to a finish. In these contests Parkin and Dick Tyldesley used to take second place. It was Mac they wanted, and they usually got all of Mac that the captain would allow.

But after the game Parkin took charge. What adventures, what wit and humour, what zest for life! That is beyond the scope of this article, but there is one tale of such an impromptu variety turn at a provincial theatre. I hope it is true. It would be a grievous disappointment if it were not true.

Where shall we see three such again on the field and off it? McDonald's death must be specially sad for his two old brothers-in-arms.

We live in a serious age, and there are many estimable people who despise cricket and lovers of cricket. But I confess freely that I looked, and still look, on a man like McDonald with open-eyed admiration.

The splendid physique, trained and adapted to endurance and highly skilful performance, is not only the enjoyment of millions of modern people. All through the ages humanity has admired such men. That most intellectual of peoples, the Greeks, gave their athletes a high place, a thing our modern "high-brows" might remember.

And I cannot conceive of a time when McDonald and his kind will not fill the eye and minds of their fellows with admiration and a generous envy of their natural gifts developed by patient toil to such strength and endurance and skill.

Bradman's One Palpable Weakness; Hassett Sets a Problem

(*Glasgow Herald*, 11 May 1938)

The Australians come first. What is their strength? It isn't too early to form some sort of judgement. I watched them very closely the other day at Oxford, batting on a perfect wicket against some bowling which I shall speak about later.

Bradman is the same Bradman, and that statement needs elucidation.

He was standing back and lashing the ball to the off-boundary in a way that lifts him head and shoulders above all other players I have ever seen. The average forcing backstroke is a wrist stroke, with sometimes a lot of shoulder in it. Being a forcing stroke, it demands quickness of eye and exquisite timing. Bradman does not need the timing. He is in position so quickly that he has time to swing the bat at the ball as if it were a thoroughly short and bad one.

Applause at one or two of these strokes was quite perfunctory. The ball seemed so easy to hit. It wasn't. The quick judgement and rapid footwork had made everything else into child's play.

That is the real Bradman, that and a nervous strength, which makes 200 for him as easy as a century for other people. I think that McCabe is quicker with the bat than Bradman is. But eye and footwork and control, it seems, are as strong as ever.

Just before Bradman got out he attempted a tap through the slips and sent the ball near to slip. And he was lbw trying to force a swinging ball to leg. I have rarely seen so amateurish a stroke from a great batsman, and I would not be surprised if Bradman was willing to get out in order to allow some of the later men to bat.

Was he then invulnerable? Nothing of the kind. He is the same Bradman, which means that just as he comes in he is liable to give a chance in the slips. I have seen him play some superb innings. In nearly all there was that ball moving down towards second slip before he had 10.

One of his greatest innings against South Africa, a double century, and another against the West Indies were both begun with this chance to the slips. He doesn't always give it. But there seems some psychological weakness at the beginning of an innings. Quick and early the ball flew off his bat to second slip this time, and the fieldsman missed it. Macindoe was the bowler, but I don't believe the bowler has anything to do with it at all. It is the enormous responsibility which must affect Bradman some way or other, the same kind of thing which made John Bright, to the end of his days, nervous at the beginning of a speech.

There is the heel of Achilles, a very small heel, I fear, but yet palpable.

McCabe made a brilliant century, but he, too, was beaten twice in the first five minutes, sending slip catches each time. He gave another chance later, but that was nothing — he hit out at a very bad ball from Kimpton and sent it straight back. But he was distinctly "feeling" for those two off which he gave the catches to slip. Otherwise he was his old self, the perfect batsman.

McCabe is a model in everything he does, with an extraordinarily quick handling of his bat to mark his genius. Whether that beautiful open style will be consistently formidable in a wet season I doubt, but on good wickets he is going to play some grand innings.

Brown and Fingleton had opened the innings. Brown was not nearly as good as he was in 1934, and although Fingleton made a century, it is difficult to say exactly what his quality is.

The Australian morale is very high — always has been, like Yorkshire's — and on such a side, with Bradman to follow, the opening batsmen have much more confidence.

While Fingleton will give a lot of trouble, I should say there must be quite a few English batsmen of his type who would do well in his place. At any rate, although he is an accomplished batsman — he could not go in first for Australia if he weren't — he did not give the impression of high class which one got from McCabe, for instance.

The man who really set everyone thinking was Hassett. The wicket was good, the bowling not too difficult, his side was in a good position. But the way this diminutive young cricketer opened was enough to make one wonder where Australia can so constantly produce these marvellous young men. Hassett was making all the strokes — right at the beginning of his innings, playing the ball off the wicket round to long-leg as if he were playing in a college match. His timing was superb either for glancing or for some truly terrific drives, and though he was welting the ball as hard as possible he was in no hurry and played some good ones with the most sober back-stroke imaginable, covering up everything. One innings does not make a great batsman, but that young man has a great future before him.

Chipperfield made some lovely strokes, but he is certainly not a great batsman. His stroke-play is not perfect, and quite a few times he was feeling for a really good ball.

After the first two overs McCabe never did anything of the kind, Hassett never at all, but that Chipperfield did shows that the bowling was not so bad as the figures showed.

The Australian batting on good wickets will be good. If Bradman and McCabe had failed, one after the other, then Hassett was quite capable of making a century, while Fingleton stuck up one end. They may have a bit of a tail, but they can afford it, for Badcock was not playing. If their man Barnes was fit, then with Bradman, Brown, Fingleton and McCabe, and the three colts — Badcock, Hassett and Barnes — they have batting more than enough.

Macindoe bowled with great spirit and has some dangerous balls on his arm, but he is as yet a youth. Else why bowl short balls to McCabe? It means 4 every time, regular as the clock. But Evans was very interesting, in himself and as a symbol. He bowled medium-pace and swung the ball away. There were times when he had each Australian playing. If there is no slow bowler available, then it seems that a good medium-paced bowler, bowling not like Goddard to a leg-trap but to three slips, will test the visitors more than most other types.

Evans had neither the steadiness of length nor the fitness, and I feel certain that Bradman could have easily played the ball that got him out, but there were certain overs bowled by Evans which made one think that it would be nice to see George Geary in his prime against Bradman and company on an English wicket in the English heavy atmosphere.

Cricket is Losing a Supreme Artist

(*Glasgow Herald*, 17 August 1938)

Frank Woolley retires this year. He is fifty-one. Think of it, fifty-one! This means by the same reckoning that Compton, if he does as well, will have reached similar eminence in 1968. What wars and revolutions will have rolled by! How many old cricketers would have left the game and new ones taken their places, and some of these gone and still others pushing eagerly in!

That is what Woolley has done.

Woolley's case is not altogether unusual. England, in cricket as in other departments of life, is the country of wonderful veterans. When W.G. Grace startled the world in 1895 with his 1,000 runs in May he was in his forty-seventh year. Eleven years later, he made over 70 for the Gentlemen, cutting the fast bowlers beautifully. Wilfred Rhodes and Hobbs played fine cricket for over thirty years.

The Australians follow an opposite course. Ponsford's career lasted only from 1924/5 to 1934, and he retired after his greatest season — that of 1934 in England. Macartney scored three centuries in the 1926 Tests and then retired. Not only from Test but from State cricket the Australians retire at the first hint of decline. Perhaps that is why they always have so fine a crop of younger players. Be that as it may: other countries, other manners.

No one wanted to see Woolley retire. Now that he is going, all would like to see him stay.

In one respect he is a unique veteran. Grace, Hobbs, Rhodes, all lost something with the years. They remained great men for a long time, but there was an audacity, a flash, a sparkle which showed that time had not forgotten them.

Of all the veterans Woolley has remained more like his greatest self than any. He gets out more quickly. He has asked to go in first to see the ball more easily as it is red. He makes 60 where formerly he made 100. But the bat swings as lazily down and the ball shoots as fiercely fast to the boundary as at any time these thirty years. He could not do otherwise. If he were lifted from his dying bed and propped up at the wicket he would make a grand stroke, or at least attempt one.

What was the secret of his success? A gifted physique — long and willowy; and muscles which have kept him slim now that he is old enough to be a grandfather. The slip that he was shows in his eye: the slow bowler who was second only to Blythe shows the physical coordination; the 2,000 runs and 100 wickets in succeeding years are proof of the sheer physical strength and resilience. The foundations of his style were laid in another age.

Whatever his virtues, no batsman of the modern school will ever play like Woolley, as no modern historian will ever write like Gibbon. Woolley played back straight with his right shoulder high; he made the drives with a full swing; he cut genuinely late. It is in the range of his strokes that he terrorized bowlers. He used to stand back to Gregory and force him to the boundary on Australian wickets. He drove the fast bowlers as hard and as fearlessly as the slow. And no array of slips checked his cuts. The bowler could not hide from him. There was a hole in his defence somewhere — the trouble for most bowlers was to have time to find it. Usually they were too busy covering up the holes in their own. Woolley found those quickly enough.

Once more, what was his secret? First of all, his height. Any mathematician can tell you that a bat truly swung by six feet hits ever so much harder than one swung by five feet. Furthermore, Woolley used his inches — every one of them. He would not stoop to conquer. Secondly, despite his wonderfully free swing, he used his wrists. Now with wrists alone a batsman can get terrific pace on to a stroke. But if he uses a long swing, a powerful forearm and at the same time uses his wrists as well, there is an accumulation of force which drives the ball like a hammer.

I have seen Woolley flick a slow long-hop into the pavilion at Old Trafford, using wrists and forearm only. But to use all these in perfect co-ordination is summed up in the one word "timing". C.B. Fry says that a batsman may make a century and never time one ball correctly. That is gospel.

A personal elucidation may help. Some years ago a cricketer was practising at an open net and a bowler bowled a medium-pace ball outside the off-stump. The batsman stepped back and decided to let it pass. At the last moment he changed his mind and dabbed down on it. He did not hit, merely tapped the ball, but playing so late the weight of the body was in the stroke and the wrist had to accelerate to reach the ball. It flew from under the bat and raced to the boundary while exclamations of delight (and, be it said, surprise) broke from the few and bored spectators around. It is twenty years now, but I can still feel that stroke in my hands.

Another day I was stepping back to play a ball outside my leg-stump. Suddenly it swung in almost from the pitch. In defence of my wicket I had to stab quickly. I saw it next about twenty yards from the boundary. Mid-on and the bowler knew even less about it than I did. These were both perfectly timed strokes, rare enough to be remembered.

Now imagine a man with all the physical gifts who has the art of constantly timing his strokes in that way, and you have Woolley. Even in a great innings by a great batsman a few strokes stand out. But in so many of Woolley's innings all or nearly all the strokes stood out. That was his special charm, and gift it was, for he has not lost it with the years.

He was not so sound as Hobbs, for instance, or Sutcliffe. In Tests, good though his record is, he did not do as well as his other performances led one to expect. He failed in South Africa. The vagaries of the matting wicket required more watchfulness and less freedom than his expansive style could stomach. Yet one day in a Test at Johannesburg, after a series of failures and the first ball having touched his wicket without removing the bails, he proceeded to make one of his most dazzling centuries. But his great innings, played in the best company, are innumerable. He was a man of lost causes. Witness his two 90s at Lord's in 1921, his last-wicket stand with Freeman of over a century at Sydney in 1924–5, when the match was hopelessly lost. He still holds the English record for the last wicket at Old Trafford.

At Old Trafford he had some tremendous duels with that great bowler McDonald. One famous match, while "Mac" bowled out the Kent team around him, Woolley hit him to all parts of the field, making over 200 runs in his two innings. Mac got him out both times, but paid the full price.

Such performances as these — even the unexpected century at Johannesburg — are not ecstatic highlights, but a part of his character. First wicket, last wicket, after failure or after success, he played the game that it was in him to play.

He was a man in his time of many parts. He bowled left-hand slow, and in eight seasons took his 100 wickets along with his 1,000 or 2,000 runs. Those who know him best say that he was, on his day, one of the great slow left-handers of his time. He was, in his prime, a superb slip. He is a fine coach, and coached Duleepsinjhi. He was a man of some humour, too. A colonial cricketer fanned the air in a series of fruitless swipes. "Say, friend, let us know if you are going to go on like this," asked Woolley from the slips, and then explained: he would have to send for his sweater to protect himself from the draught.

Hobbs relates that in South Africa a mayor, filling an unaccustomed post, proposed the toast of the WCC as a substitute for MCC, whereupon Woolley laughed so much that he fell under the table.

He often disagreed with umpires who gave him out. No doubt he felt it was a sin not to have him at the wicket as long as possible!

It was. He was one of the great cricketers of his time, but he was more than that. He gave to thousands and thousands of his countrymen a conception of the beautiful which artists struggle to capture in paint and on canvas. They would probably have resented it if you told them that. But so it was. They recognized in him something beyond the average scorer of runs, some elegance of line and harmony of movement which went beyond the figures on the score-board. That, indeed, will give him his place in the game, a place higher than many who won more matches for their side.

For if the game of cricket were ever put on trial for its life, its advocates would bring Grace and Bradman and Ranjitsinhji and a few others as evidence on behalf of the defence. But they would bring Woolley too. And if they were clever advocates they would play him as their strongest card. For if he could not win the sympathy of the jury then what other cricketer could?

1950s

James devoted the years in the United States, 1938–53, to an intensive study of Marxist philosophy and political activity. By the end of the 1940s he had arrived at a position which he expounded fully in two important works: *Notes on Dialectics* (1948) and *State Capitalism and World Revolution* (1950). Having achieved this intellectual and political clarification, James was now free to make explorations into the realms of culture. He had cleared the way for the writing of his classic cricket memoir which appeared some ten years later as *Beyond a Boundary*.

Although he had not seen a single cricket match for fifteen years, James had followed the game through English newspapers, *Wisden's Almanack* and other publications which he had been able to obtain in America. Cricket still remained a fundamental part of his thinking, and he explained this experience as follows: "I thought constantly of cricket because I could not see it. I was constantly thinking about cricket in this foreign environment. It gave cricket an existence of its own with the elements of a beginning, middle and an end. Whence this volume [*Beyond a Boundary*]. I did not write in the United States but by the time I came to England I had what for me in writing is an imperative necessity: a sense of structure."*

James was expelled from the United States in 1953, following a period of internment on Ellis Island where he completed his study of Herman Melville. It was published that same year, as *Mariners, Renegades and Castaways*.

On his return to England he published in the *Manchester Guardian* his reactions to cricket as it appeared to him after many years of only reading and thinking about, but not seeing, the game. He followed this with a season of cricket reporting for the paper. During 1954 James retraced his steps of the 1930s by travelling to the different grounds to report county matches, including the tour made that year by a Pakistani Test team. But his days as a cricket reporter were over and he was anxious to concentrate upon a much more fundamental examination of the game of cricket. The preoccupation with this project was clearly reflected in the correspondence over the decade between his return to Britain and the publication of *Beyond a Boundary* in 1963.

*Interview with Anna Grimshaw, London, September 1985.

In particular James maintained a very full correspondence with the Facing Reality Group, of which he had been a leading member while in the United States. In 1958 his collection of essays entitled *Facing Reality* was published, dealing primarily with issues arising from the Hungarian revolt of 1956.

The writing of *Beyond a Boundary* during the 1950s lay at the heart of James's new orientation towards questions of culture. Politics were central to this orientation, but James had by now definitively stated his position and evolved his method. What was needed henceforth was a development from this position to an interpretation of cultural forms. The bibliography of his work after 1950 indicates clearly the original contributions James's writings made to debates in literature, art and popular culture.

In 1958 when the manuscript of *Beyond a Boundary* (at this time called *Who Only Cricket Know*) was almost complete, James was invited back to Trinidad by his former pupil, Dr Eric Williams. Williams was leader of the People's National Movement (PNM) and his party was set to lead Trinidad to independence from British rule. James was offered the editorship of the *PNM Weekly*. The *PNM Weekly* was discarded and James founded a new paper, *The Nation*. He also became secretary of the Federal Labour Party, which represented the idea of a West Indies Federation. The return in 1958 was the first trip made by James to the Caribbean since his departure in 1932. He had spent twenty-six years abroad.

For James the imminence of independence and the publication of *Beyond a Boundary* were intimately connected: they were part of the same historical moment. Although the achievement of independence in the West Indies had not been the culmination of a struggle comparable with the experience in Africa, and perhaps because of this, several important political problems were pressing when James returned to Trinidad. A number of these issues were reflected in cricket and they were extensively debated in *The Nation* at James's instigation: specifically the question of a West Indies cricket tour of South Africa and the appointment of Frank Worrell as captain of the Test team. *Beyond a Boundary* was completed amidst, and as a part of, these political struggles.

Return of a Wanderer:
Comparisons between 1938 and 1953

(*Manchester Guardian*, 7 October 1953)

I played cricket uninterruptedly in the West Indies from the time I was four until 1932, when I came to England. Here I spent the summers reporting county and international matches, first for the *Manchester Guardian* and later for the *Glasgow Herald*. From the time I learned to read I read everything on cricket I could put my hands on. I had played cricket for many years with international cricketers, and knew some of them intimately. Then in 1938 I went to the United States and my long and close association with cricket was broken — I did not see a cricket match for fifteen years. I returned to England in the middle of the summer and have seen much of the Leeds Test on television, the Oval Test in the flesh, and a number of county matches. I have devoured *Wisden* for the years between. How does the game look after this long interval?

The most startling new feature is the routine leg-side slip field for fast bowlers. I had never seen this before, and I am immensely impressed with it. I say this because in the old days many an innings did not edge to the slips a single fast ball swinging away. But almost every batsman I have seen play this strange attack has made one or more streaky strokes through these leg-side fieldsmen or played at balls at which, it seemed, he did not want to play.

It is batting, however, which has undergone a revolution. The basis of defence to slow bowlers seems to have shifted from back play to bringing the left foot forward and from there watching the ball off the pitch carefully on to the bat. L.N. Constantine, with whom I have discussed it, is full of arguments against the technique, but I notice that when I question him about this or that slow bowler whom I have not seen he says as often as not, "You have to play him out here," and outlines the slow forward motion.

There are usually good reasons for what a lot of experts do, but every mode has its advantages and disadvantages, and I shall have to watch a long time before I can accustom myself to it and come to some balanced judgement. I notice, however, that the Australians (except for Miller) play back more in the old style, and two curious dismissals have given me food for reflection. May for Surrey at Lord's and Hutton at the Oval Test were both bowled by slowish yorkers when well set. Both batsmen seemed pinned on the left foot very early in the flight, so that when the ball dipped into them late they were, so to speak, in their own way and could not get the bat to the ball.

In stroke play there seems to be a decided increase of boundaries off the back foot. A few like Bradman, Hammond and Constantine always made the stroke, but however hard the ball went to the boundary it was in essence a defensive stroke. As I have seen it these days the batsmen are making a forcing stroke, the counterpart to the defensive forward stroke.

The Hutton of 1938 I never thought of at any time as a younger player, whatever his birth certificate might say. The change in his play has, therefore, delighted me. Every great player brings something peculiar to himself and unique to the game. From the tough Yorkshire foundation came first Sutcliffe, whom I remember as the most aristocratic of modern batsmen, and now I see a Hutton transformed. Who, in 1938, could have envisaged in the grim young Yorkshireman who scored 364 against Australia at the Oval the dignity and elegance which now characterize him?

Two new players interest me enormously. One is May, whose off-driving is unprecedented in my memory. Bradman, McCabe, Hammond, Sutcliffe all drove hard enough, but in the modern manner, that is, they never seemed to forget that the ball might swing or do something in the last few inches of its flight. May reminds me of a West Indian player, Joe Small, who startled Old Trafford in 1923 with his driving. He hit from the shoulder in a way I do not remember in any Test player and I have an idea that here for the first time is a reincarnation of the old pre-1914 off-side hitting of which we have heard so much.

The other young player is Harvey. My private measurement for judging a new player used to be first and always the way the ball left his bat in purely defensive strokes. When the ball always moved away strongly, it was a sure sign of accurate foot-work, fine balance, and playing very late which brought the bat sharply up against the ball. Long, long ago I read C.B. Fry's statement that a batsman need not remove his feet until after he has actually seen the direction the ball has taken, not through the air, but from the pitch. I know nothing better to read on cricket than C.B. Fry analysing batsmanship, but I was always sceptical of this particular point and always trying to test it. Harvey has fired my interest anew in this problem. I have rarely seen a young player who approached so closely to Fry's ideal.

The fielding as I have seen it is more flashy in the pick-up and return than it used to be, but the catching seems pretty bad in comparison with the old standards as I remember them, and this does not exclude the Australians in the Oval Test.

But far more interesting than the changes in the players on the field are the changes off it. There are many more women in the crowds, and many of them are older women, whom I do not think were watchers in 1938. The spectators applaud more. Listening to them and watching them, I am doubtful if they really know as much about the intricacies of the game as the crowds of 1938 — at the Oval I saw many who seemed to enjoy being present at a great event even if they did not follow everything.

Cricket is more a part of the national activity than it used to be. The journalists have less space in the press and are more flamboyant. More seem to be writing in the style C.B. Fry was making popular in the late thirties. I am overwhelmed by the number of books on cricket — it seems to me that in the years since I went away more books on cricket have been published than in the whole previous history of the game. Statistics, solid if narrow causeway in the dangerous swamps of critical appraisal, are far more comprehensive and ingenious than before, and, I have no doubt, as misleading as they ever were. But as a lifelong addict who has been long deprived I can testify to their increased fascination.

The broadcasters, who were more pioneers in the late thirties, and the television commentators, who are quite new, have perfected their technique and are splendid, if somewhat on the cautious side. I can understand it, for public pressure is far greater on the game than it used to be. It affects even the players. Hobbs and Sutcliffe, Bradman and McCabe played cricket as diplomatists of the old school carried on diplomacy. They were Olympians. The players I have seen this year, like modern diplomatists, are aware of their public.

Looking at the volatile Lock, I thought for long minutes of the very different figure of his predecessor of 1938, the always-to-be-remembered Verity. It may be merely temporary, but I feel that games and players are less remote, closer to ordinary humanity than in 1938. Hopes, fears, jokes (and anger) are shared by players and spectators, and through the highly developed media of mass communication by millions of people who were formerly excluded. All this makes the game far more interesting to look at than it was in 1933.

Letter to George Headley

8c Tanza Road,
Hampstead,
London, NW3

11 February 1954

My dear George,

Here is the manuscript.* A copy has gone to Learie for him to take to the publishers. I am sending you a few clippings. I expect that in Jamaica you all are getting statements of the English press. But Crawford White, Charles Bray and the rest of them are all singing one song — the miserable pushing and lack of aggression in the English batsmen. That makes your chapter on Batting absolutely marvellous and suitable to the present moment. I believe I can do something here with that chapter and a newspaper editor. But I will not attempt it without your permission. To write would be a waste of time. Cable me as follows:

IN THE CAUSE OF AGGRESSIVE BATTING USE CHAPTER 8.

Already there has been some publicity about the book. I enclose it.

Hope you are doing fine and enjoying your stay. One last word. I would suggest if you are making arrangements for West Indian publication in the press of certain chapters that you hand it over to some agency and let them make the arrangements right down the line.

As ever,
C.L.R. James.

Letter from George Headley

23 February 1954

Dear Nello,

I'm looking through script. I observe that subject to your approval in chapter 8 on Batting, page 14, a statement made

*Headley's autobiography, on which James advised.

could be a little more clarified not to cause too much controversy and I would like you to add: "For nobody living can bat better than Worrell — From a point of technical perfection."

Also Chapter 1. My tough apprenticeship at the bottom of page 12. Please insert the following:

That it is not generally realized the almost insuperable obstacles the average cricketer in the West Indies has to overcome, I was comfortable compared to many I knew, whose lot was unemployment, half-fed, and in dire circumstances. The powers that be make no attempt to help such fellows, but, when the occasion demands, they are expected to bowl or bat for five or more days.

See you soon, Topper, chapter 8 certainly a classic.

Your pal,
George.

P.S. Regards to Learie.

Pakistanis in Good Form

(*Manchester Guardian*, 10 May 1954)

The Pakistanis, scoring 374 for 8, were off to a flying start here today in the first match of their tour, against Worcester. The weather was excellent, the wicket perfect and easy-paced, and the ground looked more beautiful than ever with new stand accommodation and a fine new scoreboard, in addition to some landscaping that had been done to prepare it for the new season.

Kardar won the toss and sent in Hanif Mohammad and Alimuddin. Hanif will not be twenty until December, but he already has a fine record in Test and representative cricket, and there is a great deal of speculation among those who know his play as to whether this tour will develop him into one of the world's great batsmen. He is short, like Bradman and Headley, with broad shoulders. His stance is not easy but concentrated, legs apart, left shoulder pointing directly at the bowler. He plays back strongly, but he moves his left foot well out to the pitched-up ball and slashes his bat at it late, beating the fieldsmen to the boundary on either side of the bowler. The stroke is perfectly controlled and beautifully timed, and this in combination with his strong back-play is a sound foundation for many runs. He put the ball up in the slips trying to force a short ball off the back foot on the off-side, and was out for 29 trying to hook another short one. Both seemed the strokes of a batsman short of practice.

The stand for the first wicket produced 54, but the best stand of the innings came when Maqsood Ahmed joined Alimuddin. Maqsood could not time the ball at first, but before he went in for lunch two lovely fours in front of him, one off the front foot and one off the back, put him right, and after lunch he and Alimuddin hit the bowling all over the place. Maqsood's driving was terrific, particularly against Ashman, a slow left-hander. Ball after ball was driven hard on the off-side, stinging the hands of the fieldsmen or getting through, sometimes even when the field was dropped back to the boundary. From one of them, hit straight at him along the ground, cover thought it prudent to retire and no one on the ground seemed to blame him for it.

Alimuddin was also driving Ashman, though not so often, and a chart of their strokes would have shown boundaries from straight past the bowler down to square drives wristed well behind point. Devereux came on with leg-breaks but Maqsood showed equal strength on the top-side, swinging him for six between mid-on and square-leg twice in the first over. He is not a big man and the power comes from fine timing. The two of them hit a hundred in sixty minutes and soon afterwards Maqsood reached his century in level time with seventeen fours and two sixes. He did not, as so many modern batsmen do, immediately settle down for the second hundred. He swished wildly at a few balls, then quietened down, and was finally out to a half-hearted stroke. Alimuddin took 220 minutes to make 142, but he showed powerful strokes all round the wicket with a range perhaps greater than Maqsood's. He gave two chances, but more than any other batsman he seemed to know exactly what he was doing.

Ghazali is described in a handbook entitled "official" as a player in "the English style of being a good front-foot player", and sure as day he played the slow bowler left foot well out and a slow defensive bat. Both he and Fazal Mahmood wisely had a good look at the bowling, but both made dashing strokes. In fact no better strokes were made all day than a straight drive by Fazal off the back foot from a half-volley and three drives by which the number 10, Mahmood Hussain, ended the day.

In estimating this score it should be noted that the visitors arrived in England only on Sunday, they have had only one practice game of a few hours and one practice of two or three hours at the nets. On the other hand, however, many of them have visited England in the last two years for coaching and experience, and quite a number have played representative cricket against the Australian Services side, an MCC touring team, the West Indies and India. They are new to big cricket in England, but they are not novices. Some of them at present feel for the ball in the forward defensive stroke and are inclined to cut rather recklessly at anything short outside the off-stump. But they have the strokes, with quick footwork and fine timing for early in the season. It is permissible even this early to expect that in a good summer they will make plenty of runs.

The Worcester bowling badly missed Jenkins, whose fingers are damaged. Grove took five wickets and deserved every one. Perks sent down many fine balls, but nothing came of them, quite a few strokes flying off the edge through the slips and some catches being dropped. But to the end of the day, in spite of heavy punishment at times, the two veterans bowled steadily and well.

Pakistanis Far Ahead; Khalid's Leg-Breaks

(*Manchester Guardian*, 11 May 1954)

The weather was still fine, but with a touch of haze in the air as the Pakistani cricketers continued to do well to-day in their match against Worcester. They took their Saturday score of 374 for eight to 428 and then dismissed Worcester for 218. In the morning Fazal, who had been 34 not out, ended up with 67. As will be seen, he is primarily a bowler, but he has a batsman's balance, body almost straight and leaning well over the ball as he plays it away near his pads.

In the fifty minutes of play that remained before lunch, Kenyon and Richardson put on 52 without being parted. The opening bowlers were Fazal, a bowler of the Bedser type, and Mahmood Hussain, reputedly a fast bowler. Both had the usual array of slips and leg-slips. But Fazal bowled on the short side, and whatever he was doing the batsmen had ample time to see it. Mahmood by his third over had worked up to a fastish pace but he always bowled well within himself. The first match of the tour is no time for a fast bowler to risk straining himself, and expert Australian opinion is that it takes a month before the touring fast bowler is really at his best.

The most interesting bowler was Elahi, a medium-paced right-hander. To Richardson, a left-hander, he bowled many balls that were real round-arm, but he swung his arm high sometimes and it was off one of these that swung away very late that Richardson just before lunch gave a chance to the slips which was not taken.

After lunch the Pakistani bowling, if it did not inspire fear, commanded respect. Elahi bowled Kenyon with a ball beautifully flighted without any noticeable change of action. He gave the impression of aggressiveness, bowling with a short run and constantly changing pace, and even getting a little spin from the off-side on that excellent wicket. He had Dews caught at deep extra-cover and would have had Richardson also had not short third man dropped the catch. His steadiness and experience were evident and will be most valuable on this tour. Fazal bowled better after lunch, but again it was noticeable that he was rarely driven, his length giving the batsman time to play him off the pitch.

At about twenty minutes before tea Khalid Hassan, the sixteen-year-old schoolboy, was put on to bowl. He sent up a number of full tosses in his first two or three overs but obviously he was spinning his leg-break. As soon as he struck a length he bowled Richardson with a ball well pitched up to him at which Richardson drove, the ball turning sharply away from the bat. Until tea, the other batsmen poked circumspectively at Khalid. It took Worcester two hours to add 75 to their lunch score of 52. Most of the runs came from Richardson, who seems to be in fine form already, being strong in his defensive strokes and scoring off all loose balls.

After tea the Pakistan bowling improved considerably. In addition to battering the batsmen with his spin, young Khalid seemed to trouble them in his flight. Later in the afternoon Grove went after him and hit him for three sixes, the fieldsmen standing in the correct places, but the ball sailing over their heads into the crowd. Khalid was taken off, but he had bowled well. The Pakistanis depend a lot on Fazal, and he did his best bowling on the day after tea. He moved the ball well from just outside the off-stump into the batsmen and could hit it on the same spot and straighten it up with increased pace from the pitch. This ball had two men caught behind the wicket. He then changed over to the other end and by a bewildering series of inswings and outswings clean bowled three batsmen.

Fazal's Fine Bowling at Worcester

(*Manchester Guardian*, 12 May 1954)

When the Pakistanis came on to the field here today for the continuation of Worcester's second innings the sun was not only shining, it was stinging. The majority of the Pakistan side discarded sweaters, and conditions were ideal for them. They celebrated by getting out Worcester this time for 244 runs, and considering that at lunch Worcester were a solid 156 for one this was an even better performance by the visitors than their play yesterday. They had plenty of time to make the 35 runs required to win and did so with nearly half an hour to spare for the loss of two wickets.

This is only the third time since the war that a touring side has won its opening match at Worcester, and few bowlers can have done better in the same circumstances as Fazal, whose seven wickets for 48 today made his total figures for the match eleven for 102.

Fazal and Mahmood opened the game this morning with a ball from which only 12 runs had been made the previous evening, and Kenyon and Richardson handled their bowling well. Both seemed at home also with the change bowling and Richardson made strokes all round the wicket. Fifty came up, and after an hour's play Kardar went on to bowl with the obvious intent of breaking the partnership. Richardson cut him for four but soon was in trouble misplaying a ball past the solitary slip and in the next over gave the same slip an easy catch. He made 44 out of 69. In both his innings in this match he was merciless on loose balls and was always ready at the slightest opportunity to force a boundary. But both times he got out when one was expecting him to stay. Kenyon and Dews seemed in command of the bowling.

Khalid Hassan bowled a maiden first over after lunch and then before adding to his score Kenyon tried to play Fazal away past point. He hit the ball hard and low to Kadar in the gully, who made a fine catch. The next ball swung in quickly from the off and had Bird lbw. Eight men gathered together round the wicket to create the necessary atmosphere for the hat-trick. Broadbent stopped it, but another quick in-swinger found his foot in front and thus the second over after lunch had taken three wickets for no runs — 156 for one, 156 for four. Thus was the back of the Worcester innings broken.

Only fine defence by Devereux saved him from being clean-bowled or lbw in the next over from another late in-swinger which left the pitch at a fierce pace. Meanwhile Khalid had shouted for an lbw and failed, but in his next over Devereux, driving at the slow leg-break well up to him, was caught at slip; he was given out on appeal and if he had not touched the ball then that spinner dropping right up on the off-stump and spinning off into the hands of slip would have been the most remarkable ball bowled in the match.

The Pakistan bowlers and fieldsmen were now on their toes in ruthless mood, but Dews cleared the air by driving Khalid to the boundary for his fifty. Yarnold, the wicket-keeper, number 10 on the score card, was promoted to stop the rot and he put a solid bat in the face of a Fazal who seemed eager to get three wickets every over.

But Kardar is an ideal change bowler, astute and with good control. He had the now aggressive Dews caught in the long field next over and Fazal was immediately put on again at the other end and finished off the innings in tremendous style. At half-past three this well-built and powerful man, whose every step both running up to bowl and walking back is charged with energy, was bowling as strongly as he had been doing at eleven in the morning. His eleven for 102 in this match, on a pitch which was consistently true and easy in pace, is a remarkable performance.

Shakoor Ahmed, the Pakistan wicket-keeper, is most competent and there are many fine fieldsmen on the side, Kardar being consistently brilliant anywhere near the wicket. The throwing, too, was strong, in fact a little too strong, for both on Monday and today there were a few over-throws. The men do not as yet know their exact places in the field, and there was an unusual amount of chopping and changing about, which made for a certain raggedness. But it was much better today than it was yesterday, and altogether the Pakistanis played both effective and attractive cricket.

"Neither Toss, Weather nor Wicket were Decisive Elements in the Defeat of Australia Last Season"

(*The Cricket Society Newsletter*, 1957)

[*A debate was held at the Cricket Society on 12 March 1957 on the above motion, proposed by C.L.R. James and opposed by John Arlott. This is the text of James's opening address. The motion was carried by 83 votes to 31.*]

Mr Chairman, Mr Arlott, Ladies and Gentlemen, I would like to begin by saying a word of welcome to my distinguished opponent, not in the ordinary sense of courtesy, but rightly so. We have heard him on the radio as a commentator and have heard him in the Press. He is a good advocate and I have no doubt he will be quite as successful in this. The game of cricket today is in a difficult situation, recognized by everyone. Some of the drastic proposals made to rectify matters are evidence of that. Furthermore, the way the games have gone in South Africa have brought home sharply to many people that the complaints are not just made by people who are concerned with comparing the players of today with those of forty years ago, but that they have a genuine basis.

In these discussions with Mr Arlott, I will be speaking to you on two levels: first, on the important matter before us and I hope to bring before you precise arguments; at the same time I am not going to disguise that the ideas which I am putting forward are governed by a definite attitude to the first-class game today. I hope you will bear that in mind.

I am not saying that tossing, weather or wicket have no influence on cricket; I am not saying either that they cannot be decisive in any particular game or any particular series. When two teams are evenly matched in all respects, these matters we are discussing here could play a decisive role in a particular game and in the ultimate decision of the series. I am saying that none of these singly or in combination played a decisive role in the 1956 series.

I want to begin with what was decisive in this series for this discussion. What happened on the Saturday morning at the Oval with Miller and Lindwall batting? Miller was caught by Washbrook at cover. It does not need much to see that he said to Lindwall: "We must get along; get these fellows in here and get four wickets down before lunch." That was his plan and Sir

81

Donald Bradman thought the same. The Englishmen came in to bat and very soon Davidson bowled an impossible ball to Cowdrey and he was out. I said: "Now the fun is going to begin." I thought this was it — Johnson praying to the gods that he should put the Englishmen in the same position as he had been for the last games. The Rev. Sheppard came out. It was very important that batsmen coming in should not have a chance to find their feet. The first and second ball bowled to him — one of the most atrocious long hops I have ever seen — went for four.

I believe he was taken by surprise; otherwise I believe he would have hit it for six. The next ball, a half-volley, was hit for four. Tension immediately slackened. Then, to my surprise, Burke was put on to bowl off-spin — I was looking for Benaud. Burke bowled extremely badly. In fact the slip field, instead of getting to the ball quickly, were now getting as quickly away from it as they could. The Australian bowling went to pieces. After lunch we had the spectacle of Miller and Archer, two fast bowlers, the spearhead of the Australian attack, bowling off-spin. Mercifully the rain came down and saved them. This is the sense of what I have to say; if at that time the Australians had seized hold of their opportunity and taken three or four wickets and had shown that they were capable of handling that situation, then this evening if I had been bold enough to attempt this side of the debate I would have been in a difficult position; because they would have been entitled to say: "You had us in that spot and we also showed you that although we do not have Laker and Lock we had the people to take care of that situation," but they did not. They failed completely to take advantage of that situation; therefore, I ask what right have we to believe that if they had been a more or less equal division of good wickets, bad wickets or turning wickets, they would have been able to win the victory in the series? They had an opportunity to demonstrate on that particular day. It was a bad wicket; one ball jumped up and another stayed on the ground. Half a dozen county sides in England would have been able to make a better showing at that particular time.

I am not saying that this match set the atmosphere. There is a certain level of competence in every department of the game below which a Test match must not fall and in that sphere the Australian side made a bad showing. Let us presume that the wickets were equally divided all through the season, I think Mr Arlott will have to find a lot of arguments to show that the Australian side had batting and bowling of such quality as to make a reasonable proposition of the idea that they would hold the series.

I believe the average Test match side needs three batsmen at the top of their form, scoring well. If they are 1, 2 and 3, for example, then 4, 5, 6, 7 will make runs in between. If none of the first three score, the other batsmen play below their form because too much responsibility is thrown upon them. The 1956 England side had such batsmen. May, a tower of strength, and Richardson, did extremely well. David Sheppard was extremely effective and Cowdrey's average, if not as good as in Australia, was extremely good. I did not see one in the Australian side. Neil Harvey is a fine Test-match player, but the plain fact is he was not the batsman he could be.

May had just had an unfortunate season, but at any rate he made runs in the other matches in South Africa; and looked as though he would make them in the Tests. But Neil Harvey did not make them in Tests or otherwise. It had a tremendous effect on the side. Burke was not very effective and he did not play up to his form. Benaud had a splendid innings at Lord's. Take the example of McDonald; can we believe that in a good season of good wickets he would have been a tremendous player of English bowling? I do not think so. In the match at Lord's he made some runs and played a remarkable innings at Manchester. In the Leeds match Trueman bowled him all over the place. I was watching the match on television. Godfrey Evans was behind as the ball curled away. Before he had played it Godfrey Evans threw up his arms — he was out! At the Oval he was out to a magnificent catch by Lock on the leg side. In the next innings he was lbw to Statham. I can only give my opinion. I do not think that batting would have dominated the English bowling. English batting made 459 at Manchester, 325 at Leeds, 188 for 3 at Nottingham; all good scores. Australia won the Test at Lord's, but look at their batting. They were 137 for one in the first innings and then with a good batting side on a good wicket, nine wickets fell for 140-odd runs. Six wickets fell for 112 runs before they were saved by Benaud in the last stage of the game. I do not see that given toss, wicket or reasonable conditions their batting was such to make me feel they could have won the series.

I want to examine the bowling. If you bring fast bowlers on tour and you have one of them about thirty-five years of age, you are tempting fortune. If you bring two you are treating fortune with contempt. Two fast bowlers of that age, one of whom is certain to be suspect from the very beginning; he may seem to bowl as well as he did. At no time did Lindwall live up to the enthusiasm of the Press in his early days; never once in the whole of 1956 did Lindwall show any capacity to do this. He took seven wickets in the whole of the series and three were at the end of an innings. At no time did he look like instilling the fear of God into the opposing side, which is one of the duties of a fast bowler. He did it often in the past. When England batsmen saw he would not be doing it any more they breathed a lot more easily. I have looked at the scores of matches in Australia against England in the previous season. I believe it should have been clear there, if not on those wickets (Lindwall, Miller and Archer were prepared for the wickets they got in Australia; they should have been prepared for the wickets they got here in England). They should have seen Archer was more effective than Lindwall. In this question of selection of players, nothing to do with the selection of those players before leaving Australia, but the use they made of the players they brought, I think Johnson was quite wrong to build the opening of his attack on Lindwall and Miller. It should have been with Miller and Archer; that is my opinion and I think figures show it. It is characteristic of what seemed to affect this Australian team from the time they came. I lay some emphasis on it as I think it is characteristic of some aspects of the modern player. Johnson began by saying that he was not interested in winning county games; he was concentrating on winning Test matches. It struck me at the time that if he brought half the concentration to winning Test matches that Don Bradman took to winning everything, he would have done well. Now criticizing a Test-match captain is dangerous and in some respects foolish. He knows what is taking place and in a way people outside cannot possibly know. He could not tell the pace of the wicket on the field unless he were near. How can you tell eighty yards away? There are other things. He has knowledge and can learn things. How one or two of his bowlers feel. He has seen batsmen against different types of bowler and found out their weaknesses. There are all sorts of unknown factors taking place in regard to judgement. One is somewhat loath to criticize the captain, but over the season and after the opportunity for reflection, you have some ideas and I am entitled for the purpose of the debate to say a few things. Johnson was feeling his way. I believe he made a serious mistake in regard to Archer, because the Number one, Len Hutton, was faced with a situation not so very different in Australia. He looked at it, came to his decision and acted!

As to the question of Australia making Craig captain of the team — here he was fighting for his place! I mention that in relation to something else. In the Selection Committee here they had little respect for the Press. They chose Washbrook, Sheppard and Compton. I did not see much of that in the Australian team, that resolution or decision, it was absent on this occasion. I want to go further into what is a very important matter, the way they attempted to play Laker, it is characteristic of the team as a whole. The same thing happened in South Africa, with regard to Tayfield. Len Hutton had a way to play spin bowling; he played forward and kept his arms loose. One thing about Len Hutton, if you took liberties you would find yourself on the extra-cover boundary. When bowlers tried to block Ranji, he replied by driving and getting more runs than he had ever done before.

Some of the modern batsmen are frightened to move. The old batsmen moved freely backwards and forwards. Hutton and the rest had some idea of controlled offence against off-spin bowlers on a turning wicket. What I could not find from the beginning to end of season was what method Australia were using against Laker. At the last match at the Oval they were worse than they had been before. I have nothing against Laker's performance, he was a fine bowler on the top of his form and he had them on the run and kept them on the run. I saw them play against Titmus at Lord's on a fairly good wicket and runs were wanted in a hurry. Titmus got many wickets. Ignore the talk of not being used to turning wickets. They were here in 1948, 1953 and 1956. In 1902, the Australian team, finding it was likely to be a wet season, decided to hit their way through and went through and won. My criticism against them this time was they decided on nothing. The same Australian team in 1902 played in South Africa on matting and turf wickets and batsmen made 100s, 80s, etc., and did not complain of change in the wicket. In the West Indies their teams are accustomed to play only one or two first-class matches in a year and have to play on various types of wicket.

The wicket did not always achieve the pitch of importance it has today. "Beauty is in the eye of the beholder." "Stone walls do not a prison make, nor iron bars a cage." The wicket is not bad because of what a bowler can make the ball do but because of what is in the hearts of batsmen as individuals. Also in the hearts of the public and press men. I believe today these matters have achieved importance in the judgement of the game which has affected play. When Hobbs and Sutcliffe in

1926 played at the Oval and batted all day and beat Australia, they would never have been able to do it unless in their hearts they had felt it were possible. The general tendency today is to raise minor issues to matters of importance, and the players themselves are being affected. I believe the Australian team has also been affected as most modern teams have, and looking at their play in general, I feel first of all that the English team were the superior in every respect and they were the weakest Australian team I have ever seen or heard of; not in actual capacity to play but in their approach to the game. That is the reason I dismiss toss, wicket or weather as decisive elements in the 1956 games. A small example of the kind of thing that took place: Johnson is one of the best players of off-spin bowling; he does not take his right foot back from the off-stump; he also has a good eye and can see certain types of ball well. At Nottingham he must have been batting for an hour and made 12 runs. Suddenly to everybody's surprise he dashed down the wicket and hit a ball to Bailey and was out. At the Oval match, Johnson placed himself high on the batting list in order to stop a crisis. I believe, modestly and humbly, he could have done that with greater success in an earlier game. The last hour or so before lunch, he batted extremely well. Here was an example of someone able to handle a situation. After lunch — up with his bat — and he was bowled. I believe that embodied in the attitude of the captain was the play of the team as a whole. There is a certain point of view I am putting forward and a certain proposition I am opening up.

I believe we live in a security-minded age. The age of pioneers which produced Lloyd George, Cecil Rhodes and even in crime, Horatio Bottomley, produced great batsmen with enterprise. Today life is at a much lower level and cricket unfortunately has absorbed some of this. Australia symbolizes this and represents this state. I never thought their misfortunes were the cause of their defeat but it was because of their methods. They themselves seemed to think so, for in their new selection they are making a clean sweep. They do not think wicket, weather or toss have anything to do with it. They are going to make a new approach to the game. I suggest to you that neither toss, wicket nor weather were decisive elements in the defeat of Australia but their own deficiencies; and we will be helping them to assist in their own rejuvenation and in the cricketers' well-being.

Letter to Facing Reality Group

31 March 1957

. . . The cricket book.[1] You may have seen the reception which it is getting from everyone. Men who have studied cricket all their lives and read everything repeat incessantly, "We have never heard anything like this." Now listen to the chapters and the general movement.

The first two or three chapters deal with my early childhood. I give Neff a challenge. A stupid one, but I'm ready to make it. I defy him to read those first three chapters without at a certain stage being moved to tears. My theme is my upbringing with English literature, cricket and puritanism. These are the three fundamental characteristics of English middle-class society. I shall show first of all that, precisely because they were not native to the West Indies, they assumed a reality for me that placed me in violent contrast with the people among whom I lived. (Lamming[2] tells me that it was worse in Barbados.) My mother and my aunts were puritans of the deepest dye.

I show the interconnections between these three to show how British the literature, the cricket and puritanism are. By cricket I mean not only the game but the code connected with it. ("It is not cricket" is a very serious business and not a joke.)

I then go on to show the cricket we played in the West Indies between 1920 and 1932 and I show unmistakably that the clubs representing the various classes of society played a certain type of cricket corresponding to the social aspirations which in a few years were to be expressed politically.

I then do a biography of Constantine, showing him as a representative West Indian man, and I show that along with his great gifts as a player he was animated by a nationalist passion all through. He is now a minister in Bill's[3] government.

I then take up the Olympic Games in Greece. I show that they were the games of the feudal aristocracy and the big bourgeosie. When democracy came in the 5th century with the participation of the masses, the great public spectacle became the drama of Aeschylus, etc. Now you do not know I suppose that public games disappeared from Europe with the end of the Olympic

1. The draft of what was to be *Beyond a Boundary.*
2. George Lamming, the Barbadian novelist, whose books include *The Emigrants* and *In the Castle of My Skin.*
3. Dr Eric Williams, then Prime Minister of Trinidad and Tobago.

Games until they came back in 1860 or so with the rise of modern democracy. But what in Greece became the drama in Britain became the organized games, and particularly cricket. However, just at this time or rather some years before, the British bourgeoisie, who were just pushing the aristocracy out of power, needed an ideology. They took over the game of cricket and in the public schools established the rigorous code as a means of uniting and disciplining their class. This they exported to all the British colonies. That is what I learnt in the West Indies.

I then take up the decline in style in modern cricket and the need for a regeneration. The game has fallen very low. The reason is that it has become professionalized and now has adopted the ideology and temper of the modern welfare state, security first, no risks, characteristic of modern bureaucracy. I explain this with an analysis of the Australians in 1956 and I will complete it with the West Indians in 1957. Behind it all is the question of what constitutes an education. The British code as an education for the British upper classes. What constitutes an education today, etc.

I can't continue with it. I have it roughly written but many of the points need research and discussion. On a scale which you can judge from this brief outline. Yet the book remains extremely simple. And, like the Ghana book, which introduces such things as Montgomery, Alabama, it knits into a unity a tremendously wide variety of historical and social topics. . . .

That Worrell Tour

(*The Nation*, Trinidad, 15 May 1959)

[*On 24 April 1959 a letter from Learie Constantine opposing a tour of South Africa by the West Indies team was published in The Nation. Constantine argued that the conditions laid down by the South African government and accepted by the West Indies team were tantamount to an endorsement of apartheid. The tour, he further believed, would be used as a means for making the apartheid policy acceptable to world opinion.*]

My reply to Learie is a statement of the political problem that is raised by Frank's projected tour to South Africa.

(1) For me the dominating issue is the African cricketers and

the African people. They are stifling in a prison. They want to get out of it. They want to know exactly how good they are, they want to make contact with Test cricketers, so that they and the world may judge. For me, here as everywhere else, that is what comes first. It is to assume a heavy responsibility to deny this desire on their part.

(2) Who is opposed? Canon Collins, Alan Paton and others of that way of thought. Learie must not mind if I say that these are political persons of a type I know well. They are dominated by opposition to the South African government and apartheid. That struggle they want to keep pure. They are holding high a banner of principle. This means more to them than the living struggle of living people. If these are harsh words, I use them because this attitude is not new to me. Many bitter criticisms have been made of the European Labour parties and trade unions for constantly compromising with capitalism instead of opposing it root and branch. They are blamed for the coming to power of Hitler. Parliament has been similarly denounced. But from there certain very honest, very sincere Socialists have drawn the conclusion: have nothing to do with them, denounce them, expose them, and only by keeping away from them can you prove the sincerity of your own views. That controversy has long been settled. The attitude of non-participation is wrong. Nkrumah in 1950 denounced the Gold Coast Constitution as a fraud and a hypocrisy, but he took office under it.

(3) The argument is: by accepting the conditions, you accept the apartheid. Do the Africans who live under apartheid thereby accept it? If Africans play West Indians under apartheid conditions, do the Africans accept apartheid? Surely that is absurd. Do our boys accept it? I cannot see that at all. I once spent six months in the USA organizing a strike of sharecroppers. I was kicked around as usual, eating in kitchens when I travelled, sitting in the rear seats of buses, etc. Did I "accept" segregation? Did I help to strengthen it? The facts are that I did exactly the opposite. The sharecroppers whom I worked with had a larger objective.

(4) Which takes us back to the starting-point. You want proof the tour is a brilliant political step? It has not yet taken place, and look at the stir it had created. The whole world is talking about it. That is good enough for me to start with. People say that the South African government is in favour of it. Are they? Put yourself in their position when they received the application. Could they say no? The whole policy is that the Africans can have all privileges, as long as they are by themselves. They

therefore laid down the most stringent apartheid conditions. I haven't the slightest doubts that some of them hoped to kill the tour. They failed, at least so far. Furthermore, if they had said no, they would have created a storm of anger: you wouldn't let them play with you, you wouldn't let them play by themselves.

Finally we must never forget that these oppressive rulers are constantly guilty of the most massive stupidities. Look at the farce of the treason trails. Look at the bloodstained, the criminal stupidity of imperialist policy in Cyprus. If even the South African savages believe that by submitting West Indians to apartheid they will gain something, let them think so. For my part, I want to see an African make a century in the first Test, a bowler bowl Sobers and Kanhai for 0 in the same over (despite the fact that I admire these two more than any living cricketer except Worrell). It will be in a good cause. It will hit the headlines in Pakistan, in England, in Australia, in the West Indies, and in South Africa too. Think of what it will mean to the African masses, their pride, their joy, their contact with the world outside, and their anger at this first proof, before the whole world, of the shameful suppression to which they are subjected. Will this strengthen apartheid? To believe that is to substitute laws for human emotions. Instead, the South African government will live to curse that this project was ever put forward.

Postscript: I call the trip political. Frank Worrell will probably deny it. In fact, he would be wise to do so. I go further. He may have had no such motive in mind. But it is already clear that this is a political bombshell. That is another reason why I am in favour. I want it to go on exploding and exploding. The only people who can be hurt are the South African jailers. I want them hurt and plenty. My personal belief is that they will try to stop the tour without coming out openly and saying so.

Without Malice

(*The Nation*, Trinidad, 30 October 1959)

I happened to get hold recently of a book on *The Art of Cricket* by Sir Donald Bradman.* For cricketers or non-cricketers, there

*London, Hodder & Stoughton, 1958.

is a chapter in it (in fact, many chapters) that are worthwhile reading. The one I refer to is his exposition of the manner in which he would have played the slow to medium off-spin bowling of Laker (to a mainly on-side field) which devastated the Australians during their 1956 tour of England.

Laker bowled, for the most part, round the wicket and had three short-legs just behind the batsman. The batsmen would repeatedly play the ball off the edge of the bat and give a dolly catch to the close-in fieldsmen.

On results, Laker was unplayable. Sir Donald, however, does not think so and he says what he would have done in the circumstances. First of all, anything short or overpitched he would have slammed into the faces of the short-legs as hard as he could, and he thinks that they would have been so busy ducking from danger and damage that they would not have been able to sight the ball to make any catch. George Headley and Learie Constantine have always insisted to me that they would slam the ball at those leg-side fielders and defy them to catch it. This was also the opinion of C.B. Fry.

Sir Donald, however, had other ideas. He said that he would stand two or three feet outside the crease. This would upset the length of the bowler. The natural thing for a bowler to do in those circumstances would be to bowl somewhat to the off or somewhat to the leg, so as to make the batsman miss the ball and so give the wicket-keeper a chance at stumping. That does not trouble Sir Donald. The off-break bowler has on the whole a leg-side field. Sir Donald says that if he bowls too much to the off, in order to try for a stumping, that gives the batsman the opportunity to drive the ball through the covers. Sir Donald proposes to make great use of his legs in covering up. And he says if the bowler bowls the ball so wide to the leg that it misses his protecting pads it would probably be too far off for the wicket-keeper to take it and stump. Cutting at the off-break, unless it is very wide and very short, he rejects entirely.

In playing defensively, when stepping back he leaves more space between himself and the ball. Thus if the ball breaks enough to take the inside edge there is himself between it and the fieldsman. If he has to play forward, he will have the front foot some distance in front of the bat so that if the ball hits the inside edge of the bat it cannot bounce from the bat to the pad and from there into the hands of the leg-side fielders. . . .

The thing which strikes me — and I have seen Sir Donald play many times and make many hundreds of runs — is the scientific, systematic manner in which he analyses the dangers, the way he works out a specific counter to them. But best of all is the way he is looking for runs, because he is concerned above all to work out methods of attacking the bowler to prevent him having the moral advantage of putting the batsman on the defensive.

If Sir Donald had been captain or manager of the 1956 team of Australians in England they would not have won the series (too weak), but under his instruction and guidance innings after innings of the Australians would not have been wrecked. I have spoken with other famous cricketers on the problem that Laker presented. The method that impresses me most was the one attributed to Wally Hammond, but I have not time to go into that now. What I wish to point out is the value of having as captain or manager a supreme strategist and great master of the game. He may not be able to make the difference between victory and defeat; but he can make the difference between defeat and disgrace. . . .

Gilchrist Before and Gilchrist After

(*The Nation*, Trinidad, 20 November 1959)

The case of Gilchrist* concerns me deeply. He is not only a splendid cricketer; he is a symbol. . . .

When I was in Jamaica I tried to find out all that I could about Gilchrist as a human being. Finally I was sent to a Mr William Stewart who did business on the Lascelles de Machado Wharf. He deals with ships and goods and warehouses. Mr Stewart is a tall, good-looking brown-skin man, whose conversation with me was punctuated with telephone calls and clerks pushing papers before him to read and to sign. He is very polite and a man of sober judgement.

He told me that he first met Gilchrist playing cricket some miles from Kingston. He played for a team at Seaforth, St Thomas. He was an ordinary country boy, a member of a large family. He had some sort of job in a machine-shop on the Vale Royal Estate. He was employed today and unemployed tomorrow and so forth. His cricketing talent was obvious. Mr Stewart

---

*Gilchrist had been suspended by the West Indies Board of Control for alleged misbehaviour while on tour in India.

felt that he was being wasted and he invited him to Kingston. He gave him a job on the wharf. He taught Gilchrist how to drive one of the small engines which carried goods up and down on the wharf and in the warehouses. It was not a difficult job but Gilchrist learned and did it well.

Mr Stewart is a keen cricketer and ran a private team, the Musketeers. Gilchrist played for this team.

I asked Mr Stewart if he had any trouble with Gilchrist on the job or playing cricket with him. He said: "Absolutely none." Gilchrist did his work and played his cricket and there was never any trouble with him whatever.

His cricket was so outstanding that obviously it was not fair to keep him in a private team. He joined one of the clubs in Kingston and played through a first-class season with them. Was there any trouble? None at all. His captain was quite well satisfied with his conduct.

Mr Stewart was not blind to the erratic behaviour of Gilchrist as a member of West Indies teams. He thinks that the meteoric rise to fame as perhaps the best fast bowler in the world today of a young man without much background might have unbalanced him. Mr Stewart has seen him on his return to Jamaica within recent years. He says that he talks to Gilchrist and tries to get him to behave in a way which would stop the severe criticisms. He is not very successful. But, he concludes, "I love Gilchrist as a son, almost as much as my own son."

Gilchrist writes to Mr Stewart. His wife is a Jamaican girl who went to England to marry him. She also writes to Mrs Stewart.

Finally, I told Mr Stewart that I believed the Board of Control was playing with fire, because if the Englishmen in an early match made 400 for two, a tremendous cry would arise from tens of thousands of throats: "We want Gilchrist."

Mr Stewart smiles. "They wouldn't have to make 400 for two," he said. "As soon as the opening bowlers fail to take a wicket in the first few overs, the shout will begin, 'We want Gilchrist.' "

I told Mr Stewart that I had noticed in England in 1957 that when Frank Worrell captained the side, Gilchrist was the most co-operative and docile of players.

"Gilchrist told me," said Mr Stewart, "that in England in 1957 Frank Worrell was his father."

I gathered that there were times when Frank went out of his way to cover up for Gilchrist.

My prevailing impression was that if Gilchrist could so earn

93

the affection and respect of an experienced and judicious man like Mr Stewart there was something in him which the Board and its various captains and managers have failed to reach.

The MCC Players as I Knew Them

(*The Nation*, Trinidad, 24 and 31 December 1959)

First of all, I want to say something to get it out of the way and for future reference. If Hall and Gilchrist were playing on this West Indian team, and Frank Worrell was the captain, I have not the slightest doubt that we would massacre the English team. People's memories are short. In 1935 England sent here the most powerful batting team that ever visited here from there. Constantine, Martindale and Hylton wrecked their batting completely. Hall and Gilchrist would be enough to win the series, especially with Ramadhin to back them. I am not able to compare the Ramadhin of 1957 with the Ramadhin of 1950. But Ram in 1957 was as fine a bowler as any captain could wish to have on his side. He was grossly mishandled. But in any case you need only a pair of first-class bowlers to win a series of Tests. Grimmett and O'Reilly, Lock and Laker (on their own wickets), Lindwall and Miller, Statham and Tyson — you need only two, a good supporting bowler and a good captain. I am not being cantankerous. I have in mind the tour to Australia in the near future. To send to Australia a team in which the captain and the manager are not people who have been to Australia and played cricket there would be an act of suicidal folly, and we have had enough of this kind of nonsense in the West Indies in the past.

Here I want to make a few observations about the MCC team as I saw them in England between 1953 and 1957 (and as I have been reading about them since). There are on the side, to my certain knowledge, one great bastman and one great bowler.

The batsman is Peter May. You will find him in a little difficulty in the first over to really fast bowling. And one year Tayfield, the South African off-spinner (one of the greatest bowlers of our time), has given him trouble. But this happens to most great batsmen at some time or other. In the days of Bradman's greatest glory I would have backed Learie to catch him in the gully two yards from the bat one out of every three innings if Bradman happened to be facing Verity. He always fumbled, or nearly always, and edged a ball in that direction. After that, of course, nothing stopped him. May's greatness consists in the fact that the tighter the situation is, the better he plays. And secondly, he will not let the bowler dominate him. Over and over again I have seen him take hold of a situation and move the game along. Unless a batsman can do that, to me he remains always of the second order.

At one time most people in England would have sworn that Cowdrey was of that type. He has made many runs in difficult conditions and will undoubtedly score. But you can pin him down for two or three hours at a time. This is no question of aesthetics. If the West Indian batting makes five or six hundred runs, we can expect that they will make them fast by modern standards. Unless the Englishmen have batsmen who can do the same, it is hard for them to win, if even they do not lose.

The other great player on the side is Statham. With various ups and downs, Statham has been the best fast bowler in England for the last five years. He hasn't the devastating pace of Gilchrist, but he is fast enough. And with that pace he has all the subtlety and finesse of a medium-pace bowler. I have seen Statham settle down to bowl out a well-set McLean at Lord's in 1955 and he did it with the last ball before lunch. I saw him do the same thing to Frank Worrell at Edgbaston in 1957. Taking the tour as a whole and judging from what I have read about his performance in Australia, he will be the most dangerous bowler on the England side and, as always, a pleasure to watch.

Another fine bowler is Trueman. Trueman, however, even in '57, was not so much losing pace (though he could bowl fast enough) as concentrating on moving the ball. Hutton, who knows him very well, says that he moves the ball away from the batsman at the very last second in a most dangerous way. Keith Miller used to do it but at a tremendous pace. Trueman, of course, may change his style on these hard wickets and in this hot sunshine. But he didn't seem to do so well in Australia.

I don't know anything about Pullar. He is a tall left-hander and when I used to see him years ago, although immature he was a stroke-maker. However, he comes from Lancashire and this means there are three things to be noted. He is accustomed to playing on wickets which are not easy. Secondly, he is likely to be tough. Thirdly, he has been trained in the school of Washbrook, the Lancashire captain, a great opening batsman in his time and one of the toughest of the tough.

The other newcomer to big cricket is Mike Smith, who last

95

season burst out with a spate of runs. I have seen Smith make plenty of runs and I know Clyde Walcott thinks very highly of him. From what I saw, I don't. English players develop slowly (but they last longer) and Smith may have developed a great deal. But more than once I have seen him very slow on his feet to real fast bowling that was moving about a bit.

Moss, the Middlesex fast bowler, has a curious reputation. He has been overshadowed by Trueman, Statham and Tyson in recent years. But I have heard it from good authority, and more than one, that particularly at Lord's Moss can be as difficult or even more difficult than any of the others, with a new ball and the atmosphere to suit him. The only trouble is that he lacks real pace. But where things are right for him he can drop the ball on the leg stump and hit the off. And that always takes a lot of playing. His trouble is likely to be that out here he will need the new ball and may not get it until after Trueman and Statham. Statham will bowl well with a tennis ball.

Barrington. Barrington is a great favourite of the family and we used to go to the Oval and wish him well. He has come on as a bowler but when we used to see him there was very little opportunity for him on the powerful Surrey bowling side. Barrington can bat. He has defence and fine strokes. Furthermore he is tough and a hard fighter. I believe, however, that his qualities were recognized but he was put into Test cricket too early, and this upset him. I remember him in a scratchy innings at Lord's against the powerful South African bowling side letting loose at Heine, who is well over six feet, and driving him down to the pavilion. Also he was always ready to hook — a little too ready. I gather that he has steadied down without losing his strokes. A fine cricketer, and I shall watch him with great interest.

Greenhough is quite frankly an experiment. Specially prepared wickets, off-spin and in-swing bowlers and leg-side fieldsmen, with batsmen who would not use their feet, took English batting to a very low level which was finally exposed in Australia. (I am glad to say I was one of those who consistently protested against it as unsound and destructive to both good bowling and good batting alike.) After the Australian tour I gather that the English selectors determined to resuscitate leg-spin bowling. Greenhough was the best they could find and they nursed him. But, barring the disaster in Australia and the need to reorganize the English team on new lines, I doubt if Greenhough would have been anywhere near an English XI. On the occasions that I saw him bowling for Lancashire he seemed commonplace enough. But to tell the truth I didn't watch him with any particular care; neither did he do anything which made me sit up and take notice.

Illingworth is a good all-rounder, but he has been around for a long time before he has finally found his place in an English team.

Swetman, the Surrey wicket-keeper, is a fine cricketer and I was disappointed that he didn't do better in Australia. He is a natural, if ever there was one. And the grace with which he takes the ball and returns enables you to watch him all the afternoon purely for that alone. Andrew went to Australia in 1957 with Hutton's team as the second keeper and we all thought that he would be the natural successor to Evans. Somehow or other he dropped out and now is back again. Both he and Swetman are real keepers, not the best that can be found to fill the spot.

Alec Bedser, who played with Subba Row for some years on the Surrey side, once said of him that he didn't think Subba Row was Test-match class because he had no style. The remark is quite legitimate. Style, in the sense of giving the impression of command of ease, is a good sign in a batsman. It means that when the bowling is difficult he can unloose strokes where another pedestrian batsman would remain bound and chained. Subba Row does not have style in that sense. However, he has something else. If you look up his scores from his days at Cambridge, you will see that at every critical moment in his career he makes runs. Oxford vs Cambridge, Gentlemen vs Players, some match or other in which people feel that his selection depends on his success, Subba comes off. He hasn't had the best of luck so far. He may make it here. The same can be said of Dexter. He is a dashing hitter and at times a dangerous bowler. But somehow he remains to this day no more than an immense possibility. At present he is nowhere near the class of that wonderful England No.6, Trevor Bailey, one of the greatest cricketers of his time and a man much underestimated.

It is pretty certain that one or more of these young men will establish himself on this tour. Who these will be it is impossible to say. Much depends on whether under May's leadership the team as a whole clicks, becomes a unit. That in turn depends on whether West Indian strategy can see to it that the team never gets hold of itself. The Australians are great masters of this business. It would be nice to feel that we are.

One of the most interesting aspects of the tour is the fact that

May is on trial and everybody knows it. He inherited the team that Surridge built. May inherited the England team from Hutton and Hutton built that team. Now May has to build his own team and this will decide his place in the hierarchy of England captains. I wish him well, which does not mean to say that I don't hope that the West Indies team will beat his team properly. He has written and spoken very sympathetically about West Indian cricketers. He is a modern man and has advocated finishing away with the distinction between amateurs and professionals, and other equally drastic changes. Yet May is a certain type, English public-school, with many if not all of its virtues. In a certain Test in England in '57 he was forcing the game, came back to cut and connected with an edge that could have been heard in the next county. Umpire said no, and May looked up as if to say: "What the hell is going on here?" In Australia, tough as the going was, when he edged the ball, he walked without waiting for the umpire's signal. Frank Worrell does the same. In a hard and increasingly standardless world, it is good to have such people around, and as captains, if even only in the world of sport.

1960s

The coming of age of the West Indies dominated James's thinking in the 1960s. He was very much stimulated by the political conditions in the West Indies, and as editor of *The Nation* he explored and debated the issues within the pages of the newspaper. From the heart of these preoccupations came a great output of writing about cricket, and he contributed widely to publications particularly in Britain and the Caribbean. These included *The Cricketer*, *Cricket Quarterly*, *New Society* and the *Trinidad Guardian*.

It was no coincidence that the arrival of an MCC team for a series of winter Tests during the early months of 1960 laid bare many of the political tensions. Most dramatically they were revealed in the crowd disturbances which occurred during the Test match played at the Queen's Park Oval, Trinidad.

However, it was the questions of Federation of the West Indies and the retention of a United States naval base at Chaguaramas which brought the growing conflict between James and Williams to a head. James resigned from *The Nation* in mid-1960, but he continued to speak publicly in a series of lectures held in Port of Spain. These were subsequently published under the title of *Modern Politics*, which Williams proceeded to suppress.

James completed his manuscript on cricket during this period in the Caribbean. The consequences of his return, the events of 1959 and 1960, were of profound significance in the final form that the book assumed. *Beyond a Boundary* perhaps illustrated most clearly the new direction which James's work had taken since his departure from the United States in 1953. It was also part of a dialogue between James and a number of West Indian writers, in particular George Lamming, Vidia Naipaul and Wilson Harris. The exchanges between the different writers and their work constituted a historical movement which established an independent West Indian identity.

None the less, the originality of James's approach to questions of culture made it difficult for him to find a publisher willing to accept his manuscript. Its very originality precluded its falling into any of the conventional categories covering books on cricket. It was finally accepted for publication by Hutchinson.

Returning to London in 1962, James wrote and lectured extensively on the Caribbean, and not least on the subject of cricket. The publication of *Beyond a Boundary* came in the following year, the year after Trinidad gained independence, and it was greeted with great acclaim by the critics. John Arlott described it thus: "In the intellectual sense, it is quite the 'biggest' book about cricket or, probably, any other game, ever written."*

James went back to Trinidad in March 1965 to report the MCC tour as a correspondent of the London *Observer* and *The Times*. He found himself placed under house arrest by Prime Minister Eric Williams, who feared James's arrival in the midst of serious labour unrest. He was released after a short time, following a huge public outcry. In 1966 James reported the West Indies tour of England for the *Trinidad Guardian*.

In the course of the second half of the 1960s James visited a number of the newly independent states in both East and West Africa. He was able to celebrate the success of the colonial revolution which he had set in motion with George Padmore during their London years of the 1930s. But this first-hand experience impressed upon him, too, the immense obstacles that lay in the path of African development, problems quite distinct from those facing the peoples of African descent in the Caribbean.

---

*The Cricketer, January 1965, vol.46, no.1 (new series).

The Captain for Australia

(*The Nation*, Trinidad, 4 March 1960)

The press says that the Board of Control is due to meet in British Guiana after the Fourth Test to select the captain and the manager of the team for Australia. Being a journalist of long standing, I do not accept that. The Board can well meet before or during the fourth Test. There is no reason whatever why captain and manager must be selected now. However, be that as it may, there are a few points which the Board should bear in mind.

1) In the explanations which persons close to the Board have tried to give to their appointment of Alexander, it is obvious that the Board is still thinking in terms of thirty or forty years ago. Their main point (and I have seen it in writing) is that the captaincy was offered to Worrell twice and having appointed Alexander they are sticking to him. The idea seems to be: "We are not prejudiced; we asked him twice."

It is pathetic to see how they miss the point. The question is: what right has Alexander to be captain of a side on which Frank Worrell is playing? What qualifications for captaincy has Alexander got which put him above Worrell for this all-important post? That is the question. The answer is on every tongue. Alexander has none.

I gather that some of his supporters were hoping that Alexander would justify himself in this series. Exactly the opposite has happened. Nobody has defended his consistent inability to grasp and to drive home the repeated opportunities that his men as individuals have given to him. If even the score was 1 for England and nothing for us after three matches, it would not matter so much if by this time the West Indies team was organized and mobilized. It is not. It is in pieces. May came here with bits and pieces, openly acknowledged. His task was to build a team. He has built one. Not a single person can fail to see what has happened to the two sides since this series has begun.

2) There is something else which the Board should know. Frank Worrell is at the peak of his reputation not only as a cricketer but as a master of the game. Respect for him has never been higher in all his long and brilliant career.

a) In England in 1957 he played one of the greatest defensive innings in the history of Test cricket, 191 not out, playing right through the innings. He followed this by taking 7 wickets in a single Test innings at Leeds. He opened the bowling in Tests. When the team needed an opening batsman he took over the job. Against Middlesex he saved the side from defeat by his bowling and batting in each innings. Such was his batting that Hutton in 1957 called him openly "the greatest of all West Indian batsmen", and he had George Headley in mind. Masterly in defence, he was second in the English averages, and scored most of his runs at 50 an hour. His bearing on the field, all grace and dignity, evoked general admiration. In every sphere, and others beside myself know this, the opinion was that he should have been the captain.

b) In India, owing to his many tours with Commonwealth sides, during one of which he took over the captaincy with great success, he is remembered as one of the greatest cricketers of the age.

But more important than this, *Australia wants him as captain.*

This is the authentic fact. When Australian critics talk of Trumper, Kippax and the few, half-dozen batsmen who have batted as if they were born to it they include Worrell. As a man he made a tremendous impression in Australia. Thousands will come out on every ground to see an old friend leading the West Indies. In fact, I am able to say that if Worrell were captain and Constantine or George Headley manager or co-manager, the coming tour would be one of the greatest ever.

c) Finally the Board should know that the eyes of the world are upon them. Yes, the eyes of the world. Not to select Worrell, and to put Alexander in charge of the most difficult of all tours, with a team on which no single member except Ramadhin would have visited Australia before, that would be a declaration of war and a defiance of the opinions and attitudes and expectations of the cricketers and the cricketing public the world over. It will be asked in cricketing circles the world over, and nowhere more than in Australia: what is it that in the face of all that I have written about Worrell, which is common property, what is it that made the Board reject Worrell and choose this novice? That is the international scandal which the Board can perpetuate or on the other hand win an international chorus of praise and approbation and congratulations from the whole cricketing world, not least from their own people here and in Australia. Alexander as vice-captain will learn a lot from Frank in Australia. He would be a natural choice for captaining West Indies in England in 1963.

Letter to J.H. Fingleton

Hislop Street
San Juan, Trinidad

4 October 1960

My dear Mr Fingleton,

Thank you very much for your kind letter. . . .

You seem to have grasped immediately what I am trying to do. Whether I succeed is another matter. I send you the last chapter.[1] Despite the fact that it would cost something extra, I wanted you to read the whole book. Any arrangements that you may make for serial publication will be agreeable to me. I only hope that it does not put you to too much trouble. We are anxiously looking forward above all else to your opinion. The book, as you will see, represents many years of thought and devotion to cricket.

I would like to say here a few words in confidence. Cricket writing has entered into the doldrums. Without flattery, I believe that you and Ray Robinson, with his use of statistics and factual matter, have brought something fresh and new. But I read the essays by twenty-one writers of the Cricket Society. And I felt that, though some of them were competent, on the whole they had reached a dead end. I am also disappointed in the history of cricket in Australia by A.G. Moyes.[2] I was looking to him to relate the style of cricket to particular periods as H.S. Altham[3] most certainly did. Somehow I missed it. All that this means is that some sort of change is on the way. The scandal books are beneath contempt and I cannot say that the slapdash journalism of Keith Miller makes any particular appeal to me. Cardus came and saw and conquered. And Alan Ross knows the game and gives a certain gloss. But something is wrong somewhere. I may write about it but my chief concern is to get this book off my hands.

I look forward to hearing from you and seeing you in England in 1961.

I am waiting anxiously to see O'Neill. I can assure you that in many respects I have never seen anything like Sobers. I hope

---

1. The manuscript under discussion was James's *Who Only Cricket Know*, later published as *Beyond a Boundary*.
2. A.G. Moyes, *Australian Cricket: A History*, Angus & Robertson, 1959.
3. H.S. Altham and E.W. Swanton, *A History of Cricket*, Allen & Unwin, 1926.

you get a good look at him. I expect that in two or three years he will be as great a batsman as I have ever seen and I gather that O'Neill is travelling the same road. I have given your regards to Learie and I shall see Mr Coke soon. Once again thanking you for the interest you showed in what is a very precious piece of work to me.

Sincerely yours,
C.L.R. James.

P.S. I have to ask you a question which I have been asking for years. How is it that no one has yet written a full-length biography of Victor Trumper? The best thing I have ever read on him are two chapters in a book by M.A. Noble [*The Game's the Thing*, Cassell, 1926]. Furthermore, people always reprint the photographs of him running out to drive. In *Great Batsmen* * there are magnificent photographs of him apart from those. I continue to hope.

Letter to J.H. Fingleton

Hislop Street,
San Juan, Trinidad

18 November 1960

J.H. Fingleton, Esq.,
Press Gallery,
Parliament House,
Canberra, Australia.

Dear Mr Fingleton,

Thank you for your letter of the 9th November, and all the work you have done for my ms [*Beyond a Boundary*]. It is unfortunate that the editors have not seen the light. But one is hardened to that by now.

I must clear up a misunderstanding which, happily, is very easy to do. Of course I know you played in the body-line Tests

* G.W. Beldam and C.B. Fry, *Great Batsmen: Their Methods at a Glance*, Macmillan and Co., 1905.

(I almost feel to protest loudly). Your book* on that series is the best account that I know, I had a gleeful hour when you recently listed your own scores in that series and showed that on runs scored you were as much entitled as anybody to speak. If you look again at the ms the phrase "If we can trust Fingleton" occurs in relation to the body-line happenings in India. And I am pretty sure I know why, routine as it is, it slipped in. It is because I have never read or seen any account of Jardine's body-line tactics in India. I wanted to make my source of information clear. In any case, the offending words will be cut out.

You say you disagree with me on body-line. May I say that I was not conscious of any acute disagreement. What I did was to try to show that body-line was a sympton of a degeneration in "it isn't cricket" which continues to this day, and that degeneration I relate to the declining standards of morals and values in the world at large.

I enclose £4, and would be glad if you could send the ms back to me by air mail. I think that should cover it.

Once more, with many thanks for your assistance,

Sincerely yours,
C.L.R. James.

P.S. On second and third thoughts, I will not refrain from expressing some concern that the book itself seems to have disappointed the expectations you had previously formed. You will agree, I hope that it pushes into areas practically untouched before. I know the risks I am running but the facts I give are irreproachable and my interpretations are not of yesterday but the result of many years of reflection. I would have welcomed above all some criticism from you as the best informed, most penetrating and objective of Australian critics. Any criticism you had offered would, I assure you, have been eagerly welcomed and carefully studied with a view to modification or more careful presentation of my views. However, I shall see that a copy is sent to you immediately on publication and I hope you will review it.

---

* J.H. Fingleton, *Cricket Crisis: Bodyline and Other Lines*, Cassell, 1946.

Letter from John Arlott

George Street,
London W1

7 December 1960

My dear C.L.R.J.,

Alas, I am sorry to have to return your typescript [*Beyond a Boundary*] — we are posting it to Mr Lamming.

Now, both John St John and I enjoyed it immensely — it seems to me a very good book indeed. Cricket book sales, however — apart from star reminiscences and the occasional Neville Cardus — are struggling nowadays, unless the writer has a fairly firm public. Thus, to break even, this book would have to do well in the West Indies. Our export manager has been there very recently and he cannot see sales of 500. There is a point at which a book "breaks even" and our experts in this matter cannot see your book achieving it. Both John St John and I are extremely sorry. On pre-war costs we could — and would — have published it.

I do hope you may have better luck with it elsewhere. I wonder if printed and published in the West Indies it might be a worthwhile proposition?

Many regrets — kindest wishes for Christmas and the New Year.

Yours sincerely,
John Arlott.

Letter to John Arlott

Hislop Street,
San Juan, Trinidad

10 December 1960

My dear Mr Arlott,

Thank you for your letter. It is to some degree a disappointment that the book is not immediately accepted, even with your recommendation. But I assure you that the only thing which would compensate for it is your generous appreciation of it. That means a great deal to me. In that book I plunged off, so to speak, into the unknown, and although I was very sure where I was going and hoped for the best, I was quite uncertain as to what the response would be of people who know the game and know cricket writing. Thanks very much.

I shall let you know how I get on with it. Curiously enough, I am anticipating with great joy choosing photographs for the book if and when it is accepted. There will be statues of Greek athletes, etc., and an attempt to parallel them with modern photographs. I look forward not only to your help but your warm collaboration in this.

With best wishes for Christmas and the new year,

Sincerely yours,
C.L.R. James.

P.S. Day before yesterday Sobers made his century in Brisbane in two hours. In the last MCC tour in Australia you remember what happened in that Brisbane match and in most of the others. I refer to time. I am keeping my fingers crossed but I hope that the West Indians in Australia this time will justify my conviction not only that they have an independent style of cricket but that the style itself is effective in the highest class of play.

Letter from J.H. Fingleton

Canberra, Australia

2 March 1961

Dear Mr James,

I do hope your manuscript arrives safe and sound and I do apologize for being so long in returning it. I had high hopes that I could get one of the team to take it back with him and give it to you personally but then I thought, afterwards, that you might not like this. I have read it again and, as on the first occasion, was most impressed by it. You have certainly put a lot of work and thought into it. I still don't agree with some of your conclusions but that is neither here nor there — a lot of people don't agree with mine.

You should have no great difficulty in securing a publisher after the [1960-1] tour here by your players — I was not certain whether you said you had a publisher for it. However, you will be able to add now a final chapter that I think will round it off — the classical success of Frank Worrell, not only as a captain and a team man, but as a diplomat. His team was a credit — and I presume it also owed much to Gerry Gomez and Max Marshall, as well as the people who chose them. The manners of them were admirable and a credit to their race. It was a grand tour — the WI certainly should never have lost — and its effects will be felt in this country for years. My good wishes to you, then, in the book. I hope it is a resounding success. Please give my best wishes to Learie.

Yours sincerely,
Jack Fingleton.

Letter to Robert Lusty[1]

Mona, Jamaica

23 June 1961

Dear Mr Lusty,

I was delighted to receive your prompt reply to my letter of June 12th. I was also extremely pleased that you and George Lamming were able to discuss the book.

Let me say at once that I have a duplicate ms which I shall prepare for press. I shall also send you some suggestions for titles.

My accident[2] has left me with no permanent damage but quite weak.

I look forward with great interest to hearing what George Lamming has to suggest on my book. I haven't the faintest idea of what other books he thinks I am engaged upon. There are always manuscripts in hand and books that one wants to write. I may have mentioned to George Lamming my intention to do a book on the West Indies in view of the coming independence

---

1. Chairman of the Hutchinson Publishing Group, London.
2. Early in 1961 James had a serious motor accident in Jamaica which incapacitated him for many weeks.

(now fixed for May 31st, 1962). However, as soon as I hear from him I shall be delighted to communicate with you.

I note with interest that you have an agreement covering the publication of *Who Only Cricket Knows** which you will be sending to me shortly. I have been working on my book and thinking about it for so many years that the arrival of a contract for publication is bound to be quite an event. May I say that the book comes out at a particularly opportune time. There is an immense excitement among the people of the West Indies at the present time about everything, particularly in print, that deals with their past. The conference in England which fixed the independence has created amongst other things a great intellectual excitement. We have not fought many battles in our history nor made great conquests, nor arranged world-shaking treaties. But among the international events in which we have fully participated is the playing of cricket with other members of the Commonwealth. In writing as I have done, I know from experience that I have expressed deep currents in the life of the West Indian people. They will recognize it. I can only hope that others will, particularly the people of Britain, for now that the moment of independence approaches I become increasingly aware of the ties that bind, apart from legislation and the speeches of politically minded persons.

Yours sincerely,
C.L.R. James.

Letter to John Arlott

Staverton Road,
London NW2

29 December 1962

My dear Mr Arlott,

I am back for good. I send you two publications which sum up my experience.

Hutchinson's will be bringing out my cricket book. As soon as it is out I shall send you your copy. I am not as well as I

* The working title of *Beyond a Boundary*.

should be. I was in a motor accident and am still feeling the effects.

I listened on Christmas Day to what you had to say on the radio about Shakespeare and the "horrible" themes he dealt with. The other day I saw in *The Times* that some critic had broken with the theory that Lear's last scene with Cordelia ennobled the play (which idea I have long opposed); but he now saw *King Lear* as an exemplification of Belsen. I am as much opposed to this as to the idea that *Lear* is a play glorifying love, triumphing over all. I do not wish to lay emphasis on casual remarks you made in reply to questions. But I have long thought that Shakespeare was not only profound but had a positive and very advanced view of society and social relations, that he was a social moralist in a very realistic way. I firmly believe that a great artist is saying something very definite about the world he lives in. I am more than ever convinced of this since my five years in the West Indies. I lectured, among others, incessantly on Shakespeare to all types of audiences. Their response was *all* I could wish for. West Indians are a modern people in an underdeveloped society that is the closest that we have today to the society in which Shakespeare wrote and the people he wrote for. Also I was teacher and lecturer in the West Indies for some fifteen years, between 1918 and 1932. I believe I have something to say very different from Granville-Barker, Wilson Knight and others of the kind. And I believe that it is correct, for 1962. I sometimes feel that this is important to say but in 1962 is not a matter for academic discussion or for academic journals. I somehow have the idea that you and I can talk about it to overseas audiences *and* to English audiences. I believe that Shakespeare today has more that matters than any creative writer. He came at a time of transition from one world to a new. We are in the same position today. That is why Hazlitt, Lamb, De Quincey and Coleridge wrote so well about him. They too knew a world moving from the eighteenth to the new nineteenth century. The same newness that West Indians bring to cricket they bring to the classic writers. I can say this to you I think.

If you think the matter worth discussing, I can come over to you any time you suggest. However, I am staying very much at home these days. We are fixing our flat up slowly, but we would be glad to have you over to lunch or dinner at any time you would care to come.

Body-line

(From *Beyond a Boundary*, Hutchinson, 1963)

Body-line was not an incident, it was not an accident, it was not a temporary aberration. It was the violence and ferocity of our age expressing itself in cricket. The time was the early thirties, the period in which the contemporary rejection of tradition, the contemporary disregard of means, the contemporary callousness, were taking shape. The totalitarian dictators cultivated brutality of set purpose. By now all of us have supped full with horrors. Today cruelties and abominations which would have immeasurably shocked and permanently distressed earlier ages are a commonplace. We must toughen our hides to live at all. We are now like Macbeth in his last stage:

> "The time has been my senses would have cool'd
> To hear a night-shriek, and my fell of hair
> Would at a dismal treatise rouse and stir
> As life were in't. I have supped full with horrors;
> Direness, familiar to my slaughterous thoughts,
> Cannot once start me."

It began in World War I. Exhaustion and a fictitious prosperity in the late twenties delayed its maturity. It came into its own in 1929. Cricket could no more resist than the other organizations and values of the nineteenth century were able to resist. That big cricket survived the initial shock at all is a testimony to its inherent decency and the deep roots it had sunk.

The violence of the cricket passions unloosed in the thirties is what strikes the observer today. There was no absolute necessity for Voce and Larwood to take the actions that they did on their return from Australia. Rather than submit to the opinions of a large majority, A.W. Carr preferred to go out of the game altogether. Jardine seemed to be at war not with the Australian eleven but all Australia. The history books tell us that he carried his relentlessness to India: there were no Bradmans in India. What objective necessity was there to introduce body-line into England after the Australian tour? Yet the attempt was made. Jardine soon went, never to return. Ponsford abandoned the game when he was only thirty-four. Sir Donald Bradman assures us that but for the intervention of the war, 1938 would have been his last visit to England, and he

111

contemplated only one more season in Australia. He was younger than Ponsford. No balls had whizzed past his head for years. Yet he had had enough.

It is in Bradman's autobiography that we can today see conveniently the mentality of the time. The most remarkable page in that remarkable book is his account of his feelings after he had conpleted his hundredth century. He had played big cricket for nearly twenty years. In that time he had scored as no one had ever scored before. He had made his runs at the rate of fifty an hour. He had scored centuries and double centuries and treble centuries in cricket of the most demanding type. He had conquered bowlers and decided series. Yet what are his sentiments after he made the hundredth run of the hundredth century? He felt it incumbent upon him, he says, to give the crowd which had so cheered his achievement some reward for its wonderful feelings towards him. He therefore proceeded to hit 71 runs in forty-five minutes. This, he adds, is the way he would always wish to have batted if circumstances had permitted him. However, as circumstances did at last permit him the luxury, he classed "that particular section of my innings as the most satisfying of my career". In all the years that I have been reading books on cricket this remains the strangest statement that I have ever read, and one to which I frequently return; to it, and to the writer. If Sir Donald Bradman was able to play "in the way I would always have loved to do had circumstances permitted" only after he had made one hundred centuries, we have to ask ourselves: What were these inhibiting circumstances?

This much at least is obvious. The game he had played between 1928 and 1947 was a game quite different from the one that had been played by Grace and Shrewsbury, Trumper and Ranjitsinhji, Hobbs and Rhodes, the game we had played in the West Indies. Grace, Ranjitsinhji, Trumper and their fellows who had played with them lost infinitely more matches and series than Sir Donald Bradman ever lost. They were painstaking men who gave all they had to cricket. Yet I cannot conceive of any of them thinking of batting in the way Sir Donald thought of it. He has been blamed for machine-like play. He has been blamed for the ruthlessness with which he piled up big scores. This is absurd. I have seen some of his greatest innings and I do not wish to see anything finer. George Headley has explained to me that people speak of Sir Donald's heavy scoring as if each and every great bastman was able to do the same, but refrained for aesthetic or chivalrous reasons which

Sir Donald ignored. Speaking with authority, Headley is lost in admiration and even in wonder at the nervous stamina and concentration which Sir Donald displayed in making these mammoth scores so consistently over so long a period. In the autobiography Sir Donald maintains that he played cricket according to the rules as he saw them. There is no need to question this. Every page of his book shows that he has been deeply hurt by what he considers unfair criticism. Every accusation that I have ever heard made against him he has taken care to answer. The slightest wound still gives pain to this tough, relentless opponent. He is conscious of righteousness. His sincerity is patent. He feels himself a victim, and a victim he is, but not of petty jealousies of individual men. The chronicles of the time (far more then than now), when re-read today in the light of after events, tell the story clearly enough. The 1930 Australian team which broke all previous records took a little time to get going and was left in no doubt as to what spectators and pressmen thought.

By 1928, when he began, big cricket was already being played everywhere with the ruthlessness that Bradman is saddled with. He never knew any other kind of cricket. Ponsford and his triple and quadruple centuries had set the tone for Bradman. If Bradman made 974 runs in Tests in 1930 he had experienced when a boy of eighteen a far more merciless 905 from Hammond in the season of 1928–9. His gifts and his cricket personality matured at a time when the ethics, the morals, the personal impulses and desires of cricketers were quite different from those who had played the game in the decades that had preceded. Cricketers already mature when Bradman appeared might want to play like Bradman. They couldn't. They hadn't the outlook. They hadn't the temper. They had inhibitions Bradman never knew.

The new ones could learn. Hutton at the Oval in 1938 showed that he had learnt well. I have never had so painful an experience at any cricket match as when watching Hutton and Hardstaff together during the England innings of 903 for eight declared. Body-line may have vanished. Its temper remained. Other men had stood out above their fellows. W.G. had. But 1865 was not 1930. The spirit which Sir Donald Bradman could release only after a hunderd centuries was present, I am sure, in every single one of the hundred centuries that W.G. Grace made, was always present in Trumper and Ranjitsinhji, Fry and Hobbs. That spirit was dead. If Hobbs had been born in 1910, or later, England would have bred another Bradman. Sir

113

C.L.R. James

Donald first ran the cricket mile in under four minutes and unloosed the floodgates. Circumstances conspired to place the blame on him. I have gathered that even in Australia the attitude to him is ambivalent. They admire him, they are grateful to him, they love him, but they know that the disregard of the compulsions of everyday life, the chivalry that was always a part of the game, began to fade at the time he came into it. Sir Donald is not to blame. He was unfortunate in his place and time. The fact remains that he was in his own way as tough as Jardine.

This was the situation faced by "It isn't cricket" in 1930. It was not only a Test series at stake. Everything that the temple stood for seemed threatened within and without. If Bradman continued his portentous career a way of life, a system of morals, faced the possibility of disgrace and defeat just at the particular time when more than ever it needed the stimulus of victory and prestige. The men who had made it their special preserve were threatened not only in cricket. They were threatened everywhere. As is usual in such cases, they fought back blindly and were driven into extravagance and immorality. The body-line upheaval shocked everyone and made the cricket world pull itself up and tread carefully. The spirit was not exorcized. The Oval match of 1938 was followed by the long-drawn-out siege in Durban. Luckily the war put an abrupt end to cricket as it was being played in the thirties. The relief was only temporary. Today the same relentlessness is abroad. Cricketers try to preserve the external decencies. The tradition is still strong. But instead of "It isn't cricket", now one hears more frequently the cynical "Why isn't it cricket?" Scarcely a tour but hits the headlines for some grave breach of propriety on and off the cricket field. The strategy of Test matches is the strategy of stalking the prey: you come out in the open to attack only when the victim is wounded. No holds are barred. Captains encourage their bowlers to waste time. Bowlers throw and drag. Wickets are shamelessly doctored. Series are lost or believed to be lost by doubtful decisions and immoral practices, and the victims nurse their wrath and return in kind. Writing in *The Cricketer* in the early twenties MacLaren said that in all his career he had known batsmen duck short balls only on two or three occasions. In the West Indies up to when I left in 1932 you took the short ball round to the leg-boundary (or you underwent repairs). Today statisticians and metaphysicians seek to impose a categorical imperative on the number of bumpers the fast bowler may bowl per over. To legislators

114

for relief batsmen of all nations, like Cherubim and Seraphim, continually do cry.

A corps of cricket correspondents functions as an auxiliary arm of their side, but is ready to turn and rend it at the slightest opportunity. What little remains of "It isn't cricket" is being finally stifled by the envy, the hatred, the malice and the uncharitableness, the shamelessness of the memoirs written by some of the cricketers themselves. Compared with these books, Sir Donald's ruthless autobiography of a dozen years ago now reads like a Victorian novel. How to blind one's eye to all this? Body-line was only a link in a chain. Modern society took a turn downwards in 1929 and "It isn't cricket" is one of the casualties. There is no need to despair of cricket. Much, much more than cricket is at stake, in fact everything is at stake. If and when society regenerates itself, cricket will do the same. The Hambledon men built soundly. What Arnold, Hughes and W.G. brought is now indelibly a part of the national life and character, and plays its role, the farther it is away from the pressure of publicity. There it is safe. The values of cricket, like much that is now in eclipse, will go into the foundations of new moral and educational structures. But that they can be legislated to what they used to be is a vain hope which can only sour on the tongue and blear the eye. The owl of Minerva flies only at dusk. And it cannot get much darker without becoming night impenetrable.

Letter to Berkeley Gaskin

Staverton Road
London NW2

April/May 1963

Berkeley Gaskin, Esq.,
Manager, West Indian Team,
Waldorf Hotel,
London, WC2

My dear Berkeley,

As a West Indian looks at things not only beyond the surface but on it, things look not so good — a very useful expression.

But I hope you will see from this book how much I am counting on this team for matters *Beyond a Boundary*. In fact I know now that if it were not for that I wouldn't have written the book at all.

In that connection I want you to know that I have full confidence that with Frank as captain and you as manager what I am thinking of is in the best possible hands, the best possible. I believe you all will make history and much more than cricket history. But I know that the only way to make history in cricket is by means of cricket itself. I say that over and over again. P.60, para. 1, p.176, para. 3, and many other places.

Best of luck, Berkeley. As I see the book it is 12th man on your side. After you all have gone through the season unbeaten, before you leave, you have to spend *a day* with us, you and anybody you would like to bring.

Yours more than ever,
C.L.R. James.

P.S. My publisher has consented to send copies to Garfield Sobers and Rohan Kanhai. I had intended writing to them some things I wanted to say. I have changed my mind. *After* the tour.

Letter to V.S. Naipaul*

1963

Vidia Naipaul, Esq.,
c/o André Deutsch Ltd,
12-14 Carlisle Street,
London, W1

My dear Vidia,

I hear you are back. Do let us hear from you.

I am not impertinent enough to tell you what *you* should think about this book [*Beyond a Boundary*]. I prefer to tell you what I think.

1. The book is West Indian through and through, particularly in the early chapters on my family, my education and the

---

*Trinidadian-born writer whose works include *A House for Mr Biswas*, *An Area of Darkness*.

portraits of West Indian cricketers of the previous generation, some of them unknown.

2. But the book is very British. Not only the language but on page after page the (often unconscious) literary references, the turn of phrase, the mental and moral outlook. That is what we are, and we shall never know ourselves until we recognize that fully and freely and without strain.

3. But that does not end it, not at all. That is only the beginning. I believe that, originating as we are within the British structure, but living under such different social conditions, we have a lot to say about the British civilization itself which we see more sharply than they themselves.

I believe I have made that clear in the treatment of W.G. Grace.

I have given a view of where I think a future for big cricket lies.

I have even ventured on a conception (for it is no more) of the theory of art criticism.

But without hammering on my chest, I have made it clear (para. 3, p.97; para. 3, p.152) that it is my West Indian origins that gave me the premises and the impetus, though it "was only in England and in English life and history that I was able to trace them down to test them" (Preface).

In the last three chapters I pose the West Indian actuality without ill temper, I hope, but without mincing matters. I indicate also the certainty of independent growth. But we can recognize our future only when we know our past.

The book is touched with implications of which I have become fully aware only after my recent stay of five years in the West Indies. I had finished it up to the end of Chapter 17 in Europe, not having seen the West Indies for 26 years. When I completed it I doubt if I had to add or change two pages in what I had written during my absence.

Let us hear from you soon. You know, I hope you will like it and say something about it, something that West Indians will hear. Curiously enough, I have little doubt that in England it will be understood. It is the West Indies that I am concerned about.

As ever,
C.L.R. James.

Letter to V.S. Naipaul

Staverton Road
London NW2

May 20, 1963

My dear Vidia,

I was delighted to hear from you, not only to know that you were back but to read the things you said about my book. I felt not only that here was someone who understood it, but what is always more precious, someone who could show to me things in it and evolving out of it of which the writer himself was not fully aware.

That you should be doing such a substantial piece in *Encounter*[1] is good luck indeed. I look forward to it. I wish we could meet and talk. However you have been making an Odyssey and you need as you say a period of rest. But, as my grandmother used to say over and over again, "There is no rest for the wicked." Include me also among the wicked here.

I read yesterday a long article by Muggeridge on India. He says much the same that you said in your article in the *Statesman*.[2] I have also read similar ideas elsewhere. It is quite a circumstance, this that seems to strike all of you. I hope you are going to establish it fully once and for all. I can imagine no one doing it better and it will come very well from one who is himself one of the breeds without the law.

Looking forward to seeing you soon,

As always,
C.L.R. James.

Cricket in West Indian Culture

(*New Society*, 6 June 1963)

All the inhabitants of the British West Indian territories are expatriates: the islands are so small that it was not difficult for

---

1. Naipaul's review of *Beyond a Boundary* was published in *Encounter* in September 1963.
2. V.S. Naipaul, "Jamshed into Jimmy", *New Statesman*, 25 January 1963.

the early invaders to exterminate the native Amerindian populations. Thus language, labour and economic processes, arts and sciences are moulded on the European pattern. Cricket has proved itself one of the most easily assimilated, most penetrating and most enduring. By now everybody plays, even women's clubs flourish.

West Indian immigrants are today probably the most active cricketers in the United States and they often invite teams of the most famous West Indian players to play games in New York. Cricket clubs are proving one of the most fertile means of integrating the West Indians into British society. The West Indian of all types takes his cricket seriously and plays it that way. That is not primarily a question of temperament. Cricket has been a permanent source of serious matters, social growth and differentiation, national unity, and social awareness.

L.N. Constantine, the famous West Indian player, told me that though his father and an uncle were international cricketers and coached him, he and his brothers as children often played with bats made of coconut branches and balls of adaptable fruit. Things are not nearly so rural now. But it is evidence of the deep roots which cricket has sunk in the West Indies that it has never been seriously challenged by a game so relatively inexpensive and simple to organize as soccer.

Cricket in the West Indies seems to owe its origin to the garrisons there. In *The Pickwick Papers* (1836) Dickens refers easily to a cricket match played in the West Indies by two British officers. Trinidad became British only in 1797, yet in 1842, not ten years after the abolition of slavery, there was a well established Trinidad Cricket Club. By 1891 there was an intercolonial tournament between Barbados, Jamaica and what has now become British Guiana. In 1894–95 the first English team visited the West Indies.

From its beginning to this day cricket in the West Indies has expressed with astonishing fidelity the social relations of the islands. The early island teams consisted for the most part of Englishmen in the colonies associated with local whites, and black plebeians who were dignified by the title of professional bowlers. These bowlers were more ground attendants than professionals in the accepted modern sense. Some of them had come to the nets where their betters practised, picked up the ball and bowled, sometimes without shoes.

The brown-skin or black middle class produced a few good players but there was a sharp social gap between Englishmen and white or light-skinned members of the upper classes and

the black plebeians who bowled so well that they were sometimes given an opportunity to make a precarious living by their
skill. (In Dickens's match a black bowler, Quanko Samba, had
played a Homeric role.) The black population of those days
seemed to accept the conditions. They welcomed the Englishmen uproariously and even seemed to support them more than
the local side.

Between 1900 and 1939 the development of West Indian
society improved the status and conditions of the coloured
middle classes with effective results in the organization of
cricket as a national expression. In addition to clubs exclusively white, with perhaps a few coloured men of wealth or
distinction, the brown-skinned middle class also formed their
own clubs. So did the black-skinned middle class. In time the
black plebeians also formed their own. These divisions (not
always in every island iron-clad) were not only understood but
accepted by players and populations alike. All these clubs
played every Saturday in club competitions and not infrequently a white member of the Legislative Council or President of the
Chamber of Commerce would be playing amicably for his club
against another most of whose members were black porters,
messengers or other members of the lowest social classes.
Cricket was therefore a means of national consolidation. In a
society very conscious of class and social differentiation, a
heritage of slavery, it provided a common meeting ground of all
classes without coercion or exhortation from above.

English expatriates and their local associates retained their
dominance in cricket not merely by social prestige and money
but by their services. The wealthier clubs of the upper classes
usually assumed the responsibility of inviting MCC teams and
arranged for West Indian teams to visit England in 1900 and
1906. The black professional players were included and by
1928 the West Indies were granted Test matches. The outstanding personality in their steady advancement of the game was a
Barbados white man — H.G.B. Austin, a fine player and very
successful business man whose father had been Bishop of the
West Indies.

Yet the expatriate Englishmen and the local white aristocracy, with some few coloured men who had won acceptance
in these circles, were not the decisive forces in the inculcation
of the cricket ethic which has so shaped and permeated West
Indian social life. This was done by English university men,
chiefly from Oxford and Cambridge. During the last third of the
nineteenth and the first third of the twentieth centuries many of

these were masters at the secondary schools in the larger territories and their social influence went far beyond their actual numbers.

At these schools for many years there were some two hundred boys, children of Englishmen and local whites, many sons of the brown-skinned middle class, Chinese, Indians, and black boys, often poor who had won some of the very few scholarships to these schools, and others, not too many, whose parents could afford it. These Oxford and Cambridge men taught us Latin and Greek, mathematics and English literature, but they also taught, rather diffused, what I can only call the British public-school code.

The success of this code inside the classrooms was uncertain. In the playing-fields, especially the cricket field, it triumphed. Very rapidly we learned to "play with the team", which meant subordinating your personal inclinations and even interests to the good of the whole. We kept a "stiff upper lip" in that we did not complain about ill fortune. We did not denounce failure but "well tried" or "hard luck" came easily to our lips. We were generous to opponents and congratulated them on victories, even when we knew they did not deserve them. We absorbed the same discipline through innumerable boys' books: books by G.A. Henty, the "Mike" stories by P.G. Wodehouse, school magazines like *The Captain*. Generation after generation of boys of the middle class went through this training and experience, and took it out into the West Indian world with them, the world of the games they continued to play and the world outside. The masses of the people paid little attention to this code but they knew it, and one condition of rising to a higher status in life was obedience or at least obeisance to it.

To the degree that cricket embodied a national consolidation so much needed by the islands, it could not fail to express the growing consciousness of social differentiation. Though for a long time in the West Indies the value of the services and the authority in cricket of men like H.B.G. Austin was unquestioned, cricket was a field where the social passions of the colonials, suppressed politically, found vigorous if diluted expression. On the cricket field all men, whatever their colour or status, were theoretically equal. Clubs of the lower middle class or black men who achieved international status were passionately supported by the mass of the population, and in return this section seemed to play with an energy and fire which indicated that they were moved by the sense of being representative which circumstances had thrust upon them.

Members of various classes gave a moral support to teams and players of their own class, though my personal experience is that this sharp racial competitiveness very rarely caused any departure from the high principles of cricket sportsmanship, and sharpened the game.

Individual players of the lower class, most often black men, became popular national heroes in whom the masses of the people took great pride. Yet it is doubtful if any player was more nationally admired and more of a popular idol than the late George Challenor, a white Barbadian and a member of the most exclusive of white Barbados clubs.

In one particular respect the growth of nationalist sentiment has invaded the cricket field and coloured public response to it. From the beginning, the captaincy of the separate island teams was looked upon as an almost impenetrable preserve of the local whites. After World War II, however, public opinion and the number of fine players emerging from the middle classes and the plebeians made this preserve difficult to maintain and before long it broke down. But the captaincy of the West Indies team remained *the* patent source of social division. The explosions during the MCC tours in 1953 and 1960 were not in any way directed against British players or as representatives of the imperial power. In fact although the 1960 explosion in Trinidad, when the crowd threw bottles on the field and brought a day's play in a Test match to a premature close, took place at the height of a great agitation for national independence, no anti-British sentiments were either felt or manifested and the British players were very popular. The social antagonists which the outburst undoubtedly expressed were completely internal. They were directed against what was widely considered to be the persistent manipulation by the traditional authorities aimed at maintaining the privileges which, natural in the earlier days, were now held to be out of place. It was widely felt that for years conscious and indefensible efforts had been made to maintain the exclusion from the West Indies captaincy of men black in skin. It needed a vigorous campaign and a massive exhibition of popular feeling before Frank Worrell, a black man, was appointed captain of the West Indies team to Australia. Now organized cricket and soccer are both democratic and popular national institutions in the West Indian territories, which badly need such institutions.

More important still, Frank Worrell has shown that a black man can be an exceptional leader. One incident on the 1957 tour illustrates this well.

One of the black fast bowlers was Gilchrist, whose career is a perfect symbol of the stresses and strains of West Indian social and political life. The twenty-first child of a rural family of twenty-one children, he was brought from the rural districts of Jamaica by a local businessman, given a job and forthwith showed his unusual energies and ability for big cricket. He went to India with the West Indies team, but had to be sent home for conduct unsatisfactory to the West Indian management. In Trinidad in 1960 posters appeared asking the public to boycott the game unless Gilchrist was selected. Regardless of the charges made or charges proved, a great mass of the population feels that Gilchrist represents them and any action taken against him is an action against them, and he has become known as a stormy petrel of the game. Yet I witnessed a most revealing incident at Hastings in 1957. Gilchrist, a member of the touring team, was told by his captain that in festival cricket one did not bowl bumpers. Determined to oblige, Gilchrist allowed himself to be driven for five fours in one over: a notably tempestuous member of a tempestuous breed, fast bowlers, Gilchrist was determined not to offend his captain for that day — a middle-class black West Indian, Frank Worrell. He alone seemed able to exercise influence over the ebullient plebeian.

In one of his novels George Lamming, the Barbados novelist, has declared in the most unequivocal terms that the educated black middle classes must accept responsibility for whatever attitude to accepted standards may be shown by the black masses: "Nor can I allow my own moral infirmity to be transferred to a foreign conscience, labelled imperialist."* The relationship between Worrell, the Jamaican Senator with an economics degree from Manchester, and the plebeian Gilchrist indicates the tensions demanding resolution in the developing future of the islands, but also what cricket can do to restore them.

The West Indian's very consciousness of his own history is a product of his cricket in a very definite sense. In Britain, Drake and mighty Nelson, Shakespeare, the Charge of the Light Brigade, the success of parliamentary democracy, the few who did so much for so many — these constitute a continuous national tradition. Underdeveloped, newly independent countries have to go back many decades, sometimes centuries, to find one. The West Indian people have none, at least none that

*Season of Adventure, London, 1960; new edition, Allison & Busby, 1979, p.332.

they know anything about. To such people, Ramadhin and Valentine wrecking English batting, the three Barbados batsmen whose names begin with W, the front-page scoring of cricketers like Garfield Sobers and Rohan Kanhai fill gnawing gaps in their consciousness and in their needs. Hence the popular passions which have on occasion overstepped the bounds. Yet when over a quarter of a million people in an Australian city came into the streets to tell Worrell's team goodbye, a spontaneous gesture of affection and respect, the West Indies, clearing their way with bat and ball, had made a public entry into the comity of nations. It has been done under the aegis of the men who more than all others created the British public-school tradition, Thomas Arnold, Thomas Hughes and W.G. Grace. They would recognize Frank Worrell as a respresentative of all they were and stood for. But juniors grow up and have to make their own independent way. In cricket, the West Indies have evolved a style of their own, even if in independence as a whole they have yet to do so.

Letter to Frank Worrell

Staverton Road,
London, NW2

Frank Worrell, Esq.,
Waldorf Hotel,
London, WC2

My dear Frank,

I have nothing to write except that I perpetually wonder that a little scrap of West Indian territory has produced Garfield Sobers and you. (Anything you feel I can or may be able to do, just let me know.)

C.L.R. James.

Letter to Garfield Sobers

Staverton Road,
London, NW2

Garfield Sobers, Esq.,
Waldorf Hotel,
London, WC2

My dear Garfield Sobers,

What I think of great batsmen is all over this book [*Beyond a Boundary*], most particularly on p.147. I have shared in one of your greatest triumphs and greatest disappointments — the innings at Leeds when Lock ran you out.

Everthing I think is in this book. I hope, very much hope, that when the Tests are over you will come over to the house one evening and talk. Meanwhile, I wish you all the luck in the world and particularly to take as much care of yourself off the field as on it. You do a lot on it, as much as any cricketer I have ever seen, and I am mortally afraid that you may not be yourself by August and September.

With best wishes,
C.L.R. James.

P.S. I am sending a copy of this letter to your manager. I never, never interfere, even with a letter, with a cricketer on tour without letting his manager at least know. I hope you do not mind.

The Departure of the West Indians
(1963)

The West Indian cricketers left London airport this morning at ten o'clock. To say that I went to see them off would be untrue. I went to see what was happening. First of all the players, for despite all the mountains of talk and the articles and the luncheons and the dinners and the speeches, what matters in a touring team is how they play, as a team and as individuals.

And, as I dare say you know by now, I watch Test cricketers very carefully, as cricketers and sometimes as exceptional human beings.

One, Frank Worrell, is now a part of the British crew of the world, not merely as a fine cricketer and a great captain, but as a person. This morning he was busy but as calm and unobtrusively graceful as ever. I believe that is what has captivated the British. I also had another good look at Garfield Sobers; when he can no longer play big cricket, we will still be hearing of Sobers, where I don't know, but somewhere. Everybody wanted to know: Was Mrs Kanhai going or not going? She *was* going. Then for certain she was not going. Then she *was* going. Finally I gathered she was *not* going. Everybody loves a wedding and a bride. I personally was very happy to speak to two Barbadians. Griffith was the same as ever, a very big, very strong, very kind, very reserved, in fact very modest man. I felt a genuine sincerity in his response to my wishing him well. Very different was Hall. He is as naturally exuberant as Griffith is naturally reserved. He went round shaking hands with everybody and I firmly believe that if he had embraced the girls and kissed them they would have accepted it from him as in the nature of things. As usual he seemed to be telling everybody: "Well, we had, you and I and all of us, a wonderful time and I am looking forward as I am sure you are to our meeting very soon again and starting off where we left."

Hall simply exudes good nature at every pore, except of course to the poor batsmen. Conrad Hunte also reinforced an early impression — a very sophisticated, assured man of the world, but still young enough to smile spontaneously and naturally. I must not forget Murray, still a QRC boy. There were others, of course, MCC officials, West Indian political people, friends and relations of the cricketers; there is no point in mentioning names. It seemed an ordinary goodbye. It was not. When the cricketers were all in the bus about to leave for the plane, a sudden hush and silence fell on everyone. Almost you could cut it with a knife. Someone said to me, "You felt that? They are nice fellows. Everyone is sorry to see them go." I think I know what he meant, but I think the sentiment was more than personal. I believe we were all silent because we recognized that the team had done more than hit boundaries and bowl down wickets. They had undoubtedly registered the West Indies as a national personality in the British consciousness.

After they left I went around the airfield. I talked to a Pakistani who told me, "I do not speak English." That much, at any rate, he had learnt. I spoke to some Indians, very eagerly to some Africans; no, they knew nothing about any West Indian cricket team. I tried one or two British porters and functionaries — yes, they knew the West Indians were leaving that morning, but that was all. I presume that they are accustomed every day and sometimes twice a day to some special group of people leaving. There were other reporters around. They asked me what I was asking them: what is happening? We could not muster a headline. Well, that was that. I settled down to my return journey. I opened my paper, and there it all was. In the paper a serious discussion as to whether South Africa and some other country would share our cricket season. This today is quite a problem, and one powerful reason is: they want us back. Another paper has a photograph of Frank Worrell, Mrs Worrell and their daughter, who is staying in England to go to school — a large, informal photograph. Worrell is now one of the British public family, that indefinable group of people about whom the British public is always willing to hear news. No West Indian, not even Constantine, has ever been so completely adopted. Frank Worrell for the British is more than a cricketer; he is a person.

Finally, a political reporter in a political paper analysed the crowds at the Test. I don't agree with everything that he said but his conclusion was acute and profound. He said that next year when the Australians come, the West Indians would be there cheering England. That also is my belief. That is the new relation that has been established. And I shan't see the crowd at the airport but there was that moment of silent recognition and I recognized also that the same thing had happened to the crowd that day at the Oval when they invaded the ground to celebrate the victory. There were two sides of the same coin. It was not that the British people had accepted the West Indians; it was far more than that. The West Indians had accepted, recognized themselves, and once you do that, other people always welcome you.

Dexter and Sobers

(1963)

If Dexter and Sobers were between them to make no runs and take no wickets in the Test, they will have done enough already to establish them irrevocably as two representative cricketers of the age — representative, as a famous philosopher would say, in a double sense: representative of our age in relation to other ages, and, more specifically, men of the countries which bore and bred them.

Dexter is a man more sinned against than sinning. Of his innings at Lord's against the West Indies modesty alone compels me to moderate my language and say I have only twice seen batting of that style before. Dexter did not merely drive the two fast bowlers or hook them. He hit them so that you (and probably they) forgot for the moment that they were fast bowlers. Dexter, the unfortunate man, makes sixties and seventies and even nineties. He does not make centuries because he has the habit of losing "concentration". Blessed word. If the other players on his side bore names like K.L. Hutchings, A.C. MacLaren, J.T. Tyldesley, F.S. Jackson, C.B. Fry and he were playing against Victor Trumper, Clement Hill and Vernon Ransford, Dexter would make his centuries and perhaps a double century or two. He is a Cavalier among Roundheads. He plays not only against opposing batsmen but against the very soul of the age. It is I presume legitimate for seasoned cricketers to agree that Dexter gets out because he loses concentration. Quite the opposite may be the case. He is playing his innings in the style of a master expressing a personal vision. Like C.G. Macartney, Dexter, a new Governor-General, is intent on hitting the ball, on hitting the bowler, to the boundary. Then suddenly it begins to dawn on him that this is a Test match and that, worse still, he is the captain of England. He begins to concentrate — on that. The result is what happens to those who try to sit between two stools, or to be more precise, a good man fallen among people whose morals are not his own.

I see Dexter as engaged in a constant struggle for free individuality in a conformist age. Public school, university, the Gentlemen, sent to fill a gap in Australia. I saw him in the West Indies in 1960, a fine Test batsman. Periodically would appear the strokes of the batsman who hit the cricket ball as if it were placed on a tee, but was watching himself. After the failure in Australia, he had to establish respectability. He blossomed in full flower only in Australia in 1962 and, sure mark of genius, against the finest and most dangerous bowling at the most critical time.

Everything about Dexter marks him as a cavalier of 1850–1914. F.S. Jackson could at times bowl some devastating overs in Test matches. Dexter does the same. He does not consistently shine as the great fieldsman does. But of the more awkward and apparently hopeless catch, the more certain he is to bring it off. There is the end to Dexter's struggles against conformity. Writing in 1957 of the men of the Golden Age, I made bold to say: "Not only their cricketing styles, but the personal careers of men like Ranjitsinhji and Fry outside the cricket world show how bold and restless was the spirit that expressed itself in their play." Dexter has recently shown that he is of the same breed. It is not that Dexter is not dependable. It is that the other players of the day are too dependable. They inhibit him. In his observations of the game, all aspects of it, he bears the stamp of a man in conflict with his age. He will leave his mark on it, certainly on the cricket field and perhaps elsewhere.

Garfield Sobers is a man of similar tempestuous temperament, but with the good fortune to be born and bred in a propitious environment. Batting like Dexter's at Lord's I can remember to have seen only twice, Sobers at Leeds in 1957. He came in first wicket down, but I was all set for his first Test century before lunch when Tony Lock ran him out for 27. The second innings was also by Sobers; it was not in a Test at all and all the more self-revealing. Between the match against Trinidad and the second Test in Port of Spain in 1960, the West Indies team played a trial match. Hall was on one side, Sobers on the other. Hall was unusually careful in bowling to Ramadhin, but perhaps for that very reason he let loose at Sobers. Sobers in turn let loose at him. Stamped for ever in my mind is one drive through mid-off, and others — they were not drives, they were hits — made very late with the bat let loose as if at a golf ball on a tee. I believe I remember too a curious hook, remaining on his original stance and swatting the ball to the boundary behind square-leg. That I believe is the inner Sobers. He emerged full-fledged in that famous century at Brisbane in 1961 but has retired since. Sobers keeps himself in restraint, certainly he is doing so in England this year. What perhaps disguises his restraint is his dazzling stroke-play. Great batsmen (not Don Bradman) are as sensitive as race horses. I believe that what Kanhai is doing (in a series, not in an innings) has a great influence on Sobers. Similarly Cowdrey to Dexter.

Sobers's history is the very reverse of Dexter's. He certainly did not win an 11-plus. There was no 11-plus to win. He was on the West Indian Test side at seventeen, a slow left-hander. The batsmen around him were Weekes, Worrell and Walcott. In such company, all born within a few miles and a few months of each other in his native Barbados, Sobers could learn to bat in the way that came naturally to him. He flourished exuberantly. But crucial to an understanding of Sobers is his participation in League cricket in England.

League cricket is Saturday afternoon cricket. A batsman with scoring strokes has to use them. But his side depends heavily on the League professional. He has therefore to develop not caution but care. Constantine has stated that the slow bowler in League cricket has to be particularly careful. In addition to one or two good batsmen on the opposing side, there are quite a few who are prepared to have a hit and make 20 or 30 invaluable runs. In this encouraging environment Sobers has learnt the full exploitation of all his strokes, and developed an individual style of fast-medium left-hand bowling. I may be wrong here but I have the impression that when things are going well with him (breathing and body control and rhythm) Sobers can get anybody out for little or nothing.

Such strange individuals are perhaps a product of our age. Sobers is only twenty-seven, a year younger than even Dexter. What he will do in the future I don't know. But I think it more than likely that he will not only leave his stamp on the cricket-field but the spirit which moves in him and Dexter with a bat or ball in their hands will find ways and means to express itself in wider fields. What do they know of cricket who only cricket know? All the world's a stage, all the world, including the cricket-field, and all the men and women merely players. These two players are not souls of our age but they certainly are the applause, the delight, the wonder of our stage. In every stroke they shake a lance, but I shall not be so rude as was Ben Jonson:

"In each of which he seems to shake a lance
As brandish'd at the eyes of ignorance."

Letter to V.S. Naipaul

September 1963

My dear Vidia,

In a day or two I shall send you a manuscript, a short story about 8,000 words long. What is to be done with it I shall let you know either later in this letter or when I send you the ms. That is out of the way.

Things are happening to me, and I feel them because I am a solitary West Indian intellectual as all West Indian intellectuals are. I shall mention only the most important ones.

a) I received your review on Thursday morning. Thanks to whoever sent it. Ever since I got it I have been developing ideas which it would take a whole volume to enclose. That I know is nonsense. I can only make a few notes here.

b) Yesterday I received an advance copy of the revised edition of *The Black Jacobins*.* It will be out in New York on September 1st. It contains the appendix "From Toussaint L'Ouverture to Fidel Castro" which I now know more clearly than ever deals with the challenge you set before me in the review.

c) Now this morning I see in the *Sunday Times* your article on India.

They are all connected. But first the review. It has one point which I am sorry I missed and on which I would have spent at least a page. You make it clear that cricket represented style, grace and other elements of culture in a society which had little else of the kind. That is a point that I regret I did not make. It answers completely the questions I have been posing more in their social and historical and only generally in their artistic emphasis. On the first occasion I get I shall do something about it. The second point is that you recognize and even seem to imply that you had not recognized it before: we are a unique people. There is nothing like us in the historical development of the modern world. That is what I emphasize over and over again in the appendix to *The Black Jacobins*. I was glad to see it in the review, and the emphasis you gave to it. Thirdly, I missed something. In your letter to me before you had finished reading the book, you referred specifically to the absence of self-consciousness in the book as you were reading it. That has been much in my mind since I received your letter. I was hoping that you would refer to it in the review, although you did more than enough, far more than I could reasonably have expected. I am concerned about it because I believe that it is the specifically West Indian characteristic of the West Indian intellectual and, in fact, of all our people. I have been watching it in the young people I have been meeting and I have been seeing it in the writers. I cannot go into that here. It is the kind of thing one has to live with and talk about. But I have a

*James's classic study of the 1791 Haitian revolution, first published in England in 1938, was being reissued in America by Random House.

reference to it in the appendix to *The Black Jacobins.* After referring to the fact that there was no anti-American or anti-British feeling in the tremendous national explosion for Chaguaramas, I end the appendix as follows:

> The West Indian writers have discovered the West Indies and West Indians, a people of the middle of our disturbed century, concerned with the discovery of themselves, determined to discover themselves, but without hatred or malice against the foreigner, even the imperialist past. To be welcomed into the comity of nations a new nation must bring something new. Otherwise it is a mere administrative convenience or necessity. The West Indians have brought something new.

> "Albion too was once
> a colony like ours . . .
> deranged
> By foaming channels, and the vain expanse
> Of bitter faction.
> All in compassion ends,
> So differently from what the heart arranged."

> Passion not spent but turned inward. Toussaint tried and paid for it with his life. Torn, twisted, stretched to the limits of agony, injected with poisonous patent medicines, it lives in the state which Fidel started. It is of the West Indies West Indian. For it, Toussaint, the first and greatest of West Indians, paid with his life.

The poem is by Derek Walcott. And I notice five significant lines, the last lines of his poem "Tarpon" in the very issue of *Encounter.* (They are very West Indian but I cannot stay to explain what I mean except to say that we are backward enough and inexperienced enough still to have imagination.)

After immense labours I have at last arrived at something West Indian which will be ours, which can be ours: I made the transition from the Olympic Games of Greece to Greek democracy. I believe that we in the West Indies will make the transition from Thomas Arnold, Thomas Hughes and W.G. to the concepts with which I conclude the appendix.

Now in regard to the article on India. I have been speaking on India recently, not specifically on India as such but on India as part of the underdeveloped countries. I recognize to the last comma the truth of what you say and I am profoundly sympathetic to and respectful of the type of writing which deals in human and subjective terms with what in reality or what must be based on economic, social and political foundations. One day when we met on Oxford Street I told you that we had a special function to do that sort of thing and I wished you would continue with it. This article is very fine. But there is one thing I have to say. I do not believe that at this stage of the twentieth century we as what we are can say the things we ought to say and can say better than anybody else unless we at the same time or within its context are penetrating into and showing our awareness of the terrible crises of Western civilization. Your review was a very West Indian review. Not that that in any way made it less. Not at all. But you remember the review in *The Times Literary Supplement* where the reviewer expressed most clearly his astonishment that I had opened up perspectives about British social history of which he had not dreamt: if I remember rightly, he said that they were fantastic and improbable but had a rightness about them.

Believe me, my dear Vidia, it is with no idea of propagandizing you but as a result of my deepest studies and feelings on the situation of the West Indian writer that I believe we have an immense amount to say about Western civilization which we more than all other writers from the underdeveloped peoples can say. We not only open up ourselves but we open them too. I see you have begun in the latest novel. But I don't believe that there is any profound difference, or rather fundamental difference, between the stage of civilization in which India finds itself and the stage in which the Britain and the Europe of Hitler and Stalin find themselves. And I believe that, effective as we are in stripping the wrappings from the underdeveloped countries, we will be more effective if, maybe not directly, but certainly we indicate that we are ready to strip or have already stripped the wrappings from Western civilization itself. I believe this is necessary for us to reach a final height from which we will be able to see and to point out all things.

I wish I saw you more often. I am sure I would benefit by it and I don't think that I would either bore or annoy you. Every succeeding day makes me more certain than ever that we have something special to say but that we remain a collective of individuals and therefore are unable to make the best of our individual selves.

C.L.R. James.

The 1963 West Indians

(*From the Journal of the Cricket Society*, Spring 1964)
[*This was C.L.R. James's address to the Cricket Society in the Tavern at Lord's on 5 September 1963.*]

On an occasion like this, it is usually quite easy to say what will at least satisfy or not dissatisfy your audience. It isn't so with me on this occasion. First of all I have to speak on what is being called by everyone the most exciting tour within living memory, and that is an unusual thing to have to speak about before it is finished, to find language and ideas to correspond. You mustn't, so to speak, let down your team which has done so well. If they can play to that extent you should at least be able to talk for half an hour, and it is by the standard of the play that what you say is going to be judged. There is another more important reason. I am in no trouble about what to say to you. As a matter of fact, my difficulty is what *not* to say to you — because during the last few years, and particularly during the last two or three, I see so many things in a cricket match and in a series of Tests which I know I myself would not have dreamt of twenty-five years ago, that I am always somewhat nervous in speaking about them to people who are not aware, from unfortunate, lengthy conversations with me, of what I am driving at and where I am coming from. Nevertheless, the only thing to do on this auspicious occasion, on which we are celebrating a great victory, is to tell you what I can and hope that at any rate, though I may bowl a few wides and a few no-balls, you will understand if I do that it is accidental and that I certainly will not bowl a short ball, a beamer or a bumper.

Now the first thing I want to say this evening is something about the technical aspects of the series, because many brilliant men, distinguished men, fine writers, have written finely and most interestingly some classic books about cricket, but to the degree that they were not preoccupied with the length of the ball and the kind of stroke, at the end of the brilliant, scintillating performance you learnt much more about them than you learnt about the game that they were describing. It sometimes was and remains very excellent but I have an instinct towards the game as it was played by the players. . . .

Was this team better than the 1950 team, or was it better than the Australian 1948 team? I don't know, and I don't know anybody else who can possibly know. But I want to say something about what I think is characteristic of this team and the game as it was played. They rose to every occasion. You had to have a very sharp eye, you had to read a lot of newspapers and listen to a lot of people commenting about it on the television, and think about it a great deal, to get exactly what was the value of this team. I don't know what your experience was. I know that on the Saturday night, after four Tests and three days of the last Test had been played, at that time, even on the Monday morning, there were very few people ready to commit themselves on the West Indian side. It is all very well after they had won a fine victory on the Tuesday morning to say: "Wonderful team. Greatly superior. England not in it," and so on. But they didn't say that on Monday morning up to half-past eleven. I know. Because I was with people who talk a lot about these things. And I went and asked. And if the day before the last day of a Test series of five, you do not find many people who will commit themselves, then it is clear, I think, that we have to look a little more closely at what the West Indies team was doing through the tour.

Now what had been going on? They played the first Test at Old Trafford and they did very well. They won brilliantly. Then came the Test at Lord's. And that game, as far as I saw it, didn't exactly deserve the criticism of some good West Indians. They said that the West Indians threw away the game. They say it was a very fine game, etc., but they had it in their hands at one time and they lost it. I don't think so. That game to me was notable for two things — two bowlers, one on the West Indian side and one on the English side. I watched the West Indian batsmen, well set, and consistently beaten by Trueman with the ball he dropped on or just about the off-stump and went towards the slips. They couldn't play it. The second magnificent performance was by Hall. I have never seen a spell of fast bowling of that kind (I have read of one by Tom Richardson at Manchester before I was born). His captain needed it and up to the last over he was going as strong as when he began. As a matter of fact I don't think he recovered from it up till the last day or the day before the last at the Oval. He was never able to bowl as he should have been able to after that tremendous day's performance.

There was that weakness in the batting. The West Indians simply could not play that ball that Trueman was moving from the off-stump towards the slips. And so they went to Edgbaston, and Trueman destroyed them completely with that same ball. A whole lot of them got out not only when their names were written in the scorebook but before. And when you are in trouble with the ball leaving the off-stump and you are putting your bat there and being not quite sure, something else happens. The ball that is coming in to you also becomes very troublesome, because you don't know which way it is. And I saw them and the trouble they were in. But I have been making prophecies, very bold ones, about this West Indies team since 1957, and in a public report I made on that match, I said this: that the ball is beating those batsmen all the time. I believe that the reason is that they have come from hard wickets in the West Indies and in Australia, and the deviation of the ball was not so sharp; in addition to which, they didn't have someone who was so completely master of that kind of business on that kind of wicket in that kind of climate as Trueman is. But I went on to say that in Frank Worrell, their captain, they had somebody who could take care of that business. And when they went to Leeds that business had been taken care of. Sobers and Kanhai batted there — Sobers, by the way, with great caution. I have seen him as he could be. He has not been that here in these Tests. At Leeds he watched that ball very carefully; he and Kanhai took care that the ball that Trueman was bowling and that had given them so much trouble in the past would be properly dealt with. And Butcher dealt with it also. So that is the characteristic feature of this team. They were able to meet an occasion, to rise to a difficulty. So they won that Test at Leeds. And the fact of their being able to rise to an occasion was also proved by what happened to Griffith. Griffith bowled at Leeds for himself and Hall, and he did what the team required at Leeds in the same degree as Hall had done what the team required at Lord's. So it was they came to the last Test.

And that last innings was a wonderful innings. They there showed this capacity that I have been talking about, to rise to meet any occasion that faced them. It wasn't only that they won by eight wickets. I think what encouraged the chorus of praise on Tuesday morning and after was this: that you felt — at least I felt, and it could only have been a feeling — that if they had had to make 400 runs they would have made them. When, after a series of tests, and the last innings you play, you give that impression, it means that the team is characterized as a team that was able to rise to whatever problems faced it. That is what I say when people ask me if they were good as the 1948 or 1950 touring sides to England. I don't know. But everything they had to face they tackled, and Trueman this year, in this awkward climate and on these peculiar wickets, was a very dangerous bowler indeed. I have watched him bowling for many years and he was never more dangerous than he was bowling during this tour. If he got 30-odd wickets he deserved them. And particularly so because when Griffith was going at one end, if even Hall wasn't getting wickets, you had to watch for yourself at the other end. Sir Leonard Hutton has insisted, and I have come to that conclusion, absolutely, you'd better have two of them, one at each end, because the batsman has no peace. Trueman had no assistance to speak of and he bowled magnificently. But that the West Indian batsmen were aware of what was happening and made themselves master of that kind of bowling gives some indication of the inner strength of that team.

Now people say in Australia that the 1960–61 visit was the finest tour they had known, and it is said in England that the 1963 tour is the finest tour: they have done that within two years and we have to ask ourselves why. I want to offer some explanation. You arrive at an understanding of these things, I find, over a long period and by talking to various people. I haven't sat down to talk for an hour or two to Frank Worrell. I assure you that is quite an experience. I haven't talked to Berkeley Gaskin, the manager. I haven't talked to any of the English players. But I have some idea as to why this team in particular has created such a stir both in Australia and in England. They are very distinctly individual cricketers. Hall is an old-fashioned fast bowler. But Griffith, as the season went on, was a very peculiar bowler indeed. There were times when he cut off the pace altogether and allowed the ball to move in the air. He could move the ball various ways and he still retained that devastating old-fashioned yorker. He has come, you know, from a long tradition. Clifford Goodman was not fast but a very fine medium-paced bowler from Barbados. Then came H.C. Griffith, the fast bowler. Then came another one from Barbados, Martindale. Then comes Hall. So that Griffith inherits a very fine tradition, and, having also a very fine physique, he bowls exceptionally well and with great variety. A very individual fast bowler. Different from Hall who (I mean no offence) merely puts his head down and lets you have it, and it's pretty hot — so that is enough to go on with!

In addition to that I have never seen a bowler like Sobers. It isn't only that he can bowl the googly, the chinaman and whatever else he bowls when he is bowling slow. But his fast-medium bowling, which is much faster than it looks, is such that I believe that I wouldn't be surprised if he got any batsman out at any time for nothing. I don't mean to say he will

C.L.R. James

do that consistently. But the bowling is extremely difficult to play. And one of the reasons it is so difficult is because it is quite an individual, new type of bowling.

I have to say also that I don't know and I don't remember very much bowling like that of Gibbs. Gibbs does not bowl the googly. But he finger-flips the leg-break. And somebody who knows the team well tells me that when he happens to hit the right spot and it comes off the finger properly, that ball goes for middle-and-leg to the off-stump at such a rate that you believe it's Hall who's bowling. That is quite distinctive. Furthermore there is something very curious about Gibbs as a slow bowler. He is faster than most slow bowlers I know. I expect you've noticed that. But he has such a beautiful action and he brings the ball from so high that he is able, even at a greater than usual pace, to do a lot of fighting, and at various times he has clean-bowled Cowdrey, he has clean-bowled Dexter, he has got out a lot of people who seemed very well settled and knew what they were about. He also is a very unusual type of bowler.

So they have one old-fashioned bowler of the good, old hot stuff and they have three bowlers whose particular style, while very effective, is not the kind that you meet every day. They are a very, very unusual lot. Their batting is the same. I don't know that anyone was more astonished than I was at some of the things that Butcher did at Lord's in his century. That ill-educated young man had 92 and went to 100 by hitting two fours down to the pavilion. You just don't do that sort of thing! In addition to that, when slow bowlers were bowling to him he kept on jumping out and driving for six. You remember the stroke when he had about 50 or 60. The average batsman does not do that. Kanhai also, in one or two innings that he played, even in the first innings in the Oval Test, made a bad stroke and then the next ball made a worse stroke and got out to it. He did that quite a few times. But that is the same Kanhai who hit 77 in ninety-three minutes, one of the most brilliant innings I remember seeing for a long time. If he is going to do the second, you have to make up your mind to accept the first. You can't have it both ways. And he makes these runs with a wonderful array of strokes all over the place. Some of the strokes he makes, I believe he has invented on the spot! I have known a few West Indian batsmen who did that. There was one leg-glance at the Oval that I don't remember him ever making before. I believe he found himself there and he wasn't prepared to let the ball go — there he was, he beat the man at leg and it went flying down to the boundary for four. And, by the way, when he is really going, he is hitting everybody, and he is hitting them everywhere. He has a special favourite. It is a six wide of long-on and he hits it and then falls down in rejoicing. He does that innings after innings. That is a very individual batsman.

The individuality of Sobers we couldn't see because after what had happened at Lord's and Edgbaston, Sobers decided, it was obvious, that they were going to have to get him out. And when he comes to that decision, you are up against quite a stone wall. But when he's really going, he plays somewhat differently.

Butcher, as I say, is a very unusual cricketer. Frank Worrell is a different kind. He makes some of the great old strokes. But he is not the Worrell that he was. But he still can make runs at odd times. And as for fielding, Gibbs could field anywhere. I rather like to see him just walk about the field. He's a remarkable physical personality. Butcher was able to field anywhere. So was Conrad Hunte. So was Kanhai. Sobers was usually at slip but he also could field anywhere.

Now what is the reason why such distinguished individuals should all congregate on the West Indian side? I'll tell you why I think so and why we don't see them to the same degree on the England side. They have all learnt to play quite naturally. They have all played as they wished to play until they were about eighteen or nineteen. So the good ones have not been merely good. The bad ones have been very bad, but the good ones have been very good because they have developed an individual style, a style that is native to them.

Consider Sobers. Sobers grew up in Barbados, 21 miles long and 14 miles broad. He grew up bowling for Barbados, a slow left-hand bowler at the age of eighteen: batting around him were Weekes, Worrell and Walcott, all born within a few miles and a few months of each other. Now that is coaching of a kind that nobody can give you. He was actually playing with these people, in West Indian sides, and later on in the Test side, playing as a bowler. So he learnt to bat as was natural to him, but with the best possible models next door. So such batsmen develop an individual style. Furthermore, after they have developed themselves and played intercolonial cricket, or inter-island cricket, and played against some people coming from abroad, most of them get the opportunity to make a very distinct stage in the development of the West Indian style. They play in the Lancashire League and in many parts of central England. Now that is a wonderful training for the West Indians and for Tests. Number one, they finish every match the same day. So they have come from West Indies with a certain style, attuned to a certain style of cricket, and they come to it in Lancashire and they continue with it. If you are a professional playing Lancashire or Cheshire League cricket, you have to make strokes or the match will never finish. They've been stroke-makers since they were ten years of age. And they get themselves in the Lancashire League and they have to continue to make their strokes. But they also are the only professional on the side, and a heavy responsibility lies upon them. So although they continue to make their strokes, they make them with a certain care and caution that the conditions under which they play demand from them. They also have to learn to bowl very carefully. Mr Constantine has told me, and he has written it in his book, that you played against a side which has one or two good batsmen and down below are three or four who are quite prepared to have a dash at you and don't care if they get out for nought and then make 30 the next time. And if one or two of them make 30 and one or two of the earlier batsmen stand up, that means 150, and 150 in league cricket is a winning score. So that this West Indian bowler in league cricket is under a great strain. He has to learn to be dangerous but he must learn also not to give away anything. Frank Worrell has told me that you have conditions so changeable from place to place and so difficult that if you set yourself to meet the standards that you have to meet, your cricket does not decline, it improves. And all of them learn as boys to make strokes. Then they live right next door in these small islands to some of the greatest cricketers of the West Indian tradition, and then the best of them come here and go through the severe discipline of one-day cricket in the leagues. The result is they are fit for Test cricket in a way that you would not be able to get if you took their antecedents purely on the surface. That league cricket that they play is a wonderful discipline and training, to nourish and to develop what they have brought with them and make it fit for the larger spheres.

Now there is one more point that I have to bring in. This originality, the distinctive, creative style which makes them so effective when a difficult situation is met, can go to pieces entirely. It can repeatedly show itself, show fine form and yet lose match after match. It has to be held in check, disciplined and, where it goes wrong, brought back by some very careful captaincy. And this time they had that captain in Frank Worrell. Frank Worrell has said, "I don't lecture them. I tell them what is wrong, if anything is wrong. I tell them what is right and leave it to them." He has great confidence in them and they in him. He has had an immense experience. He did his best to go to South Africa in charge of a Negro team but they wouldn't let him come. But he has been everywhere and he knows the game well. He knows the West Indian style and the West Indian method and the West Indian temperament. And therefore this remarkably creative individual style which they all have that enables them as a team to meet an occasion, is held in order and disciplined by one of the finest cricket minds that the game has known. . . .

Now I want to say a few words about the England team. The person I choose to talk about is Dexter. He is symbolical of what the England team is not. And he is worth a close and, if I may say so, a rather sympathetic examination. Dexter made 70 here at Lord's against the West Indies team in a Test match. I have never seen a finer innings — never. Kanhai had perhaps a greater variety of strokes but he wasn't making them against Hall and Griffith, both on at the same time, and then against Sobers's curious ins and outs, and Gibbs's peculiar flights and spins. I have never seen and I don't want to see better batting than Dexter did on that day. . . . I don't believe it at all. I call Dexter a Cavalier among Roundheads. The young man has had to fight his way towards an individuality which is not in harmony with what is going on around him. He makes 70 and he makes 90 not because he has to play a faster game to please the crowd that has paid the money! I have never heard a more ridiculous analysis of what cricket is or should be. A great batsman makes his runs and plays his game to please himself. That's how he feels, that's what he requires to do justice to his powers, and that's what he does. When Dexter has reached 70 or, worse still, 90, now his concentration begins. He says, "I am the captain of England and these others are not likely to do so well so I must be serious, I really must now get down to business." Then he starts to concentrate and in between he gets out! I saw him batting there at the Oval for an hour for 6 runs. Well, there we have a fine example of doing what comes unnaturally. . . . It is because there is so much care and so much caution and so much scientific cricket around him all the time that he cannot play his own natural game. That is the problem of Dexter as I see it.

Now I hear sometimes that the West Indians have a sharp eye and sharp reflexes. Well, if so, something has happened to Englishmen during the last fifty years. They have lost a sharp eye and sharp reflexes because before 1914, R.H. Spooner, the young Jack Hobbs, K.L. Hutchings, Frank Woolley, A.C. Mac-Laren and all these, they seem to have had very sharp reflexes because they used to play just as these West Indians are playing. The West Indians learnt it from them. I don't believe in this theory of sharp tropical eye and sharp tropical reflexes. I think it's a lot of nonsense. Before 1914 the English batsmen against the Australians had these sharp eyes and sharp reflexes. They made all these extraordinary strokes. But something has happened to English county cricket. And it grinds you down. I see it happening to Dexter. I have seen it happen to two others. I saw Cowdrey bat against the Australians at Lord's in 1953 for the Gentlemen of England, and I said to myself — well, here we are, Archie MacLaren is back again. I had never seen MacLaren play, but I'd read about him and I saw the style, the power and so forth. I saw him. I was reporting cricket next year (in 1954) and I used to see him at Oxford and in other games, and therefore I was very satisfied when they sent him to Australia at the end of 1954. From all the accounts that I have read and one or two things that I have been told, there hasn't been better batting than from him and Peter May about the third Test against Lindwall and Miller on that Australian field, particularly an innings that Cowdrey played at Melbourne. But the fact remains that, while any country to which he goes now will put him right away in their Test team, he has not in my opinion become the commanding batsman that he seemed to be set for in 1953 and 1954. And I am not a psychologist. I don't work out all the influence of the father and all that. I put it to the fact that he is playing under certain circumstances which quieten you down. You fit into a groove. I believe the same thing happened to Peter May. In '53 and '54 and even '55 there was something which he had lost a little later, I think. I believe one batsman severely affected by what is going on, and who has not been able to find himself and what he is capable of doing, is Graveney.

Nowadays we have a lot of those excellent gentlemen, the Press (I have the honour and privilege of being a minor member); we have the commentators: we have them in the morning, we have them in the evening, we have them at noonday; we have them at lunch and at tea. So the cricketer today cannot go in and make a bad stroke and get out cheerfully and get ready to go in next time. He's aware that every bad stroke he makes is labelled, in fact photographed for everybody to see at half-past eight that night or ten o'clock when the news is being told — exactly what he did. Now that is very hard on the average player. And when selection committees begin to wobble about and they play a batsman in the first Test and they play him in the second and they don't play him in the third, and it is uncertain whether they will play him in the fourth but they play him in the fifth, and they send him on the next tour but don't send him on the one after, something happens to him and I believe it has happened to Graveney. I hope it doesn't happen to Sharpe. I hope it is recognized that there is a Test batsman and he's put in and made to feel that he's in.

There's another man, whose opinions I respect, who tells me what I have believed, and this makes me feel very good, that Parks should be playing in that team and should have been playing for some time as a batsman, not as a batsman-wicketkeeper. He's a stroke-maker and he has never been afraid to lift his bat and put it on Griffith and Hall, however fast they are bowling. C.B. Fry used to say that he would pick a team at the beginning of the season and that is the Test team he would play to the end. I agree, with only one proviso — that the person picking them should be a Fry. This "wobbling about" that goes on nowadays (and I'm sure it's television and commentators and journalists: they didn't used to have so many of them before), and this constant criticism and so forth; I don't say it is bad, I'm not even saying it's good. But it keeps going, and it puts a strain on the cricketer — he can't go into bat, they interview him before he goes in, they interview him after he comes out. I think the next thing they'll do is to interview him while he's batting out there! That is the only thing that is still waiting for him! It is rather difficult under this pressure, and I believe in general the atmosphere and style of play to which English cricketers have to submit themselves in the county games robs them, even when they obviously have it, of that individuality which a great Test player should have.

There are one or two brief remarks I have to make on other things. I will just make them, leave them with you, and if even some of you throw them back at me, I'm able to dodge; I have been skilful at that for a long time!

I want to say a few words about cricket as an art, and art form. I have recently come here from about five years in the West Indies and I went as usual to the National Gallery; I have been back to see the Tate, I have gone to see a West Indian artist, I went to see an exhibition of American paintings, a whole hundred of them. That, if you please, that's what they say are the fine arts. And they had some authentic fine art at the National Gallery and at the Tate. I'm not saying there was not

C.L.R. James

fine art in the American paintings, only I wasn't fine enough to see them! I have had very vivid memories of certain cricketers and certain strokes that I have seen since I was about six years of age. They are now permanent parts of my mental outlook. I had two such experiences during the series: Dexter batting at Lord's and Kanhai batting at the Oval. And I want to say this, that I see Hall after he has caught the ball taking his magnificent body back down to his starting place, throwing the ball up and down, full of vital, unspent energy. Then he turns and starts to run up, moving quietly at first. Then he moves into his tremendous delivery. That is quite a sight. And then there is Dexter standing up waiting, and there is a sudden rapid movement of the feet and a balance of the body and a flick of the wrist and the ball is flying to the square-leg boundary. A fieldsman picks it up, throws it to Hall, Hall comes back again, and Dexter goes out with another balance entirely, and the ball is flying down toward the pavilion. And all I want to say is: that is an experience I have had. And I want to know what you, Mr Art Critic, mean by saying that when I go to the National Gallery or the Tate, that is the fine art. What do you think this is? What do you call it? He says nothing about it.

Now I have opened an attack on these gentlemen, and the attack is not asking for more recognition; I have no time for that. I have read enough of art criticism to be thoroughly mystified by it. And I have written this and I say it again: you all are in a bit of a mess. That is obvious because you say so yourselves. It isn't only that other people say it about you. And until you understand that what 35,000 people come to see when Hall is bowling at Dexter, Dexter flicks him round to the square-leg boundary and then drives him down to the pavilion, until you understand that that also is definitely an art form and an artistic expression, that is felt by many people in an artistic manner, you will never be able to write properly about the art criticism of Michelangelo and Raphael. That's my belief. And it was very clear to me in watching these Tests. Not always, but at times. I keep on talking about Dexter. Every now and then, he might be getting out for ten, but he would make a stroke; he made an off-drive at Leeds. I don't know if any of you were up there to see it. He was out within the next two or three balls but it's in a flash of lightning like a tremendous piece of sculpture in movement. I remember it and I will continue to remember it. There was another stroke that I remember in the Oval match by the little wicket-keeper, Murray. He came in and Trueman or somebody bowled him a short ball. And then he got back on his

144

right foot and put him through extra-cover to the boundary. Soon he was out but that stroke had been made. And I see these things and I remember them. I have remembered some of them for nearly all of my life. And I'm not going to stand anybody talking to me and telling me, "Oh, that's mere entertainment: when you go down to the National Gallery what you see is fine art." I'll tell him, no thank you. I have a lot to say about that. I'm not going to say it now but I just want you to know I have been looking at that.

There are other things I have been looking at. I have been looking at this game and I have had in mind what many serious people and many hard-working people seek to achieve, what they call and what I have been writing about, the integration of West Indians into English life. Now the various clubs that they have, their welfare officers and all that is very good, but I am certain that at Lord's on one day that I remember, and in those days at the Oval, more integration took place spontaneously than by twenty years of organizations and individual people. It was a tremendous public show. And I will tell you one or two of the things that I noticed. These West Indians are far more noisy and talkative at Lord's or at the Oval than they are in Bridgetown or in Jamaica. That is an absolute fact. They now feel here that they have to do their share also and the best they can do is to talk. The boys on the field will bat and bowl and they will keep it up behind them. They don't do that and they haven't done that in Trinidad; I have seen them. Furthermore, they talk a lot more and they say a great deal. They make the English people understand more what they are and respect and respond to it and they also change the habits of the English people themselves. I heard some cheering at Lord's in the Test match that I am sure was a response to the West Indians' cheering. "You are not going to get away with it. We are going to make some noise ourselves." There was an occasion at the Oval — Hall got out somebody and then he bowled Lock first ball for 0 and all the West Indians got ready for the hat-trick. When Statham came in and played the ball through for 4, I heard in the English applause the following: "Not this time. You're wrong. You're not getting any hat-trick." They were telling them back. They were making themselves felt. In addition to which the West Indians express themselves in word and in manner which are not only witty but would make an impression on all who hear them. In 1957 I saw that one day a few feet in front of me. There was a West Indian of the upper proletarian class, I would say. And around him were certain

145

English people, a bank clerk and one or two others. So this fellow sat down there and he was talking a great deal. And after two or three hours they got very interested in what he was saying and the kind of remarks he was making and whenever he was about to say something they would turn and listen to him and he would say it and there would be general laughter. And he, with a good audience, felt himself and he went on. Until some time about half-past four the West Indians started to lose; the early batsmen started to get out, so he had to be quiet, poor fellow, and his friends were looking at him somewhat and were throwing one or two remarks and he just could not flourish any more. Then Statham bowled a ball to Walcott and Walcott got back on his right foot and hooked him magnificent-ly to the square-leg boundary. There was a great deal of applause and then the ball was thrown back to Statham and he started to walk back to the beginning of his run. And the moment he reached there our loquacious friend stood up, said nothing but signalled for all to see a boundary. He got more applause then than he had ever had before. He had been placed right back in the game, his confidence had been restored and they were all more integrated than ever. I watched them the whole afternoon. I was very much struck by it.

I would like to mention two other episodes which are very significant and distinctive of the West Indians. One was the Test at Lord's this year. There was a West Indian talking all over his face and he was talking in the West Indian dialect, the West Indian style all the time because his audience liked to hear that. And then an English batsman drove a ball, I think through the feet of Hall or one of them and this West Indian revelling in his language suddenly said, "Gor blimey." He hadn't learnt that in the West Indies! That he had learnt here. In other words, you see, when he was expressing himself as a West Indian to a lot of English people he was as West Indian as he could be. But after all he was living here and when something happened in which he was making a natural re-sponse he fell automatically into the language, into the lan-guage of the people around him: "Gor blimey," he said. And it was very peculiar coming after his previous language.

Then finally one man who waved at us in the bus after the Oval Test. And what he said I found most revealing. All he said was this: "*Lord* Kanhai, *Sir* Frank Worrell, *Dr* Conrad Hunte." He had distributed honours to the deserving. And I expect he would not have given those honours to them in the West Indies. He may have called one a governor-general or a premier. But in

England he thought of lord, sir, doctor — he thought that was the best he could do.

Now those are the examples that I have taken. I can't give you any more. I don't want to. But I am sure that is going on all over the grounds as long as these Tests are going on. That's what they are doing all the time. And there is a real integration going on for which the game of cricket is responsible.

I want to say something more about the West Indian tour here. As I say, nowadays when I watch any cricket match I see infinitely more than I saw some years ago. And I watch that West Indian team playing in the Test at the Oval and I saw very clearly the future development of the West Indians as a political and social entity. In the last words of something I have recently written and published, I used these words: that Thomas Arnold, Thomas Hughes and W.G. Grace after the tour in Australia of the West Indies, would have recognized Frank Worrell as "their boy". By that I brought to a climax what I have made very clear, that the middle classes in the West Indies have been brought up within a mental and moral framework which is best represented by those three men — Grace, Thomas Arnold, the headmaster of Rugby, and Thomas Hughes, the author of *Tom Brown's Schooldays*. But that must come to an end. The West Indies have reached where they are because certain of them have had the opportunity to absorb to a large degree, and to adapt to their own uses, a certain definite tradition. But they have to bring something of their own now to the life that they have to live, and I believe in the cricket that they have been playing over the last two or three years they have found something of their own.

Reflections on the Late Series

(*The Cricket Quarterly*, 1964)

The Owl of Minerva flies only at dusk. Which being translated means that the bright light which will illuminate, clear away the darkness, appears only when the darkness is pretty dark. There is not only no need to despair of Test cricket. There is every incitement to be full of hope in view of the signs of regeneration sprouting near and far. Regeneration? Yes. R-e-g-e-n-e-r-a-t-i-o-n. First, negatively: it would be hard to find more than one commentator, either with pen or voice, who says a good word for the present series of Tests. The repudiation is complete. Note, however, that no one is resigned to what is taking place. Everyone has a vision, not only what he would like to see, but of what ought to be seen on a cricket field. Even the most gloomy cannot disguise or repress a secret hope that things will change. It is when matters reach the stage of universal protest, embodying not a vague dissatisfaction, but a definite vision, that one feels confident that something new is on the way.

The second power for regeneration is not in the commentators, but in the public. England, facing a total of 656 by the Saturday afternoon, had scored 178 for 2. Yet 21,000 people turned up on the Monday morning. What came they forth to see? One argument was that they had already bought tickets, or had made arrangements to spend the Monday seeing cricket, and therefore did what they were set for doing, irrespective of what they were likely to see. That is a legitimate if debatable point. There is no possible debate about what happened on Tuesday of the Oval Test. On the Tuesday morning it rained. It kept on drizzling right up to half-past eleven. Yet for well over an hour before, there was a queue outside the Oval, four or five broad stretching for nearly half a mile. They faced the possibility of more rain, the umpires periodically. inspecting, and re-inspecting the pitch, of the game fizzling out in a draw as depressing as the weather. Yet they came and stayed. Passing along the queue, one could hear them talking about the prospects of play, and nursing a cheerful faith that the weather might allow the game to go on. What they came forth to see there was no doubt about. They had come long before 11 o'clock and were preparing to stick it out in the damp and drizzle till 5.30. In other words, certainly in London, the capital, where are accumulated all the special attractions of the age, cricket, like David, can still slay in tens of thousands. Test cricket has not to create an audience. The audience is there waiting, in the damp and drizzle.

From the point of view of the game as a social expression, the batsmen and the bowler are secondary. What matters obviously is the spectator, whether he comes or not. He comes primarily to see the brilliant, the great, dazzling performer, and that, whether his own side wins or not. The scintillating personality who draws thousands at the mere prospect of seeing him scintillate, was noticeably absent from this series. There was definitely only one such. That was Dexter. Undoubtedly many would go with the hope of seeing Dexter in full cry. In this respect, the one on the Australian side who, at the beginning of the series, raised hopes was O'Neill. He was not only disappointing, his dismissals were obviously due not to bad luck but technical deficiencies. His hooking was as often a hit as a mis-hit. On the Australian side, the cricketer who set the nerves tingling was a newcomer, Veivers. How good he actually is, as batsman or bowler, it is not easy to say: he would need two sides much better than these two really to test the best that is in him. But not only in county games, but in the Tests, he always made a creative and technically adequate response to a particular situation. He was a natural hitter not of mere fours but of sixes. He could bowl for long spells on a good wicket and could use a turning one. He could tie up a great batsman: at Leeds, he not only kept Dexter on poking, defensive and very uncertain attempts to drive him; he finally had him hitting the ball almost resignedly into the hands of a mid-on placed specially for just a stroke. Veivers could defend at a critical time as he did at Lord's. He could not merely hit hard, but he could make fine strokes. There was no finer stroke play seen throughout the series than the four strokes he made at the Oval past cover off Cartwright. The balls were not loose, Cartwright does not bowl any. But Veivers watched a series of balls carefully, and judging the length early and accurately, got into position and hit Cartwright to the left, and to the right, of cover off the back foot. Cartwright moved over to the leg-stump, and again Veivers watched him carefully, and carefully chose a ball that was not a bad ball and hit it to the leg boundary.

Apart then from Dexter and Veivers, there was no cricketer who was a performer to bring expectant thousands to the ground. Barrington, uncertain at first, ended the series not only with heavy scores, but with a noticeable recapture of command, of authority. Trueman, alas, was not the bowler who had taken nearly 300 wickets in Tests. But the manner in which he went from 297 to 301 at the Oval had all the customary appurtenances of the fiery and indomitable Freddie. It was not merely the figure 300 which created the excitement and enthusiasm: a stranger, ignorant of cricket, might well have believed that Trueman had somehow or other attained the ripe age of 300 years. Pleasantly reminiscent was the enthusiasm of the West Indians who turned up in numbers at the Oval. They not only cheered and encouraged fiery Fred, they appealed regularly against the two Australian batsmen, who showed no enthusiasm whatever for being the three-hundredth sacrificial victim. The West Indians went further. They not only appealed, but not infrequently gave out the batsmen. This was not at Headingley, Trueman's native Yorkshire. But it would have happened on any cricket ground in the world where Trueman had played. A testimony not only to his skill and sturdy independence of character, but a testimony also to what the crowds came forth to see. A technicality: Trueman got those last wickets when he had not only shortened his runs, but abandoned the attempt to recapture a pace which he no longer had. That, particularly at Leeds, he was so often hit to the on-boundary and past cover, was due to the fact that he was pitching the ball where he had always pitched it, but would not recognize the fact that it no longer came off the ground as of old.

The dazzling personality, the startling event is still the main attraction of a game so ritualistic as cricket: there is never so deeply felt a response from the crowd as when the home side gains an overthrow — something for nothing. Yet, it is as well to face the fact, and a very pleasant fact it is, that whatever the style of play, Test matches, particularly England against Australia, are an established constituent of English life. If these two sides were lacking in dazzling players, at least one of them gave a striking example that could be appreciated by all, the function of a captain in building a side. Simpson is small, but well built and very present on the field. Very obviously from the beginning of the season, he set himself to make the best use of some not very promising material. He succeeded remarkably. In this respect, the bowling of Corling and of Hawke, at the end of the series of Tests, was something very different from what it was at the beginning. Simpson nursed them along and the number of balls per over that they sent down well wide of the off-stump was obviously under their captain's direction. Simpson leaned heavily on Veivers, and if, as at Leeds, the England batsmen would not hit at him, Simpson brought long-on in, and Veivers continued to pitch the ball well up, with only one token fieldsman out. Simpson took every obvious opening and was always looking for others. He was ready to go on himself, and present a number of juicy long hops to the opposite batsmen in his first two overs. That he had his bowlers all keyed up to a high pitch as members of a Test team was shown not only by their careful use of their limited resources but by noting what the batsmen of Essex and of Kent did to them, once the Test series was over. Perhaps the most notable demonstration of the team spirit which Simpson not only built up but embodied was the way his side pulled itself together at Leeds, when Australia at 178 for 7 seemed to be losing the match. Burge, at all times a capable confident batsman, not only went on to 160, he seemed quite untroubled by the fear that he would not get the support he needed. And not only Grout (who has made runs before), but Corling and Hawke rallied to the occasion and helped Burge to build up the score in a manner that did great credit to the Australian captain and to their side as a whole. As a matter of fact, Hawke's innings approached greatness in the sublime confidence with which he played down the line and then scampered for a single not infrequently off the inside edge.

Simpson was always doing something and seemed to know always what he was doing. His 311 at Leeds was not a masterpiece of batting, but he had a job to do as batsman and as captain, and he did it. The few men who have made 300 in a Test are always not far from twenty years of age. Simpson is the first nearer thirty. On television, explaining what he did and why, he was even better than on the field. Simpson played the game according to the rules, and if the result was a mess, change the rules, do not blame Simpson.

Simpson in almost every match played almost the one eleven. All the disadvantages of a home side overwhelmed Dexter, who seemed unable, either on the field or off, to decide what role he wanted his team or the individual men to play. C.B. Fry was said to believe that at the beginning of a season, twelve men including the captain should be chosen for the Test side, and be made to understand that they would represent England for the rest of the season. That is unquestionably the high peak of policy. It gives collective co-ordination and individual self-confidence. The only thing is that it requires a C.B. Fry to make the selection. No one, least of all, the members of the team themselves, seemed to understand what aims and ideas governed the heterogeneous body of men who were repeatedly thrown together to form an England XI. At times it was impossible not to believe that men were chosen on form, i.e. the latest number of runs scored, or wickets taken just before the selection was made. That was particularly true of the list of mediocrities who succeeded one another as the England fast bowlers, a gratuitous encouragement to Australian batsmen. The Selection Committee could not decide whether Trueman could bowl well enough to be on the English side or not. It seems that there is a considerable body of opinion which believes that Statham was better than all those who were put in the position of substituting for him. To do better than they was not in fact very difficult. The one class bowler who emerged on the English side was Cartwright. It remains to be recorded why he was not selected from the first Test, and made a permanent part of the England XI. After he had made nearly 350 runs against Cartwright, Simpson still did not know which way Cartwright would move the ball. Cowdrey was the most asccomplished batsman on either side, the most accomplished, but the most lacking in that will to conquer which he had in 1953 and 1954. What is the real worth of Barber? We shall know only after he has gone to South Africa. Certainly, at the Oval Test, Dexter did not know what to do with him. For all this, Dexter must bear the moral responsibility. A captain who cannot impose a sense of direction upon a Selection Committee has no right to be captain. The storm of criticism which fell on Dexter for changing from spin bowlers to Trueman at Leeds was most unfair. How many would have advised against it, not next morning but at the time? The Australian tail was batting. The ball was new. Trueman needed three wickets to reach 300. It was his home ground. Surely if ever a captain was justified in handing the fast bowler the new ball, Dexter was justified. It is often unwise and frequently unjust to criticize a particular technical move by a captain, especially after you have seen the result. The gravamen of criticism of Dexter is this — when his side faced 656, it responded with 611. Going into bat nearly 200 behind, the side made 381 for four. *When it knew what it had to do, it could do it.* At other times it didn't know what it had to do, or who it was. It was never a side. Simpson's men were noticeably a side.

It is Hegel who stated that the owl of Minerva flies only at dusk. It is Kant who sums up the aims of mankind in the following terms: "What do I know? What must I do? What may I hope?" After this series, what do we know? We know that the technique of the game has dropped one if not several pegs lower than what it used to be. In his day, Sutcliffe was looked upon as a dependable but somewhat slow batsman. Today he would be a dazzling hero. In individual quality, the young Yorkshireman, Boycott, seems to be of the same stamp as his famous forebears, Herbert Sutcliffe and Sir Leonard Hutton. He will have to get rid of a certain awkwardness and crouching in his forward defensive. But against the Australians in particular, he seemed able to mobilize all his not inconsiderable resources. He conquered their bowlers. On the Australian side, McKenzie, it must be remembered, is only twenty-three years of age. Traditionally, the great fast bowlers, McDonald, Gregory, Constantine, Lindwall, Trueman, Davidson were at their best when nearer thirty than twenty. McKenzie seems destined to be a very great fast bowler indeed. He is still working out what he can do. He already has a wonderful rhythm. In the second innings of the English side at the Oval, Barber was playing the ball very strongly off his legs. Coming on a second time, McKenzie had him lbw by the unexpected pace that he could get from the pitch. Dexter, characteristically determined to keep the score moving, was deceived by McKenzie's pace, cut two or three times and missed, and finally connected only to edge him to the slips.

Titmus played the cricket of a classical English professional cricketer. He fielded finely. When called upon to do something with the bat, he was usually able to do what his captain wanted, and his bowling depended above all things on length. He didn't seem to spin very much. He didn't dramatically move the ball the opposite way, but seemed able to go on hitting the ball on the right spot for ever, and to such, much is forgiven.

Symbolical of what is not only depressing in itself, but the cause of depression in other men, was the batting of Lawry. I was fascinated on television by Lawry, batting against Glamorgan. Shepherd bowled him half-volley after half-volley. Lawry stuck his front foot out and put his bat on the ball immediately it touched the ground. That I would swear to on oath before a jury, because he did the same thing for hours at the Oval. There is a great deal of talk about wickets: it seems that groundsmen today have at last discovered the secret of the unimpeachable pitch; I, for one, simply don't believe it — there have been perfect pitches before. Much ink is also spilt on the assorted evils springing from seam bowling and other technicalities. All such matters are effects, not causes. They can flourish unchecked because players think and play in a certain way, submit themselves to conditions in a way their ancestors did not. We can see and hear signs all round us that modern "scientific" cricket is on its way out. In 1960 in Australia, and in 1963 in England, the West Indians showed that another golden age is with us if we want it. I have never seen a finer driver than Dexter between cover's right hand and mid-on's left, and from the first Test, at Trent Bridge, whenever he went to the wicket, the game began to crackle. At Old Trafford, Dexter's 178 showed that although he could play the stodgy cricket that too many critics today seem to think the ultimate sign of Test-match quality, even while doing that, he could still make strokes that one will remember to one's dying day. Off a fast bowler, he makes a square cut to the boundary past point, the like of which I have never seen: only the ball racing to the boundary enables it to be stigmatized as short. He also has a quality that F.S. Jackson was reputed to have. He goes on to bowl and gets valuable wickets. Veivers and Titmus showed that, in their different ways, what stirred in cricketers fifty years ago can still move in them. And now from South Africa there is news that certain young men there with bat and with ball have decided and proved that it is still possible to play Test cricket in a manner that will startle and delight both the connoisseur and the thousands who queued up on the fifth day outside the Oval.

What do we know? We know that present-day Test cricket is not what it used to be. What can we do? We can in all ways that are possible keep away from the pessimistic philosophers and the legislative reorganization of the game (tampering is the word), and keep our eye (and the eyes of others) on the signs of something new sprouting in a game, that after all has held its own for well over a hundred years. That we can do, and do with hope. The new sprouts are not merely sprouts. Though surrounded by the desiccated remains of an arid time, they are already recognizable if not quite in full bloom. Coming back for a solitary reappearance at the end of the season, Washbrook, like an echo from a vanished world, reminded us that in the right hands a bat is a sword, not a shield.

Sir J.B. Hobbs

(*The Cricketer*, 1964)

Of the late Sir Jack Hobbs I have some particularly West Indian memories. I saw him bat only once — in 1933. It was for Surrey against the West Indians. He made over 200. One stroke made his past alive for me. In 1933 he was near the end of his career and he was scoring off the fast bowlers chiefly by deflecting to the on-side. Griffith (Herman), I think it was, put an extra man on the on-side leaving mid-off open. Next ball Hobbs moved out at him and drove him through mid-off for four. He was a bit stiff but he wasn't going to stand for wide spaces left open in the field!

He never visited the West Indies but he had much influence

in West Indian cricket, physically and morally. He influenced Constantine in particular. Himself one of the greatest of cover-points, he told Constantine in 1923 that he was faster to the ball than anybody he had ever seen, but he gave him some useful hints on technique, how and when to throw at the wicket, particularly the under-arm flick. He influenced Constantine and all West Indian cricketers in another way. Our "Saturday afternoon boys" were startled in 1923 by the deadly serious-ness of first-class cricket.

The English county players asked for no concessions, gave none. But more than one West Indian has told me that while Hobbs gave nothing away he was always calm, courteous, even gracious. By the mere fact of his existence he taught them that what they had was viable in big cricket. They still have it.

Of his skill others will tell. But I have read all I can about him and talked to as many people as I could. And I give my opinion for what it is worth. Others might have exceeded him in runs made in general. But at his best, on any wicket, under any circumstances, no one ever batted better than he or gave more pleasure to spectators and players alike.

In the thirties I often sat with him in the press-box. Now C.B. Fry usually dominated the press-box, reciting lines of poetry, warbling bits of opera, recalling great cricketing events, and all the time looking at the game and writing his column. Neville Cardus was lively and talkative, full of wit and humour. Jack Hobbs as he was then sat quiet, saying little, speaking usually only when spoken to. But how he watched the game! He never took his eyes off it.

And I have since learnt what I think he was doing even in the press-box. I have learnt that when on the field he (and Frank Woolley) never took his eye off the ball. Wherever it went, beyond the boundary, thrown in by a spectator, they never took their eyes off it. And now, looking back, I think that Hobbs was doing that — even in the press-box!

I learnt much from him. In the press-box he was always ready to tell you in his quiet voice what you wanted to know, what you had seen and not *noticed*. He himself missed nothing. Small friends of mine used to ask me to get his autograph for them. He always obliged, as cheerfully and calmly as when making one of the innumerable centuries.

Jack Hobbs was more than a great cricketer. He was a remarkable human being. His influence will not die with him. Even at the end he leaves a characteristic remembrance. He died as he had played, resisting his opponent to the last but quietly and with that dignity and reserve which will now be imperishably associated with him.

Sobers' Greatest Days are Ahead

(*The Cricketer*, July 1964)

The recently appointed captain of the West Indies cricket team, Garfield St Aubrun Sobers, was born in Barbados on 18 July 1936, and is therefore not yet twenty-nine years old. Any visitor to any West Indian island in those days may have seen him and dozens like him at the side of any street, playing cricket with a bat hacked out of wood and a succession of sour oranges deputizing for balls. Constantine and George Headley began that way and Sobers, a generation later, was no different.

The foundation of all speculation about cricket must be the ball as bowled and the stroke as played. Sobers holds the record for the highest score made in a Test match. He is within a few wickets of the unique Test double of 4,000 runs and 100 wickets. In Australia he established records unknown there before he began to play professional cricket for the state of Victoria. He has developed a unique style of bowling, changing at will or at need from fast-medium to the chinaman as well as the traditional slow left-hander's spin. Whether he is the best all-rounder the game has known is a matter for stimulating if necessarily indecisive discussion. It is sufficient for any cricketer (and his period) that the claim can be made. And yet Sobers's greatest possibilities are in front of him.

Much of the cricket into which his natural skill has developed comes from three significant sources. He began Test cricket bowling slows at the age of seventeen. He was uncoached but learned to bat with his eyes on his fellow Barbadians, that original and dazzling trio, Weekes, Worrell and Walcott. His responsibilities as a professional in cricket in England enabled him to combine the freedom of a Saturday afternoon game with the careful experiments needed to get the opposing side out as expeditiously as possible. Two seasons in Australian state cricket have seasoned him in Australian toughness. And this wide and varied experience has had the benefit of the vigilant but magnanimous sympathy and advice of that stern upholder of cricket's best traditions — Sir Frank Worrell.

Sobers will probably be the youngest captain to head a touring cricket team to England. Yet he remains a charming and unspoilt person.

What can cricket — not merely West Indian cricket — expect from his new responsibilities? It seems fair enough to say that a regeneration of the Test game is on the order of the day. The West Indies in Australia in 1960 and in England in 1963 jerked Test cricket to its feet. That something is in the air is proved by the recent uninhibited play of the young men of South Africa in Australia. It is not too much to hazard the opinion that, as all pioneers, they have spontaneously revolted against the type of Test cricket which they saw around them as they grew up. It is at this exciting stage that Sobers enters into West Indian captaincy. What he will bring to the Test game no one knows and no one can know. But the time and the place — West Indies v Australia in the West Indies sun and before enthusiastic crowds — are propitious. The time and the place are well set for the man.

There is more to this captaincy than meets the eye. There are forces expressing themselves in contemporary West Indies cricket, difficult to assess statistically or even objectively, which nevertheless have exercised an influence which may reach their fullest manifestation in the Sobers of the next few years. Apart from the churches, cricket has undoubtedly been the most powerful and most deeply felt social influence in the shaping of West Indian society, even in its ethical impulses. So far its captains, beginning in 1900 with Aucher Warner (Sir Pelham's brother), have been either English public-school or university men (it so happened that the professional Worrell became captain only after he had graduated from Manchester University). H.B.G. Austin, the Grand Old Man of West Indian cricket, was President of the Chamber of Commerce of Barbados, senior elected members of the Barbados House of Assembly, Chairman of the Board of Education. His father had been Bishop of the West Indies.

Sobers is the first unambiguously native West Indian who has arrived at that exalted position. Exalted it is. Writing quite recently of modern Australian captaincy, John Arlott said:

> The title "Captain of Australia" gives its bearer an eminence in his own country which English people sometimes find it difficult to appreciate. The word "cricket" is understood beyond the need to mention it. Nor is it to be dismissed as "only a game", for it is a major aspect of Australian tradition, pride and expression — especially when it is cricket against "the Englishmen".

In Australia, the Test captaincy is almost like a peerage, distinguishing its holder long after his playing days are done.

True of Australia, it can be far truer of the West Indies, cricket being the social expression that it is there. The West Indian people are very conscious of the role of their cricket in their search for a national identity. They will look at Sobers's appointment as a stage in their national development. His captaincy has an immense potential for the future of the game. Only a potential. But it will be able to do its best for cricket if the West Indians of all classes make him aware that his future success and achievements can mean much more than the winning of a series. It can play a role in national consolidation at home, and national consideration abroad, in spheres beyond the applauding crowds at Lord's and the Oval.

West Indies

(From *The World of Cricket*, edited by E.W. Swanton, Michael Joseph, 1966)

When an MCC team visited the West Indies in 1930 West Indies had perked up enough to win the series. Roach fulfilled all his early promise and George Headley of Jamaica took the field. Only twenty years of age, he made a century three times and practically won the Test at Georgetown against time on a wearing wicket. West Indies seemed to have made some ground but a tour of Australia showed that they had not. Woodfull's 1930 team was too much for them. The side never caught itself until the last State match against New South Wales. The tour was saved from inconsequence by the full blossoming of Headley, who was hailed by the best judges in critical Australia as a batsman *sans peur et sans reproche*.

Perhaps here we can look at a West Indies weak spot — captaincy. In 1900 H.B.G. Austin had been fighting in South Africa. R.K. Nunes of Jamaica had not endeared himself to the 1928 team. The new captain, Jack Grant, a Cambridge blue, met many members of the team for the first time when they gathered together for Australia. As Test bastman and as Test captain, Grant had to start from scratch and in both spheres contributed to the first-ever West Indies Test victory abroad which came in the last game of the tour. But West Indies in England in 1933 were no stronger than in Australia. Headley was better than ever. Constantine, now a League cricketer, could only play intermittently and the side achieved little of note except that in Martindale Barbados produced yet another great fast bowler.

By 1935 maturity had come and in fact the West Indies teams of 1935–9 have never been appreciated at their intrinsic worth. In 1934 the English batsmen had concluded an exceptionally successful season against Grimmett and O'Reilly. In the West Indies in 1935, facing the pace of Martindale, Constantine and a newcomer, Hylton of Jamaica, the English batting failed in match after match. In Tests Hendren (who had had a spectacular previous tour in the West Indies) and Roy Kilner failed to pass 50. Wyatt and Holmes did that much only once and Ames alone reached a century. Headley atoned for his scores of 93 and 53 by a mammoth 270 not out. J.E.D. Sealy, who as a boy had gone to Australia, at last came into his own. Constantine in Tests did a belated justice to his batting and the West Indies convincingly won the series. In 1939 much the same team visited England. They lost the first Test at Lord's, Headley adding yet another to his apparently unending list of laurels by making a century in each innings of a Test on the famous ground. Martindale was not the bowler he had been but Constantine played the full season and with less pace but more guile was successful throughout. By the last Test the side had found itself. England made 352 and West Indies replied with a vigorous 498. West Indies now aimed to bowl out the English side and had Keeton and Oldfield for 77. But Constantine, in addition to 78 from ninety-two balls, had taken five wickets in the first innings. Martindale failed to get a wicket and Hammond and Hutton put on 264. The West Indies players would have liked nothing better than to meet England again. The confidence so painfully acquired would help to shape future West Indies teams.

The international cricket played between 1928 and 1939 had been of inestimable value. The foundations had now been properly laid, and during the war a new generation playing by themselves made some colossal individual scores whose significance was not fully appreciated until the West Indies tour of 1950. MCC sent a poor team to the West Indies after the war. Outstanding form was shown by Frank Worrell, already playing league cricket in England. He apart, no one on either side stood out, and of the four matches, West Indies won two, showing a clear supremacy. Worrell did not participate in the West Indian visit to India in 1948–9. Everton Weekes had not

159

done exceptionally well in 1947–8. However he scored a century in the last Test and did the same in his first four Test innings in India. He seemed certain to make it six in succession when he was run out at 90; his five successive Test centuries remained a record. The West Indian batsmen all scored heavily. The bowling, though adequate and able to defeat India, was for the most part medium to fast and seemed inadequate for the England tour due in 1950.

The 1950 team to England created a sensation. Jeffrey Stollmeyer, one who played a great part in that tour and later captained the West Indies, had toured in 1939 and he believes that in 1950 English cricket was still far below its accustomed standards. The 1950 team accomplished some mighty deeds. Contrary to all expectation the most striking successes were the two slow bowlers, one twenty in April, the other twenty in May. Ramadhin from Trinidad (he had played only two first-class matches) spun the ball both ways and batsmen seemed unable to detect his changes. Valentine from Jamaica (coached by Mercer) could get more spin from a sound wicket than any left-hander playing. The two of them bowled West Indies to victory in three Tests out of four. 1950 also saw the triple efflorescence of Weekes, Worrell and Walcott, born within a few miles and a few months of each other in the island of Barbados. Worrell was all grace and style, Weekes a terrific punisher of all bowling, Walcott a giant who could hook anything and off either foot was equally powerful in front of the wicket. The 1950 tour established "the three Ws". Weekes's first three centuries were double centuries. Good judges believed that better batting could not be seen than his partnership in the Nottingham Test with Worrell, who ended with 261. Stollmeyer and Rae, a left-hander, always gave a good start. Whatever might be further needed was supplied by Gomez, a canny all-rounder. Goddard, the captain, could produce dangerous off-breaks and was able to stand anywhere and catch anything.

With this tour West Indies cricket had at last arrived. Yet the team failed in Australia in 1951–2. Gomez alone seemed to have consistent staying power with the bat. Gomes also bowled well above his usual form. Yet Valentine, with 24 wickets, again proved himself to be the best left-hand spinner in the game. One Test was won and the other four lost. India visited West Indies in 1952. Weekes regained all his consistent brilliance, Walcott surpassed himself and Worrell atoned for some uncertain scoring by a brilliant double century in the last Test.

Despite other successful batting only the three Ws were really able to master the twenty-three-year-old Gupte who here began his career as a master of the googly. To him Worrell and Weekes left the crease, Walcott on the other hand trusted to his great height. Recent cricket in India makes it interesting to note that, despite the three Ws and some good batting by India, West Indian wickets could not put life into a dreadfully slow series. Ramadhin on a fast wicket gave West Indies one victory.

There was only one notable omission from the 1953 MCC team to the West Indies, the finest bowler in England, A.V. Bedser. The team otherwise seemed the best available. After two games, however, West Indies seemed set for another victorious series against England. They won the first Test and declared the second innings of the second Test closed at 292 for 2, to win by 181 runs. Walcott, better than ever, made a dominating 220. Holt also scored heavily. MCC's batting was so drab as to evoke derision from Barbados schoolboys. Hutton, however, pulled his side together, won the next Test, drew the fourth and won the last to even the series. Compton and May helped Hutton to restore the prestige of English batting but the outstanding batting feat of the tour was in Trinidad when all three Ws set the seal on their collective reputation by each scoring a brilliant century, Weekes reaching 206. Bailey, always a dependable cricketer with both bat and ball, excelled himself in the last Test by taking seven for 34 in the first innings. Hutton crowned his now impregnable batsmanship by making 205. The youthful Statham's bowling impressed all and if Valentine did little, Ramadhin took 23 wickets.

In 1955 the Australians, warmly welcomed by West Indian crowds, won three of the four Tests and drew the other two. Ramadhin and Valentine failed and in Tests nine Australians averaged from 107 to 37. Walcott scored a century in each innings of a Test twice, scored yet another century and ended with a total of 827. Weekes repeatedly showed the Australians the dazzling form he had failed to show against the same bowling in Australia. Worrell, however, seemed to have lost the habit of heavy scoring.

Striving to blood young players, early in 1956 Goddard was sent to New Zealand with an experimental side. Of the three Ws only Weekes went. The young players (including Sobers) did little but Weekes's first five innings were centuries. Against his all-conquering stroke-play and with Ramadhin and Valentine effective as a pair, New Zealand did well to win one Test of the four.

Once again West Indies, in 1957 in England, did not fulfil early expectations. Leading England by 288 runs in the first innings, West Indies seemed to have the first Test well in hand. A tremendous stand of 411 runs by May and Cowdrey for the fourth wicket nearly won the match for England. From this the West Indians never recovered. Neither Weekes nor Walcott showed consistent form, Worrell both with bat and with ball brought off some noteworthy performances, but Ramadhin, devastating as usual against the counties, in Tests never seemed to be able to recapture that first fine carefree rapture with which he had bowled out England in the first innings of the first Test. Valentine was in and out of form, mostly out. The wicket-keeping was not good, and in the end three Tests were lost and two drawn. Goddard was unable to cope with an English batting side seven members of which averaged over 50 runs per innings. "Collie" Smith twice scored centuries in Tests. Full of courage he hit a long ball. His flighted off-spinners could not infrequently penetrate the defence of well-set Test batsmen. He fielded brilliantly anywhere. He was a brave cricketer and charming personality. His death in a motor-car accident while a League player in Lancashire was a loss not only to West Indies cricket but to cricket as a whole. In 1958 Pakistan visited the West Indies. Sobers had begun years before as a slow left-hander, had rapidly worked his way up, doing well with the bat in England in 1957. He now came to maturity, made 824 runs in Tests and by scoring 365 not out at Kingston passed the record individual score in Tests which Hutton had held since 1938. The two maestros, Walcott and Weekes, seemed to recover their old form and very welcome was off-spinner Lance Gibbs, who took 17 wickets and headed the averages. There was some fine play by Pakistani players but everything took second place to Hanif Mohammad in the first Test. Pakistan following on 473 behind, Hanif saved the game by making 337 out of 657 for 8 declared. In 1958–9 West Indies went to India and Pakistan. Worrell could not leave his studies at Manchester University and thus Hall, who had failed to impress in England in 1957, squeezed into the side. Against India Hall took 30 wickets and in three matches against Pakistan 16. In India another newcomer, from Jamaica, Gilchrist, bowled perhaps faster than Hall and took 26 wickets. Sobers and Kanhai, Butcher and Solomon showed that already West Indians had replacements for the three Ws. Three Tests against India were won and two drawn. Pakistan lost the last Test but won the other two.

An MCC team visited the West Indies in 1959–60. Four Tests were drawn and MCC convincingly won the second by 256 runs. Sobers made 709 runs in Tests, scored a century three times and averaged over 100. No other West Indies batsman scored half as many. Ramadhin bowled well at times but Valentine lost his place and the fast bowling of Hall and Watson, though it raised plenty of dust, could not prevent the first five batsmen on the England side averaging over 40 runs per innings. Dexter made over 500 runs and though careful in defence not infrequently showed what powers were yet to come with maturity. Cowdrey after a dismal start missed scoring two centuries in one game by only three runs.

In 1960–1 West Indies visited Australia. Frank Worrell took over as captain from Alexander, who continued as wicket-keeper. Although the side lost two Tests and won only one, history was made. The first Test at Brisbane produced a tie, the only one in the whole history of Tests. Gibbs soon took and more than adequately filled Ramadhin's place as the spin bowler of the side. Sobers, Kanhai and Hunte batted splendidly and were surpassed in figures by a new Alexander. Valentine bowled well if not as well as in 1951. Worrell showed exceptional form both as batsman and captain. In its style of play the team restored to Test cricket the *élan* of the Golden Age. Half a million citizens of Melbourne turned out spontaneously to say goodbye and to speed an early return, a demonstration unprecedented in cricket history. India visited the West Indies in 1962 and West Indies won all five Tests, maintaining their Australian form in every department. After the uninspiring tour of the MCC in Australia in 1962–3 it was openly said that the future of Test cricket would depend on whether the West Indian team would evoke in England the revival they had initiated in Australia.

Many West Indian individuals have played fine cricket all over the Commonwealth but undoubtedly the most valuable service they have given is as league cricketers in Lancashire and other areas of Great Britain. Constantine in 1929 set the pattern and the great majority of West Indian cricketers have found in the Leagues a means of developing themselves which would have been a problem otherwise. At the moment when West Indies cricket was about to assume a not separate but equal status as an independent contributor to the development of the game, a decent respect for the opinions of all interested in a great national creation of the British people requires that the causes of such historic achievements be declared. The West

Indies Cricket Board of Control has always been sustained by clubs in each territory which are lineal descendants of the old aristocratic clubs of the plantocracy and commercial magnates. Their services in West Indies cricket, all proportions strictly guarded, can legitimately be compared to that of MCC in Britain. In the early days they bore the financial risks, they have been tireless in arranging what are now quadrangular tournaments and visiting groups of first-class cricketers. They have organized coaching from Australia and from England. They have managed to adjust themselves to the rising self-consciousness of the West Indian community without irreparable conflicts. Best of all, no part of the Commonwealth in proportion to their numbers has produced a finer body of players. To repeat E.W. Swanton: in the West Indies the cricket ethic has shaped not only the cricketers but life as a whole. If the masses of the West Indian people were now second to none in their almost fanatical devotion to the game, both as players and spectators, it has been largely due to a century of unceasing labour and devotion by this outpost of British society.

In 1963 the West Indies made the tour in England which again lifted Test cricket to a pitch of public interest and excitement which for some years it had been losing. The team consisted of Frank Worrell (Jamaica), Conrad Hunte (Barbados), David Allan (Barbados), Basil Butcher (British Guiana), Michael Carew (Trinidad), Lancelot Gibbs (British Guiana), Charles Griffith (Barbados), Wesley Hall (Barbados), Rohan Kanhai (British Guiana), Lester King (Jamaica), Easton McMorris (Jamaica), Deryck Murray (Trinidad), Seymour Nurse (Barbados), Willie Rodriguez (Trinidad), Garfield Sobers (Barbados), Joseph Solomon (British Guiana), Alfred Valentine (Jamaica); the tour manager was Berkeley Gaskin. A.W. White (Barbados) joined the side in mid-tour. The games are recent enough for scores to be familiar. West Indies won the first Test at Manchester and a magnificent game at Lord's ended in a draw which could easily have been a tie. The match at Edgbaston was lost but West Indies won convincingly at Leeds and, having to make over 250 in the last innings at the Oval, made them for the loss of two wickets. Sobers and Kanhai were great batsmen. Butcher was not far behind and Hunte did all that was required from an opening batsman. Hall maintained his reputation as a fast bowler in the great tradition and Griffith, a newcomer with real pace, showed a subtlety and adaptability which constantly broke up stands by English batsmen. Gibbs was a master of off-spin and flight. Sobers bowling either fast or a bewildering mixture of slows could have been played for bowling alone. A youthful wicket-keeper, Murray, a last-minute selection, had the honour of taking the largest number of wickets by a wicket-keeper in Tests. On the England side Trueman bowling at reduced pace forced a place for himself in the great English tradition of Barnes, Tate and A.V. Bedser. Dexter at Lord's hit the powerful and varied West Indian attack as if they were minor county bowlers: some such innings of 70 must have been played at Lord's by Reginald Hankey over a hundred years ago. West Indians in the crowds contributed much to the renaissance. Yet in a great season the finest cricket on display was the captaincy of Frank Worrell. By his easy mastery of strategy and tactics, his command of his team, his respect for the traditions of the game, and his personal distinction on and off the field he won the admiration and affection of the British public. This stimulating impact of the West Indian visit reached a fitting climax in the chorus of approbation which greeted his knighthood. So strong was the desire to see West Indian cricket again in England that arrangements have been altered so that a team will be here again in 1966.

Kanhai: A Study in Confidence

(*New World*, Guyana, 1966)

Writing critically about West Indies cricket and cricketers, or any cricket for that matter, is a difficult discipline. The investigation, the analysis, even the casual historical or sociological gossip about any great cricketer should deal with his actual cricket, the way he bats or bowls or fields, does all or any of these. You may wander far from where you started, but unless you have your eyes constantly on the ball, in fact never take your eyes off it, you are soon writing not about cricket, but yourself (or other people) and psychological or literary responses to the game. This can be and has been done quite brilliantly, adding a little something to literature but practically nothing to cricket, as little as the story of Jack and the Beanstalk (a great tale) adds to our knowledge of agriculture. This is particularly relevant to the West Indies.

A great West Indies cricketer in his play should embody some essence of that crowded vagueness which passes for the history of the West Indies. If, like Kanhai, he is one of the most remarkable and individual of contemporary batsmen, then that should not make him less but more West Indian. You see what you are looking for, and in Kanhai's batting what I have found is a unique pointer of the West Indian quest for identity, for ways of expressing our potential bursting at every seam.

So now I hope we understand each other. Eyes on the ball.

The first historical innings (I prefer to call them historical now) by Kanhai was less than 50, for British Guiana against the Australians of 1956. Kanhai had not as yet made the West Indies team. He played well but what was remarkable about the innings was not only its promise but that he was the junior in a partnership with Clyde Walcott as senior.

It is a commonplace what Clyde Walcott has done for the cricket of British Guiana. In reality, in truth and in essence, the thing should be stated this way. The tremendous tradition of Barbados batting, the fount and origin of West Indies cricket, through Walcott had begun to fertilize another area in the Caribbean. Kanhai was the first-fruit. Some like to lay emphasis on the fact that he comes originally from the Courantyne, the home not of depressed sugar-workers but of independent rice farmers. There may be something to this. I do not know British Guiana well enough to have on this matter an opinion that is worthwhile. I prefer to remember and to remind of the fact that Christiani coached on the Courantyne. Now Christiani was one of the most brilliant of the brilliant school of West Indies batsmen. Of an innings of 107 not out that he played for the West Indies against the state of Victoria in 1951–2, A.G. Moyes said that it was the most dazzling innings of the Australian season. So that the burgeoning Kanhai inherited not only the universality of Barbados batting but was able to absorb also the individualism of one of the most brilliant of West Indies individualists.

Kanhai played effective innings which resulted in his being selected for the 1957 West Indies tour in England. I am not making a chronicle. I remember, however, the batting that he showed in all the Tests in England. West Indies was scrambling for openers and much of this responsibility was thrown to Kanhai. He bore it without disgrace, with spasms of alternate toughness and brilliance which only later we were to learn were fundamental constituents in his character.

Yet the innings in 1957 that future events caused me to remember most strongly was his last ten innings at the Oval. He faced Trueman and immediately hit him for two uninhibited fours. Gone was the restraint which held him prisoner during all the previous innings against England.

Kanhai, I know now, had made up his mind to have a final fling at the English bowlers. But either he wasn't yet good enough to play such cricket in a Test or he had not shaken off the effect of months of restraint. He was out almost at once. Altogether in 1957 it was the failure of Weekes, Worrell and Walcott to repeat the Victorian cavalry charges of 1950 which threw such burdens on Sobers, Kanhai and Collie Smith. The burden fell most heavily on Kanhai. But the future batsman was there to be discerned.

The next innings that helped to build the Kanhai personality was played as far away as Australia. It was an innings of over two hundred made in one day. Kanhai simply went to the Melbourne wicket and from the first ball hit the Victoria bowlers all over the place until he was tired at the end of the day. It is my firm belief that here again the great Barbados cricket tradition was at work.

In Australia, Frank Worrell made West Indians and the world aware of what West Indians were capable of when their talents had full play. That is Worrell's gift to the West Indian personality. We are much given to individualism (it would be a miracle if we were not). But the West Indians under Worrell could not let themselves go, be their own coruscating selves, knowing that the interest and needs, opportunities and perils of the side as a whole were being observed and calculated by one of the shrewdest minds that the game has known. They could have complete confidence in their captain, go their own way, yet respond immediately to any premonition or request. That the smiting of Victoria was not the kind of brilliant innings which all good batsmen play at some time or other was proved by the fact that Kanhai continued to play that way all through the season. When he made a century in each innings against Australia, he was within an ace of making the second century in even time. Hunte being run out in an effort to help Kanhai towards the century, Kanhai was so upset that it was long minutes before he could make the necessary runs.

Kanhai continued to score, in the West Indies, in India, in Pakistan, but the next great landmark of his career was his innings against England at the Oval in 1963.

All through that season he had never been his new, his Australian self. In Tests he got into the nineties twice, but, while always showing himself a master batsman, something was wrong somewhere; if something was not wrong, at least everything was not right. Then at the Oval, with the fate of the match depending to a substantial degree on his batting (especially after Sobers ran himself out) in this his last test innings in England, Kanhai set off to do to English bowling what he had done to Australian.

Perhaps I should have seen its national significance, its relation to our quest for national identity. Here was a West Indian proving to himself that there was one field in which the West Indian not only was second to none, but was the creator of its own destiny. However, swept away by the brilliance and its dramatic circumstances, I floated with the stream.

1964 was a great year, perhaps the most important year in the steadily growing facts and phenomena I was automatically accumulating about the fascinating Kanhai. High on the list was an opinion which was the climax of many other opinions. All through the Tests of 1964 I sat in press-boxes, most often between Sir Learie Constantine and Sir Frank Worrell. We were reporting England against Australia; there was a lot of talk about cricket and naturally about West Indian cricketers. About Kanhai, for quite a while the only thing notable said was by Worrell. He made a comparison between Kanhai and Everton Weekes as batsmen who would stand back and lash the length ball away on the off-side or to the on-boundary. Then at Leeds, Kanhai himself turned up and came and sat in the press-box. Learie had a long look at him and then turned to me and said: "There is Kanhai. You know at times he goes crazy."

I never believe that an intelligent man or a man whom I know to be well informed about a subject is talking nonsense. I knew that Learie had something in mind. I waited and before long I learnt what it was. I shall try as far as I can to put it in his own words.

"Some batsmen play brilliantly sometimes and at ordinary times they go ahead as usual. That one," nodding at Kanhai, "is different from all of them. On certain days, before he goes into the wicket he makes up his mind to let them have it. And once he is that way nothing on earth can stop him. Some of his colleagues in the pavilion who have played with him for years see strokes that they have never seen before: from him or anybody else. He carries on that way for 60 or 70 or 100 runs and then he comes back with a great innings behind him."

That was illumination indeed, coming from someone who knew all about batting which aimed at hitting bowlers all over the place. It was obvious that at times Kanhai's audacity at the wicket had earned not the usual perfunctory admiration but the deep and indeed awesome respect of Constantine. We both were thinking of the 1963 innings at the Oval. He had hit the English bowlers all over the place, he gave no chance and never looked like getting out. Yet I knew Learie was aware of something in Kanhai's batting that had escaped me. At off times I wondered what it might be.

Going crazy. That could be Greek Dionysius, the satyric passion for the expression of the natural man, bursting through the acquired restraints of disciplined necessity. I played with that idea for a while. Tentatively. I settled for a West Indian proving to himself that henceforth he was following no established pattern but would create his own.

Certainty came at the end of the 1964 season. Sir Frank Worrell led a team of West Indies players against England elevens at Scarborough and Edgbaston (a third game at Lord's was rained out). I reported both games. Kanhai made a century in each, and what I saw no one has written about: nor have I met anyone who appears to have noticed it.

At Scarborough Kanhai was testing out something new. Anyone could see that he was trying to sweep anything near the leg-stump round to fine-leg to beat both deep square and long-leg. He missed the ball more often than he connected. That was easy enough. But I distinctly remember being vaguely aware that he was feeling his way to something. I attributed it to the fact that he had been playing league cricket all the season and this was his first first-class match. Afterwards, I was to recall his careful defence of immaculate length balls from Trevor Bailey, and, without any warning, or fuss, not even a notable follow-through, he took on the rise and lifted it ten feet over mid-on's head to beat wide long-on to the boundary; he never budged from his crease, he had barely swung at the ball. Yet, as far as he was concerned, it was a four predestined.

We went to Edgbaston. Bailey's side had six bowlers who had bowled for England that season. If the wicket was not unresponsive to spin, and the atmosphere not unresponsive to swing, the rise of the ball from the pitch was fairly regular. Kanhai began by giving notice that he expected test bowlers to bowl a length; balls a trifle loose so rapidly and unerringly paid the full penalty that by the time he had made 30 or 40 everybody was on his best behaviour.

Kanhai did not go crazy. Exactly the reverse. He discovered, created a new dimension in batting. The only name I can give to it is "cat-and-mouse". The bowler would bowl a length ball. Kanhai would play a defensive stroke, preferably off the front foot, pushing the ball for one, quite often for two on the on-side — a most difficult stroke on an uncertain pitch, demanding precision footwork and clockwork timing. The bowler, after seeing his best lengths exploited in this manner, would shift, whereupon he was unfailingly despatched to the boundary. After a time it began to look as if the whole sequence had been pre-arranged for the benefit of the spectators. Kanhai did not confine himself too rigidly to this pre-established harmony.

One bowler, to escape the remorseless billiard-like pushes, brought the ball untimely up. Kanhai hit him for six to long-on off the front foot. The bowler shortened a bit. Kanhai in the same over hit him for six in the same place, off the back foot this time. Dexter, who made a brilliant, in fact a dazzling century in the traditional style, hit a ball out of the ground over wide mid-on. Kanhai hit one out of the ground some forty yards further on than Dexter. He made over 170 in about three hours.

Next day, Brian Johnston in the *Daily Mail*, Crawford White in the *Daily Express*, John Woodcock in *The Times* — men who have watched critically all the great players of the last thirty years — made no effort to contain themselves: they had never seen such batting. Here and there some showed that in their minds the Everest conquered by Bradman had been once more scaled.

They were wrong. Kanhai had found his way into regions Bradman never knew. It was not only the technical skill and strategic generalship that made the innings the most noteworthy I have seen. There was more to it, to be seen as well as felt. Bradman was a ruthless executioner of bowlers. All through this demanding innings Kanhai grinned with a grin that could be seen a mile away.

Now to fit his cricket into the history of the West Indies. I saw all his batting against the Australians during their tour of the West Indies in 1965. Some fine play, but nothing in the same category as Edgbaston.

At Melbourne in Australia in 1959, he had experienced a freedom in which his technique could explore roads historically charted, but to him unknown.

He had had to wait until the last Test in England in 1963 to assure himself that his conquest of Australia was not an accident. *Now in 1964 at Scarborough and Edgbaston he was again free; to create not only "a house for Mr Biswas", a house like other houses, but to sail the seas that open out before the East Indian who no longer has to prove himself to anybody or to himself. It was no longer: anything you can do, I can do better.* That had been left behind at the Kennington Oval in 1963. Now it was fresh fields and pastures new, not tomorrow but today. At that moment, Edgbaston in 1964, the West Indian could strike from his feet the dust of centuries. The match did not impose any burdensome weight of responsibility. He was free as few West Indians have been free.

Cricket is an art, a means of national expression. Voltaire says that no one is so boring as the man who insists on saying everything. I have said enough. But I believe I owe it to the many who did not see the Edgbaston innings to say that I thought it showed of the directions that, once freed, the West Indies might take. The West Indies in my view embody more sharply than elsewhere Nietzsche's conflict between the ebullience of Dionysius and the discipline of Apollo. Kanhai's going crazy might seem to be Dionysius in us breaking loose. It was absent from Edgbaston. Instead the phrases which go nearest to expressing what I saw and have reflected upon are those of Lytton Strachey on French Literature: "[the] mingled distinction, gaiety and grace which is one of the unique products of the mature poetical genius of France".

Distinction, gaiety, grace. Virtues of the ancient Eastern Mediterranean city-states, islands, the sea, and the sun. Long before Edgbaston I had been thinking that way. Maybe I saw only what I was looking for. Maybe.

Long may Windies Flourish

(*Sunday Guardian*, Trinidad, 26 June 1966)

"God! I wish I was there." That is the ultimate response to a great cricket match. Not merely for the great stand of Sobers and Holford, one of the greatest the game has ever known. No, you cannot abstract a high moment from five tense days of cricket. Every ball was worth seeing and demands reflection. First, therefore, *before* the game. Next, *during* the game; and thirdly, *after* the game.

Naturally, after Old Trafford, no one expected us to lose. Our batting seemed solid enough. Conrad Hunte should be given a title, Old Everlasting. Our No.7, Holford, had proved himself a good batsman. Any side that got Sobers out for less than a hundred in one innings was doing well. Kanhai might appear

171

to be out of form. But that maker of centuries is a law unto himself.

Yet though Carew might be making good runs, he didn't seem to be of the quality required. At any rate he was better than McMorris. At Leeds in 1963, all McMorris seemed able to do was to put the bat to the fast-medium balls moving in the air and hope for the best. The best, however, systematically eluded him.

Hall seemed unable to find form and further he had not bowled well against Australia in the West Indies. There might be mountains of talk about Griffith, but Griffith, even at fast-medium, was still a very fine bowler, particularly in the heavy English atmosphere.

Gibbs was Gibbs and Sobers was Sobers. Holford, as in his batting, showed great promise. The all-round brilliance of our captain was an inspiration to his men.

On the England side Cowdrey, a batsman of great competence, does not today inspire others. Again, everybody knows that he does not want to be captain, and that he ought to but will not go in first. Milburn alone scintillates. The odds were with us.

Such was the spirit in which one could approach the great event, for a Test match at Lord's is a great event.

From early the crowds filled the famous ground and none could regret a second of the time spent.

West Indies were 3 for 53 and how we recovered is the very essence of what we have restored to the game. Kanhai hit 25 in thirty minutes and Butcher and Nurse did not for one moment go on the defensive as an English or an Australian pair would most certainly have done. Our batsmen are always making strokes. A bowler is not at his best when he knows that the slightest shortcoming on his part is going to be despatched to the boundary.

Next day West Indies reached 269, Holford again playing a promising innings. England seemed to go right ahead with 145 for 2 at the end of the day.

Saturday showed the West Indies side at its best. The England batsmen, with 145 on the board and 8 wickets in hand, needed only to add another 100 runs and then pile on the agony towards the end of the day.

They were not allowed to do it.

Cricketers all over the world must have rejoiced to see Hall coming back into his own with 4 wickets. Gibbs bowled 37 overs for 48 runs and Sobers obviously had a firm grip on his side. It was quite clear that if England had to make more than 200 runs to win in the last innings, at Lord's they would have a lot of trouble to make them against our bowling.

Next day, we faced disaster when 5 wickets were gone for 93 and we were less than 10 ahead. But Kanhai and Nurse did not create a situation in which the batsmen were on the defensive and bowlers in the ascendant.

Sobers and Holford may have had little to follow. At no time did they ever seem unduly troubled. In fact Cowdrey kept four men on the boundary for Sobers, and one can reasonably suppose that Holford's unsuspected technical skill was morally fortified by the mastery opposite to him and the respect which it inspired. No greater appreciation could be paid to them than the guard of honour which the English players formed for the pair as they walked in.

The question arises whether Sobers was not soft, not to say sentimental, in allowing Holford half an hour to move from 90 to 96. It is difficult to say. Sobers may have been fortifying his team by nursing another Test-match batsman. Gary is apparently easygoing but in reality is a very tough customer. If he chose to let the youthful Holford go on to the century, then that is what he did and that's all there is to it.

But this amazing match had not yet finished with the incidental excitements of which it was so prodigal. England, set 284 to win, were 4 for 67. Griffith knocked the wickets of Barrington flying, to the immense satisfaction of all who have resented Barrington's remarks about Griff's action. But while Graveney held up an end Milburn smote the bowling in the manner that English batting so much needs, and England with 197 ended with colours flying.

Barring the calculated malice of the weather, the West Indies should not lose another Test. There is only one gap in the armoury, a batsman to open the innings with Hunte. We may find one.

Higgs is obviously a formidable bowler but he is alone, Graveney may restore his personal reputation, but he cannot give English batting what Milburn alone cannot give it. The odds are still heavily with us. Reason cannot ask for more.

This game, however, has been remarkable for us not only because of the brilliance of our individual players but because it shows as sharply as ever who and what we are. Ever since Frank Worrell had led West Indies at Brisbane in 1959 we have been the catalyst in a succession of great cricket matches. That is what we of this generation have brought into this game which when others play it seems to be on its last legs as a public entertainment.

In these recent games the people of the West Indies are finding themselves, what we have been in the past and may be in the future. Worthily Barbados dominated this game. It is a reasonable calculation that a Barbados eleven with Bynoe, Lashley and Brancker could meet all England or all Australia on equal terms.

May I be allowed to quote from a recent article on Kanhai. I first noted Kanhai's brilliant double century in Australia against Victoria and I placed it in its relation to the great tradition of Barbados cricket:

> But the West Indians under Worrell could let themselves go, be their own coruscating selves, knowing that the interest and needs, opportunities and perils of the side as a whole were being observed and calculated by one of the shrewdest minds that the game has known. They could have complete confidence in the captain, go their own way, yet respond immediately to any premonition or request. That the smiting of Victoria was not the kind of brilliant innings which all good batsmen play at some time or other was proved by the fact that Kanhai continued to play that way all through the season.

This for West Indians.

Yet for Englishmen the most endearing (and enduring) memory of this game may well have been first the West Indians pouring on to the field (and this at Lord's) to congratulate Sobers and Holford personally; and, not to be outdone, Englishmen pouring on to the field to give their personal felicitations to Milburn when this Englishman had made his century.

There was a time when one could hear at Lord's: "We don't have that sort of thing here." But first they had it, then they liked it, and now they are taking part in it.

Floreat Antilles.

After that Nottingham Defeat . . . .

(*Sunday Guardian*, Trinidad, 10 July 1966)

In cricket you always have to keep your eyes on the game. Now we have to add our ears. Two new players have entered into this England *vs* West Indies series. They score boundaries every hour every day; for example:

"Do you know that although Cristopher Columbus discovered the West Indies he never represented it at Lord's?"

"That is a fact, a most interesting fact. But you don't seem to know that in addition to Denis Atkinson and De Peiza holding the world record for the seventh wicket, two West Indians, George Headley and C.C. Passailaigue, have held the world record, 487, for the sixth wicket, since 1931–2."

"A MOST interesting fact. I have looked it up while you were talking and I see that it is correct. Do you know. . .?"

All I know is that these gentlemen will be in a lot of trouble to keep this going for two more Tests. They have done pretty well so far but they seem to have exhausted their range already.

However, sufficient unto the day is the good thereof. And although they were an intrusion they had virtue. A word or two later about the English *commentators*.

Now to begin with the teams. The West Indies team was not only superior in every respect but (risky though it is, I am prepared to take the risk) we should not lose another Test, barring whatever malicious (and chauvinist) tricks the English weather may play against us in a particular game.

There seems to have been a feeling about in England that for three days England held the upper hand. Unless you are there to see, your impressions are always second-hand. But though second-hand they can nevertheless be solidly grounded. Never at any time did I feel that England was on top.

Yes, they got us out for 235. Terrible? Even shameful? Indulge in your masochism as freely as you please. Not only did we on the same day get out three wickets for 33. But there was always our second innings. And I stick firmly to my belief that I do not see the English bowlers who can get us out twice for small scores in five days.

Our batting proved itself more than adequate to any strains that may be placed on us. That D'Oliveira and Underwood made a last-wicket stand which gave the Englishmen a lead of 90 would not have caused any flutter in the mind of any mature West Indian.

The English batting on the whole was not good enough for Test cricket. Cowdrey and Graveney made a fine stand. But before them there was nothing; and after them there was little. The England second innings was almost as bad, in fact it was worse. That some member of the side made over 70 runs was quite natural. Somebody always does. But batting, in the sense of command of the bowling, there was the stand in the first innings, and in the second innings there was none.

For comparative judgement, just look at the line of our batsmen in this Test: Hunte, Lashley, Kanhai, Butcher, Nurse, Sobers, Holford.

We can reasonably expect that Lashley at No.2 will do his share in the fourth and fifth Tests. In his second innings, Holford showed himself to be in command of the situation, brief though it might have been.

As a team there is nothing in the England batting to correspond. It is the same thing when you come to the bowling. Our bowling was not only able to meet all strain or to reassert itself after any check. When it was most needed, Griffith in the last innings reasserted his old self not only with 4 for 34, but with the wickets of Boycott, Graveney and D'Oliveira. Our bowling and our batting have reserves which can emerge at any moment that seems to demand it.

About the fielding I am rather confused. Both sides seem to have dropped catches which should have been held. There is only one catch about which we can be concerned. On Monday afternoon, from the last ball of the day, Lashley dropped Milburn. It was most disappointing.

Your captain declares and gives the other side half an hour's batting, against fast bowling. Every nerve should be stretched to its full height. You are on the tips of your toes.

In those circumstances you can add a foot or two to your reach and take catches that in other circumstances you would miss. Particularly the last ball of the day is important. As is the last ball of any session. The batsman is likely to relax and feel that he only has to play one ball and then go in.

I could give many examples of how important is this last ball of a session, particularly to new batsmen and fielders in the slips or near the wicket, during the last half-hour of the day. It is to guard against this menace that we have the nightwatchman.

As to strategy, against Cowdrey, I have nothing to say. There are those who blame him for not taking more advantage of the situation at such and such a point. Those people are romantics. Cowdrey did the best he could with what he had.

It is not the business of the bowlers to bowl maiden overs, but to get batsmen out. Besides Cowdrey's temperament of going on the defensive is known. I would say that the best thing for England is to select a new team, new captain and all, and let the twelve men know that they will play in both coming Tests.

In regard to West Indian strategy, Gary Sobers was magnificent, all things to all men on his side, to the England team an avenging angel. Only one point arises: the monotonous forward defensive of Kanhai on Saturday afternoon. Distance lends enchantment to what may have been actually very irritating to the view.

But there never should have been any misunderstanding as to what was going on. Kanhai hit 23 in thirty-two minutes. In the next two hours he made 17. From the beginning, the reason was quite obvious. It was when Lashley got out that Kanhai closed down. It is certain that during the interval he must have had instructions from Sobers, who would not have allowed so sharp a change in the game without expressing his wishes. The thing was to make sure that Nurse, and Sobers himself, would come in on the Monday. Kanhai and Butcher were not to get out and allow the English bowlers after a rest on Sunday to start off all cock-a-hoop on the Monday. That was what the situation required and that was done.

Two more points only, in reality, one. The English commentators play a great part in the game for us who are listening. Yardley is as usual quite cautious. Freddy Brown is, as he always has been, more adventurous. These men are former captains of England. Whatever they say is worth listening to. They are quite fair and when England is doing well all that they allow themselves (or what happens to them) is an increasing excitement in the selection of incident and heightened pace and pitch in the voice.

The only real reporter is John Arlott. Arlott may seem to show a special interest in the volatile West Indian members of the crowd. That is not really so. He has always been interested in the responses of all cricket crowds.

He had a special warmth for the success of D'Oliveira. I shared his feelings. About racialism in cricket I have had this to say to those who deplore it: "Those exquisites remind me of ribaldry about Kant's Categorical Imperative; there was racialism in cricket, there is racialism in cricket, there will always be racialism in cricket. But there ought not to be!"

"Ought not to", indeed! The whole of Africa was watching D'Oliveira's success and the majority, in South Africa, in particular rejoicing at this demonstration of the irrationality which prevents such a man from playing for the country of his birth. I am not African but I revelled in it.

Does anyone follow Kant with his "ought not to be"? Better not, or you will be bowled down with a yorker faster than Griffith's fastest.

A Question of Cricket Approach . . . and the Journey Homeward to Habitual Self

(*Sunday Guardian*, Trinidad, 14 August 1966)

Two issues dominate the fourth Test match, the one negative, the other positive.

The negative issue is the defeat of the English team. The English have not only been beaten, they have been disgraced. The results read very much like England versus New Zealand in 1965.

The question is: Why? To think or to say that they did not have men good enough, or (which is the same thing) that our players were immeasurably superior, is to say what is immediately, even superficially, obvious and commonplace. There is more to it than this.

The English failure was due to what Neville Cardus said about them in Australia, 1936–7: weakness of technique and weakness of character. It is my personal view that when fifty million people present eleven men who consistently fail technically, at the back of this failure can be discerned the weakness of fundamental character. Needless to say, character is in their approach to the game.

First example. The West Indians had made 324 runs before Cowdrey thought that he could try Barber. Now Barber is a bowler, a leg-break and googly bowler. He has been spinning off his wrist for some years now with more rather than less success. In 1963, Barber, in first-class matches, took 50 wickets, at a cost of 28.66 each. In South Africa in 1964–5, he took 21 wickets at a similar cost.

It is not only that, at Leeds, he got out Sobers, it is that he bowled well and his average of 14 overs for 55 runs compares favourably with all other English bowlers. Yet it took over 300 runs to give him a chance.

You get a glimpse into the difference between those two teams when you see that in the second innings Sobers very rapidly put on Lashley, who is no kind of bowler at all. Whereupon Lashley got out one of the strongest batsmen on the English side at the cost of one run. This is no mere mistake of judgement or oversight on Cowdrey's part. In 1966, that is the way the English play. They have acquired a certain routine and they stick to it. Emergence from that routine is an adventure. Whether it succeeds or fails, it is merely a flash in the dark, preliminary to a return to routine, the journey homeward to habitual self, the safe harbour of the often tried. Which can be dignified by the routine phrase of:"Well tried."

This is by no means new. In 1964, Dexter was the English captain. The Australians would make 200 runs and it would never cross Dexter's mind to try Barber.

Instead, it seems that the retreat has sunk deep into the well-worn grooves. Today, the English bowlers earn their "Well tried" by bowling maiden overs. An English bowler will bowl twelve overs, of which eight are maidens. For this, he receives the approval, if not the plaudits, of commentators and writers. Now at times this bowling of maiden overs can mean a demoralization of the batting side. There are occasions when batsmen have been so tied up in defence that when a full pitch or long hop came along, they were so confused that they made a stupid stroke and got out. They are so wound up for defence that they cannot unwind for aggression. In 1963 this happened to the English team in Barbados.

But nothing like that is happening to the West Indian batsmen. After those maiden overs, the West Indian batsmen are stroke-makers always looking for runs. And this long succession of maiden overs, with the bowler ultimately getting no wickets, looks suspiciously to me as if the bowlers have set out to bowl maiden overs. They concentrate on maiden overs, i.e. on not being hit. Which means that they are leaving it to the batsmen to get themselves out.

A similar routine is taking place in regard to English batting. The man who has shown it up so far for what it is, is D'Oliveira, who climaxed his consistent batting with an 88 that included four sixes. But for him (and Higgs) we would have been left with an entirely false idea of the unplayability of the West Indian bowling.

Our bowlers are good, in fact very good, but they are not that good. D'Oliveira, that South African, is not dominated by the defensive routine of English batsmen. He has grown up in a different world and he plays a different game.

The English critics and the English public have their eyes fixed hungrily on Milburn. They are fascinated, and rightly so. Because Milburn is obviously one who is ready to break through all routine and regulations and to handle a bat as if it is a sword and not a shield.

The feeble character and feeble technique of the English

batting is further proved by the scoring of Higgs. Higgs, it is obvious, is a man of limited batting technique. He plays down the line and scoops the ball to the on-boundary, whenever he thinks he can get away with it. That is not very competent batting. But first of all, he is a bowler and, from all appearances, a fine bowler. His batting, therefore, is for him an adventure, a means of self-expression on which his place on the side does not depend. No routine or regulations for him with his bat in his hand. The result is that, as has always happened in the history of the game, he makes runs when they are needed.

The success of Higgs as a bowler points to one fundamental weakness of the England side. What Higgs needs is another bowler. In a series of Test matches you do not need anyone more than a pair of bowlers. Two are enough. Gregory and McDonald. Francis and John. Grimmett and O'Reilly. Lindwall and Miller. Ramadhin and Valentine. Hall and Griffith. You need only two.

The other bowlers on the side set themselves to fill in the gaps and, under the umbrella of genius, they usually manage it. The difficulty with Higgs is that he has at the other end not bowlers, but machines made to order for bowling maiden overs. And I am not so sure that the English selectors are looking for a partner for Higgs, someone who with him will form a pair.

That, then, is the weakness of the England side. It is a weakness that has been known for years.

At present leading the battle for a renaissance, for a reformation in the attitude of the English Test players to the game, is a West Indian, Sir Learie Constantine. One of his recent broadsides is an article in the 1965 Wisden entitled: "Cricket — an Art not a Science."

Let us note that South Africa went that same way for years. But McLean, their great forcing batsman, set himself to change it. He argued, lectured and coached. The result is that in Australia two boys, Pollock and Barlow, startled the world by the brilliance of their play. They were in England in 1965. People who saw them have told me that they reminded spectators of nothing so much as the descent of the three Ws on England in 1950.

So much for the negative. We shall now accentuate the positive.

The most positive feature of the West Indian victory, of the whole game, is the incredible, the transcendent, the ineffable Garfield Sobers.

Now a great deal is being said and written (including some

particularly vapid adjectives) about Sobers. So far I have not seen or heard the things which I think matter most.

His bowling. Sobers is able, either with his fast balls or his slow, to bowl any batsman out at any stage of his innings. I have seen him do it, repeatedly. The only other bowler that I can remember who had this quality to such a degree was the Kent bowler, Douglas Wright. The only trouble with Wright was that his fast leg-break often beat batsman, wicket and wicket-keeper, some of his finest deliveries going for four byes. Sobers is as devastating but less excessive.

Sobers's batting. Critics are now talking about his driving. His driving is a testimony to his unique mastery of batting. When I say unique, I mean unique, i.e. something I have not met before. In 1958–9, when the Englishmen were here, Sobers like every great batsman made strokes all around. But, like most great batsmen, he had one stroke unique to himself. The most dangerous ball to a left-hander was the ball from a fast-medium or a fast bowler which hit on the off-stump or middle and off and went away. To this particular ball, Sobers developed a scoring stroke.

From the back foot he put it away past cover's right hand, and such was his precision and timing and mastery that round about the stroke grew the phrase: "Not a man moved!" You remember it, I don't doubt, the phrase if not the stroke.

In time bowlers have learned that to try to get him there meant more often than not a certain four. To pitch the ball shorter meant that he would cut it, make the stroke past the bowler, or even hook. They therefore have got into the habit of avoiding his back stroke and try to pitch the ball between the good length and the half-volley. Mark now how Sobers has countered.

People talk about his driving. What he is really doing is going to meet the ball, off the front foot it is true, but *he is taking that ball on the rise.* He sees it drop, sees it rise and then, from his high back lift and with a tremendous swing, he puts it away through the covers, or through the mid-off. It will seem as if the bowler is bowling half-volleys, but he is not.

I listen to the accounts and get the impression that to escape this uninhibited driving the bowlers are shortening the length somewhat, whereupon once more we are back at: "Not a man moved." The style, the method and the result are the very reverse of English routine.

His fielding. I have heard nobody say that a great deal of the menace of Lance Gibbs's bowling, especially to the right-handed batsman, is the batsman's consciousness of the sinister figure of Sobers, three or four yards behind his back, not in metaphor but in actuality a fieldsman ten feet tall.

This is not the place to speak of his captaincy, or his effect on his own men and on the opposing side. The capabilities of his own men he multiplies by two, his opponents' he divides.

E.W. Swanton compares Sobers to F.S. Jackson, who captained England in 1905 and headed the batting and bowling averages. But Jackson was a change bowler (as indeed was W.G. Grace). A change bowler Sobers is most certainly not.

I prefer now to speak of what must be his impact upon the public which watches cricket. I do not think I can do better than to quote from the poem written by Lorca to express his sorrow at the death of his friend, a great bullfighter:

> There never was a prince in Seville to compare to him, nor a sword like his sword, nor a heart so true. Like a river of lions was his astonishing strength, and like a marble torso his outstanding discretion. An air of Andalusian Rome gilded his head, on which his smile was a tuberose of wit and intelligence. What a great bullfighter in the ring! What a good countryman in the Sierra!

In the cricket ring that we know there was never such a great fighter, never. But is he, or will we find him to be, a good countryman in our sierras? That, we must know, depends more upon us than on him.

Why Windies Fade in the End

(*Sunday Guardian*, Trinidad, 28 August 1966)

What in the name of heaven happened to the West Indies team in this last Test? We have been beaten. But anybody can be beaten in a Test. To repeat a phrase, we have been beaten, and it looks perilously as if we have been disgraced. I do not think so, however.

What happened to them is a stage in their development. We are the kind of team for whom the last Test of a series is always a crucial matter, and I shall spend most of my time today showing first of all that this is so and, secondly, attempting some speculation as to why this should be so.

The history of this series of Tests is as follows. We began

splendidly and continued that way. More than once we worked ourselves with great self-confidence out of the mess in which every team finds itself at some time or other. We established an unquestioned superiority over our opponents and then crumbled to dust in this last Test.

With this in mind look now, please, at the 1965 series against Australia. At Sabina Park, we had first innings on the Sabina wicket and made only 239. We then went on to 373, 429, 386, 355, 180 (when we were 166 ahead and were piling on the runs helter-skelter), 573, 242 for 5. By this time we had won the series; and note what happened to us then. We got in the first innings 224, of which Kanhai made 121, and in our last innings we were all out for 131. I remember the bails of Kanhai and Sobers flying in the air as if you or I were batting. After we had won the series we simply didn't have it in us.

We do not play much first-class cricket together. Our men are mobilized to play Test matches only at the cost of great tension. And the moment we have achieved the objective we fade away at once into eleven individuals who go through the routines and are no longer a Test side.

That is what I think has happened. If we had to play England another game, I am confident we would give them a sound beating.

Knowing what we now know, let us look back at two series, 1959–60 in Australia and 1963 in England. In 1959–60 in Australia the West Indies players had at last, under Worrell, found themselves.

In the fifth Test the series is still hanging in the balance. The tension of Test-match self-mobilization remains and in this last Test against Australia they play a tremendous match. They scored 292 and 391 and, although Australia scrambled home by two wickets, everybody knows that during the last hour we dominated the game and fought the Australians as they have never been fought before.

To repeat: the series was still in question and we remained mobilized.

In 1963, in England, the same thing happened. When we played the last Test at the Oval, the series was still in question. England actually led us by 29 runs on the first innings. The wicket and the weather were not dependable. On the Saturday night and over that weekend many people were in doubt as to whether we would make the 250 runs required. In the fourth innings of a Test, that is a big score and especially so at the Oval.

We rose grandly to the occasion and knocked off the runs for the loss of only two wickets. Not only that. We played in such a way that people could see (and say) that if we had 500 runs to make we would have made them.

That then is my summary of this disintegration in this fifth Test of 1966 — for disintegration it was, not defeat nor mere collapse, a total negation.

A few marks about certain players on our side. Kanhai made a century. I was as certain as anyone could be of an individual in cricket that he was going to make a century in this Oval Test. Secondly, when the top batting had failed, Hall and Griffith recovered some of what the team had lost, the two of them put their heads down and batted in genuine Test-match style; that is, for bowlers.

For the Englishmen, Graveney's innings of 165 run out was actually and historically one of the great Test-match innings and I shall be able to deal with Graveney more fully and adequately in a summary of the five Tests. I also accept completely the great innings of Murray. Murray can bat, and there have been many instances where a good batsman, in a central situation and aided by high-class batting at the opposite end, rises to a status above his habitual self. This happened to Murray; and, indeed, with the series lost, everything to gain and nothing to lose in this last match, many a beaten team plays up at its absolute best as the Englishmen did so, particularly when led by a captain of militant reputation.

However, what I believe tells us the complete story of this last Test is the last-wicket stand of Higgs and Snow. To be quite frank, I couldn't take it. I would turn off the radio for about fifteen minutes and turn it back on, presuming that by that time one had been dismissed. I did that three or four times, but it seemed as if these two bowlers would bat for ever. I had a lot of time to think.

Now that last partnership can stand serious examination. Remember, please, that the bowling side is the best bowling side in the world today. Note also that Sobers, the West Indies captain, had never lost grip of his side. Repeatedly, when the situation seemed to be getting out of hand, he himself came on to bowl and dismissed a batsman threatening to give trouble. Yet this last wicket put on 128 runs.

We have to look statistically at what they did and who were the men who did it. The best last-wicket stand by Englishmen against the Australians is 130 by R.E. Foster and Wilfred Rhodes in 1903–4. Not only was Rhodes already a sound batsman but Foster, a great batsman, had been hitting the Australian bowlers all over the place. He ended with a score for the innings of 287.

The Australian record for the last wicket is 127, made over forty years ago in 1924–5 by J.M. Taylor and A.A. Mailey. Taylor also was unquestionably a great batsman; all Mailey had to do was to keep his end up.

Now if we look at West Indies Test scores for the last wicket we find that we have never made a century. The closest we ever reached is 96, with Frank Worrell one of the batsmen. The best we have ever reached against England is 55 and Frank Worrell that day made 191 not out. Against us England's record score for the tenth wicket is 56, made in 1947–8 in Port of Spain by Jim Laker and H. Butler; and in his early days Laker could bat.

But look at these two who have made 128 against one of the finest bowling teams within living memory. You look at the English averages for 1964. The qualifications for admission to the batting list is 10 runs per innings. Neither Higgs nor Snow reached this peak. Snow's top score for the season was 28, Higgs's was 43 with an average for Lancashire of 8.47. For 1965 they made it. Snow got in from the bottom with an average of 10.07 and a top score of 27.

In other words this stand that they have made is something that, when all the circumstances are taken into consideration, is a feat unprecedented in the whole history of Test matches.

Graveney hitting, and one of them defending, yes, but the two of them! All I can take refuge in is a phrase: "the glorious uncertainty" of the game. All honour to them.

If a man does something then, it is necessary to presume that he is the kind of man who can do such a thing.

But I remain obstinate in my belief that they caught the West Indies at a bad moment and that in future not only the captain but our whole side should recognize that we have a tendency, when we have won a series, to relax and run a serious risk of going to pieces.

Two Cricketing Societies — Glorious Windies and the Defensive English

(*Sunday Guardian*, Trinidad, 4 September 1966)

In the summer of 1966, two civilizations, at different stages of their development, met in sharp but friendly conflict on the cricket fields of England. The West Indies, one of the contestants, won a decisive if not completed victory. Whereby we learnt much not only of the cricketing abilities, but of the past, present and future alternatives of both these societies, each of which is so important to us.

As a team (the first consideration) and as individual players, we of the small, in fact minute, West Indian territory established an unquestioned superiority.

Most noticeably at Lord's and elsewhere (except in the last Test) we showed the hallmark of a superior team, the capacity to fight our way out of a dangerous situation, in fact one trembling on the brink of catastrophe. At Leeds we showed the capacity to be contemptuous of mere safety from defeat, to estimate that we could take a chance and win, and do it with banners flying.

Our disintegration in the last Test does not worry me. As far as I am concerned the ancient rules of arithmetic still hold good. One from five leaves not nought but four, and our play in the first four of the Tests is the standard by which we must and shall be judged.

In batting we had five men for whom I would not exchange one (except perhaps for Graveney) on the opposite side. Our bowling is the same. I do not want to exchange our bowling team or any individual member of it. From all accounts our fielding was always good, at times magnificent.

To crown all this we had one cricketer who stands unique among all cricketers within living memory, surpassed by none in any department of the game. There have been comparisons between Sobers and the three Ws and Bradman, etc.

To all such petty mathematics I turn a deaf ear and blind eye. A batsman can only bat against the people who bowl at him. A bowler can only bowl at batsmen who stand in front of him.

Those who are pertinacious praisers of the players of past times are forced to accept that much. What they do not seem to understand is that to compare Higgs and Snow to Lindwall and Miller, and by that to judge the quality of Sobers, as a batsman, is to commit a gross logical and historical error. How do they know that against bowling superior to that which he faces at the present Sobers would not expand and produce even more wonderful batting than he does now?

There are players (not many) of a style and personal history of whom it can be said that both physically and spiritually they would achieve mastery of any problem set them. There are a few people like that and Sobers is definitely one of the breed.

That much being said of the actual play and players, we may now look at the societies which in 1966 were expressing themselves on the cricket fields of England. That is what cricket is and that is what it does.

The symbolical episode that constantly recurs to me about these Tests is the West Indies making 300 runs for the loss of four wickets before Cowdrey put on Barber to bowl. It is not merely that Barber bowled well, got out Sobers, and in the last Test was notably successful. That sort of thing can be seen as a mistake in judgement, and such things constantly happen in cricket, large as well as small, and in all departments of life. What makes the incident illustrative was because, first, from the time the score was about 100 I kept on saying to myself: "He ought to put on Barber. I am certain of that, but I am equally certain he will not."

He didn't. Next morning in the *Daily Telegraph* E.W. Swanton commented on this disinclination to deviate from the normal. He said that he doubted if M.J.K. Smith, the deposed English captain, or D.B. Close, the prospective captain, would have put on Barber before Cowdrey tried him. He thought that each would have ignored Barber just as Cowdrey did. Such tactics, he went on to explain, were part of the defensive attitude characteristic of English cricket today.

This is not a matter of exposing the personal deficiencies of Cowdrey. If it were, I would not single out a very fine cricketer and a quite gallant gentleman for opprobrious notice in this way. It is a social expression which we are watching.

Wisden's Almanack for some time now has been firing all its guns at the defensive attitude which in cricket has overtaken England and, for that matter, cricket everywhere except in the West Indies. It subsumes the very technique of cricket today. Listen to this:

> So now the left foot instinctively moves forward — before the ball is bowled, the left elbow cocked, and in that position unless the ball is pitched up to the batsman he cannot drive, nor can he hook, and the cut provided he chooses to make it becomes a slash.

187

In fact almost all the strokes in that early movement increase the margin of error and because the intention is to reduce — not increase — the margin of error the stroke is entirely eliminated.

On the other hand the bowlers who have been trying from time immemorial to equate the situation between batsmen and themselves, finding that only bad balls are punished — if at all — have devised the scheme of bowling short of a length, waiting for the prods and pushes which have become the standard shots of the day.

That is the defensive style which now dominates English play. So that the defensive, dignified as the scientific, has become a ball and chain on the feet of English cricketers.

It is not that England does not produce men of the calibre of A.C. MacLaren, Johnny Tyldesley, F.S. Jackson, R.H. Spooner, S.F. Barnes, Hirst, Rhodes and the great men of the golden age.

Cowdrey was born one of those. I saw him in 1953 playing for the gentlemen of England against the Australians at Lord's, and I remember saying to myself: "Well, MacLaren has come again." What has happened to him? Here is an account in *Wisden* of 1966:

> Of Cowdrey also there are many who feel that, great as he is, he might be greater. It seems impossible that a bowler should ever keep within bounds one who is so immensely strong whether off his back foot or his front, who plays so straight and so close to his legs and who is such a fine on-side player; and indeed on his great days few bowlers can do so.
>
> No bowler likes being dealt with as Cowdrey can deal with him or bowls so well if he is.
>
> Alas! too many of his innings both for Kent and England have been played at a time when his failure would mean disaster for the side.
>
> How different his approach might have been had he come in after Hardinge and Ashdown, with Woolley. Ames and Chapman to follow.
>
> Still, at his best he and he alone of recent Kent players can remind one of the great days of the past.

I dismiss that excuse, of not having great batsmen on his side, dismiss it absolutely.

I have watched the spirit of the age conquer Cowdrey. It was inherent but not inevitable. There is a very great batsman in England who is avoiding it by carrying on warfare against everybody and everything in the cricket world of which he does not approve.

There are many things that Dexter says with which I do not at all agree. I believe that he is not a good captain. But behind it all

I can see a man striving to maintain the genius of his individuality against the swamp of the prevailing shibboleths.

The idea that Cowdrey's style was altered by the fact that he did not have a line of great batsmen to precede or follow him is quite untrue.

C.B. Fry used to call George Headley "Atlas", Atlas because he carried the whole West Indian side on his shoulders. Yet in his last year Headley was what he had always been (and in my mind still remains), "the one and only George".

What has happened to English cricket? And what has *not* happened to cricket in the West Indies? I shall have to be brief and summary but the thing has been done already at great length and can stand up to concentration.

First the English. And then ourselves.

The English had a great period of cricket, from 1895–1914. That was also the last stage of the domination of Western civilization by Britain, and the preparation for the new stage of the British struggle for their place in the sun. The upheaval produced several remarkable men, including the great adventurous and creative cricketers known as the men of the golden age. 1914 was the end and since that time, and more than ever since the end of World War II, Britain is on the defensive.

In cricket they play down the line and bowl short. That is merely a reflection of their struggle to adjust their former grandeur to their present limitation. Politically Harold Macmillan was an adept at playing down the line and Harold Wilson is an expert at the ball of good length but short.

Nothing is wrong with Englishmen as such. Nobody I have seen has ever played a more brilliant innings in a Test than Dexter. Higgs is obviously one of the great ones, a potential, as was Cowdrey in 1953. But unless the whole cricketing climate of Britain changes Higgs will be tamed, as Cowdrey has been tamed, and as Peter May was being tamed.

We, of the West Indies, are now passing through our golden age. Ever since the Moyne commission reported in 1945, a great social upheaval has been taking place in the English Caribbean. It has produced some remarkable men, above all the writers and the cricketers. When it will stop, when and how we will meet our 1914, I don't know.

But Sobers is not an accident of the cricket field. He is the West Indian potential expressing itself in a sphere where the circumstances are made to order. Sometimes you have yourself to make the circumstances. And that is very hard.

But the British, the Australians, the South Africans, have

created the Test-match milieu. We are inheritors, not creators, but we are keeping alive a great tradition, and doing so in the only way that is ever done, by adding something of our own, remaking it anew.

This type of analysis can be easily misused. Take the case of Graveney. Graveney, in 1966, is in the great tradition. This is how. He grew up and came to maturity in Gloucestershire, the county of Walter Hammond, the sole Englishman between the wars who was authentically of the golden age.

A tradition can count enormously. Behind Sobers are the three Ws, Derek Sealy, Challenor and Tarilton. When, oh, when, will a history of West Indies cricket be written? Much of our social history is locked up therein.

George Headley

(From *Cricket: The Great Ones*, edited by John Arlott, Pelham Books, 1967)

The bare facts about Headley are striking enough. They are not only illuminating in themselves. When fitted into a wider scope and more organic reference they impose formidable, almost terrifying questions.

Here are the facts: born in Panama of Jamaican parents, Headley is sent to Jamaica about the age of ten in order to be sure to get a British education, at least an education in the English language, and not in the Spanish native to Panama. In Jamaica he begins to play cricket as did all little boys in Jamaica in those days. He does so well that in 1928, not yet nineteen years of age, he is brought to the notice of the cricket authorities in the island. He does so well in trial matches that he is given an opportunity to play for Jamaica against a visiting English first-class team. He makes 78 and follows it up with 218. Continuing to score heavily, he is an early choice for the West Indies Test side against the 1929–30 MCC team. Not yet twenty-one years of age, Headley makes 24 and 176; 8 and 36; 114 and 112; 10 and 223.

Naturally, he was a certainty for the West Indies trip to Australia 1931–2. He made 1,000 runs in the tour, two centuries in Tests, and from the beginning of the season he established a reputation as being in the full tradition of the great line of attacking batsmen. He came to England in 1933. West Indies played three Tests. Headley made 50 in the first at Lord's, 169 not out at Old Trafford and before he could get going at the Oval in the third Test, he was stretched out flat on the turf, having missed a hook off Clark, the fast left-hand Northants bowler. He was third in the English averages for the season at 66 per innings to the 67 of Hammond and Mead.

In 1934–5 a powerful English team visited the West Indies. Headley did not score quite as usual. To begin with he made 44 and 0; 25 and 93; and then 53. That was good enough for most batsmen, but not George Headley. In the last Test in Jamaica England begun by making a mighty score of 849. Headley came into his own with 270 not out, and the Englishmen having to catch a boat, the game was left unfinished. He came to England with the West Indies team in 1939. He scored a century in each innings at Lord's, 51 on a wet wicket at Manchester and 65 run out at the Oval when there was scarcely a man on the ground who would have laid odds against his making at least one century. There his career really ended. In Test matches he scored 2,190 runs in 40 innings with an average of 60.83. Only Bradman's figures stand above this. In 40 innings he made 10 centuries, again approached only by Bradman. And those centuries were made against England and against Australia. Headley never collected centuries against New Zealand, Pakistan or India.

That historical account is, for historical purposes, quite adequate. However, it leaves unanswered the question of questions: how comes it that a little West Indian boy untaught, either by instructor or the associations of public school, university or county, how comes it that before he was twenty-one such a boy would have made himself into a cricketer who would have been welcome in any eleven that has existed in England or Australia between 1866 and the present day?

That is the problem which we have to face. For when all allowances are made for qualitative individuality, for historical idiosyncrasy, we still remain face to face with a miracle. And with a miracle one either faces up to it or evades the issue behind a barrage of words of mystification of phrases.

We shall face up to the miracle of George Headley on three grounds:
1. His individual uniqueness.
2. What he learnt of the game.
3. How he managed to learn it.
The three points are more tightly intertwined, closer to being

strands of a unity, than they appear at first sight. But as Napoleon used to say: first you engage and then you see. Let us engage.

Headley's uniqueness made itself effectively felt nearly fifty years ago when he was a boy in Panama and continues to be a notable feature of his personality to this very day.

George may have been eight, he was certainly no more than ten, when he stood on a field in Panama watching some men play a game of rounders (a sort of baseball with a soft ball). George did not understand what they were doing but merely looked on interestedly. Suddenly the ball was hit in his direction and the attention of the whole field was concentrated on it. Somehow he knew that he was to catch it. At any rate he went at the ball, jumped into the air and pulled it down to the applause of the surrounding spectators.

To George's surprise he was surrounded by many of the players, grown men, who asked him if he had played before. George said: "No." They wanted to know, at least some of them did, if he would play for their side in what appeared to be a big match due on the Sunday coming. George said that he could not decide, they would have to ask his parents. The leaders of the team accompanied George to his home to ask his parents if they would allow George to play with them on the Sunday coming. Somewhat bewildered but convinced finally that there was nothing illegal nor illicit involved, George's parents agreed. So next Sunday his new comrades in arms came for him and took him off to the field of play. George's instructions were very simple: he was to stand in a certain place and if the ball came in that direction he was to catch it. George obeyed orders. Still somewhat vague as to what it was all about, he stood where he was placed until the ball came sailing through the air in his direction. He ran for it, leapt at it and pulled it down amid jubilant cheers especially from those who had backed him: it seemed that the catch was made at a very criticial stage of the game. George was loaded with presents and was taken home by a triumphant body of players who sang his praises to the delight of his still somewhat bewildered parents.

Headley has told me this story himself. And although he was already a famous cricketer when he was telling it to me, it was obvious that he was still nearly as mystified as he had been at the time. There is one great point which he missed and it can be missed to this day. The men who saw him make the first catch had no doubt whatever that if another catch came his way he would most certainly make it. Even at that age, on the field he gave the impression of competence, control and complete readiness for whatever fortune or misfortune might send his way. Never at any time during George's career was there a feeling among his colleagues or spectators that there was any situation on the field which he could not handle. He had this quality at the age of ten, and to us who knew him in the past, he has it up to this day.

To this day: I was in Jamaica in January 1964, and naturally went to see George. He had put on a little weight, but his figure was as neat and as trim as ever. In May he would be fifty-five. As usual we talked a lot about cricket, and before I left I asked him: "Do you still play?" He laughed a little self-consciously. "No," he said, "I sometimes demonstrate to my pupils at the nets, but I can't play in any matches. My problem is in my knees. I can't run and when and if I should manage to run a single, to turn for a second would be quite impossible."

George was quite untroubled by this deficiency. There was no nostalgia, no sentimentality. That was how it was and he accepted it. But I know my man a little better than to accept at face value what he says about himself. I made further inquiries about his playing, and this is what I was told by more than one person. He does not play matches and maybe he can't run between wickets. But when he stands up in the nets with bat in his hands and pads on his feet, you still can see "the one and only George Headley". I more than expected it.

If ever there was a natural batsman, Headley was one. However, in a West Indian island, George was surrounded by cricket to be absorbed at every pore, to a degree that I am sure he himself does not appreciate.

To begin with the technique of batting. In 1926 George was just fifteen years old and, West Indian fashion, still in short trousers. Now, for many years it has been a tradition for county players, including some Test players, to visit Jamaica regularly for a few weeks of cricket in the spring. George was an inheritor of this tradition. In 1926 one such team came down including Ernest Tyldesley. In one innings Ernest made over three hundred runs and George sat and watched him make them.

Now, at his best, nobody played finer cricket than Ernest Tyldesley. Unfortunately he was not always nor even often at his best. But recalling that famous occasion George says: "I watched him all day."

And the gravity with which he imbued those words showed that on that day a landmark had been reached and passed. George Headley implied that he had learnt all that he had required to know about batting from watching Ernest Tyldesley.

There was, however, another landmark. The second and last terrace in George's education was ascended in Australia. When he went to Australia in 1931, George already had a great reputation as a batsman. He had scored four centuries in four Tests against England, and against Lord Tennyson's eleven in Jamaica he had made 334 not out. This was the occasion on which Passailaigue (261 not out) helped George to a stand of 487 for the sixth wicket, which to this day remains the sixth-wicket world record.

Apparently armed and fully equipped, George set off for Australia and began the season with scores of 25 and 82; 131 and 34. The 82 he made against New South Wales, and the 131, against Victoria in even time, was acknowledged by habitués to be an innings unsurpassed on that famous field. Then came for Headley a moment of truth. So far he had been his natural self, master of all strokes on the off-side with a special West Indian penchant for hooking short balls, especially off fast bowlers. Now, however, after his flamboyant mastery of everything on the off-side, the word went round in Australia (according to George): "Keep away from his off stump. You will never get him there."

To keep away from the off stump meant to concentrate on the leg stump, and in innings after innings George faced this entirely new type of attack. The result was a period of crisis and unrelieved failure — 27 and 16; 0 and 11; 3; 14 and 2; 19 and 17. But by this time George had mastered the technique of attacking this new type of bowling: that is what mattered to him as a batsman, to be able to attack a bowler. He refers particularly to a great stand that he saw by Archie Jackson and McCabe against Grimmett bowling for South Australia. Each batsman made a century and George speaks about the innings with the same conviction of a landmark reached and passed, as when he watched Ernest Tyldesley.

"They played him one way all the time. Either back and forcing him away on the on-side, or, when he flighted the ball, they left the crease and gave him the full drive."

Whatever George had to learn he learned it well because henceforth his scores in Australia were: 102 and 28; 77 and 113; 75 and 39; 33 and 11; 70 and 2; 105 and 30.

George by now was such a master of on-side play that Grimmett considered him to be the greatest master of on-side play whom he ever bowled against, and Grimmett bowled at length to both Hobbs and Bradman.

Those were the techniques that George learnt on the road to becoming a master batsman. Both of them are indelibly linked with players foreign to Jamaica: in 1926 English batting, and in 1931–2 Australian bowling. But now I open a window into fields as yet uncharted. What made Headley the batsman he became, in fact the cricketer he was, he learnt above all in and from his native West Indies.

Headley learnt from the West Indies respect for the game; and secondly, a wholehearted belief that distinction in cricket was equal to distinction anywhere else. The whole personality, individual and social, could be devoted to it.

The deep inner respect for the game which distinguished Headley and his generation was made known to me through an accidental remark by George. He was captain of the West Indies side against Allen's team in 1947 and George, as the home captain, had to spin the coin in the first Test in Barbados. George found himself sweating after spinning the coin and it took him some time to find out why. George does not gamble but he loves to have a flutter, particularly in English racing. In the West Indies, in his generation, the sentiment was very strong that gambling, and particularly that type of gambling which involved the spinning of a coin, was something wrong, something immoral, done outside the pale of decent society. So that when he found himself spinning a coin as preliminary to a serious decision on some aspect of cricket, he instinctively felt that he was doing something very wrong and broke out into a cold sweat.

He had to pull himself together and force himself to recognize that for a captain to spin a coin at cricket was not in any way a form of gambling. I knew the feeling and how widespread it was, and maybe still is, among West Indian cricketers. But I never realized how much it was part of the cricket personality until George related his experience to me, an experience which he obviously found quite inexplicable.

Yet the deepest response to cricket that was made by George Headley was the response to the ordinary people of Jamaica. Some attempt must be made to convey this background of the generation which made West Indian cricket what it is. And here I shall make the attempt to convey what today is very vivid and organic to me but which I find little evidence of being appreciated elsewhere in the way that it should be. Unfortunately, I cannot give saws and instances from Jamaica itself. I have to depend upon experiences elsewhere. But what I shall

C.L.R. James

now relate is characteristic of the whole British Caribbean from at least the last decade of the nineteenth century. Without some knowledge of it there is no understanding of what West Indian cricket is, or of how and why it grew.

In the last decade of the nineteenth century in a West Indian village of some three or four thousand people, there were two cricket clubs. One of them consisted of a body of young men who had adopted what was for them, a new style of over-arm bowling. In the village was another club which stuck to under-arm and consisted of gentlemen who were not exactly young. They had had time to build a cricket reputation and despised the young team with its new-fangled method of bowling.

The younger men challenged the older ones to a championship match. The ancients refused; they would have nothing to do with these upstarts. However, after a year or two it happened that both clubs joined a competition that had its centre in the capital of the island.

They therefore were compelled to play against one another. They applied for and got permission to play their competition match at home. The outstanding batsman of the young Turks was a teacher and assistant master of the government school. He was a favourite of the headmaster, who had been a great cricketer in his time and an under-arm bowler. The headmaster, however, was a supporter of the new style and he took it upon himself to coach the batsman who was his assistant. His method was somewhat unusual. But it was successful and is worth recording.

Every afternoon after school he had some of the older boys bowling over-arm at the batsman. He himself, however, bowled under-arm in the style that the rival team would bowl on the Saturday coming. He instructed the batsman not to make any stroke but merely to play forward or back, defensive, and that went on from Monday to Thursday. On the Friday afternoon he changed tactics and called upon the batsman to open out, to make strokes, all round the wicket. The batsman found himself in wonderful form. On the next day he went in first wicket down, made 48 not out and his side beat the under-armers by nine wickets.

A great supporter of the under-armers was Mr Blenman, the butcher. Old Blenman was himself past the age of playing, but he had made himself into a special protector or guardian of the reputation and status of the under-armers.

"Robert," he said to the young batsman, "you all have beaten

196

us. But I am not finished with you yet. We will play you another game."

"Ready for you any time," said Robert, and forgot the threat.

About a year later, however, old Blenman turned up with a new challenge. He had a team, and would like to play the young men again. The young men were very ready, and on a day the match was played.

In his team old Blenman had brought a stranger. Nobody knew anything about him. But they soon learnt. The stranger could bat. He hit the bowling of the young men all over the place and if he hadn't been run out when 95, God knows how many he would have made. But the newcomer could bowl as well. And bowling over-arm, he proceeded to bowl out the young Turks. They were badly beaten and old Blenman's triumph was complete.

It was a year or two before the young men learnt who had so routed them. When the West Indies team of 1901 was chosen for England the young Turks recognized the name of C.A. Ollivierre. He played so well on tour that he remained in England to play for Derbyshire.

Old Blenman may have had some connection with St Vincent. At any rate he knew something about this famous cricketing family of the Ollivierres. It seems that the old man had got into touch with Ollivierre and himself paid the expenses of one of them to come to Trinidad — not an unadventurous journey in those days.

That was the spirit that permeated their attitude to the game. That was the cricketing atmosphere over the whole Caribbean. That was the air that George Headley breathed and fitted him to learn what Ernest Tyldesley and Grimmett had to teach him, and to bat probably in much the same way that Johnny Tyldesley batted.

In 1928 Headley's parents, having gone to the United States from Panama, had sent to Jamaica for their son to come to the United States to study a profession. Headley sent to Panama for his papers and if they had come in time he would not have made 78 or 228. He would not have played at all. He already would have left for the United States.

But there was some delay and therefore the visit of the English team found him still in Jamaica. However, after scoring 78 and 228, he was persuaded to give up the idea of going to the United States to study a profession, and to stay in Jamaica to play cricket.

Note, please, that there was no professional job which he

could be offered. He was not offered any job at all. But he was obviously a fine cricketer, and therefore everyone took it for granted that he should stay in Jamaica and play cricket.

We must now have a look at George Headley at the wicket. There we shall be able to learn what he contributed to cricket. We don't intend to inflict new or old quotations on the reader. Let George himself speak:

"When I think of the things I used to do, I tremble and marvel at myself.

"There was a time in my early days when I was always down the crease and hitting the sight-screen first bounce over the bowler's head. I couldn't do it now if I tried. In fact I could not try. I suppose it was youth and inexperience.

"But I have to say this. I used to go down and very rarely used to miss. . . ."

Headley took this spirit into Test matches. Hear him again on the third Test against England's team in 1930:

"It was the last innings of the match and *we had to make runs against time*. Wilfred Rhodes had a wicket to suit him and on it he was still a dangerous bowler.

"He was dropping the ball on a worn spot outside the off stump and spinning it away, with the off-side well packed. It was impossible to get runs in the ordinary way. *Yet we had to win that match*. What to do? *I knew I had to do something*. So I decided to get down to Rhodes as soon as he delivered the ball and hit it full-pitch somewhere on the on-side boundary. Now I could not wait to judge the flight and choose the ball I would go down to. Rhodes was not giving the ball any air at all. I therefore had to make up my mind to depend upon his length, and periodically, once or twice an over, as soon as the ball was out of his hand, I dashed down the pitch and depended on his length for me to reach him full pitch. I did it all the afternoon and we won the match. That was the Test in which I first got a second century in the second innings.

"However, I did not catch Rhodes napping. Once I dashed out and when I was well outside the crease, I saw the ball dropping feet in front of me. It dropped and spun away. I could do nothing and thought I was gone. But the ball spun out of the rough so quickly and so wide that the wicket-keeper bungled, and I was able to get back."

Headley remembered also his last innings in Australia. He had by this time, completely mastered Grimmett and going in first-wicket down, in less than two hours he had made a brilliant century. He knew it was an outstanding performance because in those days the fielding side did not applaud, in routine fashion, a 50 or a century by the batsmen. As a matter of fact they did not applaud at all. But this day when Headley reached the century, Bradman, Ponsford, Kippax and the rest broke into spontaneous applause.

As the years went by and the responsibility increased, Headley became perhaps less aggressive, less determined to break the spirit of bowlers. But he always remained a man who knew that the only way to be safe at the wicket was to establish domination over the bowling.

Headley at the wicket is best explained by Headley himself, sitting in his office in Kingston in the year 1964.

He gave me a vivid account of what constituted fine batting and I have never known him to be so consistently passionate as he was on this occasion. To explain himself he walked about the room using a flat bamboo ruler one foot long to illustrate the motions of the bat.

It seems that two famous players had come to Jamaica the year before and paid him a visit. George switched the conversation to modern defensive batting.

"I told them: what is this business of opening batsman batting for two hours and making 40 or 60 runs? I told them that to do that was to play in the hands of the bowlers and captain of the fielding side. When an opening batsman behaved in that way and got out he left the bowlers and fielding side in full command of the situation. The business of opening batsmen is to break up the bowling and make it easy for the batsmen who follow. They gave me some explanation which I could not accept."

"What do you thing is wrong, George?" I asked him, because this has now been a point of heated discussion in England for a number of years.

George began to swing the ruler in his left hand up and down.

"The point," he said, "is in the left hand. Too many of these modern batsmen are playing the ball in front of the wicket off their right hand. That is quite wrong."

Over the years I had never seen him so emphatic.

"Every stroke in front of the wicket has to be guided, controlled, and given its force by the left hand and the left wrist;" the bamboo ruler swung up and down.

"All you have to do is to get there in time and then whatever the pace of the bowling you use the left wrist and left hand and you can put the ball wherever you please.

"For strokes behind the wicket you use the right hand and

the right wrist. But as long as these batsmen are playing the ball in front of the wicket off the right hand and the right wrist, they will never be able to make runs off the fast bowling, it will always pin them down."

I expect George was so heated because he could not give a demonstration in the field as when we used to talk in the old days.

I have recently noticed that the Jamaican government has given him three months' notice of its decision to end his job as cricket coach. What they will do for a cricket coach, I do not know. But in my view they will have to search far and wide before they find another cricketer so firmly based on first principles and at the same time, so easy and natural among them. It will be a long time before I forget his left wrist swinging up and down and the bamboo ruler showing how the fast ball should be driven through the covers. It was almost as good as seeing him in the old days.

However gaily and spontaneously Headley had danced down the wicket to hit the ball first bounce to the sight-screen, by the time he had reached maturity, this habit of going at the bowling had been incorporated into his technique and his conception of what was good batting. That can be seen most clearly in his attitude to batting on bad wickets. Headley has a reputation similar to that of Johnnie Tyldesley for the way he handled first-class bowling on bad wickets. His record here, until clearly examined, is quite beyond belief.

In England on wet wickets in 1933 and 1939, Headley played 13 innings, made 50 seven times, only three times scored less than double figures, and in his other three innings scored 25, 35 and 40. His average is 39.85. For a similar series the average of Bradman is 16.66. What is noticeable about Headley and wet wickets is that he simply loved to bat on them. And his reason was that on them you could not play defensive cricket: you are compelled to attack the bowling; if the bowler pitched up, you had to drive; if he pitched short, you had to hook. "No nonsense," said George, and it is obvious that by nonsense he meant uncertainty as to whether to attack the bowler or not. When you are talking constantly to a great batsman or to a notable artist in any field of endeavour you remember not only what he says, but when he said it and how, and how often. And the two things that I remember most clearly in George's conversations are these:

First of all the wonder, perhaps nostalgia, perhaps — who knows? — a sense of guilt in the young batsman who danced down the wicket so happily to hit the bowlers first bounce to the sight-screen. And secondly, the elder statesman full of concern at what he considered a steep decline in a business in which he had been himself a great master, and was certain that he knew the remedy for the present discontents. In 1964 the bamboo ruler swung back and forth almost as flashingly as his bat between the wars.

To sum up, what George Headley gave to the game of cricket was this. Just at the time when the game was about to sink into its present defensive spell, Headley, in the West Indies and from the West Indies, restored to it the glamour of its best days, adding to modern technique the naturalness which gave his cricket an apparent spontaneity which added to its appeal.

Now after all this analysis, the opening of historical avenues of investigation, and so on, the entity which makes all the information and perspective alive, that entity is George Headley, the unique individual who has brought all these material facts into an existential vividness, the entity without whom they would be mere statistics or observations on a piece of paper. Where the social and historical factors end and where George Headley the individual begins, I simply do not know. But I think that this sketch would be incomplete unless I give a picture of George Headley, the unique human being as he had his being. He and I watched part of the Manchester Test against Australia in 1938. During this Test O'Reilly did a superb piece of bowling. George had been watching him closely, and after O'Reilly had taken some three wickets in four balls, George shook his head and, as quietly as ever, remarked: "He is the best bowler I have ever seen."

George does not throw superlatives around and I was profoundly impressed particularly because I had already come, with many others, to similar conclusions about O'Reilly. I expected it was my consciousness of George's self-control that prompted me to twit him. "George, if you had to play him tomorrow, you would be a bit scared." George turned to me, his reserve, as it rarely did, becoming gravity. "He is the best bowler I have ever seen, but if I had to play him tomorrow he would be just like any other bowler I have played against."

George, the unflappable. My problem is whether he was born that way or whether he began with instincts of the kind and his experience of cricket and his life of almost unbroken successes added to and fortified a natural inclination. There are other aspects to his character; an incredible modesty about his own play; a disinclination to go into any detail about his conflicts with West Indian cricket authorities; a vivid memory of personal kindnesses shown to him in Australia and in league cricket in England. But it is this unshakeable calm which, surprisingly enough, is the most striking hallmark of this West Indian batsman who did everything that he was called upon to do.

We know too little as yet of West Indies cricket to be able to speak with more certainty, but once we engage we shall learn in time. Meanwhile, we will console ourselves by the fact that two thousand years ago, Horace, facing the same problem could find no answer:

> Some think that poets may be formed by art,
> Others maintain that nature makes them so,
> I neither see what art without a vein
> Nor wit without the help of art can do.

There is one point without which I would not like to conclude.

As we wrestle with, and probe into, the development of West Indian cricket, what we shall find will most certainly illuminate cricket and the cricketers who established the game before the West Indies learned it.

Sir Frank Worrell: The Man Whose Leadership made History

(*The Cricketer*, 5 May 1967)

Dying at the tragically early age of forty-two, Sir Frank Worrell had already written his name imperishably in the annals of cricket. In practice and theory combined, C.B. Fry dominated the first twenty years of the century; similarly Sir Donald Bradman before 1948; after 1960 in Australia Frank Worrell succeeded to the proud position.

Worrell was no accident. The merchant-planter class of Barbados made cricket into the popular artistic expression and a social barometer of the West Indies. That was the environment which moulded the future Worrell. He was a prodigy, at the age of thirteen playing for his school against cricketers like Martindale, whose pace at the time was too much for most English batsmen. Barbados selected him as a slow left-hander, but, sent in as a night-watchman, he at once earned his place as a batsman. Before he was twenty he had scored 300 runs in a first-class match. But the Barbados social discipline was very firm. Even when playing for the island as a schoolboy he had to attend school every morning until play began.

He could not adjust to Barbados and went off to make his home in Jamaica. Early in 1948 he scored 294 runs in three Tests against G.O. Allen's team, and for the next few years probably had no equal anywhere. In the winter of 1949 he went to India with a Commonwealth team. In 1950 he came to England with the West Indies team and that winter he was again in India with a Commonwealth team. There was no memory of anyone scoring runs in every class of cricket with such grace and power. Of many historic innings he himself preferred 223 not out and 83 not out in an unofficial Test at Kanpur in 1949–50. To his mastery of bat and ball Worrell, in 1950–1 substituting for the ailing Ames in India, led his side with notable skill. In Australia in 1951–2 he alone of the three Ws lived up to their reputation. During that tour Worrell's form did not advance and against India and against Australia in the West Indies, he was demonstrably ineffective both with bat and ball: curiously enough, whether scoring or failing he remained a stroke-player without peer. In England in 1957 Worrell recaptured form. He played through the innings at Nottingham for 191 not out; bowling now fast-medium at Leeds he took seven for 70. After an absence of two years from first-class cricket, against England in the West Indies in 1959–60 Worrell at once played an innings of 197 not out. He did little else of note in the series but at its end was appointed captain, the result of a successful attempt to dislodge the mercantile-planter class from automatic domination of West Indies cricket.

Worrell as captain entered a decadent Test cricket. Captains sought to ensure the avoidance of defeat, batsmen to remain at the wicket, bowlers to avoid being hit. Worrell made the tremendous decision to restore to Tests the spirit of the game he had learnt in Barbados. Already experienced in India at building a team of disparate individuals, he was able to weld his West Indians from dispersed areas into a disciplined unit. Having rapidly created his instrument, Worrell initiated a regeneration. Benaud, the Australian captain, met him halfway and the result was the most exciting Test series in living memory.

In the MCC tour to Australia in 1962–3, Test cricket seemed to sink back into the doldrums and everyone awaited with anxiety Worrell's team to England in 1963. They repeated the renaissance begun in Australia. George Duckworth believed that "No more popular side has ever toured in the old country," and in the words of the Lord Mayor of London: "A gale of change has blown through the hallowed halls of cricket."

This was no casual achievement. Behind the singular grace and inherent dignity of his manner, Frank Worrell was a man of very strong character. He had himself confessed his strange inability to feel at ease in the society of Barbados. His relations with the West Indies Board of Control earned him the title of a "cricket Bolshevik". What is by now obvious is that he was possessed of an almost unbridled passion for social equality. It was the men on his side who had no social status whatever for whose interest and welfare he was always primarily concerned. They repaid him with an equally fanatical devotion.

It was typical of his particular origins that in 1958, planning his future after cricket, Worrell studied sociology at a university to emerge with a degree in 1959. He was a combination of most unusual gifts. His unobtrusive skill, his reserve and his dignity on the field made him a great favourite with the British public who saw in him the embodiment of qualities which they admired: after the 1963 tour he was knighted. But with the Australian public it was the same. The population of Melbourne turned out in 1961 to give Worrell's team a send-off "the like of which is normally reserved for Royalty and national heroes". Australia presented the Worrell Cup so as to ensure the memory of a historic tour.

His captaincy will stand on his record and on the evidence of the men who played with him and against him. But it is my duty to record that he had an altogether exceptional acuteness and intelligence of mind. I had long conversations with him and in 1963 I wrote publicly as follows:

> Worrell is one of the few who after a few hours of talk have left me as tired as if I had been put through a wringer. His responses to difficult questions were so unhesitating, so precise, and so took the subject on to unsuspected but relevant areas, that I felt it was I who was undergoing examination. No cricketer, and I have talked to many, ever shook me in a similar manner.

If his reserve permitted it, this remarkable, intelligence could be seen in his views of West Indian society. To us who were concerned he seemed poised for applying his powers to the cohesion and self-realization of the West Indian people. Not a man whom one slapped on the shoulder, he was nevertheless to the West Indian population an authentic national hero. His reputation for strong sympathies with the populace did him no harm with them, and his firm adherence to what he thought was right fitted him to exercise that leadership and gift for popularity which he had displayed so notably in the sphere of cricket. He had shown the West Indian mastery of what Western civilization had to teach. His wide experience, reputation, his audacity of perspective and the years which seemed to stretch before him fitted him to be one of those destined to help the West Indies to make their own West Indian way.

When all this has been said, it must never be forgotten that Frank Worrell was a great cricketer on the field of play. His greatest years had been between 1948 and 1951 but it was characteristic that as a captain he remobilized himself and personally led the renaissance in Australia in 1960–1. He began the season with 1, 37, 65 not out and 68 not out, 82, 51, and 0 (absent hurt), 65 and 65 (first Test), 0 and 0 (second Test), 18 and 53, 22 and 82 (third Test), 71 and 53 (fourth Test). It was Worrell who set the tone for Sobers and Kanhai and the whole team, and the words of A.G. Moyes on his batting in the third Test should be recorded: "Technically, he was the finest player in the West Indies side and in this innings he simply could not be faulted. If ever a man deserved a century it was Worrell that day, for he entered the arena when three had fallen for 22 and right from the start he batted with a superb mastery that reduced Davidson in a couple of overs to mediocrity." He was a notable personality of our century and it was cricket which had made this West Indian what he was.

Letter to Colin Cowdrey

Staverton Road,
London, NW2

16 May 1968

My dear Cowdrey,

Hearty congratulations, not only on being appointed captain of the England team but for initiating the practice of a captain being appointed for the five tests.

May I add that I firmly believe, with C.B. Fry, that the players for the Test series, perhaps 13 of them, should be selected for the first Test and (excepting strange developments) be made to understand that they would continue more or less to play in the whole series. I have always believed that abstractly but, watching England teams in the last few years, I am certain that they have suffered by being chopped about, and that one of the reasons for the success in the West Indies is that it was impossible to change the team, as could have been done if they had been at home.

Anyway, I look forward to the time when we will talk about this and other things, but the best of luck both for the team and for yourself in the coming series.

Sincerely yours,
C.L.R. James.

Letter to E.W. Swanton

*Staverton Road,
London NW2*

31 May 1968

Mr E.W. Swanton,
Editor, *The Cricketer*,
178–202 Great Portland Street,
London, W1

My dear Swanton,

I see that Cowdrey has spoken of the "natural ability" of the West Indian cricketer. And I see also that Lord Cobham has delivered a broadside which you subtitle "Where English cricket has gone wrong".

It is a long time that I have been insisting that the fundamentals of batting as I have known it are as far as possible "play back or drive", which Lord Cobham states as a counsel of perfection but surely should be the aim of all cricket aspirants. I am afraid I have a long quarrel with people who think that there is a special physical quality of West Indian players.

I would like to do an article showing how we grew up, the models that we had and the mental attitudes which had been instilled in us for over half a century. I believe the article would be worthwhile and very relevant. I have had it in mind for quite a while but I hesitated because I thought perhaps that we had had enough of the West Indies in *The Cricketer*. But these two statements in these two articles have stimulated me to say quite a lot, and I would be glad if you would accept the idea that such an article would be of some value at the present time. If you do I could let you have it within a very few days.

With best wishes,
Very sincerely yours,
C.L.R. James.

Letter to Colin Cowdrey

Staverton Road,
London, NW2

18 July 1968

My dear Cowdrey,

The 100 during the hundredth Test shows once more that truth is stranger than fiction. I am very sorry about your illness but I have to say that there were strokes in the second part of the innings that were better than those in the first part. In fact I have never seen better.

I hope you get out for the fourth Test. In any case I believe that the England side outplayed the Australians at every point and it would be very hard indeed if you were not in, not only at the next games but at the victory.

As usual, best wishes.

Sincerely,
C.L.R. James.

Letter to John Arlott

Staverton Road,
London, NW2

24 July 1968

Mr John Arlott,
Headingley,
Leeds,
Yorks

My dear John,

I have been wanting to say something for a long time and the only way I can think of saying it is writing to you a private letter.

I believe, for example, that a player like young Amiss, *if people look at him and think he has it in him*, should be played in three games or assured of two at least. This playing someone in one game and his future depends on success, especially in these days where there is so much publicity on the performance of a player, that I think is sure to bring out the worst instead of the best of a batsman. As I remember cricket in the West Indies, we played so little first-class cricket that, as a rule, when a young fellow is in, he is in for two or three games at least.

Which brings me to the question of Dexter. I believe that Dexter should have been made to understand from the very beginning that once he had made the 200 he would be in for the next two Tests. I believe that it would result in increased confidence and a certainty that he could play his own game which we so much require at the present time.

I am sorry that I am not able to be up there, particularly because at the beginning of August I am off on a lecture tour to Uganda and therefore will have to read about it in the papers. Allow me to say that you seem to have added a new dimension to your reports in the *Guardian*: You seem to have made a sharp distinction between talking during the day on television and radio and writing a column and a half for a more serious daily paper.

As ever,
C.L.R. James.

Not Cricket

(*Transition*, Kampala, 1968)

There are perhaps three cricketers in England whose names should come before D'Oliveira's in the selection of a Test team. The first and most important thing is to prove his status on the field of play.

D'Oliveira was brought to England in April 1960 chiefly at the insistence of English people who were determined that a non-white South African should get a chance to prove his worth at cricket in England. As was natural he began in league cricket, where his performances were exceptional but not unique. He began to qualify by residence for Worcestershire but played a few first-class matches outside of the county championship. As is usual with him (and this must never be forgotten in any estimate of his play), in these incidental first-class games he made 119 against the Australian team touring in England that year. From that registration of himself as the man to seize an occasion he has never departed.

By 1965, which mind you is only three years ago, he had qualified to play for Worcestershire in the county championship. He made nearly 1,700 runs, being sixth in the English batting averages. He scored six centuries, only one man scoring more than he (Edrich with 8), and took 38 wickets. Going in at number 5, with Graveney at number 4, these two repeatedly rescued a creaking Worcestershire batting so that Worcestershire again won the championship. Of his play for the county, *Wisden* said: "Few newcomers can have made such an impression in the opening season as did D'Oliveira, the first non-white South African to participate in county cricket." This was recognition *in excelsis*: *Wisden*, it must be remembered, has been recorder and judge of cricket for over a century. And earlier, of his partnership with Graveney: "Had they come together earlier in their careers (this) might well have become as famed a combination as was Compton and Edrich." Since 1918 no batting combination in English cricket has been more famous than the Compton-Edrich combination.

This, mind you, was D'Oliveira's first year in first-class cricket. Next year he did everything that anyone could have expected and more. He was tenth in the averages for the season and took 73 wickets. But he established himself as the man for the big occasion by his play for England in four Tests. His

209

C.L.R. James

scores were 27 run out, 76 and 54, 88 and 7, and 4. He not only was high in the Test averages for batting but took 8 valuable wickets, being the most successful of the seam bowlers of medium pace. He made three consecutive Test innings of over 50. In the fourth Test he made 88, hit four sixes and eight fours, including one straight drive for six off Hall, the fearsome West Indies fast bowler. He not only scored against the devastating West Indies bowlers on a losing side but he hit them in a manner that more than ever distinguished his play as being essentially the play for the big occasion.

D'Oliveira had now established himself both as a county cricketer and Test cricketer as forcing batsman, good field anywhere and more than useful medium-pace seam bowler; this in his second year of first-class cricket.

In 1967 Indian and Pakistan made joint tours in England. Against India for Worcester D'Oliveira opened the season with 174 not out. He went on to score in the Tests 109, not out 24, 33, and was left out — for some reason which I do not know — of the third Test. But against Pakistan he returned to his Test-dominating self with 59 and not out 81 in the first Test. He failed in the second and third, in each of which he had only one innings, being run out for 7 in the second. For his county, with Graveney he headed the averages.

Such has been the record of a man in his third year of first-class cricket, after a nondescript experience in South Africa in the critical years of his development. To spend a little time on this unusual early experience: in 1967 *Wisden*, after his two years in first-class cricket, included him as one of its five cricketers of the year. It began the story of D'Oliveira as "a fairy tale come true"; and further, a truly astonishing statement coming from a traditional publication: "No Test player has had to overcome such tremendous disadvantages along the road to success as the Cape Coloured D'Oliveira." Altogether, apart from the figures and the obvious capacity to rise to an occasion, there is this continuous recognition by seasoned criticism that here was a man who in the face of extraordinary difficulties made himself into a cricketer of a high order. Now for a glimpse at his cricketing origins.

He was born in Cape Town in 1934 and until he was fifteen the only cricket he played was in the street. His father, a devoted cricketer for many decades, gave him some coaching but in those early years, *Wisden* informs us, D'Oliveira thought nothing of walking ten miles to play on his home ground. From the ringside he studied the great players from abroad who played in South Africa. He learnt so well that, because of his tremendous scoring in the kind of cricket that he could play in South Africa, he attracted the notice of cricket-lovers in England. John Arlott, the writer and broadcaster, took an interest in him and Arlott and friends managed to get him to England to play league cricket. Graveney saw him, thought he was good enough for county cricket and thus he went to Worcestershire.

The only blemish in his first-class career is his failure on the MCC side to the West Indies both as batsman and fieldsman. But the failure as fieldsman showed that for some reason or other he was not his real self. It is not too much, especially by those who know the nervous strain of transition from one type of society to another, to realize that he was at last feeling the reaction of the tremendous readjustment he had had to make from South Africa to English society. In any case, I know only four cricketers who over the years have never failed in a series of Tests. They are Jack Hobbs, Don Bradman, George Headley and Garfield Sobers.

But, as often happens, the temporary failure was soon dispelled and, in D'Oliveira's case, spectacularly. There is now no need merely to repeat that D'Oliveira made a hard-hit 87 not out in the first Test against the Australians, was left out of the next three, was brought back for the last one and made 158. He not only made all those runs but he hit the Australian bowlers, which most of the English batsmen failed to do. These two successes, coming after the career that we have outlined, should make anyone understand what we mean by saying that when it comes to selecting a Test team of English players today there are no more than three players in England whose names could be placed before his.

Now with the past of D'Oliveira in mind, we can place in perspective the failure to select him. Here are two first-class cricket journalists, experienced, capable, authoritative and dealing with the matter on its immediate merits. First, John Arlott in *The Guardian* of 29 August 1968:

> So England's tactical need is for a Test-class batsman who is a reliable bowler at medium pace, or above, to make the fourth seam-bowler: Only D'Oliveira, of our current players, meets that demand. He was top of the English batting averages in the series against Australia just completed, and second in the bowling. The latter may seem a statistical quibble, but when he bowled Jarman on Tuesday he made the breakthrough which brought England their close win in the fifth Test.
>
> He is a useful, if not great fieldsman at slip or in the deep.

Decisively, to the objective observer, he has the temperament to rise to the challenge of an occasion, as he proved against the West Indian fast bowlers, and in both his matches against Australia this summer. His behaviour in what might have been difficult situations has always been impeccably dignified and courteous.

Next is Alan Ross of *The Observer*:

D'Oliveira last week, as both batsman and bowler, was crucial in winning an historic Test match. The conditions for the greater part of it were similar to those that may be found in South Africa. It is inconceivable in the light of this that he could not find a place among the 16 players chosen for the tour, had all else been equal.

Michael Parkinson in *The Sunday Times* 1 September 1968 drew the politically obvious conclusions:

Last Wednesday a group of Englishmen picked a cricket team and ended up by doing this country a disservice of such magnitude that one could only feel a burning anger at their madness and a cold shame for their folly. The dropping of Basil D'Oliveira from the MCC team to tour South Africa has stirred such undercurrents throughout the world that no one but the impossibly naïve can any longer even think that politics and sport do not mix, never mind believe it.

I am convinced that the MCC selectors who made the decision and the MCC Committee that blessed it acted without thought of racial or political motive. I also believe that by reaching their conclusions over Basil D'Oliveira they stand today in the eyes of many white men and many more coloured men condemned as racialists of the worst kind and we are all tarnished by their shadow. To hear D.J. Insole insisting with patent honesty that the selectors had done their job as cricket experts was to be outraged by the man's naïveté. I will not even waste space discussing D'Oliveira's qualifications to tour. I will simply state that in my opinion he was the finest player of his kind in the country.

The Reverend David Sheppard took great pains to achieve the impossible, condemn the behaviour of the selectors, but not to offend anybody!

"I am opposed to D'Oliveira's omission, but I do not personally think that the MCC have been dishonest," said Mr Sheppard. "I do believe though, that the MCC have mishandled the whole affair. The issue should have been cleared up before the session started this summer, and the political principle should have been cleared in public one way or the other."

I have left the strictly political issue for the last because many today are making statements not too unlike those of Reverend

Sheppard. The best you can say of them is that they betray a political amateurism. To talk about racialism is politically equally futile. The non-selection of D'Oliveira is not an example of racialism. Selectors in Britain would have been glad to play him in Britain against South Africa, would have sent him to Australia without hesitation. What has happened is much worse than racialism: it is a political demonstration.

Its result is to let South Africa off the hook on which they would have been in having to welcome a man of colour on their pitches and in their pavilions hitherto reserved exclusively for white people. That is a concern equivalent to an endorsement of the South African regime. As Mr Parkinson has pointed out, it will have immense consequences among all people all over the world. And this recognition that the South African regime is being protected from the consequences of its racialism by selectors in Britain is a matter which deserves adequate recognition by the British organization responsible, the MCC. Analysis of whether the persons responsible were honest or dishonest — that is not in the slightest degree important. To request also that the tour be discontinued, as MCC members are requesting, is I believe a political mistake. It is not likely to succeed, and if the question of the validity of any tour to South Africa is raised it should have been raised before and thus today be an additional stone in a structure that was building up. What, then, is to be done? I think that what should have been requested and could still be requested is this: To remove from the posts which they have abused the original body of selectors responsible for this quite unnecessary blow. Make it clear that because they have so signally failed to live up to the requirements of their responsibilities they can no longer be considered for holding similar positions in the future.

Letter to John Arlott

Staverton Road,
London, NW2

8 October 1968

My dear John,

I felt that you had gone away to restore yourself from the strains of the summer and am glad that you seem to have done well.

About the photographs, I don't know what to say. What I have in mind is to include them with corresponding material in a book that I am due to finish by the end of the year. It may be that they are worth a separate publication or preliminary publication in one of the Sunday journals. Or perhaps independent publication with some photographs included of Cowdrey today and Hobbs before 1914, whom I remember thinking for many years as the nearest thing to those super Trumper photographs that are in *The Great Batsmen*. I have been thinking about this for a number of years but left it where it was until somebody gave me an old copy of *Great Batsmen* which enabled me to get these pictures and not destroy my own volume.

I am leaving on Thursday for Canada for a conference and am likely to go to the United States for a series of lectures which will keep me there until the end of November. Nevertheless, I shall continue to be in the closest touch with Staverton Road and I shall be very glad if when you think something about these you drop me a line as if I was here. It will be immediately sent on to me and assist me to deal with this question which I have been thinking about so long. I am tempted to write more about them but I don't think I will do that for you, that should be for the ordinary person. So *in tuas manus commendo*.

About D'Oliveira, I have written an article for a journal in Uganda who asked me to. I am supposed to write another but I have been putting it off because I am disinclined. I am finding all sorts of excuses why I have not done the article but I know really I don't wish to be involved in this business except in a manner which would not be at all suitable.

By the way, I want to mention that one of the things that has struck me about this season is the fact that I now have been able to include in my select category, a very select category of great batsmen, Graveney on the front foot. But some day I hope to be able to talk to you about that and other things.

With best wishes and warm regards,
Very sincerely yours,
C.L.R. James.

Driving the Ball is a Tradition in the West Indies

(*The Cricketer*, 1968)

In a summer number of *The Cricketer*, Lord Cobham, under a fearsome title "Where English Cricket has gone wrong", decrees it as a fundamental premise that batsmen play back or drive. I shall not quote C.B. Fry and Don Bradman in support; I have other quotations to make. Here is one of them. In 1963 I had occasion to write the following: "Following my master C.B. Fry, experience and observation, I fought for backplay. I enjoyed a serene mind on this vital question until 1938. I came back to cricket in 1953 to find that battle being fought all over again, with Sir Leonard Hutton at the head of cohorts far more formidable than my schoolboy opponents."

Sir Leonard has been joined by a formidable array of modern pundits. However, I remain convinced that this is a fundamental issue. For one thing, without it West Indies cricket cannot be understood.

The first finished batsman that I knew in Trinidad was a man called André Cipriani, member of a wealthy middle-class mulatto family. He was educated somewhere in Essex, and told us that he had played scratch games quite often with Percy Perrin and C.P. McGahey.

Now in Trinidad before World War II we played upon coconut matting, which always took spin and gave a much higher lift than turf. Cipriani stood sideways. To a ball even a little over the good length he brought both feet back and over the middle stump, toes towards point. From there, left elbow high, he played a dead-bat defensive stroke. But quite often he had time to push the ball between short leg and mid-on for an easy single. Pushed away remorselessly, the bowler would bring the ball up a bit, whereupon Cipriani, a tall and physically very strong man, would drive him to extra cover, straight or to long-on, for four, not infrequently for six. He could cut, and a ball on the body he could play away. But I have described his fundamental method and I thought then and still think that at his best there was no cricket in which he would not have distinguished himself. In *Great Batsmen: Their Methods at a Glance*, there is a photograph of McGahey playing back: it is Cipriani to the life.

Still sticking to Trinidad, I take a bowler, Victor Pascall, the

C.L.R. James

West Indies slow-to-medium left-hander.

Pascal dropped the ball on the off-stump, breaking away (with every now and then one coming in). For this attack he always had one man on the extra-cover boundary and one straight behind. *He had to.* At times Pascal attacked the leg stump. Whereupon he moved the man from extra cover to the deep square-leg boundary. Pascal knew, and everybody knew, that you could not bowl slow to medium pace without two men out, even on a wicket that always turned sharply enough. Even if a batsman played more or less a defensive game, if those spots were left open, a stroke greeted the omission. To this day I see mediocre slow left-handers in English county cricket bowling on a good pitch, without a man more than fifty yards away from the wicket. A West Indies bowler dared not do that in the West Indies even on the matting wicket.

The last reference I wish to make is to Clifford Roach, the West Indies opening batsman. In local cricket I often opened the innings with Roach, and one of our most serious opponents was a fast-medium bowler by name Yeates. He could move the new ball late into you and move it away. In the tropical atmosphere and on the matting wicket, the shine on the ball lasted at most five or six overs. Now, Yeates knew that if he bowled short to Roach, he would end up on the boundary, off or leg. He had to keep the ball up. I took strategic singles so as to give Roach the bowling. Roach used to play Yeates back. But the moment Yeates overstepped Roach would come out at him and drive that ball past mid-off or mid-on so fiercely that it was impossible for any fieldsman to stop it unless it came straight to him. In a 1930 Test in Barbados he did *exactly* the same to Voce, making a century in the first innings and 70 in the second.

That was the way we had learnt the game, that was the way we played it. But I came to England in 1932 and in 1934 saw Waite and McCabe opening for Australia. Except for Walters, I used to watch the other batsmen, on absolutely beautiful turf wickets, making McCabe and Waite into deadly bowlers. On our matting they would not have lasted the precious six overs of the new ball.

I will end with a statement from a lecture on *The Artist in the Caribbean* that I delivered at the University College of the West Indies in Jamaica on 3 November 1959. Sobers had already made his 365 but some who had seen him in 1957 in England had already prophesied that here in embryo was the greatest batsman of the age.

I believe that Lamming is as gifted for literature as Garfield Sobers is for cricket, and I do not believe that in the whole history of that game (with which I am very familiar) there are more than half a dozen men who started with a physical and mental equipment superior to that of young Sobers. But Sobers was born into a tradition, into a medium which though transported was so well established that it has created a Caribbean tradition of its own. *That is what I am talking about.* There are no limits to what Sobers can achieve.

Cowdrey believes that West Indians are naturally gifted for cricket, and Sobers is undoubtedly a very gifted man. It is admitted that West Indies Test players play in a special "manner". Physique? I don't think so. It is the product of a tradition and that tradition, we in Trinidad used to see reinforced when Barbados batsmen came to Trinidad. In principle they played back or they drove. Nearly all West Indies Test players today have played Saturday afternoon league cricket where they do not lose but have to develop the home style.

I was not only happy to see Lord Cobham's dictum, but welcomed the heading of his article.

Letter to Learie Constantine

Staverton Road
London NW2

9 January 1969

Lord Constantine,
11 Kendal Court,
Shoot-up Hill,
London NW2

My dear Learie,

I want to put it in writing that while I have no truck whatever with lordships, etc., I am very happy to congratulate you in particular on making what is definitely a step up the ladder for most people. If anyone with our skin would fill that post with positive achievements and as little of the dangerous possibilities which surround it, I think not only that you are the person but that most people, particularly black people, would accept you as the one most fitted. All I could wish you is not good luck but a steady hand and a sharp eye for all the traps which will now increasingly surround you. Know, as usual, that if there is anything that I can do that can be of any assistance to you, you can depend upon me as it has been these 50 years.

I have two essays coming out in a volume Arlott is bringing out called *Great All-rounders*, one on you and the other on Gary. I am audacious enough to believe that you will be pleased at what I have written.

Remember me to Norma and give her my hearty good wishes.

As ever,
C.L.R. James.

Garfield Sobers

(From *The Great All-Rounders*, edited by John Arlott, Pelham Books, 1969)

The pundits colossally misunderstand Garfield Sobers — perhaps the word should be misinterpret, not misunderstand. Garfield Sobers, I shall show, is a West Indian cricketer, not merely a cricketer from the West Indies. He is the most typical West Indies cricketer that it is possible to imagine. All geniuses are merely people who carry to an extreme definitive the characteristics of the unit of civilization to which they belong and the special act or function which they express or practise. Therefore to misunderstand Sobers is to misunderstand the West Indies, if not in intention, by inherent predisposition, which is much worse. Having run up the red flag, I should at least state with whom I intend to do battle. I choose the least offensive and in fact he who is obviously the most well-meaning, Mr Denys Rowbotham of the *Guardian* of Friday, 15 December 1967. Mr Rowbotham says of Sobers: "Nature, indeed, has blessed Sobers liberally, for in addition to the talents and reflexes, conditioned and instinctive, of a great cricketer, he has the eyes of a hawk, the instincts and suppleness of a panther, exceptional stamina, and apparently the constitution of an ox."

I could not possibly write that way about Garfield Sobers. I react strongly against it. I do not see him that way. I do not see Hammond that way. I see Sobers always, except for one single occasion, as exactly the opposite, the fine fruit of a great tradition. That being stated, let us now move on to what must always be the first consideration in writing about a cricketer, what he has done and what he does: that is, a hard look at Sobers on the field of play.

For Sobers the title of all-rounder has always seemed to me a circumspection. The Sobers of 1966 was not something new: that Sobers of 1966 had been there a long time. The truth is that Sobers for years now has had no superior in the world as an opening fast bowler.

Here are some facts to substantiate this apparently extravagant claim: which even today many of the scribes (and there are among them undoubted Pharisees) do not yet know.

It is the business of a fast bowler, opening the innings, to dismiss for small scores two or three of the first-line batsmen on the opposing side. If he does this and does it dramatically, then good captaincy will keep him in trim to make short work of the last two or three on the side, so ending with five or six wickets.

In 1964, his last session for South Australia, Sobers, against Western Australia, bowled batsman No.1 for 12, and had batsman No.2 caught by wicket-keeper Jarman for 2. Against Queensland Jarman caught No.2 off Sobers for 5, and Sobers bowled No.3 for 1. Against the history-making New South Wales side, Sobers had Thomas, No.1, caught by Lill for 0. He had No.2, Simpson, caught by Jarman for 0. He then had Booth, No.4, caught by Jarman for 0. He thus had the first three Australian Test players for 0 each. In the second innings he bowled Thomas for 3.

South Australia's last match was against the strong Victoria side. Sobers had Lawry, No.1, caught by Jarman for 4; Potter, No.3, caught by Lill for 0; Stackpole, No.5, caught by Lill for 5. In the second innings Redpath, No.2, was caught by Jarman for 0; Cowper, No.4, was caught by Hearne for 0; Lawry, No.1, was caught by Jarman off Sobers for 22. (Let us note in passing that in this match against Victoria, Sobers scored 124 and had also scored 124 in the game against New South Wales, the same in which he dismissed the three Test batsmen each for 0.)

It is impossible to find within recent years another fast bowler who in big cricket so regularly dismissed for little or 0 the opening batsmen on the other side.

His action as a pace bowler is the most orthodox that I know.

It is not the classical perfection, above all the ease, of E.A. McDonald. Sobers gathers himself together and is obviously sparing no effort (a rare thing with his cricket) to put his whole body into the delivery. The result is that the ball leaves the ground at a pace quite inconsistent with what is a fast-medium run-up and delivery. It would be worthwhile to get the pace of his delivery mechanically timed at different stages, as well as the testimony of observant batsmen and observant wicket-keepers.

There is nothing of the panther in the batting of Sobers. He is the most orthodox of great batsmen. The only stroke he makes in a manner peculiar to himself is the hook. Where George Headley used to face the ball square and hit across it, Denis Compton placed himself well outside it on the off-side, and Walcott compromised by stepping backwards but not fully across the hitting, usually well in front of and not behind square leg, Sobers seems to stand where he is and depend upon wrist and eyesight to swish the short fast ball square to the leg boundary. Apart from that, his method, his technique is carried to an extreme where it is indistinguishable from nature.

You see it in both his defensive and offensive strokes. He can, and usually does, play back to anything about which he has the slightest doubt. More rarely he uses a forward defensive stroke. But he never just plays forward to put the bat on the ball and kill it. He watches the ball off the pitch and, even in the most careful forward defensive, plays the ball away; very different from that modern master of the forward defensive, Conrad Hunte. Hunte from the advanced front foot (never advanced too far) plays what Ranjitsinhji used to insist on calling a back stroke. His type of mastery of the forward defensive gives us the secret of the capacity of Sobers to punish good length bowling on anything like a reasonable wicket. He does not need the half-volley of a fast or fast-medium bowler to be able to drive. From a very high backlift he watches the ball that is barely over the good length, takes it on the rise and sends it shooting between mid-on and mid-off. That is a later acquisition to a stroke that he has always had: to move back and time the good length through the covers.

The West Indian crowd has a favourite phrase for that stroke: "Not a man move." That stroke plus the ability to drive what is not a half-volley is the basis of the combination that makes Sobers the orthodox attacking player that he is. His aggressive play is very disciplined, which is shown by his capacity to lift the ball straight for six whenever he feels like it. But as a rule he reserves these paroxysms for occasions when the more urgent necessities of an innings have been safely fulfilled. It is possible that Sobers at times plays forward feeling for a slow ball, more often to a slow off-spin bowler, pitching on or just outside his off-stump, going away. But I have to confess that I saw this and remembered previous examples when I was searching for a way in which as a captain I would plan to get him out.

Yet I have seen the panther in Sobers. Not when he opened in a Test and hit Miller and Lindwall for 43 runs in fifteen minutes. The balls were just not quite there and this neophyte justly put them away. No. The panther one day saw the cage door open. In 1959–60, MCC visited Trinidad in the course of the tour of the West Indies. In between the match against the territory and the Test match the players of the Test side had a practice game, Hall on one side and Sobers on the other. Ramadhin was on the side of Sobers and Hall bowling to him was extremely careful to bowl not too slow but not too fast and always at a good length: he was not going to run the risk of doing damage to one of the main West Indies bowlers. But when he bowled at Sobers, Hall made up for the restraint enforced when bowling to Ramadhin. He ran to the wicket and delivered as fast as he could, obviously determined not to forgo the pleasure of sending Sobers's wicket flying.

Sobers returned in kind. I have never seen a fast bowler hit back so hard. It was not a forward push, it was not a drive. It was a hit. Sobers lifted his bat right back and did not lift the ball. He hit one or two of these balls to the on-boundary, almost straight drives. Hall did not fancy it and bowled faster. Sobers hit him harder.

But in competitive cricket Sobers did not play that way. I saw on the screen shots of the famous century in the first Test against Australia in Brisbane in 1961 and also in the latter part of a day's play at Sydney in the third Test. All have agreed, and I agree with them, that at no time was there anything but orthodoxy carried to the penultimate degree when orthodoxy itself disappears in the absolute. There is no need here to give figures. One episode alone will show what the batting of Sobers can mean not only to spectators but to seasoned Test players. The episode will, I am certain, live in the minds of all who saw it. In a recent series, West Indies were striving to force a win against Australia in Barbados. On the last day with less than an hour to go, West Indies had to make some 50 runs.

Sobers promoted himself in the batting order, and as he made his way to the wicket, as usual like a ship in full sail, the feeling in the crowd grew and expressed itself that if this was to be done, here was the man to do it. But somebody else was thinking the same. Simpson, the Australian captain, put Hawke on to bowl; he himself stood at slip and he distributed the other eight men about the boundary. Obviously Simpson felt that if he left one gap in the field unprotected, Sobers would be able to find the boundary through it. I have never seen or heard before of any such arrangement or rather disarrangement of a cricket field.

Sobers had a look at the eight men strewn about the boundary, then had a look at Simpson standing at slip. He accepted Simpson's homage with a great grin which Simpson suitably acknowledged, altogether quite a moment. And an utterly spontaneous obeisance before the fearsome skill of the super batsman.

Two more points remain of Sobers on the field, his close fielding and his captaincy. Sobers has one most unusual characteristic of a distinctive close fielder. The batsman is probably aware of him at short-leg, most probably very much aware of him. But the spectator is not. Constantine in the slips and at short-leg prowled and pounced like a panther. Sobers did not. Of all the great short-legs, he is the most unobtrusive that I can bring to mind. To Gibbs, in particular, he seems to stand where there is no need for him to move; in making the catch he will at most fall or rather stretch his length to the right, to the left or straight in front of him. But he is so close and so sure of himself that I for one am not aware of him except to know that he will be there when wanted.

His captaincy has the same measured, one might say classical character. Don Bradman has written how embarrassing it is for a junior cricketer, even a Bradman by 1938, to captain a side containing his seniors. Sobers has had to contend with similar pressures native to West Indies society.

I awaited his handling of the captaincy with some trepidation. Not in any doubt about his strategic or tactical ability, not at all. I could not forget a conversation (one of many) with Frank Worrell, immediately after the return from Australia. We had talked about the future captaincy of the West Indies. Worrell was as usual cautious and non-committal: yes, so-and-so was a good man and capable; and so on. Then, when that stage of the conversation was practically at an end, he suddenly threw in:

"I know that in Australia whenever I had to leave the field, I was glad when I was able to leave Sobers in charge." The timing, the style of the remark was so pointed that I felt I could push the unlocked door right open.

"He knows *everything*?" I asked.

"Everything," Worrell replied. For me that settled one aspect of the question. The other I would be able to see only on the field. I saw it at Sabina Park at the first Test against Australia in 1965. Sobers was completely master of the situation from the moment he stepped on to the field, most probably before. He was aware of everything and at no time aware of himself. He was more in command of his situation than the far more experienced Simpson, though he did not have to face the onslaught that Simpson had to face, a problem not only collective but personal, Hall at one end and Griffith on the other. To see in the course of one day Sobers despatch the ball to all parts of the field with his bat, then open the bowling, fielding at slip to Hall or Griffith, change to Gibbs and place himself at short-leg, then go on to bowl slows, meanwhile placing his men and changing them with certainty and ease, this is one of the sights of the modern cricket field. I cannot visualize anything in the past that corresponds to it.

It was jealousy, nay, political hatred which prompted Cassius to say to Caesar:

Why, man, he doth bestride the narrow world,
Like a Colossus, and we petty men
Walk under his huge legs and peep about,
To find ourselves dishonourable graves.

Certainly in the press-box watching Sobers a mere scribe is aware of Hazlitt's: "Greatness is great power, producing great effects. It is not enough that a man has great power in himself, he must show it to all the world in a manner that cannot be hid or gainsaid." Of a famous racket-player: "He did not seem to follow the ball, but the ball seemed to follow him." Hazlitt would not have minded the appropriation of this acute simplicity for Sobers at short-leg to Gibbs.

At the end of 1966 Sobers had scored over 5,000 runs in Tests and taken well over 100 wickets. Prodigious! Is Sobers the greatest all-rounder ever? The question is not only unrhetorical. It is unhistorical. Is he? I do not know. And nobody knows. I go further. Alert I always am to the reputation of West Indian cricketers; about this I do not even care. Sobers exceeds all I have seen or read of. That for me is enough, but I keep that well within bounds. There are pedants who will claim that he does not face bowling or batting of the temper and skill of previous generations. The argument errs on the side opposite to that which bravely asserts "the greatest ever". Sobers has so far met and conquered all opposition in sight. How can anyone say that if he had met this bowling quartet or that batting trio he could not have conquered them too? My presumption is that he would have dealt adequately with whatever problems he faced. Sir Donald Bradman is reported to have contested strongly Sir Stanley Jackson's dictum that George Lohmann was the greatest of medium-pace bowlers. Sir Donald gave first place to O'Reilly because O'Reilly bowled the googly and Lohmann did not. Despite the eminence of these two gentlemen I beg to disagree with both. Lohmann had no need to bowl the googly. He had enough in his fingers to dismiss the men whom he bowled at. He needed nothing else. To compare him with other bowlers who had other problems and solved them can lead to missing what really matters and what cries for comparison. And what really matters is this: I believe Garfield Sobers has it in him, has already done enough to become the most famous, the most widely known cricketer of the century and of any century barring of course the Telstar of all cricket, W.G. This is not so much a quality of Sobers himself. It is rather the age we live in, its material characteristics and its social temper.

Let us go back to the weekend, more precisely the Sunday, following the first three days of the Oval Test in 1966. West Indies, in their second innings, had lost wickets and still had to make runs to avoid an innings defeat.

On that Sunday over half the world, was that a topic of discussion? Not at all.

The topic was: would Sobers make 200, vitalize his side and so enable West Indies to win? That he could no one doubted, a situation that only one word can express — the word *formidable* as the Frenchman uses it, vocally and manually.

I borrow here a thought from Sir Neville Cardus. Visualize please. Not only in the crowded towns and hamlets of the United Kingdom, not only in the scattered villages of the British Caribbean, people were discussing whether Sobers would make the 200 or not. In the green hills and on the veldt of Africa, on the remote sheep farms of Australia, on the plains of Southern and the mountains of Northern India, on vessels clearing the Indian Ocean, on planes making geometrical figures in the air above the terrestrial globe. In English clubs in Washington and in New York, there that weekend at some time or other they were all discussing whether Sobers would make the 200 required from him for the West Indies to win the match.

Would he? No one knew. But everyone knew that he could. And this was no remote possibility. It was not even 50–50. It was nearer 60–40. I have never known or heard anything like it, though I suspect that in 1895 when W.G. approached the hundredth century the whole cricket world stood on its toes and held its breath. But the means of communication in 1895 were not what they were in 1966. A man must fit into the expanded technicalities of his age. Garfield Sobers does. We are the second half of the twentieth century, heading for the twenty-first, and the word global has shrunk to a modest measure.

In 1967 I saw Garfield Sobers captaining a World XI at Lord's. He not only had been appointed. He fitted the position. No one would challenge either his competence or his moral right to the distinguished position. I confess I was profoundly moved as he led his team on to the ground and fixed his field.

I thought of cricket and the history of the West Indies. I cannot think seriously of Garfield Sobers without thinking of Clifford Goodman, Percy Goodman, H.B.G. Austin (always H.B.G. Austin), Bertie Harragin and others "too numerous to mention" (though not very numerous). They systematically built up the game, played inter-island matches, invited English teams to the West Indies year after year, went to England twice before World War I. I remember too the populace of Trinidad & Tobago subscribing a fund on the spot so that "Old Cons" would not miss the trip to England; and that prodigious St Vincent family of the Ollivierres. The mercantile planter class led this unmercantile social activity and very rapidly they themselves produced the originator of West Indian batting, George Challenor. In 1906 he was a boy of eighteen and made the trip to England. He saw and played with the greatest cricketers England has ever known, the men of the Golden Age. Challenor returned to set a standard and pattern for West Indian batting from which at times it may have deviated, but which it has never lost. That history is a history of its own, going deep, too deep for the present area of discourse.

The local masses of the population, Sobers's ancestors and mine, at first looked on; they knew nothing about the game. Then they began to bowl at the nets, producing at that stage fine fast bowlers. Here more than anywhere else all the different classes of the population learnt to have an interest in common.

The result of that consummation is Garfield Sobers. There is embodied in him the whole history of the British West Indies. Barbados has established a tradition that today is the strength, not only of Barbados, but of the West Indian people. But if there is the national strength there is also the national weakness. Sobers, like the other great cricketers of the present-day West Indies, could develop his various gifts and bring them to maturity only because the leagues in England offered them the opportunity to master English conditions, the most varied and exacting in the world. Without that financial backing, and the opportunity systematically to consolidate potential, to iron out creases, and to venture forth on the sea of experiment, there would be another fine West Indian cricketer but not Garfield the ubiquitous. When Sobers was appointed captain of the West Indies he was the first genuine native son to hold that position, born in the West Indies, educated in the West Indies, learning the foundations of his cricket there without benefit of secondary school, or British university. And there he was, just over thirty, with no serious challenge as the greatest cricketer of his generation.

The roots and the ground he now covers (and can still explore further) go far down into our origins, the origins of all who share in the privileges and responsibilities of all who constitute the British version of Western civilization.

For to see Sobers whole one must place him in a wider framework than meets the eye. Research shows that cricket has been a popular game in England for centuries, but the modern game that we know came into its own at the end of the eighteenth century, and the beginning of the nineteenth. It was part of the total change of an agricultural type of society that was developing into what are now known as the advanced countries. Perhaps a most unexpected and therefore arresting exemplification of the change is to be found in a famous piece of writing.

Few books in English literature are more noteworthy than *The Lyrical Ballads*, a joint publication in 1798 of William Wordsworth and Samuel Taylor Coleridge. In addition to the poems, known today to every schoolboy, Wordsworth wrote a preface, now classical, in which he said what he and Coleridge were trying to do and what had impelled them to do it. Civilization had reached a certain stage of decay and they set out to offer an alternative. It reads as if written yesterday:

> For the human mind is capable of being excited without the application of gross and violent stimulants and he must have a very faint perception of its beauty and dignity who does not know this, and who does not further know, that one being is elevated above another, in proportion as he possessed this capability.

It has therefore appeared to me, that to endeavour to produce or enlarge this capability is one of the best services in which at any period a writer can be engaged; but this service, excellent at all times, is especially so at the present day.

For a multitude of causes unknown to former times, are now acting with a combined force to blunt the discriminating powers of the mind and unfitting it for all voluntary exertion to reduce it to a stage of almost savage torpor.

The most effective of these causes are the great national events which are daily taking place and the increasing accumulation of men in cities where the uniformity of their occupations produces a craving for extraordinary incident, which the rapid communication of intelligence hourly gratifies.

To meet these new chaotic conditions, Wordsworth and Coleridge wrote about simple things with a simplicity that sought to counteract these new dangers. Wordsworth was certain that there were "inherent and indestructible qualities of the human mind" which would survive "this degrading thirst after outrageous stimulation".

That was the period and those the circumstances in which modern cricket was born. In its own way it did what Wordsworth was trying to do.

And this is the enlargement of our historical past and the savannahs of the future which this young man now impels into our vision of ourselves. For he is one of us. We are some of him. I have met his people, listened to his mother talk about her son; he is a West Indian of the West Indies. But he is also a citizen of the world today. Sobers has played not only in the cricketing countries of the wide, wide world. E.W. Swanton has taken him to Malaya and, the other day, Yorkshire took him to play in Canada and the United States.

More than ever today the English game is a most powerful resistant to the "outrageous stimulation" of our age, stimuli far more powerful and far more outrageous than they were in Wordsworth's time.

And of all those who go forth the world over to maintain and develop the beauty and dignity of the human mind which Wordsworth was so certain would survive all challenges, cricketers are not the least. This is the age of Telstar and whatever the engineers do for cricket, there is one all-rounder whom we may be certain will meet their challenge. Such is the social temper of our age that of all cricketers, the ubiquitous all-rounder Sobers, native West Indian, sprung from the people and now treading the purple with unfaltering steps, is the cricketer with whom people living over thousands and thousands of far-removed square miles, in London, Birmingham, Sydney, Calcutta, Nairobi and Capetown, can most easily identify.

In writing about cricket you have to keep an eye on the game, your own eye on the game that is before you, not on any other. Sometimes it is, it has to be, play and players reconstructed in the imagination. Garfield Sobers as a small boy most certainly played cricket barefooted in the streets with a sour orange for a ball and a piece of box or a coconut branch hacked into an approximation of a bat. All of us in the West Indies did that. I have owned a bat since I was four years of age and I do not remember ever being in a situation where I did not own a pair of shoes. But in the early years of this century there were not many, if any, motor cars about, cork balls were easily lost and could be bought only at the nearest small town; and to this day, far less than thirty years ago when Sobers was a boy, from convenience or necessity, future players at Lord's may be seen playing barefooted with a piece of wood and a sour orange in some village or the back street of a small town in the Caribbean. In the larger islands, once you show unusual capacity, people begin to watch you and talk about you. Sobers stood out easily and people have told me that even as a lad he conferred distinction on his club and people were on the lookout to help in any way he needed. In the West Indies the sea divides us and, in any case, when Sobers at the age of sixteen played for Barbados, I could not possibly see him because I was far away in England. Though as a personality he could mean little to me, I read the accounts, as I always did (and always will if I live in Tierra del Fuego). I couldn't help noting that he was only sixteen years old and that he had taken seven wickets. The scores showed that all were bowled or lbw. Very interesting but no more.

Later, however, I saw what I did not see at the time. In the second innings he bowled 67 overs with 35 maidens for 92 runs and 3 wickets, this when India scored 445 for 9. This was a boy of sixteen, obviously someone that would attract special notice. But in those days Valentine filled the bill for slow left-arm bowling. He took 28 wickets in the series so that one could not take Sobers very seriously as a slow left-arm bowler.

Followed the visit of MCC to the West Indies. Sobers did little for Barbados with the ball, but this youth, it seemed, could bat. His 46 in the first innings was the second highest score and he made 27 in the second. After the third Test,

Valentine did not play and Sobers came into the fifth Test, taking four wickets in one innings and scoring 14 and 26 not out. So far, very useful but nothing to strike the eye of anyone far away. He goes into the list of youngest Test players. When he played at Kingston he was only seventeen years and 245 days.

So far there was to the reading eye only promise, but now against the Australians in the West Indies there could be no failure to see that a new man had arrived. Sobers took only six wickets in 93.5 overs. But Valentine in 140 had taken only five. Ramadhin in 139 had taken the same paltry number. Sobers was second in the bowling averages and in batting, in eight innings, had scored 38.50 runs per innings. One began to hear details about his style as a batsman and as a super slip more than as a bowler. In the last Test in Jamaica he made 35 not out and 64. I was informed that from all appearances he would have gone on to the century in a partnership with Walcott which added 79 runs. Sobers was completely master of the bowling but not of himself. Lindwall with a new ball bumped one short at him, Sobers could not resist the hook and found deep square-leg waiting for the catch.

Then came a setback that startled. Sobers went to New Zealand as one of the bright stars of the junior Test players. In four Tests his average was 16 runs and with Valentine doing all that was needed from a left-hander he took only two wickets. In first-class matches his batting average was below 30 and in all first-class matches he took four wickets: far below the boy who had done so well against the full strength of Australia before he was twenty. But for a West Indies team in Port of Spain against E.W. Swanton's team, Sobers had three for 85 and three for 49, and made 71, second only to Weekes with 89. New Zealand was a distant dot on the Sobers landscape.

West Indies came to England in 1957 and obviously Sobers was someone I had to see as soon as possible. I went down to Lord's to see the team at the nets but this was my first glimpse of the three Ws and I don't remember noticing Sobers, except for his fine physique. I missed the Worcester match but found myself at Northampton to see the second game. Curiously enough, as he did often that year, he played second fiddle to Worrell, in a stand of over a century of which his share was only 36. But great batsman was written all over him, and I think it was Ian Peebles who referred to him in terms of Woolley. I remember noting the stroke off the back foot that sent the length ball of the pace bowler past cover's right hand. There was another stroke, behind point off a pitched-up fast ball. The ball was taken on the rise and placed behind point to beat the covers, now packed. Here obviously was that rare phenomenon, in cricket or any other form of artistic endeavour, someone new, who was himself and like no one else. There are vignettes in 1957 that are a permanent part of my cricket library. There was an innings against MCC at Lord's in which Sobers came as near as it was possible for him to look like Constantine in that with monotonous regularity the ball flew from his bat to all parts of the field. In the first Test at Birmingham, he made over 50 in little more than an hour and I remember in particular my being startled at the assured manner in which he glanced — I think it was Bailey — from the middle stump to square-leg and so beat the man at long-leg. The same determination to thumb his fingers at the covers lifted Lock or Laker overhead to drop in front of the pavilion for four; batsmen didn't do these things in 1957.

In the last Test at the Oval West Indies collapsed before Lock and Laker and there came fully to the surface the element of stubbornness which Sobers had shown in the last innings at Kingston in 1953 in his partnership with Walcott, and which I had glimpsed at his batting with Worrell at Northampton. Out of a total of 89 he made 39 and in the second innings out of 86, 42. I believe I saw how famous men of old made runs on impossible wickets. To Laker in particular Sobers played back, always back. When Laker had him playing back often enough, he would drop a ball just outside the off-stump going away from Sobers to cut: there was a long list of West Indian casualties to this particular disease which appeared most often in the records as "Walcott c. Evans b. Laker". Sobers, however, it would appear was waiting for Laker. Time and again he could get across and cut the ball down past third man.

In a review of the season Skelding, former county fast bowler and now umpire, was reported in one of the annuals as saying that the Sobers he saw in 1957 would be one of the greatest batsmen who ever lived. I could not go quite so far but I have it down in writing of 1958 that if Sobers developed as he promised in 1957, he would be the greatest of living batsmen. So that the 365 which exceeded Hutton's 364 and the tremendous scoring which followed filled out a portrait whose outlines had been firmly drawn. No need to go through 1963. I saw and felt what I expected to see and feel. However, there was one piece of play in the field which I have seen mentioned only in Wisden and not commented upon elsewhere. That was his bowling in the Oval Test. The famous feat of fast bowling in 1963 was Wesley Hall at Lord's in the second innings when his figures read 40 overs, 9 maidens, 4 wickets for 93 runs. He bowled during the three hours and twenty minutes which play was in progress on the last day. I believe that on that last day he bowled 35 overs.

Now in the Oval Test Sobers bowled in the first innings 21 overs, 4 maidens, for 2 wickets, 44 runs. I remember these two wickets. He had Bolus caught by keeper Murray (33) and Edrich, caught Murray, for 25. Hall and Griffith had tried in vain to break that partnership and Sobers, struggling mightily, dismissed both of them well set. In the second innings he did even better; again he dismissed Bolus at 15, again well set, and Dexter when at 27 he seemed poised for one of his great innings. Sobers bowled 33 overs and took 3 wickets for 77 runs. At the time and to this day I measure that performance and Sobers as a fast bowler by his approximation at the Oval to Hall's far more famous feat in the Test at Lords.

There is one episode on the field which for some reason or other sticks in my mind as representative of Sobers. He came out to bat at the Oval against Surrey early in 1963. He came to the wicket and some Surrey bowler bowled him a short ball. It went to the square-leg boundary. A dead metaphor can sometimes be made to live again: that ball went like a flash. As far as I remember the same over saw another ball, short, but this time outside the off stump and rising higher than usual. That ball streaked to the off boundary. Sobers had not scored any runs in the south and everybody including myself believed that here was the beginning of one of the great innings. It was not to be. Two or three balls later he was out to the almost audible lamentation of the crowd which had been keyed up to a pitch in the belief that we were going to see what we had come forth to see.

Sobers today is a captain and I believe it would be worthwhile to give some hint of what I have been able to detect of the personality behind that play. I do not know Sobers as well as I knew Constantine, George John and Headley and the men I have played with. But there are certain things that one can divine. I saw Sobers in 1957 make 27 at Leeds and then get run out not through anybody's fault but by some superb fielding by Tony Lock. Finer batting it is impossible to imagine and that day nothing was more certain than a century before lunch in a Test. But this is not why I remember that day. What remains in my mind is the fury, the rage of Sobers at having been dismissed when he obviously felt that history was in his hands for the making. His walk back to the pavilion made me think of those hurricanes that periodically sweep the Caribbean. I caught a glimpse, by transference so to speak, of the aggressive drive which expresses itself in his batting and fast bowling. I have already referred to the demonic hits with which he greeted Hall's attempt to bowl him out in a practice game. In the Test which followed that practice game Sobers drove too early at a wide half-volley and was caught for 0. Again on his way back to the pavilion I saw the gleam of the damped-down furnace that raced inside of him. Therefore when I read his detailed protests against what he considers the unfairness of British reporters and commentators in their diatribes against his team of 1966 in general and Griffith in particular, I take it much more seriously than most. The protest is not a formality, or something that ought to be put on record, parliamentary fashion. He feels it personally, as a man feels a wound. I suspect that that is the personality which expresses itself as ubiquitously as it does on the field because it needs room. A man of genius is what he is, he cannot be something else and remain a man of genius.

I think of Sobers walking down the pavilion steps at Lord's, captain of an international cricket team. Sixty years ago it would have been Pelham Warner, another West Indian, and thirty years before that it would have been Lord Harris, yet another cricketer of Caribbean connotation. Whoever and whatever we are, we are cricketers. Garfield Sobers I see not as a fortuitous combination of atoms which by chance have coalesced into a superb public performer. He being what he is (and I being what I am), for me his command of the rising ball in the drive, his close fielding and his hurling himself into his fast bowling are a living embodiment of centuries of a tortured history.

Learie Constantine

(From *The Great All-Rounders*, edited by John Arlott, Pelham Books, 1969)

Constantine is probably the only all-rounder in cricket who could win his place in a Test side by fielding alone. That will not be easy to demonstrate on the page of a book. In baseball, errors and brilliant playing in the field are statistically recorded; not yet in cricket. Not as difficult but not very easy to record is the place he has won in other spheres of this great and important game: both on and off the field he did not leave the game where he found it. To very few has it been given to do this.

Constantine is not a Test cricketer who played in the leagues. He is a league cricketer who played Test cricket. It is not enough to do justice to league cricket. Justice must be seen to be done. League cricket today is what he made it. As far back as 1963 I referred to the coverage of league cricket by the national Press as "caves, dark and unfathomed". It was only in 1965 that Wisden extended its section on league cricket. We shall therefore begin with league performances of this greatest of league cricketers.

Here are the figures of Constantine's play during his great years in the Lancashire League, 1929–37. In the nine seasons that he played with Nelson, they were league champions on seven occasions, runners-up twice. His first season, in 1929, broke all records, for £2,380 was paid in gate records to watch this great professional play with a great team. A higher record was created in away matches, for these gates totalled £2,659. Of course, Nelson were again champions. Learie in his final analysis had scored 820 runs (average 34.16) and taken 88 wickets at 12 runs each.

Although Nelson were only runners-up in 1930, he headed their batting and bowling averages, with 621 runs (average 38.81), and 73 wickets at a cost of 10.46 each. Nelson won again in 1931 and added to this victory the Worsley Cup. Learie's figures read: 961 runs (average 51), 91 wickets (average 9.54).

In 1932, the figures were: 476 runs (average 22.66), 91 wickets (average 8.15). In 1933 but for missing two matches (to play with the West Indies team) he would surely have done the double unheard-of in this league, of 1,000 runs and 100 wickets. Only four wickets short, his final analysis was: 1,000 runs (average 52.63), 96 wickets (average 8.5). In 1934 Nelson won both cups. Learie's analysis was 807 runs (average 40.17), 104 wickets (average 8.12).

In 1935, victory again. Although Learie missed seven matches, his analysis was: 493 runs (average 30.81), 79 wickets (average 10.5). It was victory again in 1936; Learie's final figures being: 632 runs (average 33.26), 86 wickets (average 11.22). 1937 was his final year. Little short of thirty-five years of age, his final Nelson analysis read: 863 runs (average 43.15), 82 wickets (average 11.41).

The concentration on Learie's figures (in relation to league cricket in Lancashire it would be wrong, unhistorical, not to call him "Learie") . . . the concentration on the figures is not simply a biographical and historical need. Constantine has written extensively on the game, few cricketers more, and wherever possible I shall let him speak for himself. In an illuminating chapter on league cricket in his first book he analyses the role of the professional in a league side. He draws in detail his special functions and value but ends by saying: "If even the professional is the essence of selfishness, and thinks only of doing well for himself, it will pay him in the end to study and help his side as much as possible; for it is with them that he has to play and no one man can consistently beat eleven others at cricket. It is a case of him who wishes to save his soul first losing it."

The figures are biographically important for another reason. So acute a critic as Sir Donald Bradman has expressed the belief that Constantine was the success he was in league cricket because he could turn the fortunes of a Saturday afternoon match by quarter-hours of fierce fast bowling and brilliant hitting. Those figures and the record in general show nothing of the kind. I saw a good many of those league matches. The cricket was tense and often it was tough. It was agreed among the players that it was harder to get a hundred wickets in the league than in county games. But tight as the cricket was, happenings were always bursting through. And I repeat here one recorded by the Nelson journalist to whom I am indebted for these figures:

One year Nelson required only a victory over Enfield in the last match of the season to enable them to retain the league cup. The Lancashire League officials came to Nelson, and sat down to witness a comfortable Nelson victory. Making full use of the glorious uncertainty, the Enfield team beat Nelson, and then raced back to the pavilion, to get the rare privilege of a look at the cup. But they were yards late. The cup and officials were speeding off to Church in a taxi. Todmorden, having beaten Church, were the new champions.

Constantine had visited England in 1923. He had come with a modest reputation. He left with little more than a promise of great things to come. Then came the 1928 visit. He scored more runs than any other member of the team, and also headed the bowling averages. In first-class games alone he scored 1,381 runs at an average of 34.52, and took 107 wickets at a cost of 22.95 runs each wicket. But even this remarkable performance, although without parallel for over a generation by any visiting fast bowler (except for J.M. Gregory in 1921), was relegated to mere statistics by something that both the public and the professors hailed with equal enthusiasm as a new dimension of play on the field. There had been and were great all-round fieldsmen. No one had so dominated this department of cricket wherever he was placed, or decided to place himself, slip, short leg, or in the covers. We have to stay here a while and place great fielding in general, and Constantine's fielding in particular, where it belongs. I do not believe it has been done before and if even it has been it is worth doing again.

We cannot do better than place ourselves in the shadow of that luminary of English life and English prose, William Hazlitt. With his usual directness Hazlitt tackles the question of the use of the term "great" in relation to physical performers. There are passages and persons it would be sacrilegious to para-phrase.

A great chess-player is not a great man, for he leaves the world as he found it. No act terminating in itself constitutes greatness. This will apply to all displays of power or trials of skill, which are confined to the momentary, individual effort, and construct no permanent image or trophy of themselves without them. Is not an actor, then, a great man, because "he dies and leaves the world no copy"? I must make an exception for Mrs Siddons or else give up my definition of greatness for her sake.

You might think that this writer of casual essays was, as is the habit of this type of writer, merely expressing a personal preference, being what the Americans call "cute". No such thing. Hazlitt is deadly serious. Elsewhere we find him saying at length what he thought of Mrs Siddons and why:

But to the retired and lonely student, through long years of solitude, her face has shone as if an eye had appeared from heaven; her name has been as if a voice had opened the chambers of the human heart, or as if a trumpet had awakened the sleeping and the dead. To have seen Mrs Siddons was an event in everyone's life. . . .

Though the distance of place is a disadvantage to a performance like Mrs Siddons's Lady Macbeth, we question whether the dis-tance of time at which we have formerly seen it is any. It is nearly twenty years since we first saw her in this character, and certainly the impression which we have still left on our minds from that first exhibition is stronger than the one we received the other evening.

The sublimity of Mrs Siddons's acting is such, that the first impulse which it gives to the mind can never wear out, and we doubt whether this original and paramount impression is not weakened, rather than strengthened, by subsequent reptition; if we have seen Mrs Siddons in Lady Macbeth, only once, it is enough. The impression is stamped there for ever, and any after-experiments and critical inquiries only serve to fritter away and tamper with the sacredness of the early recollection.

If only Hazlitt had reported cricket matches. (He wrote fabulously on boxers and on a great fives-player.) But in his writing you glimpse some representation of what people see when they are dazzled by the sunburst (especially in the bleak English weather) of a great cricketer at his best, and particularly of a fieldsman. In 1928 people learnt to come to see Constantine field and to this day some have never forgotten what they saw. I know I have never forgotten single episodes I have seen at cricket: a great number by Constantine, batting, or bowling, or fielding. It is a conception I am trying to drive home: one day in 1954 at Sheffield I saw an England fast bowler bowl a length ball to Freddie Trueman. What spirit moved through that strong-willed, strong-armed bowler of fast balls I do not know, but he drew himself up to his full height, put his left foot forward in a most majestic manner and taking the ball on the rise drove it through extra-cover (nearer to mid-off), for a classical perfection of a four. His follow-through was just high enough to make the stroke a drive and not a forward-stroke. Having finished his stroke he remained poised just long enough to show that he knew he did not have to run. Whereupon he returned to normality, this being for him an old-style number ten or eleven who might or might not connect with his sporadic heaves at the ball. The point about Constantine's fielding is that you came to the ground and looked at him expecting the moment of artistic truth and were rarely disappointed.

But more than that. That year he could register indelibly on the spectator's consciousness on the field, with bat and with ball, right through a three-day match. Against Middlesex he went in at 79 for 5. In twenty minutes he had scored 50 and 86 in less than an hour. Then in 6.1 overs he took 6 wickets for 11 runs. In the second innings West Indies were 121 for 5. He hit 103 out of 133 in an hour, 50 of them in eighteen minutes. All through the season he was performing similarly. It is sufficient to say of this series of displays that they defied the accepted logic of past history. That year the only outstanding player with any pretensions of pace who did the double was Maurice Tate who took 165 wickets and scored over 1,400 runs. But whereas Tate bowled well over 1,500 overs Constantine bowled little over 700. He took thirty catches. Tate was a tremendous cricketer, definitely a greater bowler than Constantine. But I do not think that any or many single efforts by him made the shattering registration on the consciousness and memory of the spectator which Constantine repeatedly did through a whole season. Figures here positively distort the actuality.

We restore perspective by noting that in 1928 Constantine failed in the last three Test matches, failed that is to say as batsman and bowler. In 1929–30 in the West Indies, he took 18 wickets with his fast bowling in four Tests. His batting was again moderate but his fielding at slip and short-leg reached heights never attained by him before or after. The account of that, however, must wait. He went to Australia in 1930–31 and though his figures were good they were not particularly striking. However, he did not fail to make spectators realize that they were watching a cricketer the like of which they had never seen before. The Australian authorities asked him for a photograph to place among their special collection of great players.

By 1933 Constantine had mastered the technique of batting and bowling in the League. But for playing with the visiting West Indies team he would have done the double. He took, you remember, 96 wickets and made 1,000 runs with an average of over 50. This was the seasoned cricketer who now re-entered the first-class game in England. He played in very few matches. Against Yorkshire at Harrogate he had 5 for 44 and 4 for 50, getting Sutcliffe for 2, Holmes for 0, Leyland for 9 (in the second innings for 10); in the whole match 9 wickets for 94 runs.

Previous to this he had come down to play for West Indies against MCC. Thousands came out to see the man of 1928. He took four wickets for 88 runs including Hearne for 12, Hendren for 6, and D.R. Jardine for 7. In the second innings he hit 51 out of 66 in twenty-seven minutes. But it was in the single Test match that he played at Manchester that Constantine, the Test batsman, appeared. He made 31 out of 36 in the first innings, the West Indies after 226 for 2 collapsing for 325. In the second innings West Indies were 2 for 132 and finally staved off defeat by reaching 225. Constantine had saved the situation by a hard-hit 64 made in fifty minutes. I know that he was spoiling for the fray in the last Test at the Oval and he complains that he was manipulated out of it. In 1934–5 in the West Indies, he was at his best. He played in only three of the four Tests but took 15 wickets at a cost of 13.13 each and made runs steadily, usually when they were badly wanted.

The next height scaled by Constantine — he always gave me the impression that he was scaling or about to scale new heights — was his re-entry for a season's play with the West Indies team of 1939. What Constantine did in 1939 can best be expressed by an experience with his fellow warrior in many a hard-fought field. I was talking to George Headley in Jamaica in 1965 and the conversation, one of the strangest that I have ever had on cricket, went something like this.

"Tell me, George, do you remember any innings that you have played that you think of with special pride and satisfaction?"

Headley's face was that of a man who was asked if he remembered the day that he was born. "No," he said, "I don't remember any of them. I just played these innings as they came."

"Nothing, George? Not even the century in each innings at Lord's?"

"No," he replied, his face still a blank.

I was intrigued. "Tell me," I said, "is there any innings played by anybody that stands out in your mind?"

"No," he said slowly, trying his best to help me. "Frankly I don't remember any of them specially. I have seen a lot of good innings but none stands out."

I decided to force him to the wall.

"Is there anything at all in your career which stands out as something you cannot forget?"

His face lightened and he became not only enthusiastic but excited. "Yes," he said, "most certainly. I often remember how Learie, the fast bowler I used to know, changed his style in 1939 and became a slow-to-medium bowler as effective as he had been when bowling fast. That is the thing about cricket that I remember most."

I had the sense not to push the matter any further. George Headley is a very honest and a very sincere man and what he had told me showed not only his own attitude to the game that he had played with such distinction, but the impact that Constantine made upon not only spectators but upon players.

In 1939, bowling a mixture of medium-pace and slow, with googlies, and of course the inevitable fast one, Constantine ended with the following: 651.2 overs, 67 maidens, 1,831 runs, 103 wickets, average 17.7.

These are among the most remarkable figures ever achieved

by any visiting bowler in England. Especially for a man of thirty-seven who eleven years before, as a fast bowler, had taken his hundred wickets in the following terms: 723.3 overs, 131 maidens, 2,456 runs, 107 wickets; average 22.95.

A cursory review of the figures of visiting bowlers who have taken a hundred wickets convey unexpected relations, even oddities, out of which Constantine's figures emerge not only with brilliance but with an abiding solidity. Take O'Reilly in 1938 and R.J. Crisp of South Africa in 1935. In 1938, W.J. O'Reilly bowled 709.4 overs, 215 maidens, 1,732 runs, 104 wickets, average 16.65. In 1935, Crisp: 690.5 overs, 105 maidens, 2,096 runs, 107 wickets, average 19.58. In 1934, O'Reilly and Grimmett each took 109 wickets. But where more than one bowler has taken that number of wickets, too much has to be taken into account before any too obvious conclusions can be drawn.

To take their hundred wickets, however, O'Reilly needed 870 overs and Grimmett 985.4. Constantine took his 103 wickets in 651 overs. We have to go back to a great bowler of pre-1914 to find comparable figures: Hugh Trumble in 1902 (six-ball overs) took 137 wickets at the low cost of 14.2 runs per wicket and needed only 912 overs, just above Constantine's wicket every six overs. However, 1902 was a notoriously wet season, made to order for bowlers of Trumble's pace and spin.

The figures of other West Indies bowlers are worth remembering and comparing. In 1933, E.A. Martindale, the West Indian fast bowler, carrying the main responsibility for piercing a heavy phalanx of English batsmen, emerged with 668 overs, 109 maidens, 2,161 runs, 103 wickets, average 20.98. For the fast bowler's business, despatching batsmen with promptitude, these figures are almost identical with Constantine's. Nothing, however, approaches Charlie Griffith's figures in 1963. His 119 wickets fell in 695 overs, a batsman every six overs, and the cost was incredible: 12.82 runs per wicket. To complete the overall outline, add the following for the West Indies team in 1966. Between them Griffith, Sobers, Gibbs and Hall took 195 wickets and to do so needed 1,962 overs, ten overs for a wicket. Apart from the deceptiveness of figures in themselves, it must be repeated that there are all sorts of imponderables which have to be taken into account, not only the year's weather but the quality and type of batting that the bowlers faced. One point, however, can be responsibly added. Robertson-Glasgow, summing up the season of 1939, in *Wisden* of 1940 reported that an experienced observer had given a considered opinion that the first dozen or so of English batsmen in 1939 were in sum the equals at least of his own time, that is about 1905–14. Robertson-Glasgow went on to say that the old freedom of stroke-play had returned. Perhaps this it was that helped Constantine's slows to get his wicket every six overs. It would be too invidious to detail the many batsmen heading the averages for their county whom Constantine's slows dismissed for little or nothing. It was a correspondent of *The Times* who noted that no other bowler was more expert at diddling batsmen out. That he had learnt in the league.

Constantine played some league cricket afterwards but we need not go into that. Two years after 1937 war broke out. He was occupied with war work and there was no league cricket again until 1946. He played for various league clubs but at no time did he attempt or could he reach the standards he had set in the Nelson years. That much he knew and although he gave great service to various clubs in other leagues, the Nelson years were the beginning and end of a period, one of the historic periods of English cricket.

It would be a mistake to ignore the fact that the glamorous spontaneity of Constantine's cricket did not have behind it an exceptionally shrewd and penetrating judgement of the generalities and refinements of play on the field. Take what would appear to be above all an explosion of hand and eye and energy — the marvellous catches. I have never seen or heard of a series of catches such as Constantine took in Trinidad against the MCC team in 1930. Some of the catches were literally created by the fieldsman. George Gunn brought to the West Indies his habit of walking down the pitch to meet a ball just as it pitched. He did this once. The second time as he started to go down Constantine, at second slip, moved fast and began walking side by side with him: Gunn did not completely control the stroke: he edged the ball slightly, the catch was a dolly and Constantine picked it up one-handed. I presume that such a response to his adventurous habits had never happened to Gunn before. That alertness was behind many of the catches. I used to watch the great Bradman playing to Verity before he had begun to score. During that initial period, more than once I saw Bradman nervous, playing forward very shakily to Verity's leg-break and edging the ball slightly towards the offside in the direction of point. Once that had happened Bradman was at once, as if by magic, completely master of himself. But after seeing the uncertain stroke off Verity and the ball drop two or three feet from the edge of the bat I said to myself, "If Constantine was on

that side you would play Verity differently or you would be
caught for 0.''

Many of the famous catches were so subtly created that, even
to a not unskilled observer, the process could only be known
afterwards when Constantine himself explained. Hendren is 98
on the matting wicket in Trinidad. Achong is bowling to him
slow to medium left hand and as is natural on the old-style
coconut matting he is turning the ball slightly from the leg.
Constantine knows the tension which Hendren, at 98, probably
feels. He is standing in the gully and he instructs Achong, his
junior, to keep the ball just outside the off-stump at a good
length and not to attempt anything else. Achong obeys implicit-
ly and Hendren remains at 98. Standing in the gully, his eyes
glued on Hendren, Constantine notices that Hendren, before
getting down to face Achong once more, takes a quick glance at
the wide spaces between gully and second slip. Achong bowls
the same ball as before. Hendren cuts to pierce the gap he has
spotted between Constantine at gully and second slip, only to
see that Constantine has anticipated the stroke and is making
what is apparently an easy catch from not a bad but an
ill-judged stroke. I saw the incident and the whole thing had
been done so discreetly and unobtrusively that I did not know
what had happened until I was told. Hendren, however, knew
and before he left the wicket expressed his appreciation to
Constantine in language not violent but personal, quite
personal.

Some more of the brain which directed the brawny West
Indies playing in Kingston. Constantine is captaining the side,
the official captain being ill. West Indies are well ahead in runs.
The problem is to get the England team out in time, in
particular Leslie Ames who is in the 90s and completely master
of the bowling. Constantine knows he has to get Ames out and
he goes to the slow left-arm bowler and tells him what he must
do. "Keep your length. Drop the ball on the off-stump, breaking
away as you have been doing. I am going to go and stand at silly
mid-off a few feet away. Now, mind you, keep the length with
the little bit of turn from leg that you are getting. Ames is going
to get his century. The moment he gets it he is going to be
looking for a chance to open out and especially to move me.
Then bowl a ball over the good length but moving it to him with
the arm. He is going to drive. The ball will hit the inside edge of
the bat and I will have a chance to pick him up. But mind you,
when I am standing there I am taking my life in my hands. You
do exactly as I tell you and we will see.''

Constantine stood at silly mid-off. Ames made his century. The bowler pitched up the ball, moving in with the arm. Ames believed his chance had come; came forward and drove. He did not connect squarely but hit with the inside edge, Constantine threw him up and the match was won. A year or two ago I saw Constantine recalling the incident to Ames at Lord's. And both of them revelled in the memory.

This standing where a full hit by a powerful batsman can seriously hurt plays a part in one of Constantine's most spectacular catches. It was in 1933 in the Test at Manchester, where a Lancashire crowd saw Learie catch R.E.S. Wyatt one-handed practically under the bat at short leg. Constantine was standing there for Martindale's attempt at body-line. Martindale pitched short, and Constantine began to move away looking to defend himself, not to catch anything but to avoid being damaged by a powerful stroke from a good batsman and bad ball. But as he was going he kept his eye on Wyatt and spotted that Wyatt was mistiming the stroke and could not possibly do anything serious to the ball. He therefore returned to his position. Wyatt hit the ball much too late, and Constantine stuck up one hand and pulled down what, from the ring, seemed to be a dazzling feat. Constantine reported it as in reality a very easy catch from a stroke that had no power behind it and from which the flight of the ball from the bat could be easily followed. That catch was made before the ball hit the bat. And this marks Constantine's fielding at slip and short leg. He preached and constantly practised anticipation. Another superb slip, Walter Hammond, preached and practised that at slip it was a mistake to anticipate. I believe there is more to this difference than merely opposition in style. Sufficient for the time being that each master achieved in his own way mastery. You cannot ask more.

There is no need to go into further details about the famous innings, the main point about them being the strokes that make them memorable. For example there is the square cut off G.O. Allen in 1928 that sent the ball high up into the stands at Lord's for six. There is another uniquely original boundary in 1933. Someone bowled Constantine a slow, high full-pitch. Constantine turned, faced square leg and hit the ball for six straight behind the wicket-keeper, another of the strokes that no one remembers having seen before or seen afterwards. Yet there is a curious misconception about the last of his innings in Test cricket, the famous 79 made in the Oval Test in 1939. Of many appreciations, every one of them in my opinion fundamentally false, the place of honour will be given to *Wisden* 1940: *Wisden* cannot possibly be affected by any sharp disagreement. This is the account of the innings:

> It was a real joy to watch the carefree cricket of the West Indies on the last day. Constantine, in the mood suggesting his work on Saturday afternoon League cricket, brought a welcome air of gaiety to the Test arena. He revolutionized all the recognized features of cricket and, surpassing Bradman in his amazing stroke play, he was absolutely impudent in his aggressive treatment of bowling shared by Nichols and Perks. While the four remaining wickets fell those two bowlers delivered 92 balls from which Constantine made 78 runs out of 103. Seldom can there have been such a spreadeagled field with no slips, and Hammond did not dare risk further trouble by changing his attack. With an astonishing stroke off the back foot Constantine thumped Perks for 6 to the Vauxhall end — a very long carry — and helped himself to eleven fours before he was last out to a very fine catch by Wood; running towards the pavilion the wicket-keeper held the ball that had gone high over his head.

The facts are correct. What I challenge is the belief invariably expressed about his innings that Constantine brought to this Test the carefree and impudent manner in which he played Saturday afternoon league cricket. That is most certainly not true. I saw Constantine year after year batting in the league. There was no air of gaiety or impudence in the innings that he played or in the thousands that he scored. There were times when he would amaze spectators by the audacity, even the daring of his strokes but it was all very seriously and systematically done: league cricket was not played for fun. At the risk of repeating myself I must give one example of this type of batting in the league.

Constantine is facing the impeccable length and direction of McDonald, the Australian who is still a dangerous bowler on a Saturday afternoon. Unable to get the ball away to a well-placed field, Constantine suddenly takes a long stride forward with his left foot and glances McDonald from outside the off-stump to long leg for four. A few balls later he brings off the same amazing stroke. Whereupon McDonald rearranges the field and Constantine does not make the stroke again. As I have elsewhere written, "In these two strokes there was not the slightest restlessness or chanciness. The unorthodoxy was carried out with a precision and care, fully equal to the orthodoxy of Mac's classical action and perfect length."

It was in the 1939 Test that Constantine played carefree, impudent cricket. West Indies had ended on the Friday 43 runs ahead, with four wickets in hand. They had seriously planned to win that Oval Test. The runs had to be made as far as possible and Constantine reverted to the spontaneous exuberance of 1928. But here, as always, it was business. And we get a glimpse of what he would have made of Test cricket if the early batsmen on his side had had names that began with the same letter, for example W.

Not only on but off the field this all-rounder made his mark. He is to be placed as an ambassador with Lord Hawke, Pelham Warner and Sir Frank Worrell. They travelled far and travelled wide, and where they passed the blossoms and flowers of cricket bloomed or sprouted.

And finally Constantine has written on the game as no other professional and few amateurs have written.

On bowling: "I am genuinely sorry when I hit a batsman but I know that I must have him aware that the ball can be made to do something. . . . If a batsman can take my short ball and hit it round to square-leg he is a fine batsman . . . for me to put a fine leg and a bunch of short-legs and then a man on the deep square-leg boundary is to reduce cricket very nearly to a farce."

On Test cricket: "The excitement, the publicity, the material rewards, all will tend to increase and so gradually to impregnate this most beautiful of all games with the spirit which resulted in the deplorable scenes connected now, it seems inseparably, with all Test matches." This he was saying as far back as 1933.

And what to do about it? Let the last words be his.

"Conditions are such in the West Indies that we shall never be able to play cricket in the style that it is played by so many Englishmen and not a few Australians, and it is my firm belief that we can learn the atmosphere of Test cricket, get together as a side in order to pull our full weight and yet as a side preserve that naturalness and ease which distinguish our game."

He has lived to see it come true. And both on and off the field none had worked harder, all round, to make what seemed to many a wish-fulfilling idiosyncratic dream into a global reality.

Letter to Rowland Bowen*

London NW2

13 March 1969

My dear Major Bowen,

As soon as I started life today, I have been squeezing in the reading of your book. I am now at the Modern Period VIII.

It is one of the most extraordinary historical analyses I have ever read, and is fully comparable to work by an accredited scholar in a particular field.

I write because I feel one gap. About Beldham, and most particularly about the famous trio, Pilch, Mynn, etc. You do not bring in the kind of strokes they make, the off-drive, the cut for which Beldham was so famous, the leaving of the crease to the slower bowlers, the particular style and pitch and pace of the regular bowlers where they got their wickets, etc. etc. I must confess that I feel fanatically that no history of cricket which does not bring these concrete matters to the attention of the readers can be said to be doing what the game, or any other game, requires. Such is my respect and indeed, admiration, for the remarkable work that you have done here, that I take the risk, even before completing the book, to tell you at once what I think would add considerably, not only to its interest, but to its historical value.

Please accept this in the spirit in which it is written, a spirit not only of admiration, but of wonder at the historical insight, and the sense of phenomena of history, not only of cricket history, but of history in general, which you here display as never before.

As ever,
C.L.R. James.

P.S. I have just finished the section on W.G. Grace and I feel more than ever that there is needed here some account of the great professional fast bowlers who dominated the game, and the technique as well as the spirit, but particularly the new technique which was introduced by W.G. Grace, etc. etc. I would make clear what I say later, but I'm merely submitting this for your consideration.

*Founder and editor of *Cricket Quarterly* and author of *Cricket: A History of its Growth and Development throughout the World*

Letter to Rowland Bowen

London NW2

25 March 1969

Dear Major Bowen,

Most unfortunately I may have to leave for the United States on Saturday coming to stay until June. Meanwhile, however, I impose myself on you by sending you the enclosed pictures and the letter from Stanley Paul. I want your opinion on them and although I doubt if you will be able to send them back to me in time, nevertheless please send them as soon as you can so that they can be sent on to me in the United States if I go.

It is to teach at a university. The question is whether the American authorities will let me in. I have been to the United States five times during the last decade but it seems that they have to overlook the question of my entry every single time. I presume that they think I may have recently learnt to throw bombs or something.

In regard to the question of technique: I am glad that you do not wish me to go into detail because some of my books are put away and especially at the present time it will be difficult to put my hands on them. But it is useful that you do not need and in fact most certainly do not require any lengthy or detailed references. The things I have in mind are comparatively simple.

1. There was a time when I am thinking that batsmen or a batsman started to move out of his crease "to run them down" and that caused more than a flutter in batting. Somewhere around the same time there was William Beldham and his cut. Others used to cut too but I have in mind that that cut was a notable stage in the development. Round about that period also there was a change in the delivery of the underhand bowling.

2. The next stage I have in mind as suitable for reference is W.G. Grace. I refer, of course, to the passage where he summed up all the techniques that men had previously used and began a new era in batting. I remember being very embarrassed to make that quotation in my book but I faced the question that it had to be done. That is a stage in the history of the batting and one might as well be embarrassed in writing about the Battle of Hastings when dealing with the early history of Britain.

About the same time, before and after, there is the change in bowling. Before W.G. the fast bowlers used to revel on the rough wickets and the players used to win match after match. But W.G. conquered them and introduced the new comprehensive style. As I see it, the whole body of batsmen followed him (which is enough for our purposes) and a generation of orthodox batsmen came into existence. But, and this is very important, by the end of the century the style had become extremely dull. The bowling was dull, the batting was dull, and in England Ranjitsinhji and C.B. Fry changed the style of batting. Backplay and forcing strokes to the onside were introduced by them and became regular features of batting technique. And what is not commonly known but I am sure is understood by you is that in Australia there was the same dullness and commonplace of batting and Victor Trumper changed the style. That is very clear in M.A. Noble's book, *The Game's the Thing*.

It was in my opinion this change in the aggressiveness of batting which developed the particular variety in bowling methods which we find between the end of the century and 1914.

I do not think that there is any need for me to take it further. I believe I have referred to the changes that mattered and which should be referred to in a book of the kind. That is all I had in mind. I shall let you know my address in the United States if I go there and hope to continue the discussion on these and other points. The Sobers matter I shall go into, both for our mutual understanding and for my information and method of going into a serious point. I am sending back the Sobers material of which I have had a copy made for myself. The text of your book I shall let you have in a day or two, most certainly before I leave, if I do leave.

Very sincerely yours,
C.L.R. James.

West Indian Cricketers in County Cricket

(1960s)

Having made themselves into a *sine qua non* in league cricket, West Indian cricketers are now embarked on what could be a comparable establishment in county cricket. As experienced a commentator as John Woodcock, who knows the West Indies not only at Lord's and at the Oval, but in their own Caribbean habitat, comments as follows (*The Times*, 4 July): "On a day when overseas players showed our own home-bred ones how to play it was between Livingstone from Antigua and Marshall from Barbados."

With all due respect to Ahmeds, Mohammads, Saeds, etc., and other oriental nomenclature, to talk about overseas players in English cricket is to bring to mind at once the West Indians. The West Indian player is a special type, *sui generis*, a type which is fundamentally the same as it has been for over seventy years.

Let me give my own experience of this peculiar phenomenon. The other Sunday I saw on television the latest import: a young man from Guyana by name Lloyd. His record in inter-territorial and Test cricket is what it is. What I saw was the embodiment of two West Indians whom England saw as far back as 1923, men whom I have known well and with whom I have played a lot of cricket. Lloyd startled the crowd and commentators by the speed and ubiquity of his fielding at cover. An experienced English observer said that it reminded him of Learie Constantine's fielding on the Edgbaston ground in matches that were played during the war. He mentioned the fact that Constantine at that time was over forty years of age. This was one more proof that the dazzlingly mobile Constantine still retained the dash and vigour which we had experienced twenty-five years before. But a few Sundays ago the Lloyd I saw at cover was the early Constantine, whose appearance added a new dimension to West Indian experience in 1922, before he came to England; but for the spectacles, Lloyd could have been passed off as an ancient telepicture of the youthful Constantine.

When Lloyd batted I saw an embodiment of another West Indian of forty years ago — Joe Small. We have and Small had the advantage of having been the subject of a famous description of West Indian batting by Mr Neville Cardus. In 1923 (after the sun had at last come out) against Lancashire, Small made 94 and 68.

No doubt one of the purposes of the West Indies cricketers' visit to this country is to get instruction into the fine shades of the game from our famous men. Well, there is one West Indies cricketer, at least, who is likely to teach our very best professional batsmen quite as much as he learns from them. . . .

This West Indian is named Small, and he is tall, well-built and black as ebony. His innings yesterday was the finest exhibition of off-driving and cutting that Old Trafford has seen since the war. . . . He came to the wicket to stop a terrible collapse — four of his side were out for 26 when it was his turn to go into the wicket.

Now, how do you suppose the average English professional cricketer would have behaved in a crisis like this? Would he not have got himself suspiciously down on the bat? Would he not have put his right leg over the wicket, using the pads as a second line of defence? Would he not have poked and pushed the ball a yard or two away on the on side all day until we were driven to weariness and blasphemy? Small had no use for these fashionable "safety-first tactics". He had as much faith in his skill as the bowlers had in theirs; he met aggression by aggression. . . .

Small went from 94 and 68 against Lancashire to 42 and 19 against Cheshire. Then he scored 71, 48, 10, 131, 85 and 0, not out 65, 50 and 47, and this in a wet season. Says Constantine who toured with him: "Over and over again players, spectators and journalists alike told us that for years they had seen nothing like it."

The difference with Lloyd is that whereas Small's aggression was based upon the front foot, Lloyd's is based upon the back. Both were strikingly individual players. Lloyd we shall see soon enough but the technique of Small was equally personal to himself. Front-foot player as he was, Small's right foot never left, nor was ever in danger of going over, the batting crease. He was an extremely tall man and even on our matting wicket, where the ball always turned and rose, Small sent his front foot right forward so that, when he made his strokes, he was balanced on both front and back foot equally. From there he took the ball on the rise and hit it through the covers, at a pace about which there are still legends in the West Indies.

Small had been a fast bowler before, during World War I, he went to Egypt with the British West India Regiment. There he learnt to bat. A man of entirely different origin was H.B.G. Austin, the father of West Indian cricket. Austin was brought up on the lightning-fast wickets of Barbados. But listen to Constantine on the style of H.B.G. Austin: "As a batsman he was essentially sound, being a master of back play, though trained on the fast Barbados ground. He made a fine drive to cover and could lift the ball over extra-cover's head to the boundary. He played that great stroke of all good batsmen, the forcing back strike wide of mid-on, a real wrist stroke, and he could get the ball away on the leg side."

Like nearly all the great West Indian batsmen, and perhaps this accounts for the example that Woodcock finds they give to English players, the foundation of their play was to play back or drive. I saw Austin batting against Astill in Trinidad in 1926; Astill bowled slow to medium pace and on the matting wicket he could drop the ball on or just outside the off-stump, spin it away and periodically bring one into the batsman: he had the off-side field well packed. Austin played back to this excellent length for two or three overs. Then, although obviously stiff in the joints — he was at that time nearing fifty — he twice jumped down the pitch to Astill and lifted him over mid-on's head for four. Whereupon the field was rearranged and Austin could play the ball on the off-side for runs. Some critics make West Indian batting a matter of race. Austin was a white man, so was S.G. Smith (of Northamptonshire and the Gentlemen), so was George Challenor, the originator of West Indian batting, and so is that other West Indian batsman, Roy Marshall of Hampshire.

I want here to refer to another West Indian, Nelson Betancourt, sometime captain of the West Indies, a member of those French Creole families who helped to establish the game in Trinidad. A great master of length was Victor Pascall, the slow to medium left-hander and Constantine's uncle. He was a master, not only of length, but of direction. When he was attacking the off-stump he had a man at extra cover on the boundary. When he was attacking the leg-stump he moved him over to deep square leg. Betancourt would watch the off-stump attack for an over or two and then unfailingly would jump to Pascall and hit him cross-batted a few feet over mid-on's head to the on boundary. I have seen him do it any number of times and never saw him fail. Pascall, by the way, never moved a man because he knew that if he had moved a man from anywhere Betancourt would most certainly begin to make strokes in that direction.

There is no need to speak about the three Ws and Garfield Sobers. I could at some future time show that the West Indies brought this style of play to England on their first visit in 1900. Sobers is the inheritor of a great tradition. I will only add the following about Frank Worrell in Australia in 1960. He was nearer forty than thirty years old.

Technically, he was the finest player in the West Indies side and in this innings he simply could not be faulted. If ever a man deserved a century it was Worrell that day, for he entered the arena when three had fallen for 22 and right from the start he batted with a superb mastery that reduced Davidson in a couple of overs to mediocrity.

To reduce to mediocrity a bowler who is carrying all before him signifies membership unchallengeable of the aristocracy of great batsmen. Lloyd and coming West Indian batsmen may make their thousands, and even their tens of thousands, but they will make them in a certain way: otherwise their country-men and spectators all over the world will be in no difficulty to discern behind the Test cap and blazer and the impressive statistics the bar sinister of the outsider, born of the blood but not of the bat.

1970s

The 1970s was a decade of teaching and lecturing for James. He travelled between England, Africa, the United States and the Caribbean. He addressed audiences on topics in history, literature, politics and cricket, which had dominated his thinking over the past fifty or sixty years.

Many of his publications at this time were part of these lecture series, strongly reflecting both James's place in the history of the twentieth century as well as his continuing participation in contemporary movements.

In 1974 James initiated the Sixth Pan-African Congress in Tanzania, but did not himself attend, in protest at the restrictions on delegates from the Caribbean. An integral part of the preparation for this Congress, however, was the publication by James of work on two important founders of the Pan-African movement: George Padmore and Kwame Nkrumah. James's assessment of their roles in this movement was explored largely in the form of essays, but a collection of articles appeared in 1977 under the title *Nkrumah and the Ghana Revolution*.

James's cricket writings in the first half of the 1970s may be seen as an extension of the great output of the previous decade. They were marked by a very strong historical sense. They were part of the emergence of a West Indian identity, an identity which was expressed through cricket and its personalities.

Walter Hammond:
An Anniversary Tribute

(*The Cricketer*, 1970)

Time dims certain figures. Others grow larger and brighter. For me, Walter Hammond is one of these latter. My thesis is a West Indian one. At least I think so. Judge for yourself.

My first experience of big cricket (not of fine cricketers) was MCC to the West Indies in 1926. Against the West Indies XI in Barbados, Hammond made 238. W. St Hill, a brilliant fields-man, fielded at cover. "Constantine," he said, "would have saved fours and singles over and over again." So H.B.G. Austin insisted that Constantine, a cover-point, play in all future matches.

In Trinidad Hammond stood exactly where he was and twice flicked Constantine off his face to fine leg. A length ball outside the off stump he pushed away with the old-fashioned English forward stroke. Nobody ever did that on the old matting wicket — nobody. Naturally we pertinaciously looked up what this dramatic new-comer had done against us in 1923. None of our players had remembered him particularly. He had made only six. He was ill in the English summer of 1926, but against us in 1928 in England Hammond, now an England player, made no striking impression. It was 905 Test runs in Australia in 1928–9 that made us aware that in 1926 we had entertained greatness incognito.

I came to England in 1932, all agog to watch and study the great man. He made brilliant runs against everybody, but in 1934 against Australia and in 1934–5 in the West Indies he never reached 50 once. So that by 1938, in my reporter's mind (statistical, historical, critical) Hammond was a large question mark. He answered it without equivocation.

First, the Test at Nottingham. He made only 26 runs but to this day I have no memory of such command and ease by any batsman. He would judge the ball early, step back and play as if someone was throwing a tennis ball. At 26 O'Reilly bowled him a ball. Hammond as usual stood perfectly straight and still before he played his stroke. I got a strong impression that he was inclined to play back, but after some hesitation put his left foot right out and pushed forward. But O'Reilly's flighted inswinger evaded his bat and clean bowled him. There were some gorgeous centuries and history made in that Test. But after Hammond's 26, *I knew*, I knew for certain that before long I would see the real Hammond at last.

If I had to repeat a Test, it would be Lord's, 1938. There were some 20,000 people lined up around Lord's an hour before the game, and I saw one policeman, a cheerful smiling fellow, doing nothing before the Members' Gate. The memory has stayed with me — 20,000 people (cricket people) and one smiling policeman. The Australians had a very fast bowler, McCormick. Hutton, Barnett and Edrich were soon out — three wickets for 31. I do not wish to use one single superlative. I can remember much fine batting, but Hammond's play that day remains in my mind as the summit of what batting could be. He was as completely in command as he had been during the 26 at Nottingham. That a fast bowler, a very fast bowler, had taken wickets bothered him not in the least. Off either foot, he distributed his strokes to every part of the field. He played a ball back to Chipperfield, low down. Chipperfield put his hand to it and left the field with a split finger.

I lunched somewhere on the ground. Near to me, one Englishman ventured to another that Hammond had played a remarkably fine innings. The second said he thought it was the best innings in a Test that they had seen at Lord's. The first said it was perhaps the best innings he had ever seen in any Test match anywhere. Ultimately they agreed that it was the best innings that had ever been seen. That was 1938. I went to the United States that autumn where I soon learnt that an American would have begun by saying militantly that Hammond's was the best innings that had ever been played. His friend would have immediately objected to such an extravagant statement. They would have hammered at each other until ultimately they would have agreed on much the same.

Hammond's last years were not easy and he died prematurely. In America at any Test match a television reporter would have introduced "the celebrity" grandiloquently and demanded a few words. In England the word would have gone round and the thousands would have stood to applaud the veteran as he made his way unobtrusively to his seat. I never exchanged a word with Hammond. He knew who I was and I regret that I didn't. I regret also that there is no spontaneous applause for me to join.

Sir Frank Worrell

(From *Cricket: The Great Captains*, edited by John Arlott, 1970)

At the beginning of this article I want to say something I feel I should not. It is my conviction and my practice that whatever is being said about cricket should begin with the game as played on the field. Nevertheless, it is the exception that indicates the validity of the rule and I will make an exception about Frank Worrell as captain. Of Worrell as captain two things must be said at once and he must be placed historically.

He lifted West Indies cricket to the highest peak possible and everybody knew that he had done it. Why he did it and how he did it is another question which we will examine. But this is the obvious, the accepted, that no one will argue about. That, however, is only the appearance of things, and a great logician, one of the greatest, has clarified the difference between the appearance of things and the essence. The appearance is not a mere superficial obviousness, that everybody can see; what our logician disdainfully calls a mere *show*. The appearance is a vital category. Because it is only by means of the appearance that the essence can manifest itself. And the essence of Frank Worrell's captaincy is not West Indian. It is that he was one of the great captains of the age, a captain of cricket, the international game, a captain who must be understood. Without this, the game as it is today and as it will be tomorrow cannot be seen in depth. This is an enormous claim and must be dealt with at once.

The twentieth century has seen three captains who have expressed a certain stage of cricket and of society. Without some grasp of what they represent, cricket is just a lot of men hitting a ball and running about in flannels. These three men are Pelham Warner, Don Bradman and Frank Worrell.

The date at which to begin is 1903–4, when the MCC sent an official touring side to Australia under the captaincy of Pelham Warner. Cricket had technically made a great stride. In England Ranjitsinhji, C.B. Fry, R.E. Foster had changed the game completely. Back-play, the on-side and the hook had revolutionized the game. The same changes had appeared in Australia. Victor Trumper, R.A. Duff, those two had changed the style of cricket to something not dissimilar from what the English genius had created.

However, there was much more to this as there is always

much more to cricket when it is seen as part of the way in which men live. 1903 is an important date. For years Joseph Chamberlain, Rudyard Kipling, Rider Haggard, to mention only three, had been building a certain conception of empire. It reached its climax in the Boer War. After the Boer War there began a counter movement. I mention (with some trepidation) the foundation of a new, a Labour, party. And it is in that environment that we must see what Pelham Warner, beginning officially in 1903, was doing until 1914 and afterwards. The game of cricket was taken systematically all over the world, making it clear that there were other things in British civilization besides the Union Jack and preparation for world power.

The next great captain is Don Bradman, and Don Bradman I see as the cricketer symbolical of the age which can be called the age of J.M. Keynes. After the crisis of World War I and the Depression, Keynes set in motion a systematic and as far as possible scientific use of what existed. He created nothing new. Neither did Bradman. Like Keynes, Bradman systematically and scientifically used all that there was, carried it to an extreme. The process did not actually begin with him. History does not work mathematically. The thing actually began with Ponsford. But Bradman not only as batsman set the seal on the incorporation and exploitation of every technique that the game of cricket had invented and which could be adapted to defeating an opponent.

That was Bradman as batsman and as captain. People are inclined to blame Hutton for what came of this. That is not only unfair; it is untrue. Despite the fact that some gifted individuals continued to express their personality, cricket followed the lines that had been laid down by Bradman. The systematic refusal to take risks, and to concentrate on what could be reasonably safe dominated cricket for years and, what was worse, did not decline but expanded.

The man who broke this, and made it clear that the game could and should return to what it had been, was Frank Worrell as captain of the West Indies Test team. It is not too much to say that in the world at large, today and in recent years, we have seen a massive instinctual rejection by people everywhere of the kind of systematized social organization which began with the organization of the economy by J.M. Keynes. This I know is somewhat difficult to accept in regard to a game like cricket, but I cannot think of it otherwise and that is the significance of Frank Worrell as a cricket captain.

A Test cricketer, above all a captain, is not an automaton, not an abstraction, not a kind of computer who responds to happenings with instruction. He is a man of passions like ourselves. And Worrell, captain of the West Indies, had one passion — not to lift Test cricket to what it was. That was an effect, not a cause. Worrell's passion was to prove that West Indian Test cricketers could be as good as other Test players. To put it negatively, nothing was inherently wrong with us. When he was appointed captain of the team to Australia in 1961–2, he knew what he had to do and he knew how it had to be done. Those of us who fought the campaign to make him captain had a feeling that he *ought* to be the captain. In addition we felt that with him the team would do better, and *in time* find itself. More than that we did not expect. Strictly speaking, that campaign for Worrell as captain was a moral issue. But beside Worrell himself there was one notable exception.

For the West Indies cricketers, as cricketers, at least one man had complete belief in them, technically and spiritually. That was Learie Constantine. For nearly forty years Constantine had bombarded my scepticism with his conviction. After 1923 and particularly after the West Indian trip to Australia in 1931–2, Constantine insisted to me, like a fanatic, that the West Indies team was as good as any other team, could play with any other team and win. "They are no better than we," was his belligerent statement, belligerent I believe because I could not be convinced and he respected my judgement and my opinions.

They are no better than we, he used to say: we can bat and bowl and field as well as any of them. To my — as I thought — devastating query, "Why do we always lose and make such a poor show?" he would reply: "We need a black man as captain." I was stupid enough to believe that he was dealing with the question of race. I should have known that it was not so, because he used to speak with the utmost respect and admiration of H.B.G. Austin as a captain. He also had an immense respect and admiration for C.G. Macartney. What he used to tell me was that the West Indian players were not a team and to become a team they needed a captain who had the respect of the players and was able to get the best out of the team. Not too far from his argument was the sentiment that a good captain would respect all the men. I remember those constant arguments very well because it was one of the questions in which I was wrong and in which I was wrong because I failed to examine exactly what was involved. I have to say also that Constantine did not explain. But it was my business as a writer and critic to understand. The captain does not only depend on fine players. He makes the best of them and he makes players who are high-class players into men who play above themselves.

That explains Worrell's captaincy on the field. It wasn't merely knowledge; it was a conviction that guided everything that he did. Over the years I have collected a number of instances and examples of what made him the captain that he was, the particular leader of a particular group of men that he was.

A captain, any captain, must select the best men at his disposal for the task in hand and make the best of them. Simple in appearance, this in essence is a tremendous task. The captain must not only choose in general. He must decide on a particular bowler for a particular situation or a particular batsman. Furthermore his is the responsibility of devising ways and means to help bowlers who are unable to dismiss a batsman, particularly one who looks as if he will win the match. (On this particular business, of devising ways and means of getting out a batsman who seems set to stay, undoubtedly the greatest of all captains whom I have known would be P.G.H. Fender. During the thirties, one of the most illuminating and rewarding pastimes was to go to the Oval and watch Fender on the perfect Oval wicket with a poor bowling side diddle out batsmen.) Every captain has to be able to do this. First of all to choose. One famous choice is that of Hutton in Australia choosing Tyson in place of Bedser on the very morning of the match. Worrell's great choice, not nearly so well-known but equally effective, was the choice of Gibbs in Australia to replace Ramadhin. In 1959–60 against the MCC Ramadhin had headed the bowling averages with 17 wickets. The other two bowlers who had taken over ten were Hall and Watson, both bowlers of pace. The talk is (there can be no question of proof in these matters) that Gibbs, already a fine bowler, played always under the shadow of Ramadhin, at that time perhaps the most famous off-spinner in the world. In Australia Ramadhin was still a very fine bowler. He headed the averages in all first-class matches, taking 24 wickets at the cost of 26.29 runs per wicket in 170.3 overs. In other words he needed only seven overs to take a wicket. Gibbs played in one or two early matches. Ramadhin did little in the first two Tests but Gibbs in other matches did not do much either, except in the match before the third Test in Tasmania. In the first innings Gibbs did nothing, but in the second he took four for 29. Whether for this or any other reason,

Worrell dropped Ramadhin and played Gibbs as his spinner in the third Test. Gibbs, recognized at last, took three for 46 in the first innings and won the match in the second innings with five wickets for 66 runs. Gibbs on the last morning took four wickets for two runs in a spell of 27 balls. Gibbs was not only the choice of his captain but Worrell had much to do with the taking of those wickets. Australia in the last innings needed to make 464 to win and after two wickets had fallen for 83 runs, O'Neill and Harvey took the score to within sight of 200 and seemed set for the day: the bowlers could do nothing against them. Harvey, however, was suffering from a pulled muscle in his right leg. Worrell knew that this could be a handicap against spinners. He brought Sobers close in at cover because wherever you expected a catch you always put Sobers, and he told Gibbs to flight the ball at Harvey. To a flighted ball Harvey went out to drive, but with his injured leg could not get to the pitch. He holed out to cover, Gibbs proceeded to take his other three wickets, and the match was won.

In the fourth Test Gibbs took five for 97 in the first innings and did the hat-trick, the first hat-trick against Australia in the twentieth century. In the last Test he took four for 74 and two for 68, the runs being scored off 41 overs — 19 of them maidens. He ended the tour at the head of the Test averages with 19 wickets in 192 overs at a cost of 22 runs each: this is a case in which averages count for something; by the end of the tour Gibbs in three Tests had bowled 192 overs, more than any other bowler on the side. There was a similar collaboration between the same captain and the same bowler at Barbados in 1961 against India. Sardesai and Manjrekar, both of whom scored over 50, had put on nearly 100 for the third wicket and India seemed set to save the match. But after lunch Gibbs got both of them out in rapid succession and in 15.3 overs, 14 of them maidens, he took eight wickets for six runs. One far-sighted indication of what Worrell as captain meant to Gibbs has now to be told. It has been pointed out to me that in Australia in 1960–61 in the very first match that the West Indies played, against Western Australia, Worrell put on Gibbs before Ramadhin in the first innings and did the same in the second. I have been told that from that time Gibbs was a changed man: he knew that his captain did not see him as automatically second to Ramadhin.

Worrell was noted, not only among spectators and critics but naturally among his men, for his sensitive handling of his bowlers. Before he took charge of the team, the fast bowlers

C.L.R. James

used to be bowled at the start of an innings so that near the end there was nothing to them. Worrell changed all that so that even the ordinary spectator knew that no fast bowler was ever likely to be over-bowled. Often he would be given three or four overs and changed immediately. At the same time, perhaps for this very reason, Worrell could call on his fast bowlers for efforts of which they did not know themselves capable. The most notable was the case of Hall in the second Test at Lord's in 1963. Hall bowled on the last day for three hours and twenty minutes, delivering 40 overs. Hall has said himself that this spell of bowling was something he did not know he was capable of: the captain seemed to want him to go on and he just went on, never losing pace nor direction. Other spells of bowling of the same kind are associated with Sobers. In the last Test in Australia, Sobers, according to *Wisden*, went on to bowl half an hour before tea on Saturday and was not taken off until the score stood at 335 for nine on Monday. He bowled slow at first but opened with the new ball on Monday and bowled all morning and for an hour after lunch. Altogether he bowled 44 overs and took five for 120. In England in 1963 Worrell called again on Sobers for a similar effort. It seemed to me that after his tremendous effort in the second Test at Lord's, Hall never recovered himself until a critical moment in the last Test at the Oval. In that Test Sobers bowled 21 overs in the first innings and 33 overs in the second. In the first innings it was Sobers who broke what seemed to be a formidable opening partnership between Bolus and Edrich. Bolus made 33 and Edrich 25 and both of them were caught by Murray behind the wicket off Sobers after some hard bowling. But this was nothing to what he had to do in the second innings. He bowled at a strong pace all through the last day, getting rid of Bolus again for 15 and Dexter for 27, Dexter caught by Murray when Dexter looked very dangerous. I remember that spell of bowling well. I had Hall at Lord's in mind and that day Hall took four wickets for 39 in only 16 overs. The man who carried the burden that day on a wicket that was by no means easy for fast bowlers was Sobers. Worrell could call on anyone for anything.

Worrell could get his men to do whatever he wanted from them because even before he became captain he had the reputation of never asking anyone to do anything which he would not do himself. In 1957 at Trent Bridge he played through the innings for 191 not out. He went in on Friday afternoon facing an England total of 619 (for 6). West Indies finished the day 59 without loss. Worrell batted all day

SIR FRANK WORRELL (1970)

Saturday and continued on Monday, 570 minutes in all. West Indies had to follow on and it was suggested to Worrell that somebody else open the second innings. Worrell refused. He was the opener and it was his duty to open. He was bowled playing the stroke of a tired man. There was a similar occurrence at Leeds. Worrell bowled fast-medium for many hours, taking seven wickets in 38.2 overs. It was suggested to him that someone else should open the batting. Again he refused: the duty of an opener was to open. He obviously was not himself and was soon out. It is quite probable that in both instances his judgement was wrong. The fact remains that that was the kind of thing for which he was known among the members of his side. He had been invited to go to India as captain after the 1957 tour. He was studying at Manchester University and could not go. When the MCC visited the West Indies in 1959–60, Worrell had been away from the first-class game for two years. However, he felt it his duty to go to the West Indies and play and found himself in the first Test at Barbados, short of any kind of first-class practice. However, he played himself into some sort of form in the Test, making 197 not out and helping the West Indies to reply to England's 482 with 563 for eight.

These qualities were a solid foundation to any captaincy, strategic insight into the capabilities of individual men and the capacity to get the best out of them, not only in general but for a particular situation. Added to this was the sentiment that Frank not only was prepared to do everything. He knew everything, at least everything that could be known. He had been a slow bowler and he had made himself into a fast-medium bowler. He had been a tremendous stroke player and now during the MCC tour had shown himself able to defend for hours. As a captain he was already legendary. On a Commonwealth tour to India the captain had fallen ill, Frank had taken over and had convinced everyone that here was a born captain. Furthermore, it was not merely the judgements of people in authority that had made him captain. He had been appointed captain of the team to Australia by what could be called a popular campaign and a popular vote.

As a result of his previous training (as a member of the black West Indian middle class of Barbados, of this more later) Frank had certain other qualities which expressed themselves in his captaincy. For one thing he was always calm and unruffled even in times of crisis. I am told that that is very obvious in the photograph of the last run-out in the famous tied Test in Australia. His team remember also at a very critical moment at the Lord's Test in 1963, that when Hall began his last over eight runs were needed by England to win the match. Off the second ball, and the third, came sharp singles but the batsmen attempted another run when the ball was played to Frank at short leg. First-class players are of the opinion that it was an open question whether a fieldsman under those circumstances would throw at the wicket or not. Frank did not throw. He ran to the wicket with the ball, determined to beat the batsman to the bowler's end and not to risk missing the wicket by a throw. Others might have thrown. His fellow players thought it natural of their captain not to take the chance.

He was noted for the care that he always paid to apparently small, but in essence highly significant, events or episodes. Take the situation at Brisbane when the scores were tied and the last Australian batsmen were at the wicket. Hall had two more balls to finish the over, and Frank from mid-on walked over to him. What he said is worth noting as being symbolical of his methods as captain: "Remember, Wes, if you bowl a no-ball, you'll never be able to go back to Barbados." Hall reports that this so terrified him that he made sure to put his foot a good yard behind the crease. Kline the batsman turned the ball to square leg and Solomon made his throw which tied the match. The team as a whole laughed at the particular kind of warning which Hall had been given by his captain — only to discover afterwards that Frank had calculated carefully what he should say. If he had told Hall seriously to be careful not to bowl a no-ball, Hall might have bowled one. But he put it with humour as a passing but necessary consideration and it had the effect required.

When Frank was appointed captain of the team to Australia he knew what Constantine always used to insist upon, that technically they were a body of fine individual players. What he had to do was to build a team. In discussing the tour in Australia, which I did very often with him, I was amazed to find that his main judgement of an individual player was whether he was a good team-man or not. It seemed that he worked on the principle that if a man was a good team-man it brought the best out of him as an individual player. He once noted to a senior player how well-disciplined the team had become by pointing to an incident with Kanhai. While the team was walking into the pavilion for an interval he happened to mention to Kanhai that he would like him to be ten yards further back for one of the two batsmen at the wicket. After the interval Frank says he looked over his shoulder and saw that for the particular batsmen Kanhai had placed himself exactly where he had been told. He was not referring to Kanhai in particular. He was referring to the fact that the team now responded to him like a musical instrument.

He watched over them carefully and they knew that he was watching over them. Kanhai and Sobers seemed unable to hit it off together at the wicket. Not saying anything to anybody, Worrell separated them in the batting order and removed Sobers down to number six. Sobers accepted completely, as they all accepted whatever their captain said. One of the team believes that after both players had matured Frank would have removed Sobers from number six and placed him again at number four. But for good or ill the belief is that Frank having placed Sobers at number six, Sobers believes that number six is his correct place. Personally I do not believe that. I believe rather that Sobers has not got the quality of complete belief in his team which Frank had and therefore bats at number six in order to see what is happening and know what kind of game he is to play. What is important is that members of the team should believe that Sobers is at number six and remains at number six because Frank placed him there.

With all this ceaseless watching of his men, Worrell was a stern disciplinarian. He spoke very harshly to one of his top players for the attitudes he showed when he disagreed with an umpire's decision. He was adamant against players walking over the pitch. Yet at the same time he was most vigilant about the interests of the team both in general and in particular. At a public dinner when the Indian team had visited the West Indies, Frank uttered some harsh words in a public speech about the fact that no one had mentioned that the West Indian team against India was the best team that the West Indies had ever fielded. A West Indian captain at the dinner shook his head in agreement. Frank also watched very carefully over the financial and educational interests of his players. He himself had had some stern duels with the authorities. They had wanted him to go to India with the West Indian team in 1949. They refused to pay him what Frank thought he, his wife and child needed and Frank refused to go. There was another set-to when the team was due to go to Australia in 1951; Frank laid down his conditions and said that if they were not met he would not go. They were met and there is a comic story of another player of Frank's rank who was absolutely astonished when he heard what arrangements Frank had made for that Australian tour. Frank used to give his players advice and help about the contracts that they signed. In addition he used to tell them that as cricketers (I believe that he saw them as West Indian cricketers) occupying a special place in West Indian society, they were people who had to think of themselves off the field as well as on it. He himself set an example by going to Manchester University to get his degree. He encouraged all who wanted to take similar or parallel steps in order to be adequate to the positions in which cricket had placed them.

Yet despite all this vigilance and attention to detail, both of play and personality, Frank was in general a conservative rather than an adventurous captain. I have two very vivid examples of that, one of which is known and the other which no one but myself knows. The first is his attitude to the change in method which Close made in his innings during the second Test at Lord's in 1963. When all the regular batsmen had gone, Close, who hitherto had played a stern defensive innings, began moving down the wicket to Hall and Griffith in order, obviously, to put them off their length and score some urgent runs. I doubt if many people would have disagreed with the change in Close's tactic. But Worrell stated publicly that he believed Close made a mistake in changing his method; he, Worrell, would have gone on playing in the normal way. It was a statement of position that I never understood until the next year. I was sitting in the press-box next to Worrell during the Test match between England and Australia at Leeds. Australia were seven wickets down when the new ball was due. Dexter took off Titmus who had been bowling very well and gave the new ball to Trueman. Trueman had taken 297 wickets in Tests. He needed only three more to get the 300. The Australian batsmen who remained seemed made to order to help him to the record and I think I can say that not a single soul in the press-box disapproved of what many people thought was a strategic move by Dexter. What actually happened was that Burge played a magnificent innings. The Australian tail-end batsman held the fort at one end. Australia made a fine score and Trueman did not get his 300 wickets. What interested me particularly was that on the following morning many, if not all, the cricket reporters expressed themselves very sharply at the expense of Dexter. You would have believed on reading these reports that there had been general disapproval of Dexter's taking off Titmus and putting on Trueman. There had been no such disapproval, except from one person, and that was Frank. When the change was made, I, as I was doing all through, asked him what was his opinion of it. He was very calm and very precise. "No," he said, "I wouldn't do that." And then he added this expression, which I believe went deep into his method as a captain: "In cricket you leave well alone." I remember him saying these words in a manner that corresponded to the weight of the expression. "In cricket, you leave well alone." It explains much that he did and which I understood only afterwards.

That was the way the famous West Indian team was built. I cannot do better here than quote what I have already written about the West Indian team which had been created at the end of that tour to Australia in 1961–2:

> The West Indies team in Australia, on the field and off, was playing above what it knew of itself. If anything went wrong it knew that it would be instantly told, in unhesitating and precise language, how to repair it, and that the captain's certainty and confidence extended to his belief that what he wanted would be done. He did not instil into but drew out of his players. What they discovered in themselves must have been a revelation to few more than to the players themselves.
>
> When the time came to say goodbye some of the toughest players could only shake the captain's hand and look away, not trusting themselves to speak. We have gone far beyond a game. This is the only way I can convey the full force of "If something was wrong I told them what was right and left it to them".

All that has been said was necessary but, as is said often in political philosophy, necessary but not sufficient. No account of Frank as captain would be sufficient if it did not lay adequate stress on his play on the field. It was not only that he scored runs and took wickets. It was that he did so in a West Indian way, in a manner that would bring out from the West Indian players what he knew to be their particular style. In the 1950 tour of England, Frank, Weekes and Walcott, and Frank in particular, had distinguished themselves by the range and vigour of their stroke-play. Frank as captain of a Commonwealth team to India had attacked the bowling constantly and played what he considered his best cricket. But the years, and presumably lack of first-class practice, had slowed him down. In 1957 he had played some hard defensive innings, and, in the West Indies against the MCC, again his play had been defensive. But when he was made captain of the team to Australia Frank recognized or at any rate seemed to recognize that if he wanted to get the best out of his men they had to play their own type of cricket, the only type of cricket which would enable them to make the best of themselves. From the very start of the tour, in State as well as in Test matches, Worrell set the example which was followed by Sobers and Kanhai, to mention only two. The figures here tell the story better than any comment can.

In the first match against Western Australia, West Indies were set 488 to make in 510 minutes. They went for the runs, Sobers hitting away for 119, but West Indies made only 395 and the last wicket fell fifteen minutes before time. Worrell himself made 37. In the next match against an Australian XI, Worrell made 65 and 68, being not out both times. In the second innings *Wisden* refers to the batting of the West Indians, including Worrell as a "revelry" — not a word that is often used about batting in first-class cricket. Against South Australia Worrell did not play and the side did not do very well. But the revelry began again against Victoria. Kanhai played a famous innings of 252 made in a day, but Worrell came in with the score at 326 for four, the innings was declared closed at nine for 493, Worrell having made 82. The West Indies failed against New South Wales, all being out for 111 in the first innings, Worrell 51. But in the first Test the West Indians continued with their revelry. They made 453 runs, scoring 4.5 runs per over. *Wisden* tells us that the West Indies attacked the bowling from the start, losing three men for 65. Not in any way deterred by these failures, Sobers and Worrell continued the attack, Sobers hitting a century, one of the best he has ever made, in just over two hours; Worrell made 65. In the second innings he scored another 65, again going at the bowling from the start of his innings. In the second Test, West Indies failed, Worrell contributing a pair. In the third Test, Sobers, after beginning quietly to 80, "launched a tremendous attack on the Australians when the new ball was taken after tea and scored 72 in as many minutes".

In this third Test, A.G. Moyes tells us the role of the captain: "Worrell's was a lovely innings. He seemed all the time to know exactly where he wanted to hit the ball and appeared able always to guide it through the gaps in the field. Technically, he was the finest player in the West Indies side and in this innings he simply could not be faulted. If ever a man deserved a century it was Worrell that day, for he entered the arena when three had fallen for 22, and right from the start he batted with a superb mastery that reduced Davidson in a couple of overs to mediocrity." In the fourth Test Worrell made 71 and 53. In the first innings he and Kanhai put on 107 in just over an hour.

What is obvious is that in their tremendous batting the West

Indies were carrying out the policy which the captain not only preached but practised, a policy which Worrell knew could be successful. For me the most striking features in this cricket were the first Test when three wickets had fallen for 65 and in the fourth Test when three had fallen for 22. It is at this point that Worrell went in and reduced the conquering Australian bowling to mediocrity.

This captaincy, not only by policy but by example, Worrell displayed also in his Test bowling. A Test player who knew him well and knew his cricket well told me in 1961, when the news was coming over, that he doubted if Frank at that stage of the game could spin a marble. Nevertheless in the fourth Test when every run counted Worrell took over from his regular bowlers and bowled 17 overs for 27 runs and three wickets. I have been told that he understood that what was required was faultless length with periodically a slight change of pace. He trusted the Australian batsmen to do the rest. In the side were Hall, Sobers, Gibbs, Valentine, all far better bowlers than the Frank Worrell of 1961, but in the last innings of the last Test he bowled 31 overs for 43 runs and three wickets. Thus in batting and in bowling Frank led the West Indians in a type of cricket which he knew they could play, which was the only game they could effectively play. This approach to Test cricket, dead for a generation, was met halfway by Benaud and the result was the finest series of Tests that had been known during the century. There is no need to go into further figures except to say that against India Worrell did the same remarkable batting, heading the Test averages.

No wonder that half a million people turned out in Melbourne to bid Worrell's team goodbye. They realized that something which had been lost was now restored to the game. Worrell and his team did it again in England in 1963. But when he went out of the game it seems that it went with him.

It is time to draw this to a close because it is possible to go on indefinitely. Let us have a look at what one of the greatest of captains wrote about captaincy at the end of his playing career, as far back as 1926. In his book *The Game's the Thing*, M.A. Noble writes about captaincy as follows:

Many qualifications are necessary adequately to equip the man selected as captain, and he may learn just so much as his mentality will allow. There is, however, one attribute that cannot be acquired; it is a gift of the gods, and may be summed up in the phrase "personal equation". When he possesses that most valuable trait, it

C.L.R. James

goes without saying that the men under his command have great personal respect for him and faith in his judgement. He becomes a tower of strength, a rock to lean upon in adversity. He inspires such confidence that they will work hard, keep "on their toes", and combine to give of their best no matter how long the way or how tired they are. His keenness and enthusiasm are infectious, and his men respond readily and without effort. It is this dominant force that is of such tremendous value to the side. Emerson once said: "There is no company of men so great as one man." In a cricket sense that is particularly true. The great leader is the embodiment of all the hopes, virtue, courage and ability possessed by the ten men under his command. If he is not, he is but the shadow and lacks the substance of captaincy. He will not last.

He adds a paragraph to which many people subscribe but do not really understand. In the case of Worrell it expresses an absolute truth.

Captaincy has much greater influence on the fate of a match than is often realized. The side possessing a capable leader has a great advantage. No two men are alike. The only times captains are reduced to the same level is in the spinning of the coin. One may have a run of luck, but he can never have a run of character; and even the toss will even itself up in the long run.

Noble most effectively and even with eloquence states what the good captain is and what he does. So does Don Bradman in his comprehensive and penetrating book on cricket. I am positive, however, that there is more to it than either of them suspects. Here goes.

Worrell was a black middle-class Barbadian from Barbados, born in 1924. In that simple sentence there is contained a volume. Unlike Trinidad and Jamaica, which are off-shoots of the South American main, Barbados is a coral island. There are no mountains, no rivers, no forests, no snakes. Every inch of the island is swept by the breeze of the ocean because Barbados is only 21 miles long and 14 miles broad. When slavery was abolished in 1833, in Jamaica and in Trinidad, there was land on which slaves could squat, or buy, and establish themselves as peasants. In Barbados there was no such land and therefore the Barbados blacks had to exploit every possibility for making something of themselves. They learnt to be strenuously effective as employed labour. Barbados had been British from the start and had never been anything else; no groups of foreigners had ever come there. There was therefore no obstacle in the way of their mastering the English language, the English religion or adopting the English ways of life. This was particularly urgent for those members of the black middle class who emerged from the black slaves. They became the finest scholars the West Indies has ever known. The population were great singers of hymns and many read music.

When the local whites started to play cricket, black Barbadians watched and the black middle class began not only to play but to form clubs. On the coral island without much difficulty excellent wickets could be prepared, and Barbados produced a line of great batsmen and fast bowlers of a high class, the only ones who could be depended upon to get batsmen out on such pitches. But the white upper classes continued to hold all the economic and political power and, more than anywhere else in the West Indies, social prestige. The blacks who emerged therefore found themselves in a not unprecedented position. They could learn all that there was to be learnt, at home and abroad, but they were as excluded from what we know today as the Establishment as the great body of Russian intellectuals were excluded from the Tsarist aristocracy and the Tsarist establishment. But, as in Russia, the black middle classes were not excluded from the grammar schools: the local government needed some of them to fill local posts such as lawyers, doctors, civil servants, schoolmasters, pharmacists, sanitary inspectors, and such. There was thus created a body of men who from their education had instinctively absorbed the principles of English liberalism, knowing that they were being unreasonably excluded from expressing themselves and making the best use of their abilities and attainments. Sir Grantley Adams, not only Prime Minister of the now defunct West Indian Federation, but one of the earliest agitators for democracy in the West Indies, told me that before he left Barbados he had read Aeschylus, Sophocles, Euripides, Thucydides and Herodotus, Plato and Aristotle and could read Greek as easily as he could read English. For him and all like him the real breakthrough came with the great strikes that ran through the West Indies from British Guiana to Jamaica in 1937–8.

Worrell, Weekes and Walcott grew up in the new environment. Barbados still offered to black men the opportunity to learn the foundations of what British civilization had to offer. They learnt but nevertheless they had to go abroad, to Britain itself, in order to express their knowledge and the principles that they had learnt. When in 1959 Frank Worrell became the first black captain of the West Indies cricket team, it was one notable climax of more than a century of social restraint and, at last, successful endeavour. Worrell knew that and it affected him far more than he knew. . . .

That will have to be developed in another place. But there is still something more to be said. After you have analysed to the last comma, there is always something which defies analysis. Worrell had told me that, as a young man, as soon as a ball was delivered he could tell the blade of grass on which it was going to drop and could therefore place his feet and body for any stroke he wanted to make. You cannot analyse that. At a certain stage a gifted person appears who can make use of environmental opportunities. But the person himself is unpredictable, a portent, from the premises known and knowable only when they appear. Worrell was such a one. And I believe so was M.A. Noble and Don Bradman. Which is why I bring it in here.

The History of Cricket

(Introduction to *Cricket: A History of its Growth and Development throughout the World* by Rowland Bowen, 1970)

This history of cricket by Rowland Bowen is a type of cricket history which I have never read before and whose forebears, either in method or material, as far as I know, do not exist. Let me add that I do not expect within the next generation to see any book of this kind and this quality again. Now I have committed myself. I have broken all the rules. I have *not* eschewed superlatives, I have indulged myself superlatively, not only in retrospect but in prospect. All I can say is what Luther said when faced with a fundamental crisis: "I can do no other."

The best thing that I can do is to try to show by example what the author is doing. Everybody knows more or less what is meant by the Golden Age of cricket. Ask anyone who has the faintest knowledge and he will tell you it is the age which began towards the end of the nineteenth century and continued at least to 1914. It was the age of a new style of batsman who took batting into reaches undreamed of by their ancestors; Ranjitsinhji, Fry, A.C. MacLaren, R.E. Foster, Johnny Tyldesley, J.B. Hobbs, R.H. Spooner. The same phenomenon appeared in Australia, Victor Trumper, R.A. Duff and Clem Hill: this revolution in batting caused a revolution in bowling and the strategy of captaincy and field-placing. Batsmen (and bowlers too) were great individualists; matches were dramatic contests, great crowds poured out to see not only Tests but lesser games as never before and never since. When Rowland Bowen writes on this period, we see what, quite uniquely, for him makes the age Golden:

> In this country it was the period when a Board of Control was set up; when Test match selection became a central responsibility; when overseas tour selection became, in a slightly different form, also a central responsibility; when the control of county cricket was also centralized; and when minor county cricket was first organized. It was a period which spanned the first South African tour to this country and the Triangular Tournament of 1912: at the beginning it almost took in the start of the Currie Cup in South Africa, and even more closely almost took in the start of the Sheffield Shield in Australia, while the start of the Plunket Shield in New Zealand came later on in the period. The New Zealand Cricket Council was established in 1895: the South African Cricket Association a shade earlier: the Australian Cricket Council just before, but ended not long after the start and was replaced after a few years by the Australian Board of Control. Its commencement very nearly saw the start of the Bombay Tournament in India: shortly after that it only just failed to see the first All-India tour to England but did succeed in seeing it just before its close, while almost throughout it saw that great Imperial symbol, Ranji. Its start just missed the rise of international touring in South America, and almost completely took in the rise of West Indian cricket. It saw the greatest age of Philadelphian cricket.

He is not as yet near the end. He continues:

> And at home, it saw the formation of the Scottish Cricket Union, the formation of county competitions in Scotland and North Wales, and the very early beginnings of what was to become the Club Cricket Conference. The serious development of League cricket came about during the period and the start had preceded it by only a few years. In legislation, the last modernizing change in the Laws took place: the six-ball over, the optional follow-on, the raising of the limit of the follow-on, the first new ball rule, and the steady extension of the period within which one could declare (not finally consummated till after the Second War), and facts were faced, however unpalatable, in recognizing that drawn matches were inevitable when points were awarded for a first innings lead towards the end of the period. Some attempt also was made to make the first-class game more popular by tentative experiments with a Saturday start. (Great matches had generally started on Mondays and Thursdays for very many years.) Finally, Yorkshire, to its praise, in this period became the first county to ensure all the year round payment for its players as well as to establish a provident fund for them when retired: a very significant social change, and

271

not hitherto attempted or even thought of by any other county and by no means fully emulated by all counties up to the present time. It is difficult to think of any other period of the game's history when so many important things happened.

That is how Rowland Bowen sees the game. That is his History, from the earliest times to the present day.

We go on to full details of the game as played from 1894 till 1914. We learn that, in 1896, Ranji beat a record that W.G. had set up in 1871. In 1899 Ranji was the first batsman to pass 3,000 runs in a first-class season and in 1900 he made another 3,000 runs. Our historian does not omit these stand-bys. We have an original glimpse of Hobbs, "perhaps the most successful opening batsman who ever lived", who was so successful, we are told, because he had "an instinctive understanding of his partner, whether it was Tom Hayward, Andy Sandham, Wilfred Rhodes or Herbert Sutcliffe". "In 1888, League cricket had commenced in the Birmingham area. Within a few years leagues had become the normal way to play club cricket in much of the Midlands and all the North of England, later spreading into Scotland and Wales. This kind of cricket was played 'harder'." This we are told was not in accordance with southern tastes, nor was it to be for nearly three generations. Those who played country-house cricket (which is fully analysed) adopted a hostile attitude towards the game as played in the leagues. We take up school cricket in that period, and club cricket. Then, and on the same scale, the author deals with 1894–1914 abroad, and abroad includes the Fiji Islands, Brazil, in fact wherever a ball was bowled. Part three of the chapter "The Golden Age" deals with "Conduct of the game and administration". But we are not nearly finished with the Golden Age despite the fact that the three sections together comprise 33 pages.

To keep our eye steadily on one period (the only way we can visualize the whole) let us stick to the Golden Age. In the appendices under Other Countries between 1894 and 1914, there are 33 entries; under Canada and the United States, there are 63; under India, 25; under New Zealand, 77 entries. For what I hope I can call without offence the big cricketing countries: under West Indies there are 57 entries; under Southern Africa there are 99 entries; under England there are 109 entries and under Australia there are 133. The first entry of the appendix for Pakistan begins in 1947, so it is obvious that there can be no comparison with other periods of the Golden Age.

I will not dare to select what interests me specially in the appendices in the Golden Age. I only point to their comprehensive and detailed character. It so happens that I find myself interested in the statistics I read there about one famous cricketer, Spofforth, the great Australian bowler. In such a plethora of detail about every country, the reader is certain to see statistics and events which interest him particularly. Spofforth interests me: for example I note that in 1878 at Lord's, Spofforth performed the hat-trick against the MCC, the first time that this had been done by an Australian in English first-class cricket. Again in 1878–9 Spofforth performed the hat-trick in the English first innings of the Melbourne Test, the first occasion in a Test match. In 1881–2 in a minor match in Australia, Spofforth took all 20 wickets for 48 runs, all bowled. In 1882 in a Test match in England, Spofforth took 14 wickets for 90. We learn that no Australian has bettered this in Test matches and it has been equalled only by C.V. Grimmett against South Africa in 1931–2. In first-class matches in 1884, Spofforth took 207 wickets at an average of 13.25 runs per wicket. He is the first of only two touring Australians to take over 200 wickets in an English touring season. Against an English eleven at Birmingham, he took seven wickets for three runs. What strikes me is that he is not only a famous man historically, but like W.G. in his great years, what he did after all these years still remains unparalleled.

I shall select, to give some idea of what they are, entries for two years in the Appendices covering England and the West Indies:

England 1902	First Tests played at Edgbaston and at Bramall Lane, the latter being the only Test ever played in Sheffield. A new match aggregate of 1,427 runs for 34 wickets set up in the game between Sussex and Surrey at Hastings. The first MCC tour to Holland, captain A.H. Hornby. *Ayres' Cricket Companion* first appeared, annually until 1932. W.H. Hyman scored the then record number of sixes — 32, in his innings of 359* for Bath Association v. Thornbury at Thornbury; the record for many years. The record six-wicket partnership in England of 428 made by W.W. Armstrong (172*) and M.A. Noble (284) for Australians v. Sussex at Hove. K.S. Ranjitsinhji (230) and W. Newman (153) made 344 for the seventh wicket, the English first-class record, for Sussex v. Essex at Leyton. Sussex made their record score of 705 for eight wickets declared v. Surrey at Hastings. Scottish County Championship inaugurated.

West Indies
1913

Second tour by MCC (captain, A.W.F. Somerset): won two and lost one of the representative matches. In the match v. Barbados, A.W.F. Somerset (55) and W.C. Smith (126) added 167 for MCC's last wicket (the West Indian record for that wicket), the Barbados pair, P.H. Tarilton (157) and H.W. Ince (57*) having already made 100 for the Barbados last wicket in the same match, a most unusual occurrence in any class of cricket. P.H. Tarilton made 1,084 runs, average 83.38, in all matches in the Barbados season, the first time it had been done in that island. Sir Hesketh Bell presented a cup for competition on a knock-out basis amongst the Leeward Islands, of which he was then Governor. The first winners were Antigua. E.R.D. Moulder carried his bat for 104* for West Indies v. MCC at Bourda, the first time anyone had carried his bat for a century in first-class cricket.

Doubtless, readers in Australia, South Africa, New Zealand, India and Other Countries will turn eagerly to those special sections which deal with them. I read the West Indies appendix recognizing much, but I read them all, and members of Other Countries would recognize me as a brother.

There is such a mass of material in this book on the game and relevant matters that I can allow myself references here to only two. The first because there is not much available about it for the ordinary reader of cricket history and, also because it is the kind of information that will startle anybody. "In the United States," Rowland Bowen writes, "this was the heyday of cricket in and around Philadelphia — cricket which sustained the game in Boston and Baltimore, in New York and even in an almost typically English country-house form in Virginia. Cricket in America is so much regarded now as a joke or a curiosity that it is difficult to realize that it was in this period that the prospect of Philadelphia actually playing Test matches one day was not to be laughed at. Let us consider a few of the events of the Golden Age of cricket as they affected Philadelphia: for four years around the turn of the century, there were two competing monthly cricket magazines in that *city* — two! Few countries are able to support one nowadays. . . . Look at the tours: from 1896 to 1914 Haverford College undertook five tours to England to play other schools, and clubs. It was many years before any English school toured abroad. The Gentlemen of Philadelphia came here three times, and each time their record was good and some of the play remarkable. Three of the constituent clubs each made tours here to play clubs and country teams and ground teams. There were six trips to Bermuda and to Jamaica. Twelve teams from these islands made tours to North America and chiefly to Philadelphia, and these included Kent, the first county to tour abroad, the MCC, and many of the leading players of the time, Ranji among them. It was an extremely pleasant ending to a cricket season to cross the Atlantic in early or mid-September and play on till October in the marvellous surroundings to be found there. There were three Australian tours, official in 1896 (when again they managed to lose to Philadelphia in one of their matches by an innings) and 1912, and unofficial but hardly less powerful in 1913. And never was Philadelphia found to be playing above its class."

Rowland Bowen goes on to say, "Philadelphia had one very great player, of world class — John Barton King", but I am not going to say a word about John Barton King because anybody who knows anything about cricket knows that this American from Philadelphia proved himself to be one of the finest fast bowlers the game has ever known.

The second point I select is the concern of the founder and editor of *The Cricket Quarterly* with cricket periodicals. Here I would only mention one instance, taken from the appendices which I find myself reading as much as the text. I see that in 1877 the *American Cricketer* was founded, weekly till the end of the century, monthly until its demise (though very irregular towards the end) in 1929, and thus the longest lasting of any cricket magazine.

Who in the name of heaven would have guessed that of a publication on cricket in America?

As much for the information as to insist upon the value of the appendices, we read that in the United Provinces (of India) instructional books on the game appeared in Urdu and Hindi; "probably elsewhere and in other languages, judging by the success of the game in the Bombay area".

Some words now, few but necessary, as to the method which the author uses. The reader of this introduction will already have felt the impact of the kind of passionate research and investigation which went into this book. We can note that cricket was recorded in France in 1478 but that, doubt having been cast on the correct reading of the document, Rowland Bowen took the matter up directly with the Directeur-General of the *Archives de France* and received the reply that, after looking at the original and consulting several specialists on handwriting of the fifteenth century, the reading "criquet" was unassailable. What I personally like, however, is the reference to one William Bedle, born 22 February 1679. He is the first man known to have achieved great prominence in the game, for when he died in June 1768, nearly ninety years of age, he was "formally accounted the most expert cricket player in England". The conclusions drawn are those of a genuine historian. The fact is unquestionable and it can mean three things: first that he was indeed a great player. Secondly, that there were means *then* of judging comparative prowess, and thirdly that his fame lasted at least a generation after he last played. The material is slight, the implications are enormous and justifiable: already the game was national.

This book means a great deal to me not merely as a history of cricket but as history. Over the last years I have been noting a new type of historical writing. In English there is *The Making of the English Working Class* by E.P. Thompson. In French there are two books, *The History of the Sans-Culottes* by A. Soboul, which deals with the ordinary people whom historians at last recognize today as primary in any consideration of the French Revolution. An Englishman, Mr R. Cobb, has written in French a history of the French Revolutionary armies of the period 1793–4, an army essentially of the *sans-culottes* and the ordinary people. A friend of mine in the United States will soon have published material which deals with the life of the slave before the Civil War, what he did as a human being, what he thought and how he adjusted himself to his difficult situation. These and other books are breaking new ground in a manner that treats their material as fundamental and not subsidiary to what we usually know as history. This history of cricket obviously does not treat the subject as if the ordinary cricketer was a *sans-culotte* but the method, the tone, the tempo, the range, show that we have here something new, not only in the history of cricket but in the writing of history. Hegel says that the owl of Minerva flies only at dusk. That is to say, one seriously examines and explores a situation, a totality, only when it is in the stage of its decline. Rowland Bowen, I would suspect from this book, even if he did not agree with this, would not disagree. It seems to me that a book like this which delves so deep and shows cricket to have been a part of every period of the history of England and the colonial territories makes one thing clear, that cricket is an integral part of the British civilization. I believe that whatever road that civilization takes, it will take cricket with it.

Not Just Cricket

(*New Society*, 18 December 1975)

Gerald Howat has written not merely a good but a valuable book.* Office-boy Constantine began in Trinidad at three shillings a day. The dynamic Constantine was carefully trained by his father, who was a famous cricketer. Local selectors recognized Constantine's cover-point fielding and general potential, resulting in selection for the 1923 team to England. Howat does not fully recognize how systematically Constantine worked at fast bowling and (a fast bowler cannot be a great cover) transformed himself from a super cover into a super slip. At the age of thirty-seven, he abandoned speed for a pragmatic medium pace, with outstanding success. In between, his play and personality had lifted league cricket in the north of England to heights undreamt of.

Cricket being over, he was natural chairman of a new populist party in Trinidad. Howat notes that half the first budget of his party's government was allocated to Constantine's ministries: that safeguarded the party from any charge of corruption.

He left the government to become High Commissioner in London. Howat is accurate and detailed about Constantine's brilliant cricket and his competence as minister and diplomat, but he is unaware of, or perhaps prefers to ignore, the fact that Constantine's premier refused to receive the man who was chairman of the party for seven years and High Commissioner for two.

He says that Constantine always had "a determined approach to money". True. But in 1931, when Constantine learnt that I planned to come to London when I had saved enough money, he immediately told me to come at once and he would take care of any financial difficulties. This he did. Without being asked, he spontaneously paid the printing expenses of my book on West Indian self-government. One day I met him by chance in Fleet Street. He mentioned that West Indian students had included him in a circular seeking money to pay for a lecture made to them by Wilson Harris. He asked me what I thought of the lecture and I told him. "Tell them to print," he said, "I'll pay." I could multiply these instances.

**Learie Constantine*, Allen & Unwin, 1975.

He wrote and spoke on the race question in order to temper race prejudice in England. He was unusually successful because there was pride but no bitterness in him.

He was a great judge of the game. Before 1938 he said that the future lay in one-day cricket. As a cricket correspondent for a London daily, he waged an unceasing battle against the routine play increasingly prevalent in county cricket. A.G. Gardiner has said that Ranjitsinhji's play made the British public aware of India. Constantine's cricket made them aware of the Caribbean in general and of black men in particular.

In 1930, during a Test series in the Caribbean, I wrote about him: "Where Hendren husbands his energy, Constantine expends his with a reckless, a positively regal prodigality. It is Europe and the Americas over again — the old world and the new."

To conclude the historical comparison: Constantine and Headley preserved the shaky West Indian status as Test cricketers. A succeeding generation, led by the unparalleled Frank Worrell, established Test cricket standards permanently in the Caribbean. Now the latest generation, today in Australia — Lloyd, Kallicharan, Boyce, Julien, Roberts — all play Test cricket in the Constantine tradition. For years Constantine maintained that despite their constant defeats, the West Indies needed only the proper leadership to play as well as England or Australia. This lack he attributed to the effect on the team of social antagonisms in the Caribbean. He himself, however, under the most depressing conditions, insisted on playing as he thought West Indians could and should play. This, perhaps more than anything else, expresses the Constantine behind the genial Learie. And Howat's biography, valuable as it is, lacks this important chapter in the history of the game.

Cricket and Race

(1975)

Commiserating with Lady Constantine about Constantine's death, I said, "For over sixty years I found him always ready to talk, always ready to listen. . . ." He died when I specially needed to talk to him.

He died on 1 July, and on 4 July the *Washington Post*

published an article on Willie Mays, the greatest baseball hero since Babe Ruth: "Mays . . . was a black athlete. He ran black, swung black, and caught black." Baseball had deteriorated into boredom. But Mays expressed on the field what James Baldwin (the famous black novelist) and others would later try to say in words: "You need to learn something again about joy and suffering, about risk and about those possibilities of uninhibited expression without which neither life nor art can survive."

I have expressed similar ideas about cricket but from this "blackness" I recoil: it is not new, it is not Black.

Wordsworth and Coleridge (*Lyrical Ballads*, 1798) first said that industrial civilization needed to reaffirm the elementary hopes and fears of simpler ages. The man who made these concerns a part in industrial England was W.G. Grace. But A.G. Steel in *Wisden* (1891) and M.A. Noble in *The Game's the Thing* (1926) recorded routine and boredom. But Noble knew who infused new life. It was a white man, Victor Trumper. The Age was Golden, not Black.

When Frank Worrell and his team tried to restore to cricket what it had lost, they were not expressing a blackness.

I believed and still believe that the generations of Grace, Trumper and Ranjitsinhji, of Worrell and his men, all were expressing powers inherent in a section of society but hitherto dormant. And where else but in South Africa, aggressively anti-Black, can contemporary cricket see the seeds of regeneration?

On 16 July I went to Detroit to see Mays. The morning after 17 July the *Detroit Free Press* noted that although Mays failed "the fans didn't mind. They were glad to see him play". Within his elegance and dignity, there is the ferocious effectiveness of Frank Worrell and I cannot see that Barbadian as an exemplar of blackness.

Does Sobers bat, bowl and field black? He plays the game of powers emancipating themselves in a field that needs emancipation.

I believe that the Constantine I knew would have been an ally against these racial ideas, benign as they may appear.

1980s

On the occasion of his 80th birthday in 1981, James returned to London at the invitation of the Race Today Collective to deliver three public lectures. He subsequently settled in Brixton and resumed regular cricket writing, which in the preceding years had hardly been possible given his geographical mobility. He began writing a column in *Race Today* and also made occasional contributions to other publications, including *The Guardian*, *The Times*, *South* and the *Journal of the Cricket Society*.

James has very much remained a source of reference in London for cricketers and cricket writers alike. He continues to read, think, watch and discuss the game. To his interpretation of the contemporary cricket scene he brings the whole weight of his historical experience.

Images of the great cricketers, of yesterday and today, are as clear in C.L.R. James's mind as are the great artistic achievements of Michelangelo and Picasso.

A Majestic Innings with Few Peers

(*South*, September 1982)

On 28 June in the second Test between England and India at Old Trafford, S.M. Patil made 129 not out. India had resumed on Sunday at 35 for three and very few people except the Indians themselves believed they would overcome the nearly 400-run deficit that separated them from the England total. To the excitement, enjoyment, and, in all probability, the astonishment of most people, the Indians recovered and ended the day with 379 for eight. The major contribution was the innings of Patil.

The wicket was very slow and the rise of the ball from the pitch was reasonably uniform. To this advantage was added the idea among the English bowlers and fieldsmen that all they had to do was attack and the Indians would crumble. In fact, the attacking bowling and close fielding produced unceasing stroke-play to all corners of the field by Patil, aided chiefly by Kapil Dev. Patil treated the England bowling, in theory a first-class attack, with majesty — if not contempt. Contempt is a strong word, but Patil hit the fast bowler and England captain Bob Willis for six fours in an over of seven balls. He went from 80 to 100 in that over, and a batsman must have a feeling of unimpeachable command to make these boundaries in such uninterrupted sequence.

I have seen many centuries by great batsmen in Tests during the last fifty years. In confidence and power, I remember few that approach Patil's century. The peak of this innings arrived with a new-ball delivery that pitched somewhat short, from Willis. Patil, it seemed to me, stepped back to hook but the ball was on him too quickly. He did not moderate his aggression, but, from his back foot, played a tennis stroke past the bowler to the boundary. I have not kept count, but I believe he found the boundary on the offside between point and cover as often as he hooked to the square-leg boundary. Altogether an innings without superior and with very few peers.

Comparison is the cricket fanatic's incurable practice. Matthew Arnold said that one should learn very well certain classic pieces of poetry and that this would help in the writing of poetry. I instinctively apply a similar principle to great innings by great batsmen.

Two innings are permanently engraved as No. 1 in my

C.L.R. James

multitudinous memories. That is not true, my memories of
great batsmen and even of great innings are not multitudinous
by any means. Such batsmen and such innings are rare, though
not as rare as the historical memory of George Headley. (I once
asked George if he remembered any outstanding innings in the
course of his long experience. He said no, he didn't. I asked him
if he remembered any of his own innings, particularly the
century in each innings at Lord's. Again he said no.) But I
remember two above all. One was the 72 made by Ted Dexter
against the West Indies at Lord's in 1963. The West Indies had a
fine all-round bowling side, perhaps the best they have ever
had. There were Hall and Griffiths, the left-handed Sobers, and
slow bowler Gibbs. From the first ball, Dexter was at home and
I remember hooks to square leg off the fast bowlers, cuts to the
point boundary when they dropped the ball off the off-stump,
and, as if according to a predestined rhythm, when they
pitched the ball up they were driven straight back to the
pavilion. Sobers got him out lbw and I believe I was not the
only follower of the West Indies who was sorry to see him go.

The other innings was by that very great batsman Rohan
Kanhai. I don't believe Kanhai is fully recognized as one of the
greatest batsmen in living memory. I was fortunate enough to
be present at one of his most creative innings. For Kanhai was a
creative batsman. Dexter's 70-odd was not a creative innings.
He simply did everything that was necessary, and executed his
strokes with natural freedom and incomparable style. But
Kanhai, so his fellow West Indian players have told me, would
go to the wicket and unloose a bevy of strokes which they had
never seen before and which they might never see again for
years. As Learie Constantine told me one day, "Kanhai sometimes goes crazy," and, coming from him, with his habit of
making unprecedented strokes, it was a description which
implied far more than it said. In 1964 at Edgbaston I saw
Kanhai play an innings of, I think, over a century and a half. I
have described it elsewhere and can do no better than to
recommend the committed historian to read the press reports of
that match. He will see that writer after writer compared the
innings to the play of the all-conquering Don Bradman. For me,
that innings surpassed anything I ever saw from Bradman.

Patil's innings was a great one. But that does not make him a
great batsman in the historic sense of that noble term. Let me
illustrate from a personal experience what the term "great
batsman" means.

Some time in the 1920s, Trinidad was playing against Barbados at the Queens Park Oval in Trinidad. Late in the afternoon of the first day, Challenor and Tarilton opened the innings for Barbados. Now Challenor symbolized batting, in every palace and hovel in the Caribbean. Challenor had made his reputation in England in 1923 as one of the great batsmen of the period. Tarilton was not as brilliant but perhaps, *perhaps* more reliable. Challenor and Tarilton greeted all cricket invaders of Barbados with a century each, specializing in inflicting this on the visiting MCC teams. So the famous pair walked to the wicket in the gathering dusk to face the bowling of Aucher Waddell. I knew Waddell's bowling well. He was captain of the club of which I was the vice-captain (he and I opened the bowling; I fielded at second slip).

So, ensconced behind the white board where I could see directly along the line between the wickets, I watched Waddell begin as I had seen him do dozens of times. The first ball was shortish and pitched well outside the off-stump. That was Waddell's way of finding his range, so to speak. The next two balls were on the middle stump, good length and of a fine pace. Challenor played a forward defensive stroke, a stroke of certainty and command. I knew what was coming next. Without change of action, Waddell increased his pace and the ball began outside the leg stump. Challenor put his left foot forward, prepared to glance, and did so. But the new ball swung into the wicket very late, eluding Challenor's bat and hitting him on the pad. There was the usual appeal, not only from the bowler but from the crowd, and I was in it. But the umpire, Toby Creighton — a very sophisticated young Trinidadian — said no. Some time afterwards I met Toby, with whom I used to talk.

"Hi, Toby," I said, "you know that Challenor was out in that first over."

"I know he was out," said Toby.

I was dumbstruck. "You knew at the time that he was out?" Toby very firmly replied that at the time he knew.

"But if you knew," I said, "why didn't you give him out?" Toby replied firmly: "Give him out? You wanted me to give out Challenor lbw for nought, opening the Barbados innings a few minutes before the close of play? Nello, you surprise me. I thought *you* had more sense than that. Would *you* have given him out?"

I found I was unable to answer yes. For the first time, I became aware of the enormous quake that would have shuddered through the body politic of the Caribbean if Challenor, of the world-famous firm of Challenor and Tarilton, had been given out lbw for nought a few minutes before the close of play. To this day, some fifty years afterwards, I have not been able to say: "Yes, I would have given him out."

For the first time I recognized what it really means in Terra Britannica to be a great batsman. That is the horizon Patil faces. To reach it he will need many more repetitions of what took place at Old Trafford last June.

Gower to Lead England

(*Race Today*, May/June 1983)

The question of the day is not who will bat for England, who will bowl for England, not even who will captain England. The question is: who will lead England? The word is *lead*. I wouldn't be surprised if many people in England, followers of cricket, do not know what I mean by placing so much emphasis on the word lead. You can appoint a captain, in fact you have to. What you really want is a person who will *lead* the side.

Now for a negative point which I have made before and make again, and I am very unhappy about it. Willis, above all, never did and does not lead England. I believe that he writes the batting order almost automatically. As for changing the bowlers, you can foresee everything he does. As I have said before, Willis is a correspondent. Something happens and he does what is obviously required. And today, above all, England needs a leader. Not merely to lead the team on the field or even off it. What is required is someone to build a team and I am of the opinion, which I do not hesitate to express, that has to be done by a person, one person, one person of character. He must know what he wants, what is the material at his disposal, what he is aiming at and having made his initial choices will alter them only as a result of a formidable crisis. You cannot chop and change a body of men without inhibiting and disrupting their capacity to co-operate.

And now I shall make two choices. I shall reject one person and propose another. High on my list of rejections is Ian Botham. I have read in the press and what is more I have seen him on television talking about the captaincy. I was against, and this time he made me more than ever certain that he was unfitted to be the England captain.

My reason for this dogmatic attitude? Not only his previous failures as captain. Not only the fact that both as bowler and batsman he needs to reorganize his own play and put them on sure foundations. His style of bowling in particular is impossible to criticize because it has no solid foundation.

When Alec Bedser came on to bowl you knew more or less what his approach, his technique and his style would be. When at the beginning of an innings the captain hands the ball to Botham you do not know exactly what he is going to do, you do not know exactly what pace he is going to bowl at. You cannot know because he himself does not know. He responds to his feelings, maybe to the batsman, maybe to the weather, maybe to the climate. People refer to him as a fast bowler. In my view he has never been a bowler of real pace. Sometimes he is a mere medium bowler.

This may seem capricious to people, even perhaps impertinent. I remain obstinate. You see, I saw him in the Caribbean a few years ago where in batting and in bowling (even perhaps in the slips) he was all over the place. That he has done the same in more than one series since merely fortifies the opinions I formed years ago.

To drive a final nail into this coffin, Botham, a few days ago, said to an interviewer that he wanted to captain England again. When the interviewer asked him why, Botham replied that he wanted to get back at the critics. He did not want to rebuild the England team, he did not want to strengthen the batting, he did not want to give dynamism to the bowling, he did not feel the need to inspire the team to look upon the opposing sides that he as captain was preparing a thunderbolt for them. Strategy of attack, of defence was further from him than it was from Willis. All he wanted was to get back at the critics. I almost wept, for Botham has fine cricketing qualities but a commonplace mind which cannot organize them and tries this and that and the other. His dominating aim, after years of failure and catastrophe, is to get back at those who criticize him. I look and listen and wonder at this unique phenomenon in this game of Test cricket.

The captain of a side must first be certain of himself. I shall go no further than that.

After such a decisive negative, I have to make a positive statement. I propose as captain of England, David Gower. He was born on 1 April 1957. That means he is just twenty-six years old. It is the one reason why I am in favour of him. The England side is badly in need of something new, that is to say the rejection of the old. Gower is a young man, but he was in the Wisden Five in 1979: in other words this young man is a most experienced cricketer playing for years in the toughest circles.

And now I come to another important feature. He has always batted well, many times, at his age, carrying the side. I saw him do it in the Caribbean. He did it in Australia and yet he is just twenty-six. That means he has that notable combination of youth and experience.

I am not going to quote all the things that have been said about Gower by critics of note. (It would be more easy to quote the things they have not said.) I will however quote G.O. Allen in Wisden (1981), p.109: "Gower twice played some fine strokes and was beginning to look the batsman all Englishmen hope and believe he would be, only to get out to two bad shots." Those were two bad ones against the infinite number of great ones he has made.

Let me conclude with that astute and steady observer, Trevor Bailey. I quote: "It is also interesting that David Gower, who is a lovely mover and has lots of time to play his strokes. . . ." I am happy in that I saw it early. I may seem here to be stressing or overstating the eye. It is not a mistake — I would not make such a mistake. It is because years ago, before an England team was selected for the Caribbean tour, there were one or two critics posing the problem about the selection or rejection of Gower. I was not only put out but even angry because Gower was obviously a boy to stick in the England team and leave him there. So I did what I could. I sent a telegram to Gower, c/o MCC, Lord's telling him that I was expecting to welcome him to the Caribbean particularly in relation to Caribbean cricket. My name counted for something and I wanted to register the fact that a representative Caribbean observer was looking upon Gower as an ornament to the England side.

Ultimately he was selected. But since that time, while he continues to be a lovely mover and to have more time than ever to play his strokes, there continues to be the question of the youthful Gower, obviously a player of genius but needing experience. How much experience did W.G. Grace have? How much experience did Don Bradman have? Gower today, at the age of twenty-six, has far more experience than they had when they burst upon the world. Gower not only has lovely strokes, he is an individual player with years of experience and still four years short of thirty. And in match after match he makes some impossible catches which point to reflexes far beyond the normal.

He can do more than lead England. He can set out to do what cannot be done by explosion: he can set out to build a team, his own batting at the centre; he can build around himself with an instinct towards youth so that before he is thirty an England team will step on to the field to the applause of its fellow countrymen and the respect of its opponents.

I could say a lot more, but finally I want it to be understood that I am here not only giving some useful advice, but expressing a grievance I have felt for some time now.

The Captain and His Team: An Injustice to Gower

(*Race Today*, October/November 1983)

Let me quote a statement by Jeffrey Stollmeyer, a man with an immense experience of cricket all over the world — in the Caribbean, England, Australia, India. In his recent book on cricket* he has the following paragraph on page 73: "I had watched the day's proceedings critically from the gallery of my room at the CCI in the company of George Headley. Our conversations that day taught me more about the tactics of the game than I was able to learn anywhere else at any one time during my future as a player. It was then that I was more resolved than ever to make a study of cricket tactics."

It is obvious that for Jeffrey Stollmeyer, Headley was a great master of the game. I can fortify that statement recalling Constantine telling me about some strategic point: "George would know that." By George, of course, he meant George Headley. I was a bit surprised and forced the issue: "Is George a master?" I asked him. "George," he said gravely, "is one of the best."

There was a fuss about Headley being made the captain of the West Indian side when his turn came. The important thing is that not only must a captain be a great master of the game but the team must recognize that. At times a captain at cricket (like leaders in all other spheres of activity) has to take decisions in which a clear answer is not obvious. He uses his experience, his knowledge, his insight and he says: "Well, in this mess I

*Everything Under the Sun, published by Stanley Paul & Co. Ltd, 1983.

think we should go this way." Very often the situation is not at all clear and much will depend on the rest of the team having confidence in the captain's judgement. They have to put their strength into the way that he has pointed out. Otherwise the uncertainty inherent in the situation becomes widespread and the team for the time being fumbles.

Now I want to come back to Headley. I knew George very well, both as a cricketer and personally. The trouble with George was that he was an utterly retiring, selfless type of person. To talk to George about batting and cricket was to be aware of a man who just batted naturally with technique and creativity. But of himself, as a personality, as a great cricketer, he had nothing of that in him. He impressed you with a bat in his hand and on the cricket field generally. He was in his manners both reserved and generous, but otherwise he was just a modest Jamaican.

Now the captain must not be that way. The captain must impress people. Of course one of the ways that he will impress people (whatever his personality may be) is that he is a great cricketer. I do not know of any batsman greater than George Headley. Nobody. I repeat this as I have done before. Nobody ever batted better than George Headley. Nobody. But he was not the kind of person to impress people with his cricket personality and knowledge. I have said enough to show that it was immense, recognized by people who played with him.

And now after this long introduction I can come to what has been my great concern for some time. I believe that the England selection committee is not only doing harm to the conception of an English side but they are striking blows, subtle but heavy blows, at David Gower. I have written before that Gower ought to be appointed captain of the England side because, number one, he is a great batsman; number two, he has an immense experience of international cricket; number three, he is still very young which means that in addition to all that he knows there are fields and opportunities for developing knowledge at his age which is still formative. He can build an England side. That is what England requires, not eleven cricket players but an England side. And only a captain (backed by management) can build a side. The England team at present is all in pieces. Willis, I have to repeat again, is for years the finest fast bowler in the world today. There is nobody at his pace can hit the ball at a good length or over and then shoot it up at the batsman's throat. He is still doing so, doing it as well today as ever he did. From listening to him, watching him on television, watching him on the field, he seems a serious and attractive man, with a cricketing personality of distinction. But to lead a team, to take charge of it, to lead it through difficulties, to create solutions to problems, to create difficulties for the other side — of all this, Willis is innocent. He is not a leader in that sense, he does not intervene to shape the team and do things to the opposite side. He does not create. He merely responds.

Now if you want to have a captain to do that you must have confidence in him and the most destructive thing in cricket selection in the last few years is what has been happening to David Gower. He plays a Test innings and the rest of the side fail. Yes, they agree, Gower played splendidly; he sure is coming along well. He is not *coming along*, the others failed, are failing while he makes the runs. But all they can say is that Gower is certainly going to be a very great batsman some day. He is always looked upon as someone who is coming and the result of that is to inhibit him.

Gower needs at the present time the encouragement and the confidence of those who are managing cricket, the encouragement and confidence of those who are writing about cricket. There should be a universal feeling that Gower is the man. I have watched him batting and watched him throughout the year and I get the impression that he would be able to do the job. I was very pleased the other day to see that experienced and sober critic John Woodcock, of *The Times*, say that Gower has the ability, character, energy etc. to be captain of England. I would not have gone so far because I did not know, I was not in contact with the cricket team as I used to be in the old days, but Woodcock is. He has been around for many years. He thinks that Gower can do it. I accept that. From my general knowledge of Gower's cricket I am satisfied that he would be able to do it, but if you keep on leaving him out and stating that England needs a captain, who can it be? It is time for Willis to go but he has not gone because we have not found anyone to put in his place and you keep on running around, avoiding the obvious fact that Gower is the man. You are not merely making a misjudgement. You are objectively attacking and demolishing the power and the gifts of David Gower.

I want to end this article by saying pretty crudely that the England team has gone from pillar to post, jumping from rock to rock somehow. The necessity is for the England team to be *led* by someone over the next few years. All these circumstances and his own abilities point to David Gower as the captain of England, *to be appointed today*. And now I conclude: if you do not do that then you are *against* him. And if you are *against* him then you should be *for* somebody else. But the state in which the captaincy, and with the captaincy the selection of an English team (the building of an England team), has arrived at today requires very serious consideration. That is why, contrary to my usual habit, I intervene with such a definite opinion into what is always a critical matter — the selection of any Test team for any particular country.

And now my friends, particularly my British friends, listen to the words of wisdom from a man from the West Indies. Richard Wright, one of the finest writers of the day, a black American, once told me: "Nello," he said, "you are from the Caribbean, you don't know what it is to be a black man in the United States. Your father tells you that you are black and therefore below normal, your mother tells you that you are black and therefore cannot have this or that, your friends at school tell you the same thing, your teacher tells you that you are black and therefore you must be careful, your parson and all people around you from the time you begin to know the world tell you that you are black, you have to be careful and be always aware of the fact that you are black." Wright continued: "You know what is the result of that? If everybody around you and all the books and papers that you read tell you that you are black and *therefore inferior*, then you begin to wonder: I am obviously black, and if all of them think we are inferior then maybe it is true. So *they* instil in you the doubt as to whether you are something that can take its place in the world."

How does this apply? You find all sorts of reasons why David Gower should not be appointed captain of the England team today. You cannot find somebody of whom you could say, if not Gower, this person; you are really striking blows at Gower and instituting in his own mind doubts about his own capacity. It is a pity. Because Gower is not at his peak as a batsman. There is still more of his batting to come. But this question of the captaincy would bring everything to full blossom. What it is doing is impeding him.

George Headley 1909–1983

(*Race Today*, January–May 1984)

George Headley is dead, is dead and has not left his peer. Poetic yes, but no hyperbole; the material facts will appear.

Meanwhile as with every cricketer — first what he has done.

In Test matches George made 2,190 runs in forty innings with an average of 60.83. He is sixth in the list of Test averages, exceeded by Bradman and Pollock, the three others who are above him have not played twenty innings each. In his forty innings George made ten centuries; curiously with him he made only five fifties to his ten centuries. Bradman scored similarly — thirteen fifties to twenty-nine centuries. That means that when George made 50 he did not get out easily, he went on to the century. But Sutcliffe, who averaged 60.73 to George's 60.83, had twenty-three fifties to his sixteen centuries.

George has another quality which he shares with Bradman alone — he never failed in a Test series. In the 1930 Tests he made 21 and 170; 8 and 39; 114 and 112; 10 and 223. In Australia, 1930–1, he made 0 and 11; 14 and 2; 102 not out and 28 (the 28 being top score); 33 and 11 (the 33 being again top score); and 105 and 30 (the 30 being second only to 34). We need not continue with detail except to say that in 1939 George made 106 and 107; 51 and 5; and 65 run out.

I did not see that run out but I heard about it from press reports, many people and from George himself. Except for malice aforethought, George that day was on his way to two hundred at least, at least.

By failing in a Test I mean, for example, Hammond who scored in Australia in 1928–9, 44; 28; 251; 200; 32 run out; 119 not out; 177; 38; 16. But followed this up in England in 1930 with 8 and 4; 38 and 32; 113 and 35; 3; 13 and 60, while in 1934 his figures are unbelievable — 25 and 16; 2; 4; 37 and 20; 15 and 43. That kind of failure in a Test series never befell Headley and the only other batsman of whom that can be said is Bradman. Sutcliffe, I admit, always maintained a high level but Sutcliffe never played the cricket that Bradman and Headley played.

Always I insist upon statistics because, utterly apart from the runs made, my claims for Headley are without restraint. I have said it before and I say it again: nobody ever batted better than George. Bradman made more runs and it is from George that I have heard the greatest tribute, not only to ability with the bat, but to the concentration and endurance which enabled Bradman to score those mountains of runs so consistently. Yet I cannot place George second to Bradman.

First of all Bradman had a powerful array of batsmen, first to open the innings and secondly to support him if he scored. George had nobody. From start to finish he carried the whole West Indies side on his solitary shoulders. George has told me himself what a strain this was and I remember the regret in his voice as he said: "Sometimes I haven't finished putting on my pads when I hear that one of them has gone."

In 1938 I watched with George the Australians playing England at Manchester. Somewhere early in the innings O'Reilly bowled a tremendous over and George admitted that he had never seen anything like it and O'Reilly was a tremendous bowler. So, tempted perhaps by his unfailing calm and control, I said: "George, if when you went in you faced that kind of attack you would be in trouble." His face changed from its normal good nature into tight readiness. "No," he said, "when I am walking down the pavilion steps, going in to bat, if I met my father I wouldn't recognize him. And once I am at the wicket I am concerned with nothing else but seeing the ball from the bowler's hand. . . ."

George stayed at my house often and we would talk cricket until the small hours of the morning. I also played common-place club cricket with George in Lancashire. I stayed at the house of Constantine and he would take me to play in the matches that the professionals arranged among themselves. George was adamant — no kind of bowling, no kind of wicket, no arrangement of the field ever put him off. Or the leg-side field and batsmen and bowlers bowling to leg? To George it was quite simple: "If when I hit it they catch it then that is OK with me." One thing disturbed him (or rather what he was on the lookout for): "In a Test match be on guard against the bad ball." Somewhat bewildered, I asked him why. He said that in the tight play of a Test when a really bad ball comes, you go at it so greedily that you can make a bad stroke and get out. And from my previous knowledge of him I knew that George was not going to make any rash stroke and get out stupidly.

One last word on this unique player. He played usually off the back foot, but so aggressive was he against all bowling that even when on the back foot for defence he would be pushing the ball through the covers or between short leg and mid-on. One of the most anticipated and keenest of my cricket enjoyments was what happened to a bowler after George had played him back and back and back; he thought he could bring up one and get George still on the back foot. But George would stick his left foot out like an English forward player, take his bat back high over his head and drive like . . . George Headley.

I have to put it that way in order not to do injustice to George Headley.

I am in a lot of trouble here. I personally believe that if I had to choose one batsman of all the great batsmen of the twentieth century I would choose George Headley. But I know there would be a chorus of objection and some people would question my judgement or my honesty, and they all would agree that number one should be Don Bradman. I agree, too, in theory. There is no batsman of whom it was more certain that he would score a century in an important match than Don Bradman. I agree, but I agree only in general.

When the wicket was wet and the ball moving around, Bradman got out almost immediately. People went so far as to try and explain it. They said that Bradman had worked out a technique, a masterly technique, which was absolutely impregnable on an ordinary wicket. But to play on a wet wicket meant an entirely different style and inasmuch as wet wickets did not come very often, Bradman was not prepared to change his style and then have to change it again. So he went on to the wet wicket, played as usual and he got out.

Now this is not mere talk. I had, some years ago, examined the figures carefully as to how George Headley and Bradman played on wet wickets — both of them flourishing at the same time from about 1930 to 1939. In fifteen innings Bradman passed fifty only once, forty only twice and fifteen only four times. His average for the fifteen innings is 16.66. George's average for the period on wet wickets is 39.85. If I can quote what I said at the time: "You need not build on these figures a monument, but you cannot ignore them." I will go on to say that Neville Cardus has stated that Headley has good claims to be considered *on all wickets* the finest of the inter-war batsmen.

I don't want to quote Cardus as my authority but I think that the history of West Indies cricket and of cricket as a whole demands what I am going to say now. Headley was the superb player that he was on bad wickets because he liked them. I have never heard of any other batsman who liked the wickets on which the balls turned, kept low or jumped. George told me more than once, because I questioned him, that he liked to play on those. When I asked him why, he said: "Because they are so difficult, because you have got to watch the ball and you can't make any mistakes." And he finally added: "You see, when you are on those you can't take any chances, if the ball is short you have to turn and hook, if the ball is pitched up you have to drive 'cause the wicket is such that you can't expect any special luck. You have to take the chances that they give you, take them as they come."

That was George Headley and that is why he scored so heavily on the wet wickets.

Now his play on a good wicket will tell you the secret of his play on a bad wicket. I have said earlier that George was a back player. That is not a clear statement of the case. George played only back. That is an extreme statement but I wanted to be extreme. He was always on that back foot in front of the middle wicket. Always. The pace of the bowler did not matter, it did not matter how fast they bowled.

He told me that you can always see that fast ball which drops and rises. The time it takes to rise to your head, you can see it all the time. He used to treat with contempt balls that rise to the head. He said: "If a ball is going up to my head it is taking a long time to get there and that means that I can see it." Therefore one of his main strokes was the cut. From that right foot he could cut square and with the late cut, in particular, the slow bowlers hadn't a chance. He would bring that right foot across and either defend or cut late down between the slips or to a third-man's left hand. If not, he would hook straight away and he hooked square. He didn't hook between mid-on and short leg. He hooked square to bowlers of any pace but to slow bowlers in particular. And one of his finest strokes was off that back foot.

As he told me once or more than once, with almost a smile he said: "I would get back there and they would believe that the ball was going to hit my foot, it was so close. But I knew that it was not going to hit my foot, my pad was in front of the wicket and the bat came down sideways at the last second. Sometimes they would appeal but after the appeal my bat came down sideways and the ball goes round to the leg boundary." That was George on the ordinary wicket. I am not speaking here of a slow wicket — that was the way he played, a back-foot player. If he did not play back he could come out to drive.

I think I have said enough. His scoring was only exceeded by Don Bradman right up to the '70s and '80s in Test cricket. I would like to end this with one or two reminiscences.

I saw George playing in 1934 against the Englishmen for the

West Indies — '34 or '33 — and he made 165 not out. What I can say about that innings is that he seemed to begin at 165 not out and all through continued as if thinking of something else. I don't remember anybody playing so easily. He wasn't scoring slow, he wasn't scoring fast — he was just scoring. He was not a man to make brilliant strokes, but he would drive hard usually to punish the bowler for thinking that he would bring the ball up.

And finally a conversation with George. It was pretty personal. We were watching the Australians play and O'Reilly was bowling. O'Reilly bowled a tremendous over in which I think he got out three Englishmen. He was bowling at a medium pace and the ball was breaking from the off and breaking from leg and coming off the pitch at times at a tremendous pace. It was obviously a tremendous piece of bowling and George stood up with me at Manchester and he said: "That fellow can bowl." I said: "Yes," and then I said: "But, George, if you were in there batting to that bowling you would be in difficulties, wouldn't you?" His face changed completely. He turned and he looked at me. I don't think he changed his face, simply something happened to him and he said: "No, Nello, I don't care what is the method or how that bowler is bowling. When I am going in to bat I am never in difficulties. I can get out for nought but I am never in difficulties."

I would like to end this statement about George with something which I think marked his uniqueness as a player — he was never, never in difficulties.

MacGregor

(*Journal of the Cricket Society*, September 1984)

MacGregor attended a school I used to run. He must have been about ten years old and he was a very slender, even notably thin, boy. When you saw him you noticed first how thin he was. He was interested in cricket. I used to do some batting at the school on a piece of concrete which ran along the side of the building and the boys would bowl at me.

MacGregor used to bowl a leg-break. His hand used to turn over and I used to watch the ball spin. He could not bowl an off-break but he got to be a very good leg-spinner. His father was very much interested in cricket and he also noted that this son of his used to bowl the leg-break which is the most difficult thing in bowling. MacGregor would keep on bowling me this leg-break and I would be quite impressed. He was not a master of it but he kept on trying and improving.

Now at times I would tell a boy to have a knock and one day I told MacGregor: "Well, you have been bowling all the time, come and have some batting." And MacGregor stood up with a bat that was almost as tall as he was and he played forward and he played back with a command and a confidence that astonished me.

MacGregor batted at times and always he impressed me. I saw that he had the foundations of batting in him.

He left the school and I went to teach at Queen's Royal College. About two or three years afterwards, one day at the beginning of the school year in September, MacGregor joined the school and he came to see me. I said: "Well, are you going to play cricket?" He said: "Yes, I have put my name down for the Fourth Eleven."

Next day the college was astir. The afternoon before they had mixed the Fourth and Third Eleven, for a match. MacGregor had gone in to bat at about a quarter past four, batted until six o'clock and made fifty-something not out. He went on playing, batting well but bowling his leg-break. Primarily he was a leg-break bowler.

Time passed. MacGregor entered his teens. His father used to talk to me always about his leg-break bowling. But I used to watch his batting and, though he did not make a lot of runs, he always shaped well.

One afternoon I was at the Queen's Park Oval, the big cricketing-centre at the practice nets where anybody could come and bowl. So MacGregor was there bowling leg-breaks. The rain started and those of us who were practising ran into the pavilion. But a few did not mind the rain. They seized the chance to do some batting. MacGregor was one of those. He had no pads and there was a boy, a bare-footed boy, a thick black boy who was bowling very fast. On that practice wicket but without pads to this fast bowling, MacGregor stood up and batted in commanding style. I called to one or two others who were in the pavilion with me. I said: "Look at that boy." They were impressed.

MacGregor became eighteen years old, he and his leg-break. He played for the island, they sent him to Barbados to play for

Trinidad but as a leg-break bowler. He went in to bat at about number nine or ten. In Barbados he took wickets with his leg-break, he made about twenty runs and everybody said that he batted well. That was all, a good twenty.

I go to England in 1932 and I am staying at Constantine's house. Every year Constantine goes to Trinidad. In 1932 he went to Trinidad and he came back in 1933 for the English season. I said: "How was it, Learie?" He said: "It was fine." I said: "A lot of cricket?" and he said: "Plenty." I asked: "Did you see a young fellow I used to know — MacGregor?" He said: "Oh, God, Nello — if you see that boy bat!"

Now you must understand that Constantine had played cricket in England, he had played cricket in India, he had been to Australia — he was an international cricketer, a man of immense experience. So he and I talked — you can understand what this meant to me. He said: "Nello — if you see that boy bat!"

I now arrive at what is an unusual piece of cricket writing — unusual for me, at any rate. I wish I could say how I saw MacGregor bat. I cannot say that, but what I have to say is the conversation that I had with Constantine after he had expressed to me his astonishment at the way MacGregor could bat. I questioned him carefully and exhaustively. By exhaustively I mean going into the question of strokes, forward play, back play, timing, different strokes to a particular ball, etc. Constantine and I had had, in the past and were going to have, many such conversations — in fact we talked about that sort of business more than we talked about anything else. But I was very anxious to hear all about this new batsman MacGregor had made himself into. And Constantine was ready to talk, particularly in answer to my questions.

I now have to disappoint. MacGregor was not in any way a unique player. He had no particular strokes — he just batted and did everything as it ought to be done. Like all great batsmen, or at any rate the majority that I have known, he was strictly orthodox. If there was one thing that Constantine seemed to emphasize it was his habit of getting singles off the back-stroke, the back defensive stroke and the forward defensive stroke. His secret with the forward defensive stroke was to play it very quietly so that cover point had a long way to get to it and he could practically walk up the pitch. On the on-side his defensive back-stroke was twisted slightly and it would constantly beat the man at short-leg, although he had to play this defence a little harder than the other one. Apart from that he was a completely orthodox, straightforward batsman.

I now have to end this article and it matters to me — *I never saw MacGregor bat in this way*. That Constantine was correct in his judgement was proved the next year when MacGregor made some seventy-odd runs against a visiting side. I heard about it and read how everybody seemed to see a new MacGregor. Unfortunately he died before I could see him play.

His death was peculiarly connected with cricket. He was not physically strong. He was batting one day and it was raining — he had been batting for some time, he was perspiring strongly and some said: "Let us stop," others said: "Let us go on." MacGregor said to go on. So from perspiring strongly he got soaking wet while batting, and when he went home he went to bed and never got out again. He seemed to have caught some kind of chill or something, and he died.

I want to add only two things. First, I understood the kind of batsman that Constantine had described to me. Constantine and I understood one another very well.

Secondly, I have always wondered what it was I saw in that boy MacGregor when he was ten years old and battling to master his leg-break. What it was I saw that kept me telling his father that he bowled the leg-break well but that boy was really a batsman — that is one of those cricket problems that I have never been able to answer to myself. There are others and we may come to them in time.

West Indies *vs* England

(*Race Today*, October/November 1984)

The West Indies team continues, in England, the series of victories won against Australia this year. It has defeated the English team in five successive Test matches — a thing that has never been done before. It is quite a feat. You do not win match after match in this way unless your team is sound, having remarkable players who respond to every occasion. But people are now saying that this is the best West Indies team that has ever visited England. Worse, there are serious people, who imply that this is the finest team ever. That I must say, quite plainly, is nonsense.

It is necessary to get down to principles. A winning team

must be well established in certain departments. The team should have a good pair of openers. It should have three good batsmen, and it would do no harm if one of these is a great super batsman. By super batsman I mean one who is not disturbed by any bowling or any crisis. There are good Test batsmen — good but not super. Super batsmen are rare, and a team can be a good team without having a man of that style.

A good team must also have a pair of bowlers — not two good bowlers, but a pair. History has recorded them — for instance, Barnes and Foster before 1914 in Australia; for the West Indies, Ramadhin and Valentine; for Surrey and for England, Laker and Lock; Australian fast bowlers.

Now the present West Indian team is singularly lacking in outstanding features of that kind. I look at their batting, and I think that there is one super batsman — that is Richards. Richards is undoubtedly a batsman who can be ranked with great batsmen of any time. But I look at the others, and I do not see any very distinguished batsmen there. Greenidge made two double centuries, but I do not believe that making two double hundreds is a sign of a super batsman. I look at the rest — Gomes is a good player, but a good player is good, not better. (The best of them I believe to be Lloyd. Going in at number five, he plays a captain's innings and holds his side together.) Apart from Richards, frankly I do not see any outstandingly great batsmen on that West Indian side.

In regard to bowling, they have some bowlers who are superior to the level of batting. For instance they have Garner and Holding, but by and large I do not think the bowling constitutes a disruptive attack upon a line of sound batsmen on a good wicket.

Now all this may sound as if I am being unduly critical, particularly of people who have been winning so many matches. But you win matches first of all on account of your skill, your own skill and, secondly, on account of the lack of skill in your opponents. I cannot speak about the skill or lack of skill in the Australians, but I have to say, with a certain regret, that the English side is very poor.

One looks at them and looks in vain for one high-class cricketer. You cannot find a high-class cricketer who has established himself as such. Botham is a very gifted cricketer. I have not known many Test players who can hit the ball so hard, and he has such wonderful all-round gifts, not least as slip fieldsman. But for some years now, Botham is a man who is continually promising to do great things, but failing. In this last

Test here, he has a wonderful opportunity in the last innings to make a fine demonstration, perhaps win the match or if not win it, play a fighting innings so as to lift the morale of his team and the supporters of the England side. He could not do it — not only could he not do it, he did not try. That hook by which he lifted the ball up to the leg boundary was a very bad stroke and would not have been made by a batsman in control of the situation. Botham, not the bowling, got himself out. I insist on this because I see no bowling which can embarrass Botham if he is prepared to take charge.

I notice that Lamb made three separate centuries in this series of Tests — few people have done as much. Nevertheless Lamb's cricket does not seem to me to promise that he will produce and maintain a high standard of scoring, against bowling of a high class or in difficult situations.

The rest of them are just plain ordinary up and down: except one. The one is Gower. Gower is a cricketer of great natural gifts. But as I have said before he has not achieved complete mastery. He still has a long way to go to make the best of the capacity he has. That he is not master of himself has been proved in this series of Tests. A batsman, who has failed in innings after innings, in his last try could have settled down to make 60 or 70: I have seen it happen in the past that the batsman says that he has failed so far and that he is going to make some runs this time. Gower is not able to do that yet.

Now it is all very well to be talking in this way, but I am not going to leave it at that. I am going to make some comparisons and some comparisons that can be made without the question of the wicket or the strength of the opposition being raised. All I will do is to name a West Indian team and certain names come to my mind at once: Weekes, Worrell and Walcott. Those are tremendous names. I do not know any cricket side that has had three such batsmen playing all the time and scoring. But we can do better than that.

In 1957, in the fifth Test at the Oval, the West Indies were bowled out for 89 and 86. I chose that match specially because the English batsmen made 412, and then the West Indies side collapsed. The West Indian side consisted of Worrell, Asgarali, Sobers, Walcott, Weekes, Collie Smith (who died), Kanhai, Alexander, Dewdney, Ramadhin and Goddard. Now that was the West Indies team about 1957 and 1958. They might have been bowled down in that last Test for 89 and 86, obviously they had been demoralized and the wicket was a mess. But this was the team at Birmingham: Pairaudeau, Kanhai, Walcott,

Weekes, Sobers, O. Smith, Worrell, Goddard (who was a very fine off-break bowler), Atkinson (a fine player), Ramadhin and Gilchrist (a real pace bowler). That was the West Indian team.

Is the present team better than that? I do not say it is the better side. All I am asking for is some restraint, and some respect for historic players.

I must add that a West Indian team was defeated by England that had on it Kanhai, Walcott, Sobers, Weekes, Worrell, O.G. Smith, Goddard, Ramadhin, Valentine and Gilchrist. I knew them all, as a team and individually. If I had to play a game against anybody, and was offered that body as my team, I would take it happily and I would not care who won the toss.

The Decline of English Cricket

(*Race Today Review*, January 1985)

The decline of English cricket as a subject of an article has been posed to me. I accept, but with a certain trepidation.

First of all, decline is not a permanent state. In two or three years the said cricket could easily take an upward form; and while you are looking for decline you must also be aware of the sprouting elements for advance. Finally the argument is, and cannot but be, historical.

With all my fortifications in order I can now join battle. Historically I find it impossible to do without remembering what happened in the decline of English cricket, 1920–21. The English team then, like this one, lost eight Tests in succession. A.C. MacLaren, a famous veteran, said that he could select a team and beat the Australians which was, if I may be allowed my rare excursion into violence, a hell of a thing to say. I cannot go into detail, but what MacLaren did was to analyse the Australian team (their fast bowling, their medium-pace bowling, their batting), to point out weaknesses and to select English players who he said could take advantage of these weaknesses.

The Australian victorious march was checked, and MacLaren's method made an indelible impression upon me. Beside MacLaren there was C.B. Fry and others. Now for me. An Australian team came to England and was beaten in Test after Test, not only beaten but disgraced. I was a reporter then, and I thought the same but I did not write it.

C.L.R. James

However, years after, Bradman tackled that year, 1956, so disastrous for Australia. They were beaten above all by the off-spin of Laker. Bradman did not complain of how badly the Australians played, but he said that he would have worked out a method of playing Laker. And now get ready: *if that method failed he would have another to try.*

I have been thinking along those lines, having been brought up on the writings of C.B. Fry. But Bradman was categorical — *you had to analyse the concrete difficulties and work out a* method. What you were not to do, and let me repeat it, *not to do*, was to keep on putting out men who had failed and putting in men who you thought would take their place. When your team is winning or is more or less equal to the other team, you can get away with that. But history and my many years of experience tell me that when you are losing constantly you have to seek why that is happening and take measures to *fill that gap* or *correct that weakness.*

What I am trying to say about the English team and the selection committee is that I see no sign whatever that there is any serious analysis of the body of the matter and a strategic attempt to strengthen weaknesses and improve strengths.

Now before you can go into proposals it is best to know the reasons for a pervading sickness. I can now only be brief, but today the kind of analysis that you used to get from the masters and reports of the journalists have disappeared. They have disappeared first because of television and the fact that after two or three overs, two or three people are on the television saying what happened and giving causes.

You cannot analyse a five-day cricket match or five five-day matches in that way. The result is that we have a series of front-page observations, dramatic moments, astonishing successes, astonishing failures — everything or nothing, governed by the remorseless claims of the television audience waiting for the event which will summarize the day's play or the morning's play.

I am certain of this because I used to participate in the old reporting and I know our discussions, unceasing, and then the way we used to read our reports the next morning and compare. There were the special players, who were our personal friends, to whom we could talk. The press and the older cricketers constantly had the feeling of responsibility for going below the surface.

Today there are no cricket reporters of that kind, but there are journalists who must catch the passing event and seek the pregnant phrase. I am not attacking a body of men for not doing what they ought to do. I am saying that modern means of communication, the pressure by other sports on cricket space, photography, love for scandals and the general absence of strategic thought (and not merely on cricket) have deeply damaged cricket reports. I do not say that the reporters do harm to the cricket but that cricket in the present age does great harm to reporting.

Botham Hitting Sixes

(*Race Today*, August/September 1985)

Botham is a unique character. I mean, naturally, that he is a unique cricketer. What his personal outlook or idiosyncrasies are, are no business of mine. Even if they became a matter of concern I would not be dealing with them in a cricket column.

Botham is unique as a cricketer and to understand that you have to know something about the history of cricket. I am fairly familiar with this history, and I believe Botham to be the hardest hitter of any Test batsman, or for that matter of any Test cricketer at all.

To be a hard hitter is not a matter of mere strength. One of the hardest hitters we have had in the West Indies was a little fellow from Barbados. For him, hitting a six was far more natural than playing the ball for a single. But let us look closer at Botham's batting.

Your really hard hitting is, as a rule, a man hitting with a cross bat. It could be a mighty cross or what we used to call a "swipe", or it might be just a trifle outside of the straight and narrow swing of the classic batsman. But, as a rule, that lapse from the regular was a sign that the batsman was depending more on physical strength than on timing. This brings us close to a distinguishing mark of Botham.

I do not believe that there is the slightest element of hitting the cricket ball with strength so as to throw it over the boundary. Not in the slightest. Botham's hitting is regulated according to custom and in the tradition of the great orthodox batsmen.

He is not exactly orthodox. A great batsman never is. The infallible sign of his greatness is that somewhere in his method

303

he is breaking the rules, or if not rules, the practices of his distinguished equals. Where Botham is different is that he does not want the real half-volley. He prefers the ball to be a little shorter, not quite up to the half-volley, but not as far back as the good length. In between. Why this is so I do not know. I would have to talk to him for a long time before I discover. But Botham knows that and, as far as I can see, too many bowlers of reputation do not know that.

For the time being, and only for the time being, I suspect that he prefers the ball a little shorter than the half-volley because by the time it reaches him (or he goes to it) the ball is a little distance off the pitch. Botham is hitting sixes and consciously lifting the ball to do so. It seems to me that he prefers the ball more removed from the pitch than the ordinary half-volley.

Let no one think that an article of a few hundred words can deal with Botham. There will be plenty more later.

C.L.R. James: A Bibliography of Cricket Writings

[An asterisk* denotes writings included in this present volume. For an extensive bibliography of other works by James see his volume of Selected Writings, At the Rendezvous of Victory, Allison & Busby, London, 1984.]

1932 "Tribute to Lord Harris", *The Times*, London, 29 March.
1932 "The greatest of all bowlers: an impressionist sketch of S.D. Barnes",* *Manchester Guardian*, 1 September.
1933 Cricket reports in *Manchester Guardian*:
 "The West Indian cricketers", 17 April.
 "A great West Indian batsman",* 18 April.
 "West Indians at Lord's", 19 April.
 "West Indians at Northampton", 8 May.
 "Good bowling by Northampton", 9 May.
 "West Indians beaten", 10 May.
 "Iddon's century", 22 May.
 "Duckworth hits freely", 23 May.
 "Drawn match at Edgbaston", 24 May.
 "What Constantine's absence means", 24 June.
 "Dull cricket", 26 June.
 "A slow match", 27 June.
 "Draw at Old Trafford", 28 June.
 "Bad day for West Indies", 7 July.
 "Lancashire at the Oval", 24 July.
 "Sibbles makes 61", 25 July.
 "Lancashire draw", 26 July.
 "Hampshire's bad catching", 14 August.
 "Mead's innings of quality", 15 August.
 "Lancashire take 5 points", 16 August.
 "Voce plays havoc with Lancs", 21 August.
 "Rain interferes at Old Trafford", 22 August.
 "Notts win on first innings", 23 August.
 "Duckworth takes command", 24 August.
 "Essex and Lancs tie on first innings", 25 August.
 "Lancashire win in a close finish", 26 August.
 "A plucky Leicestershire stand", 29 August.
 "Leicestershire helpless before Hopwood", 30 August.
 "An uncertain wicket at Blackpool", 31 August.
 "Lancashire in danger of defeat", 1 September.
 "Lancashire's last match drawn", 2 September.
 "West Indians' last game", 11 September.
 "West Indies fail", 12 September.
 "West Indians lose", 13 September.
 "West Indian cricketers", 22 September.

C.L.R. James

1933 "West Indies cricket",* *The Cricketer*, Vol. 14, 6/13/20/27 May, 3/10/17/24 June.

1933 "Chances of West Indians in first Test",* *Port of Spain Gazette*, Trinidad, 15 June.

1933 "The West Indies cricket team", *The Keys*, London, vol.1, no.1, July.

1933 "Our clubs don't play the game", *Daily Herald*, London, 21 July.

1934 Cricket reports in *Manchester Guardian*:
"Watson's century", 7 May.
"Two Lancashire centuries", 8 May.
"Leicestershire bat all day", 14 May.
"A dour struggle at Leicester", 15 May.
"Leicester save the game", 16 May.
"Hopwood makes 220 at Bristol", 7 June.
"Parkinson and Moore bat brightly", 8 June.
"Lancashire's big victory", 9 June.
"Lancashire again exceed 400", 11 June.
"Worcester out twice in a day", 12 June.
"Lancashire play fine cricket", 14 June.
"Lancashire's sound recovery", 15 June.
"Mead alone resists Hopwood", 16 June.
"A short day at Old Trafford", 22 June.
"A match of 'might have beens' ", 23 June.
"Even play at Old Trafford", 25 June.
"Lancashire beaten by Kent", 26 June.
"Hopwood's great bowling feat", 28 June.
"Lancashire rout Glamorgan", 29 June.
"Merry batting by Lancashire", 5 July.
"A gallant stand in vain", 6 July.
"E. Tyldesley's great record", 9 July.
"Lancashire again winning", 10 July.
"Lancashire win easily", 11 July.
"Lancashire's poor day at Blackpool", 12 July.
"Lancashire's one salvation", 13 July.
"Lancashire beat Worcester", 14 July.
"Australians and Yorkshire", 16 July.
"Bradman smites Yorkshire", 17 July.
"Wood saves Yorkshire", 18 July.
"Lancashire's bad day at Lord's", 19 July.
"Notts visit Old Trafford", 23 July.
"Iddon 200 at Old Trafford", 24 July.
"Lancashire and Notts draw", 25 July.
"Lancashire bat admirably", 26 July.
"Short day at Old Trafford", 27 July.
"Lancashire's grand victory", 28 July.
"Tyldesley again", 30 July.
"Leicester to follow on", 31 July.

"Leicestershire's brave effort", 1 August.
"Lancashire in strong position", 17 August.
"Nichols saves Essex in fine game", 18 August.
"Lancashire's bleak cricket",* 20 August.
"Spirited batting by Kent",* 21 August.
"Lancashire draw with Kent",* 22 August.
"Lancashire in difficulties", 23 August.
"Lancashire's first innings lead", 24 August.
"Lancashire's cricket to arithmetic", 25 August.
"Bradman's remarkable century; Australians' huge total",* 10 September.
"Cricket at Scarborough; Australian bowling can be hit",* 11 September.
"Australians' easy victory", 12 September.

1935   Cricket reports in *Manchester Guardian*:
"Lancashire's spirited victory", 21 May.
"Lancashire's bowling chastised", 27 May.
"Iddon's century", 28 May.
"Leicester win", 29 May.
"Hopwood's day of success", 4 June.
"Lancashire's quiet batting", 6 June.
"Many delays at Blackburn", 7 June.
"Kent bowlers in generous mood", 15 June.
"Farrimond hits with spirit", 17 June.
"Holmes makes excellent hundred", 18 June.
"Langton's catch; Lancashire collapse at Aigburth",* 20 June.
"Lancashire and South Africans draw", 22 June.
"Paynter shows his England form", 24 June.
"Lancashire in sore peril", 25 June.
"Lancashire batting all day", 1 July.
"Worcestershire follow on", 2 July.
"Lancashire win easily", 3 July.
"Lancashire's hard task", 9 July.
"Lancashire draw at Buxton", 10 July.
"Lancashire's fine recovery", 11 July.
"Booth and Duckworth beat Essex", 12 July.
"Lancashire's poor position", 15 July.
"Hard task for Lancashire", 16 July.
"Lancashire sadly fallen", 17 July.
"Lancashire lead Gloucester", 18 July.
"Short day at Old Trafford", 19 July.
"Lancashire win", 20 July.
"Lancashire's splendid fielding", 20 July.
"Lancashire tormented by Smart", 26 July.
"Fine cricketers seen at Swansea", 27 July.
"Fine bowling by Sibbles", 29 July.
"Lancashire's good position", 30 July.
"Lancashire's exciting match", 31 July.

"Lancashire bat all day", 8 August.
"Somerset have to follow on", 9 August.
"Somerset's fine recovery", 10 August.
"Dull batting by Kent", 19 August.
"Lancashire behind at Dover", 20 August.
"Great win for Lancashire", 21 August.
"Clark's battle with Lancashire", 22 August.
"Bakewell twice bats finely", 23 August.
"Lancashire gay and dour by turn", 26 August.
"Morning play at Old Trafford", 27 August.
"Wellard rings down curtain", 28 August.
"Sorry plight of an England eleven", 3 September.
"An England eleven's feeble batting", 4 September.
"Pleasing play at Scarborough", 5 September.
"A.D. Baxter's bowling success", 6 September.
"Won in last over", 7 September.
"South Africans' poor day", 9 September.
"South Africans in trouble", 10 September.
"South Africans avoid defeat", 11 September.

1937   Cricket articles in *Glasgow Herald*:
"Enthusiasm must come from the players — exciting cricket depends upon exciting personalities",* 28 April.
"Can Yorkshire regain the counties title?", 5 May.
"Freer style of cricket promised",* 12 May.
"Building up an England side", 19 May.
"Rich week in English cricket", 26 May.
"Nothing wrong with cricket", 2 June.
"Better days ahead for Essex", 9 June.
"Choosing an England team", 16 June.
"New Zealanders put to the test on Saturday", 24 June.
"Cricket's decline at the universities", 7 July.
"Cricketers of genius who miss the limelight", 14 July.
"Young men not realizing early promise", 21 July.
"The greatest of modern fast bowlers — E.A. McDonald's example of perfection of style",* 28 July.
"Mystery of England's Test Disappointment", 4 August.
"The rise of Lancashire in county cricket", 11 August.
"Middlesex or Yorkshire for championship", 18 August.
"Argument in favour of the challenge match", 25 August.

1938   Cricket articles in *Glasgow Herald*:
"Cricket season awaited with eager anticipation", 27 April.
"Bradman's one palpable weakness",* 11 May.
Test Match comments, 16/27/30 June.
"One of the greatest matches in game's history", 16 June.
"Hammond is England's Bradman", 27 June.
"England has not forced home advantage", 30 June.
Test match comments, 6/20/25/28 July.
"Have the selectors gambled?", 6 July.

"Restore the natural wicket", 14 July.
"Leeds may be fore-runner of five-day matches", 20 July.
"The odds are on England now — and at the Oval", 25 July.
"Flat-footed England were at mercy of spin", 28 July.
"Cricket — Test and non-Test at the Oval", 10 August.
"Cricket is losing a supreme artist",* 17 August.
"Victory within England's grasp", 23 August.
"England have now mastered Australian bowling", 26 August.
1953   "Return of a wanderer: comparisons between 1938 and 1953",*
       Manchester Guardian, 7 October.
1954   Cricket reports in *Manchester Guardian*:
"Smith's sound batting for Oxford", 3 May.
"Oxford routed by Trueman", 7 May.
"Oxford's narrow escape", 8 May.
"Pakistanis in good form",* 10 May.
"Pakistanis far ahead",* 11 May.
"Fazal's fine bowling at Worcester",* 12 May.
"Hard day for Lancashire's bowlers", 13 May.
"Lancashire well behind", 14 May.
"Lancashire in exciting finish", 15 May.
"Two fine stands against Surrey", 17 May.
"Stout reply by Surrey", 18 May.
"Surrey's narrow win over Sussex", 19 May.
"Middlesex in sound position", 20 May.
"Somerset fight back", 21 May.
"Somerset hunt Middlesex home", 22 May.
"Pakistanis testing day", 24 May.
"Pakistanis in good form", 25 May.
"Pakistanis struggle at the last", 26 May.
"Doggart defies Pakistanis", 27 May.
"Pakistanis just lead", 28 May.
"Warwickshire well placed", 7 June.
"Surrey soon in trouble", 14 June.
"Keen struggle at Old Trafford", 15 June.
"Ups and downs at Bath", 21 June.
"Hard day for batsmen at Bath", 22 June.
"Lancashire use worn patch at Bath", 23 June.
"Yorkshire's good day", 24 June.
"Essex saved by Gibb", 25 June.
"Great start for Oxford", 5 July.
"Stout-hearted reply by Cambridge", 6 July.
"Two keen attacks at Bramall Lane", 12 July.
"Yorkshire lead Surrey", 13 July.
"Yorkshire held by Surrey", 14 July.
"Notts profited by their patience", 15 July.
"Lancashire punish Notts attack", 16 July.
"Lancashire's stirring failure", 17 July.
"Little play at Lord's", 19 July.

"Hard day for Middlesex's bowlers", 20 July.
"Middlesex fall to fast bowlers", 21 July.
"Surrey saved by Stewart", 22 July.
"Essex just lead Surrey", 23 July.
"Colchester game drawn", 24 July.

1957 Debate with John Arlott, "In the opinion of this house, neither toss, weather nor wicket were decisive elements in the defeat of Australia last season",* 12 March, reprinted in *Newsletter of the Cricket Society*, no.48 (3).

1957 "Cricket and contemporary life", *The Cricketer*, vol.28, no.5, June (appears in *Beyond a Boundary*, pp. 208-13).

1959 Cricket articles in *The Nation*, Trinidad:
"Frank Worrell must be captain", 28 February.
"Without malice" (on Worrell tour), 10 April.
"That Worrell tour",* 15 May.
"Without malice" (on Bradman), 30 October.
"Gilchrist before and Gilchrist after",* 20 November.
"Some of the MCC players as I knew them",* 24/31 December.

1960 Cricket articles in *The Nation*, Trinidad:
"Homage to English cricket", 15/22 January/5 February.
"MCC: Without malice", 22/29 January/5 February.
Open letter to Queen's Park Cricket Club, "Make Worrell captain", 12 February (in *Beyond a Boundary*, pp. 233-40).
"The Jamaica Test", 19 February.
"The same wretched story", 26 February.
"West Indian Board of Control: the captain for Australia",* 4 March.
"Without malice" (on British press coverage), 11 March.
"Without malice", 18 March.
"West Indies v. Australia", 8 April.

1963 Publication of *Beyond a Boundary*, Stanley Paul/Hutchinson Publishing Group, London.

1963 Foreword to *Cricket Quarterly*, vol.1.

1963 "Cricket in West Indian culture",* *New Society*, 6 June.

1963 "The departure of the West Indians",* previously unpublished.

1963 "Dexter and Sobers",* previously unpublished.

1964 "The 1963 West Indians" (address at Lord's, 5 September 1963),* *Journal of the Cricket Society*, vol.II, no.2, Spring.

1964 Review of *Frank Worrell: The Career of a Great Cricketer* by Ernest Eytle, *Cricket Quarterly*, vol.2, no.1, January.

1964 "Sir J.B. Hobbs",* *The Cricketer*, vol.45, February.

1964 "Sobers' greatest days are ahead of him",* *The Cricketer*, vol.45, no.11, July.

1964 "The inheritors", in souvenir programme commemorating Sir Frank Worrell's West Indies XI Tour, 1964.

1964 "Refelections on the late series",* *Cricket Quarterly*, vol.2, no.4.

1965 "McKenzie and Hawke rout West Indies", *The Times*, London, 18 May.

1965 "West Indies v. Australia", *Cricket Quarterly*, vol.3.

1965 "Cricket in the West Indian islands", unpublished.

1966 "First Test at Old Trafford", *The Vanguard*, Trinidad, 10 June.

1966 Cricket articles in *Sunday Guardian*, Trinidad:
"Long may Windies flourish",* 26 June.
"After that Nottingham defeat, England must find 12 new players to battle WI",* 10 July.
"A question of cricket approach ...",* 14 August.
"Why Windies fade in the end",* 28 August.
"Two cricketing societies",* 4 September.
"Sobers – a man who fits into the expanded technicalities of his age", 11 September.
"From the spectators came Sobers", 18 September.

1966 Articles from the *World of Cricket*, edited by E.W. Swanton (Michael Joseph, London): "Australia v. West Indies"; "West Indies";* biographies of Challenor, Goddard, Gomez, Hall, Headley, Kanhai, Ramadhin, Smith, Sobers, Stollmeyer, Valentine, Walcott, Weekes, Worrell.

1966 "Kanhai: a study in confidence",* *New World*, Georgetown, Guyana Independence issue.

1967 Review of *King Cricket* by Gary Sobers, *Cricket Quarterly*, vol.5, no.3.

1967 Obituary: Sir Frank Worrell, "The man whose leadership made history",* *The Cricketer*, vol.48, 5 May.

1967 "George Headley",* in J. Arlott (ed.), *Cricket: The Great Ones* (Pelham Books, London).

1967 "Cricket and history", unpublished.

1967/8 "How West Indies cricket was built", *The Cricketer*, Winter Annual, vol.48, no.12.

1968 "Not Cricket",* *Transition*, Kampala, Uganda, vol.7, no.37.

1968 "West Indies cricket", unpublished.

1968 "Cricket season of 1968", unpublished.

1968/9 "Driving the ball is a tradition in the West Indies",* *The Cricketer*, vol.49, no.12.

1969 "Learie Constantine",* in J. Arlott (ed.), *Cricket: The Great All-Rounders* (Pelham Books, London).

1969 "Garfield Sobers",* in J. Arlott (ed.), *Cricket: The Great All-Rounders* (Pelham Books, London).

1960s "West Indian Cricketers in County Cricket",* previously unpublished.

1969/70 "Sobers and the future", *The Cricketer*, Winter, vol.50, no.12.

1970 "Walter Hammond: an anniversary tribute",* *The Cricketer*, vol.51, no.8.

1970 Introduction* to Rowland Bowen, *Cricket: A History of its Growth and Development throughout the World* (Eyre and Spottiswoode, London).

C.L.R. James

1970   "Sir Frank Worrell",* in J. Arlott (ed.), *Cricket: The Great Captains* (Pelham Books, London).

1975   "Beyond the Boundary", *Race Today*, vol.7, no.7, July.

1975   "Not just cricket",* review of *Learie Constantine*, by Gerald Howat, *New Society*, vol.34, no.689, 18 December.

1975   "Cricket and race",* previously unpublished.

1980   "Australia v. West Indies", with Tony Crozier, in E.W. Swanton (ed.), *Barclays' World of Cricket* (Collins, London).

1980   "West Indies", with P.D.B. Short, in E.W. Swanton (ed.), *Barclays' World of Cricket* (Collins, London).

1982   "A majestic innings with few peers: Sandip Patel",* *South*, September.

1982   "Comparison of Botham, Khan and Kapil Dev", unpublished.

1983   "Cricket notes", *Race Today Review*, vol.14, no.5, January.

1983   "Cricket notes", *Race Today*, vol.14, no.6, March/April.

1983   "Gower to lead England",* *Race Today*, vol.15, no.1, May/June.

1983   "Cricket notes: Gower and Richards", *Race Today*, vol.15, no.2, August/September.

1983   "The captain and his team",* *Race Today*, vol.15, no.3, October/November.

1984   "Reminiscence", review of *Everything Under the Sun* by Jeffrey Stollmeyer, *Race Today Review*, January.

1984   "George Headley 1909-83",* part 1, *Race Today Review*, January; part 2, *Race Today*, April/May.

1984   "Caribbean views from the top", review of *Everything Under the Sun* by Jeffrey Stollmeyer, *The Guardian*, London, 6 January.

1984   "A princely gift to England's game", *South*, July.

1984   Review of *As I Said at the Time* by E.W. Swanton, *Race Today*, July/August.

1984   "West Indies cricket team in England 1984", *Sunday Tribune*, Dublin, August.

1984   "It's still cricket, lovely cricket", *The Times*, London, 26 September.

1984   "MacGregor",* *Journal of the Cricket Society*, vol.12, no.1, September.

1984   "West Indies v. England",* *Race Today*, vol.16, no.2, October/November.

1984   "The decline of English cricket",* *Race Today Review*, January.

1985   "Caution in Comparisons", *Race Today*, May/June.

1985   "Botham still hitting sixes",* *Race Today*, vol.16, no.5, August/September.

1986   "Botham and Gower", *Race Today*, July.

Index of Names

Achong, E., 35-6, 241
Adams, Grantley, 269
Aeschylus, 40, 87, 269
Alexander, F.C.M., 101, 102, 163, 300
Alimuddin, 75, 76
Allan, David, 164
Allen, G.O., 53, 56, 203, 242, 286
Alletson, E.B., 19
Allom, M.J.C., 10
Altham, H.S., 103
Ames, L.E.G., 31, 43, 188, 203, 241-2
Amiss, D.L., 208
Andrew, 97
Archer, R., 82, 84
Aristotle, 269
Arlott, John, 81, 82, 106-7, 109-10,
    157, 177, 208, 211-12, 213-14, 218
Armistead, H., 8
Armstrong, W.W., 273
Arnold, Matthew, 281
Arnold, Thomas, 115, 124, 132, 147
Arnott, T., 10
Asgarali, N., 300
Ashdown, W.H., 188
Ashman, J.R., 76
Astill, W.E., 11, 28, 30, 31, 250
Atkinson, D., 175, 301
Austin, H.B.G., 17, 18, 19, 22, 24, 25,
    26, 27, 28, 121, 157, 225, 249, 250,
    253, 257

Badcock, C.L., 64
Bailey, T.E., 86, 97, 161, 169, 230, 286
Balaskas, X.C., 51
Baldwin, James, 279
Barber, 152, 153, 178, 179, 187
Bardwell, G.R., 16
Barlow, E.J., 180
Barnes, S.F., 5, 7-10, 25, 64, 165, 188,
    299
Barnett, C., 56-7, 58, 254
Barrington, K.F., 96
Barrow, I., 32, 36, 37
Bartlett, E.L., 29, 30-1, 32
Bedle, William, 275-6
Bedser, A.V., 77, 97, 161, 165, 258,
    285
Beldam, C.A., 16
Beldam, G.W., 104
Beldham, W., 245, 246
Bell, A.J., 51, 52

Bell, Sir Hesketh, 274
Benaud, R., 82, 83, 203, 267
Bennett, R.A., 19, 20, 25
Betancourt, Nelson, 250
Bird, R.E., 80
Birkett, L.S., 32
Blazo, Sir Thomas, 14
Blenman, 196-7
Blythe, C., 65
Bolus, 231, 260
Booth, 51
Booth, B.C., 219
Bosanquet, B.J.T., 19
Botham, I.T., 285, 299, 303-4
Bottomley, Horatio, 86
Bowen, Rowland, 245-7, 270-6
Bowes, Bill, 45, 46, 51
Boyce, K.D., 278
Boycott, G., 152, 176
Brackley, Lord, 19, 20, 26
Bradman, Sir D., 10, 12, 43, 45-6, 47,
    48, 53, 55, 57, 62-3, 64, 68, 72, 73,
    75, 82, 84, 90-2, 94-5, 111-15, 129,
    170, 186, 191, 195, 199, 200, 202,
    211, 215, 222, 224, 234, 240, 243,
    255-6, 268, 270, 282, 286, 291-2,
    293, 294, 302
Brancker, 174
Bray, Charles, 74
Bright, John, 63
Broadbent, R.G., 80
Bromley-Davenport, H.R., 15, 16
Brown, Freddy, 177
Brown, George, 24
Brown, F.R., 35, 45, 63, 64
Browne, C.A., 24, 25, 30
Browne, C.R., 24, 26, 27, 28-9, 32
Burge, P.T., 151
Burke, P., 82, 83
Burton, D.C.F., 17, 18, 19, 25, 26
Bush, 15
Butcher, B., 136, 138, 162, 164, 172,
    176, 177
Butler, H., 185
Bynoe, 174

Cahn, Sir Julian, 11
Calthorpe, Hon. F.S.G., 11, 28, 31, 32
Cameron, B., 21, 52
Cardus, Neville, 5, 103, 106, 155, 178,
    224, 248, 293

Carew, Michael, 164, 172
Carr, A.W., 111
Cartwright, T.W., 149, 152
Chalk, F.G.H., 42
Challenor, George, 21, 23-4, 25, 26, 27, 28, 29, 30, 122, 190, 225, 250, 283
Challenor, R., 25
Chamberlain, Joseph, 256
Chipperfield, A.G., 46-7, 64, 254
Christiani, R.J., 166
Cipriani, A., 3, 4, 5, 24, 25, 215
Clark, 10, 191
Close, D.B., 187, 264
Cobb, R., 276
Cobham, Lord, 206, 215, 217
Coke, 104
Coleridge, 110, 226-7, 279
Collins, 28, 30
Collins, Canon, 89
Compton, D., 55, 56, 64, 85, 161, 209, 220
Constantine, Sir L.N., 2, 3, 4-5, 8-9, 27, 28, 30, 31, 32, 33, 34, 36, 71, 87, 88-9, 91, 94, 102, 104, 119, 127, 130, 140, 152, 155, 156, 159, 168, 169, 180, 217-18, 222, 230, 231, 232-44, 248, 249, 250, 253, 257, 262, 277-9, 297-8
Constantine, L.S., 2, 17, 18, 19, 21, 22-3, 24, 25, 119
Cooper, 56
Corling, 150, 151
Cowdrey, Colin, 82, 83, 95, 129, 138, 142, 152, 162, 172, 173, 175, 176, 178, 187, 188-9, 205-7, 214, 217
Cowper, 219
Cox, P., 17, 18
Craig, I.D., 85
Crawley, L.G., 28
Creighton, Toby, 283
Crisp, R.J., 51, 239
Cumberbatch, C.P., 16, 17, 18, 20, 25

Da Costa, O.C., 35, 36, 38
D'Ade, 16
Dales, H.L., 28
Davidson, A.K., 82, 153, 266
Davies, 39, 41, 42-3
Day, A.P., 21
De Boissière, Ralph, 2
De Caires, F.I., 22, 32
Denton, D., 21
De Peiza, C.C., 175

De Quincey, 110
Devereux, L.N., 76, 80
Dewdney, 300
Dewhurst, G.A., 26, 28
Dews, G., 78, 79, 80
Dexter, E.R., 97, 127-30, 138, 141, 142, 144, 148-9, 151, 152, 153, 163, 165, 170, 179, 188-9, 208, 231, 260, 264, 282
Dickens, 119, 120
Dillon, E.W., 19
Dobson, 25
D'Oliveira, Basil, 175, 176, 177, 179, 209-13, 214
Dolphin, 21, 49
Douglas, J.W.H.T., 28
Dowson, E.M., 19
Drake, 123
Duckworth, G., 40, 41, 42, 47, 48, 51, 204
Duff, R.A., 57, 255, 270
Duleepsinhji, K.S. 67
Durston, 11

Ebeling, H.I., 47, 48, 49, 50
Eckersley, P.T., 41, 42, 52
Edrich, W.J., 56, 209, 231, 254, 260
Elahi, Ikbal, 78
Emerson, 268
Euripides, 269
Evans, Godfrey, 64, 83, 230

Fagg, A.E., 42
Fane, F.L. 19
Farnes, K., 45, 46, 47
Farrimond, W., 52
Fazal Mahmood, 76, 77, 78, 79, 80
Fender, P.G.H., 28, 30, 36, 258
Fernandes, M.P., 26, 27, 29
Fingleton, J.H., 63, 64, 103-5, 107-8
Fleetwood-Smith, L., 48, 49, 50, 51
Foley, C.P., 19
Foster, R.E., 184-5, 255, 270, 299
Francis, G.N., 18, 26, 27, 28, 31, 32, 33, 180
Freeman, A.P., 39, 40, 41, 43, 48, 67
Fry, C.B., 66, 72, 73, 91, 104, 113, 128, 129, 143, 151, 155, 189, 202, 205, 215, 247, 255, 270, 301

Gardiner, A.G., 278
Garner, J., 299
Gaskin, Berkeley, 115-16, 137, 164
Geary, G., 64
Ghazali, M.E.Z., 76

Gibbon, 65
Gibbs, 25
Gibbs, L., 138, 139, 141, 162, 163, 164, 172, 181, 222, 223, 239, 258-9, 267, 282
Gilchrist, R., 92-4, 95, 123, 162, 301
Gillingham, Rev., 30
Gimblett, H., 55, 57, 58
Glover, 37
Goddard, J.D.C., 161, 162, 300, 301
Goddard, T.W., 64
Gomes, Albert, 2
Gomez, G.E., 108, 160
Goodman, Clifford, 16, 18, 137, 225
Goodman, Percy, 17, 19, 21, 22, 24, 225
Gover, A.R., 58, 59
Gower, D.I., 284-7, 287-9, 300
Grace, W.G., xi, 18, 24, 54, 58, 65, 68, 112, 113, 115, 117, 124, 132, 146, 182, 224, 225, 245, 246-7, 272, 273, 279, 286
Grant, G.C. (Jack), 32, 33, 34, 36-7, 38, 158
Granville-Barker, 110
Graveney, T.W., 142, 143, 173, 175, 176, 185, 186, 190, 209, 210, 211, 214
Greenhough, 96-7
Greenidge, C.G., 299
Gregory, J.M., 60, 66, 152, 180, 235
Griffith, C.C., 126, 136, 137, 141, 143, 164, 172, 173, 176, 177, 180, 184, 223, 231, 232, 239, 264, 282
Griffith, H.C., 31, 32, 33, 35, 36, 154
Grimmett, C.V., 12, 94, 159, 180, 194, 197, 198, 239, 273
Grout, A.T.W., 151
Grove, C.W., 77, 78
Gunn, George, 31, 240
Gunn, William, xi
Gupte, S.P., 161

Haggard, Rider, 256
Haig, Nigel, 11
Hall, W.W., 94, 126, 129, 135, 136, 137, 138, 141, 143, 144, 146, 163, 164, 172, 180, 184, 221, 223, 231, 233, 239, 258, 260, 262, 264, 267, 282
Hammond, W.R., 28, 29-30, 53, 55, 57, 61, 72, 113, 159, 191, 219, 242, 243, 253-4
Hankey, Reginald, 165

Hardinge, H.T.W., 188
Hardstaff, J., 113
Hargreaves, 21
Harragin, Bertie, 20, 22, 225
Harris, Lord, 232
Harris, Wilson, 99, 277
Harvey, Neil, 72, 83, 259
Hassett, A.L., 63-4
Hawke, Lord, 15, 16, 18, 20, 244
Hawke, N.J.N., 150, 151, 222
Hawkwood, 51
Hayes, 19
Hayward, Tom, 57, 272
Hazlitt, 110, 223, 235-6
Headley, G.A., 5, 10-12, 19, 32, 33, 57, 74-5, 91, 102, 112, 156, 158, 159, 175, 189, 190-202, 211, 220, 231, 238, 282, 287-8, 291-4
Hearne, J.W., 24, 219, 237
Hegel, 152
Heine, 96
Hendren, E.H., 12, 31, 48, 50, 159, 237, 278
Henry, P.J.T., 15
Henty, G.A., 121
Herodotus, 269
Heseltine, C., 16
Hesketh-Pritchard, A., 19
Higgs, K., 173, 180, 184, 185, 186, 189
Hilder, A.L. 10
Hill, Allen, 58
Hill, Clement, 128, 270
Hirst, G.H., 188
Hitler, 89
Hoad, E.L.G., 29, 30, 31, 32
Hobbs, J.B., 28, 35-6, 37, 54, 57-8, 61, 65, 67, 72, 85, 112, 113, 142, 154-6, 195, 211, 214, 270, 272
Holding, M.A., 299
Holford, D.A.J., 171, 172, 173, 174, 176
Holloway, 24
Holmes, E.R.T., 28, 29, 30, 56, 159, 237
Holt, J.K., 27, 29, 161
Hopwood, 39, 43, 44, 51, 52
Horace, 202
Hordern, H.V., 29
Hornby, A.J., 272
Howat, Gerald, 277-8
Hughes, Thomas, 115, 124, 132, 146
Human, J.H., 47, 48, 49
Humphreys, E., 25, 26

Hunte, C.C., 126, 139, 146, 163, 164, 171, 173, 176, 220
Hunte, E.A., 32
Hunter, C.V., 26
Hussain, Mahmood, 76, 77-8, 79
Hutchings, K.L., 128, 142
Hutton, Sir L., 71, 72, 84, 85, 95, 97, 98, 113, 137, 152, 159, 161, 162, 215, 230, 254, 256, 258
Hylton, 94, 159
Hyman, W.J., 273

Iddon, J., 39, 40, 44, 51, 52
Illingworth, R., 97
Ince, H.W., 22, 25, 26, 27, 274
Insole, D.J., 212

Jackson, Archie, 194
Jackson, F.S., 128, 154, 182, 188
Jackson, Stanley, 224
Jameson, T.O., 28, 30
Jardine, D.R., 105, 111, 114, 237
Jarman, B.N., 211, 219
Jenkins, R.O., 77
Jessop, G.L., 19
Jingle, Alfred, 14
John, George, 18, 24, 25, 26, 27-8, 29, 180, 231
Johnson, 82, 84, 86
Johnston, Brian, 170
Julien, B.D., 278

Kallicharran, A.I., 278
Kanhai, R.B., 90, 116, 124, 129, 136, 138-9, 141, 144, 146, 162, 163, 164, 165-71, 172, 173, 174, 176, 179, 183, 184, 205, 262-3, 266, 282, 300, 301
Kant, 152, 177
Kapil Dev, 281
Kardar, A.J., 75, 79, 80
Keeton, W.W., 159
Kenyon, D., 77, 78, 79
Keynes, J.M., 256
Khalid Hassan, 78, 80
Kilner, R., 28, 30, 159
Kimpton, 63
King, John Barton, 275
King, Lester, 164
Kinneir, S.P., 21
Kipling, Rudyard, 256
Kippax, A.F., 12, 102, 199
Kline, L.F., 262
Knight, Wilson, 110
Knott, D.H., 40-1

Laker, J.C., 82, 85, 91, 94, 185, 230, 299, 302
Lamb, 110, 300
Lamming, George, 87, 99, 106, 108-9, 123, 217
Langton, A.B., 51, 52
Larwood, H., 31, 111
Lashley, 174, 176, 177, 178
Lawry, W.M., 153, 219
Lawton, A.E., 21
Layne, 20, 21, 24
Lee, G.M., 10
Leveson-Gower, H.D.G., 16, 45, 46, 47, 48, 49
Levett, W.H., 42, 43
Leyland, M., 46, 48, 50, 237
Lill, 219
Lilley, A.A., 21
Lindwall, R.R., 81, 84, 94, 142, 153, 180, 186, 221, 229
Lister, W.H.L., 40, 44, 52
Livingstone, 248
Lloyd, C.H., 248, 249, 251, 278, 299
Lloyd George, 86
Lock, G.A.R., 73, 82, 83, 94, 129, 230, 231, 299
Lockwood, Ephraim, 10, 12, 58
Lohmann, G.A., 224
Lorca, 182
Lusty, Robert, 108

Macartney, C.G., 37, 65, 128, 257
McCabe, S.J., 46-7, 48, 49, 50, 62, 64, 72, 73, 194, 216
MacCarthy, Desmond, 8
McCormick, 254
McDonald, E.A., 58-61, 67, 83, 152, 180, 220, 243
McGahey, C.P., 215
MacGregor, 2, 295-8
Macindoe, 63, 64
McKenzie, G.D., 153
MacLaren, A.C., 34, 114, 128, 142, 188, 270, 301
McLean, R.A., 95, 180
Macmillan, Harold, 189
McMorris, E., 164, 172
Mailey, A.A., 185
Manjrekar, V.L., 259
Maqsood Ahmed, 76, 248
Marriott, C.S., 39, 41, 42, 43
Marshall, Max, 108
Marshall, R.E., 248, 250
Martin, F.R., 29, 30, 31, 32, 36, 37, 38

Martindale, E.A., 34, 35, 36, 94, 137, 159, 202, 239, 242
May, P.B.H., 71, 72, 83, 94, 95, 97-8, 101, 142, 161, 162, 189
Mays, Willie, 279
Mead, Philip, 55, 191
Mendes, Alfred, 2
Mercer, 11, 160
Merry, C., 36, 38
Michelangelo, 144
Milburn, C., 172, 173, 174, 176, 179
Miller, K.R., 71, 81, 82, 84, 94, 95, 103, 142, 180, 186, 221
Mitchell-Innes, 56
Mohammad, Hanif, 75-6, 162, 248
Mold, A.W, 17
Morrison, C.S., 21
Moss, A.E., 96
Moulder, E.R.D., 25-6, 274
Moyes, A.G., 103, 155, 205, 266
Muggeridge, Malcolm, 118
Murray, D.L., 126, 144-5, 164, 165, 184, 231, 260
Myers, 21
Mynn, A., 245

Naipaul, V.S., 99, 116-18, 130
Napoleon, 192
Neff, 86
Nelson, 123
Newman, W., 273
Nichols, M.S., 11, 45, 46, 47, 48-9, 50, 243
Nietzsche, 171
Nkrumah, Kwame, 89, 252
Noble, M.A., 104, 247, 267-8, 270, 273, 279
Nourse, A.D., 51, 52
Nunes, R.K., 27, 29, 30, 158
Nurse, S.M., 164, 172, 173, 176, 177

O'Connor, J., 31
Oldfield, W.A., 48, 50, 159
Ollivierre, Charles, 17, 18, 20, 197, 225
Ollivierre, Helon, 20
Ollivierre, Richard, 20, 21, 22, 25, 26, 225
O'Neill, N.C., 103-4, 149, 259
O'Reilly, W.J., 47, 49, 50, 51, 94, 159, 180, 201, 224, 239, 253, 292, 295
Osment, 20

Padmore, George, 3, 252
Pairaudeau, B.H., 300

Palairet, R.C.N., 16
Parkin, C., 60
Parkinson, 40, 41
Parkinson, Michael, 212, 213
Parks, J.M., 143
Pascall, V., 26, 28, 29, 30, 216, 250
Passailaigue, C.C., 175, 194
Patil, S.M., 281, 282, 284
Paton, Alan, 89
Paynter, E., 40, 44, 52, 57, 58
Peebles, Ian, 229
Perks, R.T.D., 77, 243
Phillips, R.L., 27
Phillipson, 42, 43, 44
Pilch, F., 245
Plato, 269
Pollard, 42
Pollock, 180, 291
Ponsford, W.H., 46, 58, 111, 112, 199, 256
Potter, 219
Priestley, Sir Arthur, 16
Pullar, G., 95

Quaife, W., 21

Roe, A.F., 160
Ramadhin, S., 94, 124, 129, 160, 161, 162, 163, 180, 221, 229, 258-9, 299, 300, 301
Ranjitsinhji, K.S., xi, 54, 68, 85, 112, 113, 129, 220, 247, 255, 270, 271, 272, 273, 275, 278, 279, 301
Ransford, V.S., 128
Raphael, 144
Ray, 30
Redpath, I.R., 219
Relf, A.E., 25, 26
Rhodes, Cecil, 86
Rhodes, W., 11, 21, 28, 31, 57, 65, 112, 184, 188, 198, 272
Richards, I.V.A., 299
Richardson, P.E., 77, 78, 79, 83
Richardson, T., 58-9, 135
Roach, C.A., 2, 31-2, 36, 37-8, 158, 216
Roberts, A.M.E., 278
Robertson-Glasgow, 239-40
Robins, R.W.V., 56
Robinson, Ray, 103
Rodriguez, W., 164
Rogers, 24, 25
Root, C.F., 28, 30
Ross, Alan, 103, 212

Rowbotham, Denys, 218
Ruth, Babe, 279

Saeed Ahmed, 248
St Hill, E.L., 11, 12, 30, 32
St Hill, W.H., 2, 26, 29, 253
St John, John, 106
Sandham, A., 31, 32, 272
Sardesai, D.N., 259
Scott, O.C., 29, 32
Sealey, Ben, 30
Sealy, J.E.D., 32, 159, 190
Sewell, E.H.D., 21
Shakespeare, 110, 123
Shakoor Ahmed, 80, 248
Sharpe, 143
Shepherd, 153
Sheppard, Rev. D.S., 82, 83, 85, 212-13
Shrewsbury, A., xi, 112
Siddons, Mrs, 235-6
Simpson, 150, 151, 152, 219, 221, 223
Simpson-Hayward, G.H., 19
Skelding, 230
Slade-Lucas, 15, 20
Small, J.A., 24, 26, 27, 30, 72, 248-9
Smith, E.J., 21, 28
Smith, M.J.K., 95-6, 187
Smith, O.G. (Collie), 162, 167, 300, 301
Smith, S.G., 18, 19-20, 21, 23-4, 26
Smith, W.C. (Razor), 25, 274
Snow, J.A., 184, 185, 186
Sobers, Sir G., 90, 103, 107, 116, 124-5, 126, 127-30, 136, 137, 139, 141, 156-8, 161, 162, 164-5, 167, 168, 171, 172, 173, 174, 176-7, 178, 180-2, 183, 186-7, 189, 205, 211, 216-17, 218-32, 239, 267, 279, 282, 300, 301
Soboul, A., 276
Solomon, J.S., 162, 164, 262
Somerset, A.W.F., 25, 274
Sophocles, 40
Spofforth, F.R., 273
Spooner, R.H., 141, 188, 270
Sproston, G.W., 17
Stackpole, K.R., 219
Stanyforth, Major R.T., 31
Statham, J.B., 83, 94, 95, 96, 145-6, 151, 161
Steel, A.G., 279
Stevens, G.T.S., 11, 28, 31
Stewart, William, 92-3, 94
Stoddart, A.E., 16-17

Stollmeyer, J.B., 2, 160, 287
Stollmeyer, V.H., 2
Strachey, Lytton, 171
Subba Row, R., 97
Surridge, 98
Sutcliffe, H., 45, 48, 49, 50, 57, 58, 67, 72, 73, 85, 152, 237, 272, 291
Swanton, E.W., 103, 164, 182, 187, 206, 227, 229
Swetman, 97

Tarilton, P.H., 22, 24, 25, 26, 27, 28, 29, 30, 190, 274, 283
Tate, M.W., 55, 165, 236-7
Tayfield, H.J., 85, 94
Taylor, T.L., 21
Taylor, T.L., 21
Tennyson, Hon. L.H., 10, 11, 28, 30, 194
Thomas, 219
Thompson, G.J., 19
Thompson, E.P., 276
Thucydides, 269
Titmus, F.J., 85, 153, 154, 264
Tomlinson, 51
Toussaint L'Ouverture, 131-2
Townsend, 31, 49, 50-1
Trueman, F.S., 83, 95, 96, 135, 136, 137, 144, 149, 150, 151, 152, 153, 165, 166, 236, 264
Trumble, H., 12, 33, 239
Trumper, V.T., xi, 10, 54, 57, 102, 104, 112, 113, 128, 247, 255, 270, 279
Tunnicliffe, J., 21
Tyldesley, E., 28, 30, 40, 44, 193-4, 197
Tyldesley, J.T., 128, 188, 200, 270
Tyldesley, R.K. 60, 61
Tyson, F.H., 94, 96, 258

Underwood, D.L., 175

Valentine, A.L., 124, 160, 161, 162, 163, 164, 180, 228-9, 267, 299, 301
Valentine, V.A., 35, 36, 39, 43
Vanloo, J., 20
Veivers, T.R., 149, 154
Verity, H., 46, 53, 73, 95, 240-1
Vincent, C.L. 52
Vincent-Brown, 17
Voce, W., 11, 31, 32, 111

Wade, H.F. 52
Waddell, Aucher, 283

Waite, J.H.B., 216
Walcott, C.L. 96, 124, 129, 146, 158, 160-1, 162, 166, 167, 180, 186, 220, 229, 230, 265, 269, 300, 301
Walcott, Derek, 132
Walters, C.F., 58, 216
Warner, Aucher, 157
Warner, Sir Pelham, 16, 17, 24, 157, 232, 244, 255, 256
Warner, Thornton, 15
Warren, 21
Washbrook, C., 52, 81, 85, 95, 154
Watson, W., 28, 30, 39, 40, 41-2, 43, 44, 51, 52, 57, 163, 258
Watt, 39, 41, 42, 43
Weekes, E.D., 124, 129, 158, 159-60, 162, 167, 168, 180, 186, 229, 265, 269, 300, 301
White, A.W., 164
White, Crawford, 74
Whittington, T.A.L., 24, 25, 26
Wight, O.S., 32
Wiles, C.A., 26, 28, 30, 37-7
Williams, Dr Eric, 2, 70, 87, 99
Willis, R.D.G., 281, 284, 285
Wilson, E.R., 19
Wilson, Harold, 189

Wodehouse, P.G., 121
Wood, H., 243
Woodcock, J., 248, 250, 289
Woodfull, W.M. 50, 58, 158
Woods, S.M.J., 16, 17, 18, 19
Woolf, Virginia and Leonard, 5
Woolley, F.E., 40, 43, 61, 64-8, 155, 188, 229
Wordsworth, 226-7, 279
Worrell, Sir F., 70, 75, 88-90, 94, 95, 98, 101-2, 108, 122-4, 126, 127, 129, 136, 137, 139, 140-1, 142, 146, 158, 160-1, 162, 163, 164, 165, 167, 168, 169, 173-4, 180, 185, 186, 202-5, 222-3, 229, 244, 250-1, 255-70, 278, 279, 300, 301
Wright, Douglas, 181
Wright, E.F., 14, 22
Wright, Richard, 292
Wyatt, R.E.S., 31, 45, 48, 49-50, 159, 242
Wynyard, E.G., 19

Yardley, N.W.D., 177
Yarnold, H., 80
Yeates, 216
Young, H., 24

THE BLACK JACOBINS

C.L.R. JAMES

"The Black Plato of our generation . . . the founding father of African emancipation" *The Times*.

This classic study of the only successful slave revolt in history is a masterpiece of historical scholarship, astute political analysis and narrative excitement.

In 1791 the Caribbean island of San Domingo, France's most profitable colony and the greatest single market for the European slave trade, found itself in the grip of revolution.

The island's slaves rebelled, embarking on a twelve-year struggle against their white masters and successive invading armies of French, Spanish, and British Troops. The final defeat of Bonaparte's 1803 expedition resulted in the establishment of the black state of Haiti.

The leader of this unique achievement was himself a slave until the age of forty-five—Toussaint L'Ouverture. Why and how the revolution happened, how it created this brilliant leader and how he in turn brought it to its triumphant conclusion are the themes of this remarkable book.

"His detailed, richly documented and dramatically written book holds a deep and lasting interest"— *New York Times*.

"Contains some of the finest and most deeply felt polemical writing against slavery and racism ever to be published, and it locates the Caribbean and Caribbean society firmly on the world stage"—*Time Out*.

"He is, quite simply, the outstanding West Indian of the century"— Caryl Phillips—*The Guardian*.

WASHINGTON BABYLON

SHELLEY ROSS

Sex, scandal and corruption are inherent in the American political system and have caused many public figures to fall from grace.

Throughout history an aggressive news media has consistently exposed irregularities and illegalities on all sides — helping to shape public opinion about politics and politicians. *Washington Babylon* names the names and sets the scenes — from almost every presidential administration — revealing history's best-kept secrets and most infamous scandals.

Here are the true stories behind some of these compelling headlines:

"THE GOVERNOR IN SKIRTS"

In 1702, Lord Cornbury, New York's English drunken, transvestite colonial Governor-General, insisted on wearing formal hooped skirts and ladies' accessories in public as a tribute to the fashionable Queen Anne.

"OVER-ZEALOUS COLONEL RAISES FREEDOM-FIGHTER FUNDS"

Oliver North's predecessor in clandestine paramilitary activities was William S. Smith, in Thomas Jefferson's administration. Intent on aiding Venezuelan freedom fighters in their struggle against Spanish occupation, he raised private funds, secured weapons, and enlisted soldiers of fortune for *his* private army.

"MA, MA, WHERE'S MY PA?"

Grover Cleveland, considered honourable by all, publicly claimed paternity for his illegitimate child three months before the election — and won!

Drawing comparisons between malfeasance in bygone times and contemporary scandals, *Washington Babylon* demonstrates how the intriguing if flawed system manages to survive — almost despite itself — and exposes the all-too-fallible men and women who take the front page by storm.

THE UPPER ROOM

MARY MONROE

"A delightful story, the life and disgraceful times of Mama Ruby, a great fat reprobate, black and poor all right, but not in the least sorry for herself or for anyone else either...A marvellous character, wonderfully bizarre, as outrageous as she is appealing..." — *Financial Times*

"An extraordinarily vivid, painful and funny record of shanty town life, dominated in this instance by the formidable Mama Ruby who thinks no more of stealing a baby than she does of dispatching unwanted visitors with the knife concealed beside a crucifix beneath her dress" — *Irish Times*

"A novel with more violence than Rocky and Rambo combined...vivid, acrobatic language...larger-than-life characters" — *Times Literary Supplement*

"Monroe is a talented writer and this is a distinguished debut...Monroe mixes a witty patois with a plot of episodic mayhem which recalls the genius of Damon Runyon...autobiographical or not, it is the quality of the writing that holds the reader" — *City Limits*

"There are novels that, from their first pages, enter your consciousness irrevocably...Mary Monroe's novel *The Upper Room* is just such a novel... There is an indescribable electricity, an excitement, a vitality in this novel that makes it unique in my reading experience. It reads like one of the stories from the beginning of the world: a parable of conflicts between white and black, illusion and reality, good and evil...It marks the debut of a remarkable talent — possibly a great one. If you can read only one or two novels this year, read this one" — Susan Fromberg Schaeffer, author of *Anya* and *The Madness of a Seduced Woman*

ISHMAEL REED

"A great writer" — James Baldwin

"The brightest contributor to American satire since Mark Twain" — *The Nation*

"Always entertaining, often provocative, at times profound" — *Washington Post*

"Reed is as close as we are likely to get to a Garcia Marquez" — *New York Times*

MUMBO JUMBO

Mumbo Jumbo is a whirlwind tour of America's eccentric culture — an almost surrealist detective novel featuring Private Eyes PaPa LaBas and Black Herman who together investigate questions that have long plagued mankind: Was Warren Harding a member of a hated cult whose rites are still practiced? Why did Sigmund Freud call the United States "a mistake"? Why do intelligent shrinks make journeys to West Africa, Haiti, Brazil and New Orleans? Why is Moses called the Bob Dylan of the ancient world in certain HooDoo texts?

The explosive, hard-hitting satiric world of Ishmael Reed's fiction is likely to take your breath away. . .

"Part vision, part satire, part farce. . .a wholly original, unholy cross between the craft of fiction and witchcraft" — *New York Times*

RECKLESS EYEBALLING

Reckless Eyeballing, Ishmael Reed's seventh novel, is the story of Ian Ball, a black playwright who has been "sex-listed" and who is trying to get back into favour with theatrical power brokers by writing a militant play for women. Supported by powerful director Jim Minsk and eminent playwright Jake Brashford, Ball seems assured of success this time — that is, until he comes up against his ideological enemies. Minsk is murdered by white southerners, and Ball finds himself at the mercy of Tremonisha Smarts, a famous black playwright, and Becky French, a feared feminist producer who would rather put her efforts into a new play about Eva Braun. It's black against white, North against South, and Ishmael Reed against everyone in this explosive, satirical tour-de-force behind the scenes of New York theatre.

"Hilarious, hideous, infuriating and brilliant" — *San Francisco Chronicle*